THE
ANIMATION
BUSINESS
HANDBOOK

THE ANIMATION BUSINESS HANDBOOK

KAREN RAUGUST

St. Martin's Press

New York

www.stmartins.com

Book design by Maura Fadden Rosenthal

Library of Congress Cataloging-in-Publication Data

Raugust, Karen, 1960–
    The animation business handbook / Karen Raugust.
       p. cm.
    Includes index (page 357).
    ISBN 0-312-28428-4
    EAN 978-0312-28428-2
    1. Motion picture industry—United States—Finance. 2. Motion picture industry—United States—Marketing. 3. Motion picture industry—United States—Distribution. 4. Animated films. I. Title.

PN1993.5.U6R365 2004
384'.83'0973—dc22

                                                              2004041816

First Edition: August 2004

10   9   8   7   6   5   4   3   2   1

Contents

Introduction

Many trends in the animation, entertainment, and commercial industries have affected how studios and independent animators do business in the early twenty-first century. After a peak of animation activity in the mid- to late 1990s—with a proliferation of films, television series, and new media opportunities such as the Internet, for example—consolidation and cost-cutting have led to more uncertainty for studios large and small.

The lowering of prices on animation equipment has enabled more animators to create a quality product on a reasonable budget. While this has increased opportunities for many, it has also led to increased competition in the market. Meanwhile, the general malaise that characterizes the current economy has led customers to ask their animation partners and vendors for more services at a lower price, exacerbating the competitive situation. While the economy rises and falls cyclically, much of the reliance on low prices (at the expense of studio profit) is likely to continue, even as the economy starts to come out of its doldrums.

Other challenges abound. The fast pace of technological change requires increased investment in order to keep up and stay competitive. Fragmentation in the television industry, a reduction in films released, more concentration in the home video and video game markets, and the failure of Internet entertainment to succeed as a standalone business have made distribution of animation properties more difficult. The globalization of the animation industry, the rise of vertically integrated entertainment companies, and the increased ownership participation by studios around the world in properties with which they're involved have combined to saturate the animation market. Cost-cutting and the need to remain flexible have created a workforce that is largely freelance, as opposed to staff-dominated as it was in the 1990s. More reliance on franchise-based properties has made it difficult for original, innovative productions to break through.

All of these developments, and others, have made the animation industry ever more complex for those doing business in it. In order to succeed studios must have more knowledge about what's happening in the global market, about alternative methods of distribution and marketing, about ways to cut costs and increase efficiency without sacrificing quality, and about the strategic moves that might keep them ahead of their competitors.

Exhibit 1.1

Animation Trends by Media Sector

Trend	Film	Television	Home Video	Interactive/ Software	Internet
Lower license fees	x	x			
Increasing competition		x		x	
Shorter lifespan	x			x	x
Franchise marketing	x	x	x	x	
Higher budgets	x	x	x	x	
Market fragmentation		x			x
Concentration of fewer hits	x		x	x	
Proliferation of outlets		x			
Increased marketing budgets	x		x	x	
Technological/format change			x	x	x

It is critical for all practitioners, whether on the creative side, the business side, or the technology side, to understand the business tools they have at their disposal.

The Animation Business Handbook is written for those animators and the executives who support them. It is for creatives who need to know about the business side of their craft in order to succeed; for the businesspeople who market, distribute, or tie in with animation properties; for the independent animators who want to gain a better understanding of how their industry works; and for new and experienced practitioners of all types looking for fresh ideas to create a healthy and growing business.

As more creators try to control their own destinies, as the vagaries of the industry make it more difficult to succeed, as more animators are finding themselves out on their own, and as more studios are taking a strategic look at the direction in which they want to move, there is a great need for a book like this. Surprisingly, no titles have been written about the business tactics involved in running an animation studio; about how to market, position, distribute, and finance animation properties in all media; or about how to price and promote a studio for both work-for-hire and proprietary opportunities. There are books on film financing and distribution, the creative side of the animation process, the history and art form of animation, and producing a proprietary animation property. (Many of these are listed in appendix 2 at the end of this book.) But none of these titles look at all aspects of managing and marketing a full-service animation studio. *The Animation Business Handbook* is meant to fill that void.

The Animation Business Handbook is divided into three parts. Part One (chapters 1 through 8) looks at the concerns related to developing, producing, distributing, pitching, and marketing proprietary properties, including staffing, budgeting, deal making, and an overview of trends. It covers all sectors where animation plays a role: television, film, home video/DVD, the Internet, and electronic gaming.

Part Two (chapters 9 through 11) addresses issues specific to the work-for-hire or contract portion of the market, including the bidding process, how to estimate prices for contract projects, how to market a studio to potential client groups, and a summary of trends. This section deals with all aspects of the contract animation business, including commercial work and special effects.

Part Three (chapters 12 through 14) highlights the issues affecting the operations of a studio, whether small, midsize, or large. These include strategic issues as well as day-to-day tactics and operations such as hiring, funding, contracts, and intellectual property protection. Part Three also contains a chapter offering an overview of global trends, issues, and market characteristics affecting the many studios that operate on a worldwide basis.

Two appendixes end the book. The first is a detailed glossary explaining many of the business terms animation executives and creatives need to know. The second is a compilation of resources, including publications, books, associations, and trade shows.

Much of the information in Part One, the most detailed section in the book, applies to Parts Two and Three as well. For example, issues related to personnel are largely the same, whether a production is done on a work-for-hire basis or as a proprietary property. Cross-references will direct readers to the relevant sections when needed.

As noted, animation has become a global business. *The Animation Business Handbook* is written from a North American perspective (using U.S. dollars in valuations, for example). Many of the trends and issues that affect North American studios also play a role in the business strategies of studios located elsewhere, and the book takes that into account. Many of the examples involve non-U.S. studios.

None of the information in *The Animation Business Handbook* should be construed as legal or financial advice. The book is intended to explain the concepts and trends that studio owners and animators need to know. Any involvement in contracts or financing should, of course, be done in consultation with attorneys and financial advisors who have experience in animation.

It should be noted that every animation production and every deal having to do with animation is unique. While *The Animation Business Handbook* offers guidelines and an overview of how studios often handle different situations, it cannot offer step-by-step instructions for how to produce, finance, market, sell, and distribute an individual property or project. It can, however, provide the information that will allow animators and studio executives to assess their own situation and create a plan that makes sense for their properties, projects, and studios. This is the mission of *The Animation Business Handbook*.

PART I
PROPRIETARY PROPERTIES

1

Overview of Proprietary Animation Projects

Proprietary animation properties are those in which the creator or a production company, such as an animation studio, owns or maintains an interest. Given the complicated negotiations and deal structures required to get an animated property made and distributed in the 2000s, many proprietary properties have more than one owner. Meanwhile, sole owners often must share the revenues from their properties with several other parties.

Most proprietary animation projects fall into the realm of entertainment, but otherwise vary significantly. They can range in length from less than one minute to ninety minutes or more, encompass one-off projects and ongoing series, and extend into all entertainment media.

FILM

Film producers released 482 films (both animated and live-action) in 2001. Together these features generated a U.S. gross box office take of $8.4 billion, according to the Motion Picture Association of America (MPAA). The box office total was up 9.8 percent from 2000, when 478 films hit theaters.

During the 1990s the number of animated films released each year grew consistently. Of the films released in 2001, twelve were animated, compared to three in 1991, seven in 1999, and ten in 2000. The twelve released in 2001 accounted for about $790 million in ticket sales, or 10 percent of the total box office take for U.S. films that year. Since they represented only 3 percent of films released, their box office totals were, on average, higher than those for live-action films. (These numbers include only fully animated films and not those that were special-effects-heavy, live-action productions, such as Warner Brothers' *Cats and Dogs* in 2001.)

Many animated films, of course, do very well theatrically, generating among the top ticket sales in any given year. According to Exhibitor Relations, which tracks U.S. box office, the top animated film of 2001 was *Shrek,* which racked up $267.6 million in U.S. ticket revenues, followed by *Monsters, Inc.,* with $244.6 million. These two films ranked third and fourth respectively in the total box office rankings of all films that year.

Most animated feature films are funded and distributed by the major Hollywood studios such as Disney or DreamWorks, or television networks with feature film arms, such as Nickelodeon, which partners with its sister company Paramount on film distribution. A few are produced apart from the studio system and sold to exhibitors through independent distributors, but these are rare.

The big studios released ten of the animated movies that came out in 2001; the top "independent" release (*Waking Life,* released by 20th Century Fox's art-house subsidiary, Searchlight) ranked number 164 in total box office for that year, selling $2.9 million worth of tickets.

Overall, animated films' ability to bring in significant revenues varies widely. In addition to *Shrek* and *Monsters, Inc.,* other animated features released in 2001 included *Atlantis: The Lost Empire* (generating $84 million at the box office), *Jimmy Neutron: Boy Genius* ($62.3 million), *Recess: School's Out* ($36.6 million), *Final Fantasy* ($32.1 million), *Pokémon 3* ($17 million), *Osmosis Jones* ($13.5 million), *Waking Life* ($2.5 million), and *The Trumpet of the Swan* ($152,525). Of course, even a low-revenue film can be profitable if its budget is small. *Jonah: A VeggieTales Movie* (Big Idea/Artisan Entertainment, 2002) generated a U.S. box office gross of over $25.5 million. The production budget was $14 million and the print and advertising budget $7 million.

In 2001 75 percent of the films that held the number-one box office ranking in their opening weekend saw revenues drop by at least half the next week. The first weekend, therefore, is critical to a picture's success, and studios spend significant marketing dollars to drive audiences to the film during its first few days. The focus on marketing a film's premiere probably contributes to the quick drop-off in attendance for most movies. At the same time, if a release fails to make a mark immediately it will be pulled from theaters; most are no longer given the chance to succeed over time.

Another reason behind the large drop-off in attendance after the opening weekend is that films are able to screen on a huge number of theaters upon their debut, enabling virtually everyone who wants to see a film to see it on the first weekend. Some films open on as many as five thousand screens.

The need to generate moviegoer interest in a film prior to its release is one reason many films—especially those intended to be blockbusters—are based on recognized franchises such as television shows, comic books, or books. Of the top ten films of 2001, as ranked by U.S. box office totals, seven were based on well-known "brands." The top three were based on books, two were sequels, and two were remakes.

In addition to relying on franchise pictures, many studios are reducing risk by decreasing the overall number of films they release each year. Universal's output fell from thirty-five to less than twenty and Disney's from thirty to less than twenty from 1998 to 2001.

One area of the feature film business that represents a small but growing opportunity for animated movies is large-format distribution. IMAX is the best-known name in this segment, operating two hundred theaters as of 2001 and planning an ambitious expansion. IMAX showed its first all-animated release, *Cyberworld,* in 2000. The 45-minute project included eight short films from DreamWorks, 20th Century Fox, Sony, and other entertainment companies.

Walt Disney became the first studio to release a film simultaneously in traditional 35-millimeter theaters and on IMAX screens in 2002 with *Treasure Planet,* after having had successful IMAX runs with previous movies, including *Beauty and the Beast* and *Fantasia.* The IMAX version of *Fantasia 2000* brought in about $50 million at fifty-four large-format theaters.

Other studios large and small have released films in large-format theaters, or are looking at large-format distribution as a potential avenue for their films, either on an exclusive basis or along with traditional theatrical outlets. Meanwhile, IMAX invested over $10 million in the CGI animation house Mainframe Entertainment in 1999. The two companies set up a joint venture to produce films for the IMAX format.

Many of the so-called "live-action" movies on the market today are actually composed of a significant amount of animated footage in the form of computer-generated (CG) special effects. Sometimes entire characters— such as Jar Jar Binks in *Star Wars: Episode I—The Phantom Menace* (1999), Dobby in *Harry Potter and the Chamber of Secrets* (2002), or Gollum in the *Lord of the Rings* trilogy (2001– 2003)—are CG creations.

Often these effects-filled films are at the top of the box office rankings in a given year. In fact, about a quarter of the $8 billion in domestic box office in 2001 was attributable to films with CG animation. That includes *Shrek, Monsters, Inc.,* and several other CG-animated releases, as well as *Harry Potter and the Sorcerer's Stone* (bringing in $317.5 million at the domestic box office), *The Lord of the Rings: The Fellowship of the Ring* ($311.7 million), *The Mummy Returns* ($202 million), *Pearl Harbor* ($198.5 million), and *Jurassic Park III* ($181.1 million).

In 2002 seven of the top ten films were dependent on effects. They included *Spider-Man* (with a domestic gross of $404 million), *Star Wars: Episode II—Attack of the Clones* ($310 million), *Harry Potter and the Chamber of Secrets* ($246 million), *The Lord of the Rings: The Two Towers* ($231 million), *Signs* ($225 million), *Men in Black II* ($190 million), and *Scooby-Doo* ($253 million). The number-nine film of the year was the all-CG-animated *Ice Age* ($176 million).

Effects are completed on a work-for-hire basis during the postproduction phase of a live-action film (see chapter 9 for more details).

TELEVISION

Television is a coveted distribution channel for owners of animation properties. Not only are there fewer barriers to entry than in the film business, which is dominated by a handful of powerful distributors, but the exposure can be greater if a show appears on a highly rated network. More Americans watch television than see movies, and they are exposed to the characters on a weekly or daily basis, rather than just once.

As of 2001 there were over 105 million TV households in the United States, according to Nielsen Media Research, with viewers watching those sets almost 52 hours per week. Over 69 percent of TV households (73.2 million) had cable service, while 32.3 percent (34.1 million) received pay cable stations. Another 12.9 million households subscribed to satellite services, up 34.4 percent from 2000.

As the number of television channels has proliferated in the United States and worldwide, there has been more demand for programming, including animation. In the mid- to late 1990s there were more than six hundred animated shows on the air on all television venues in the United States, according to estimates, compared to just seventy-five in 1980, when the market was dominated by three networks. The amount of time devoted to animation has grown even more since then, although it is hard to pin down an exact nationwide number for this fluctuating market.

Cable has become more influential than broadcast in terms of animation, with Nickelodeon and Cartoon Network attracting larger groups of viewers than the networks in many instances. In May 2001 Nickelodeon garnered a 4.8 rating among viewers aged 2 to 11 on Saturday mornings (translating to 1.9 million kids), according to Nielsen, compared to a 3.0 rating for the top broadcast network at that time period, the Kids' WB! Following these two, in order of ratings strength, were the broadcast channel

ABC, cable's Cartoon Network, and broadcaster CBS. As of early 2001 Nickelodeon and Cartoon Network, which are on the air 24 hours a day, controled 84 percent of all the children's rating points available each week.

While the growth in the number of channels has led to more opportunities for animation producers to sell to television networks, it has also become more difficult for any single show to succeed. Children's viewing time is scattered over many offerings—as is adults'—reducing the chances for an individual show to break out of the pack and attain "hit" status, with all the ancillary revenues that entails. While programs such as *Bob the Builder, SpongeBob SquarePants, The Powerpuff Girls,* and *Pokémon* can still make a mark, it is difficult for most programs to become bona fide hits.

Another significant development occurred in the children's television market in the late 1990s and early 2000s. The formerly important syndication market, which enabled producers to distribute their shows to local markets for early morning and after-school airing, dried up. The increased strength of cable networks as an alternative to broadcast was one factor in its decline.

An even more important impetus, however, was that most previously independent local stations became affiliated with new networks such as the WB and UPN, along with the slightly older Fox. These new networks were associated with entertainment conglomerates, and they had programming divisions that provided shows to their new affiliates and squeezed out independent studios. Much of the remaining time has been filled by programming blocks from a few large independent producers and distributors who have formed alliances with the networks. 4Kids Entertainment has supplied Fox with its Saturday morning programming since 2002, while Discovery Networks has done the same for NBC, as has Nelvana for PBS. All of this leaves little time available for syndicated programming.

These trends, as well as a downturn in television advertising in the early 2000s and competition from non-TV-related media such as video games and the Internet, have combined to drive license fees down. Studios that are able to get their programs on the air receive a much lower payment for those shows than in the past. Whereas in the mid-1990s a U.S. television license fee would cover all or most of the cost of a show's production budget, that is no longer true. This situation has necessitated the rise of international coproductions, which will be discussed in detail throughout this book.

Aside from traditional half-hour and hour-long series, broadcast and cable networks also purchase animated shorts to be used as interstitials (30- to 60-second productions that air between shows). The classic property *Gumby* was reintroduced to modern audiences in 2001 as a spokescharacter for the ABC network's children's programming, during which the characters appeared in interstitials. The success of the property in this venue led to its being developed into a movie of the week. The interstitial exposure helped spur demand for licensed merchandise and home videos as well.

Television-distributed, feature-length, original animated movies are another opportunity for animators. In 2002 a leading independent animation studio, DIC Entertainment, signed a deal with Nickelodeon for thirty-nine original DIC films under "The Incredible DIC Movie Toons" banner. All were spinoffs of existing DIC franchises, including *Sabrina the Teenage Witch* and *Inspector Gadget*.

Although the broadcast networks, Nickelodeon, and Cartoon Network account for most of the animation on television, other networks are increasingly purchasing cartoon programming that appeals to their audiences. The Christian Broadcasting Network launched an animation division to produce series such as *The Storyteller Cafe*. *Fox News Sunday,* a program on the cable network Fox News Channel, has used animation to explain news stories during broadcasts. The Sci Fi Channel acquired its first animated show, *Tripping the Rift* (a CG series produced by CineGroupe in association with the property's originator, Film Roman), in 2002. Playboy TV commissioned its first animated series, *Playboy's Dark Justice,* in the early 2000s, while The History Channel licensed short films featuring rapping versions of the U.S. founding fathers from JibJab, a New York–based production company, as a way to promote a documentary on the actual people involved in the country's early days.

Interactive television is another opportunity for animation producers, although it is just emerging as of this writing. A Danish company, ITE, has developed several interactive television shows, including *Hugo the Troll* and *The Nelly Nut Show,* which utilize 2D-animated characters that are able to interact in real time with viewers who call or e-mail. Most companies in this market use proprietary software systems and develop their properties internally, but are likely to consider ideas and characters created by outside firms, especially after the technology becomes established.

HOME VIDEO/DVD

Home video has traditionally been viewed more as an ancillary product or secondary distribution channel for entertainment properties, rather than as a first-run venue for animation. Yet home video's and DVD's importance as initial distribution channels has grown, especially as a means of supporting existing franchises with new means of exposure.

Rental and sell-through revenues for home video and DVD reached $20.6 billion in 2002, according to the Video Software Dealers Association (VSDA). The sell-through portion of that (the revenues attributable to videos that were sold, rather than rented) was $12.4 billion, or 60 percent of the market. Ninety-five percent of U.S. television households possessed a VCR, while 35 percent of TV households had a DVD player. The latter number continues to grow exponentially.

A growing proportion of the videos and DVDs released each year, especially for the sell-through market, consists of original video productions. Animation comprises a small portion of these titles; according to *The Hollywood Reporter* just forty-six, or 2 percent, of the two thousand direct-to-video productions released in 2000 were animated. But animation is powerful when it comes to sales. Adams Media Research found that forty-eight original video titles in 2000 achieved sales levels of fifty thousand units or more. Twenty-three, or 48 percent, of those were animated, with the year's top release being Disney's *The Little Mermaid II: Return to the Sea,* a 5.5-million-copy seller.

Many of the major studios have developed strong direct-to-video initiatives, comprised of sequels to theatrical films or original movies based on television shows. Disney started the stampede with its *Aladdin* sequel, *The Return of Jafar,* which was released as an original video production and sold 4.6 million units in its first week; a later sequel, *Aladdin and the King of Thieves,* surpassed that with 6 million sold in its first week. Warner Brothers, 20th Century Fox, and other studios have had success with theatrical sequels, while Warner and others have developed video programs for their classic TV franchises (in Warner's case, *Scooby-Doo* and *Looney Tunes*). All of the twenty-three top-selling original animated videos mentioned above were based on existing franchises: eight on film properties, ten on television series, three on books or comic books, and two on classic song titles.

Franchise-based original videos tend to earn good placement in stores; they maintain consumer awareness, which helps them attract notice on retail shelves; and they are often heavily marketed, since the studios feel the investment is worthwhile. All of these factors help boost sales. Meanwhile, the cost of production for an original video is usually much less than for a theatrically released feature, which means profits are often higher for a direct-to-video sequel than a theatrical one, at least in the children's market.

The five top-selling original videos of all time, as of late 2002, according to *Video Premieres Magazine* (which changed its name to *DVD Premieres Magazine* in 2003), were all franchise-based. They included *The Lion King II: Simba's Pride* (1998, 14 million units sold), *The Return of Jafar* (1994, 11 million), *Aladdin and the King of Thieves* (1996, 9 million), *Beauty and the Beast: Enchanted Christmas* (1997, 8 million) and *The Little Mermaid II: Return to the Sea* (2000, 7.5 million), all from Disney. The top eight all-time best-sellers were from Disney; numbers nine and ten were the second and third installments in Universal's *Land Before Time* franchise.

Marketing support for original video productions based on franchises can rival those for theatrical films in both their cost and the number of impressions generated. A 2000 direct-to-video production tied to Warner Brothers' *Batman Beyond* television series, *Return of the Joker*, attracted theatrical-level promotional partners that included Dairy Queen, Coca-Cola, Hasbro, Scholastic, and Orange Julius, all of which—along with Warner's internally funded advertising activity—created significant impact at retail, in schools, and in all advertising channels.

In general, the big studios look at their direct-to-video program as opportunistic: if a property lends itself to video and there is some indication it will sell well (such as a track record in licensed products or other consumer markets), they will produce and release it as a direct-to-video production. This activity is not necessarily part of an ongoing strategy, however; there are no objectives requiring a studio to produce a certain number of original videos per year. Even franchise-based original videos find it challenging to stand out in a crowded market, so studios are selective about which properties warrant an original video production requiring a high-profile marketing kick-off.

While the major studios release the best-selling original video titles, some independent animation houses are also active in this sector. DIC Entertainment produced a series of four direct-to-video films as a key element in the relaunch plan for the classic property *Strawberry Shortcake*. Video distributor Artisan Entertainment, along with toy maker Mattel and animation studio Mainframe Entertainment, released an original video starring the doll Barbie in a production of *The Nutcracker Suite*, shipping nearly 3.5 million VHS and DVD units to retailers; an estimated 93 percent of those were subsequently sold to consumers. The production's success boosted sales of tie-in products from Mattel and other partners, and spurred production of a sequel, *Barbie as Rapunzel*, the next year and subsequent releases thereafter (now distributed by Lion's Gate).

While producing and marketing a video without franchise backing seems a nearly impossible task, it can be done. If an independently produced, wholly original title can gain shelf space and generate positive word of mouth, it can succeed over time. More than 2 million copies of *Annabelle's Wish,* produced by Ralph Edwards Film, were shipped to retailers in 1997, for example.

Probably the best example of a nonfranchise-based direct-to-video success is Big Idea Productions' *VeggieTales,* an inspirational series that began its life on videos sold exclusively through the Christian bookseller market. After three years in Christian stores, the franchise was popular enough that Wal-Mart and other mass merchants began to carry the line. From 1993 through early 2002 Big Idea sold more than 25 million videos, not to mention 3 million musical recordings.

One reason smaller studios can succeed in the video market, even with nonfranchise-based original productions, is because their assessment of "success" is different from that of the studios. Whereas a major Hollywood oufit might need to generate at least $100 million from a single video production to deem it a success, a smaller producer might be happy with sales of just $1 million.

One of the most important trends in the video market in the early 2000s has been the rise of the DVD format. In 2002 DVDs accounted for 65 percent of video/DVD sell-through sales, or $8 billion, representing a 51 percent increase over the previous year, according to the VSDA. The VHS format continues to dominate the rental side of the market, but its share dropped from 83 percent to 65 percent of rental revenues in 2002. The market for DVDs has grown twice as fast as the VHS market did in its early years; some publications are predicting the demise of VHS in the near future as VHS users purchase DVD players and move to that format.

As of 2002, major chains such as Blockbuster are devoting nearly half their new-release shelf space to DVDs. Sales of the video/DVD version of the theatrical film *Spider-Man* skewed 80/50 toward DVDs, while the breakdown for *Monsters, Inc.* was 50/50. These developments have caused studios large and small to release videos in DVD and VHS formats simultaneously, rather than waiting to see how the VHS did before considering a DVD, as was the case as the format emerged. They are also rereleasing earlier films, especially classics, on DVD.

The home video/DVD sell-through market is cyclical, with the bulk of sales occurring in the fourth quarter of each year. Some of the major studios have reported that nearly half their revenue from videos and DVDs comes from sales occurring in October, November, and December.

INTERNET AND WIRELESS ANIMATION

The Internet has grown significantly as a channel for animation since the late 1990s. There were 69.1 million computer households in the United States in 2001, according to the U.S. Census Bureau—66 percent of all households had a computer. Of those, 87 percent had Internet access, according to the Census Bureau, and 12 percent had high-speed/broadband access, according to Jupiter Communications.

Although the Internet did not turn out to be viable as a primary distribution channel or business model for animation companies—many entertainment-centric Web sites have folded—it remains a means of exposing a property to the trade and consumers. Producers and distributors of animated TV shows and films also enhance their off-line productions by creating convergent Web sites featuring interactive entertainment and activities.

The Internet is an effective "incubator" for new properties. Online exposure can generate immediate feedback, allowing the creator to alter the property so it becomes more marketable for mainstream media. For example, the creator might stress certain elements that fans like or de-emphasize unpopular storylines. In addition, since online production is relatively low-cost, it is easy to experiment with little risk. Positive online feedback, as well as strong viewership levels, can help a producer sell a property to a television network or film studio. Web users tend to tell each other about properties or sites they like, so word of mouth can help build a following among core fans. Many producers try to encourage word of mouth by implementing so-called "viral" marketing efforts, such as sending an e-mail with a link to an original animation, in the hopes that recipients will forward it to their friends.

Few Internet-origin properties make their way to mainstream media, but there are examples that illustrate how the Web can be a successful incubator. Showtime was one of the first networks to purchase an Internet show with its acquisition of *Whirlgirl* from Visionary Media. The episodes aired first on the network's Web site sho.com starting in 1999. The cable network TNN acquired *Gary the Rat* from MediaTrip and expanded it into a 30-minute television series. Mondo Media's *Happy Tree Friends* has moved from the Internet to DVD and cable, as well as into ancillary merchandise.

UrbanEntertainment.com, a Web entertaiment producer and distributor, has had success translating its Internet-developed properties into mainstream media. It sold its series *Cisco & Ripple,* an animated movie review program, to the premium movie channel Black Starz!, which has an audience with similar demographic characteristics to UrbanEntertainment's. The studio also sold its webisodic series *Undercover Brother* to Imagine

Entertainment, which developed it into a live-action feature film released by Universal in 2002.

In rare cases properties originating on the Internet have become multifaceted franchises. Spring House Entertainment, a digital production company in Taiwan, attributed much of its nearly $3 million in revenues in 2001 to its animated character *A-kuei,* a main feature on its Web site. Spring House had 300,000 paid subscribers to its site across Asia, but also generated revenues from Video CDs of its cartoons. *A-kuei* inspired licensed merchandise such as stationery and appeared in advertising and as a guest on television shows. An *A-kuei* feature film was planned for 2003.

Studios of all sizes have set up Web sites to gain exposure for their lesser-known properties. Pixar, recognized for its CG-animated feature films, set up a Web site to spotlight some of its 3D-animated shorts, which otherwise would have little chance to be seen except at film festivals. Similarly, U.K.-based stop-motion studio Aardman Animations, producer of *Wallace & Gromit* and *Chicken Run,* introduced an Internet-exclusive property, *Angry Kid,* in 2001. Twenty-five 1-minute episodes attracted over 1 million views in their first two months online; the series was available on Aardman's site and on the Web entertainment destination site Atomfilms.com. Aardman also released ten new short *Wallace & Gromit* films, under the *Cracking Contraptions* banner, for online-only distribution.

In order to increase traffic to animation sites and raise exposure for individual properties among both consumers and the trade, several companies have set up online film festivals. Yahoo! Internet Life and the Sundance Film Festival were among those sponsoring online film festivals as of 2001. (See more film festival listings in appendix 2.)

Despite the demise of high-profile entertainment-destination sites ranging from Pseudo.com to Pop.com, there are sites that continue to specialize in online entertainment that includes animation. Internet sites tend to have far less exposure than a television series or other mainstream vehicle of course; Film Roman's Level13.net had 25,000 registered users in early 2001, more than a year after its launch. Most sites target a narrow audience, with the majority going after young adult males. Yet, there are destination sites for nearly every demographic group.

Entertainment-destination sites are not the only distributors or purchasers of animated content. Corporate and sports-related sites, for example, seek animation to entertain their visitors, to encourage viewers to come back to the site, or to educate or demonstrate. Many of these sites commission the work on a contract basis and own all rights, while others acquire or license properties from independent producers. An example of the latter is

The Kellys, an auto racing–themed series developed by SportsBlast and acquired by nascar.com in 2001. In its first ten days online the series generated more than 100,000 downloads. Turner Sports Interactive produced and distributed *The Kellys* on behalf of SportsBlast.

Technology companies often include animation on their corporate sites to demonstrate how their software products can be used. One Belgian company, Imagination in Motion, created a character called *Night Knight* to demonstrate its RealActor brand of 3D streaming software. The property began in 2000 as a couple of 30-second webisodes produced for less than four thousand dollars each, targeted at kids aged eight to twelve. The company planned to develop the property for a CG television series, interactive gaming, interstitials, and interactive television, as well as syndicating it to other Web sites and creating licensed merchandise.

An important venue for Internet animation is comprised of "convergent" sites set up by film studios, television networks, and others to enhance fans' experience with their off-line entertainment properties. The company ties its off-line and online activities together to drive traffic back and forth. This strategy reinforces the company's brand(s), allows for cross-promotion of online shows on-air (or on-screen or in-game) and vice versa, and creates more advertising opportunities for the company's partners. The online venue also allows low-cost testing of limited licensed products and new entertainment productions, and generates feedback on both the online and on-air content. The online and off-line staffs work together to convey the same message about the brand and ensure complementary programming choices. Macromedia's Flash software, used to create most online animation, can be used easily and cost-effectively for television animation as well, which allows for content sharing.

Egmont Imagination, the animation subsidiary of the European publishing giant Egmont, was among the many producers and networks to promote the convergent aspects of its programming in the early 2000s. For example, it pitched its Flash-animated series *Solve the Mystery with Inspector McClue* at the television trade show NATPE in 2002. The concept allows children to discover clues to the mystery by watching the show and then to solve the mystery online. The program, coproduced with TV2 of Denmark, had a successful history on Danish television.

Online Challenges

Although the total universe of computer users is large, there are many challenges facing those whose business model relies on the Internet as a distribution or revenue-generating channel. One barrier has been the lack of widespread broadband access. Online entertainment files are often large and therefore slow to download or view. This is one of the reasons that Flash animation has become so popular; its animation style is simple and file sizes are small. Greater broadband penetration will allow for much more sophisticated Internet animation—similar to video-game or television quality—without sacrificing speed and frustrating viewers. The number of households with broadband is increasing quickly, and more access will enable increased sophistication and variety in online animation and may create an environment where Internet animation can attract revenues.

Another barrier—one likely to remain—is that online viewership is highly fragmented, meaning that audiences for any one site are too small to attract mainstream advertisers. And due to the low barriers to entry (just about anyone with a computer can create animation for the Web) quality is an issue. Online-only companies (known as "pure-play" operations) originally had business models driven by advertising; they hoped they could create low-cost content and attract viewers and, in turn, advertisers or sponsors. Eventually the novelty of the Internet wore off and all the bad animation began to alienate viewers. Audience sizes have not grown to a level that would appeal to most mainstream advertisers.

To be successful, Internet animation must be interesting enough to make people stay a while. It must also be ever-changing, so viewers will want to visit the site repeatedly. And it must generate enough "buzz" to create word of mouth, so audience size increases. Sites that can achieve these goals over a long enough period of time to amass a large and loyal audience may be able to make money from their efforts and create a viable business model.

Wireless

Wireless communication is an emerging business, especially in the animation sector. The consumer base in the United States, Europe, and most of the rest of the world is small for uses outside telephone communication, and the technology is such that animation is very simple and of poor quality. Wireless technologies include WAP (wireless application protocol) and MMS (multimedia message service), neither of which have been embraced fully by consumers. New "smartphone" models allow Java- and BREW-based animation and gaming; the better quality may attract new consumers over time. Wi-Fi, or Wireless Internet, took off in 2003 and holds promise as a mainstream technology.

Japan is one of the few countries where wireless has made a mark in the animation industry. Telephone company DoCoMo markets i-mode phones that allow connectivity to the Internet as well as the downloading of small entertainment files. In Japan 25 million users as of 2001 owned i-mode phones, representing about a quarter of the population. More people regularly use i-mode than the Internet, although its usage fell off somewhat in 2002. (E-mail use continues to grow.)

Because a significant number of people already own these phones, some Japanese content providers have focused their businesses on creating animation and games for i-mode phones since 2001, when the first animation became available for the technology. DoCoMo collects fees from its customers for each information "packet" downloaded and passes along a percentage of the fee to its official content providers. (Unlike on the Internet, all DoCoMo content providers are officially sanctioned, preventing content oversaturation.) Consumers' fees for general phone service are low, but their bills can add up if they download a lot of information. This model gives content providers a significant potential revenue stream; they do not need to sell advertising to survive.

Games accounted for 90 percent of content downloads during 2001, but some content providers have successfully marketed animation packets. One company, Cybird, was licensed by Disney to create animation based on its characters; the Disney site was one of twenty-four Cybird sites that offered various types of character animation for the i-mode.

Some observers believe the production of animation for cell phones, handheld computers, and personal digital assistants (PDAs) may become a bigger business in the U.S. and elsewhere than it is now. Some content providers are marketing animation for wireless devices in the early 2000s, including Eruptor.com and 3D Pulse, which supported PocketPC units. Viral marketing (efforts to spur word of mouth via e-mail) to encourage additional downloads is a key promotional tool in this market.

GAMING

Gaming, for video game consoles, computers, and wireless devices, has become a larger industry than filmmaking in terms of total revenues (including both hardware and software). In 2001 U.S. sales of computer and video game software alone reached $6.35 billion, with $4.6 billion (72 percent) of that from console video games and $1.75 billion (28 percent) from computer games, according to the Entertainment Software Association and NPDTechworld.

There are differences between the console and computer game sectors in terms of dominant consumer groups and sales. In video games the top genre was sports, accounting for 22.2 percent of the market, followed by action games, with 19.8 percent, and strategy/role-playing games, with 17.6 percent. In computer games the top genre was strategy games, accounting for a 25.4 percent share (role-playing added another 8.8 percent), followed by children's games at 14.2 percent, and family titles at 11.5 percent of the market. According to Forrester Research, 58 percent of consumers with a home-based personal computer use it for playing games.

Revenues from interactive games rivals that of other entertainment vehicles for some multifaceted studios. In fiscal 2002 Sony Corporation's worldwide revenues for game consoles and software exceeded $8.4 billion, while motion pictures and television generated $5.3 billion and music $5.39 billion. Sony has long been active in the interactive game market, starting in electronics before moving into entertainment, but all the studios have joined Sony in viewing interactive software as an important business.

The gaming industry offers many opportunities for CG animators, who create both 3D character animation for the game itself and in-game cinematics (that is, animated scenes that further the story and/or reward gamers for reaching certain levels). Many of these animation sequences, which can reach five minutes in length, are created by outside companies on a work-for-hire basis. The games themselves are proprietary to the company that created them, and are often the basis for further entertainment such as films or merchandise.

Keeping up with technology is a struggle in gaming, probably more than in any other sector of the animation industry, as the major console manufacturers continuously introduce new platforms. Not only do game developers have to spend to keep up with the new authoring tools (the technologies used to create the game) in order to stay current, but they must continue to support older technologies that are still being used by consumers.

Some of the leading platforms as of the early 2000s include Nintendo's GameCube, Sony's PlayStation 2, and Microsoft's Xbox, plus several handheld games, a number of older consoles, and PC and Macintosh computers. (This roster excludes games created for arcades and cell phones.)

Acquiring the rights to create and sell games for multiple platforms helps a game developer or publisher spread its risk, but this strategy is expensive. Some studios lack the financial or human resources to embark on this path, and choose to specialize instead. As of 2001 Sony had the largest number of consoles in homes, and therefore offered the most profit potential for its developers. As would be expected, it had the greatest number of developers on board, with three hundred companies making games for Sony machines. Each company has its own characteristics—such as how difficult it is to program games for its platforms, how responsive it is to developers' needs, the size of its installed base, and its prospects for future growth—which developers and publishers must weigh before approaching each for a license.

A typical title in the violent *Doom* franchise, released by Id Software, sells more than 1 million units; the same company's *Quake I, II,* and *III* titles sold 4 million copies as of early 2003. Blizzard's *Diablo II* generated sales of over 2 million units in its first three months on the market, while its *Warcraft II: Tides of Darkness* moved almost 2.5 million units on a global basis. The first two games in Ubisoft's *Rayman* franchise sold over 10 million games. *Duke Nukem,* a violent franchise developed by Apogee/3D Realms, has generated $250 million in sales over its lifetime. Mainstream titles containing less violence, such as *Final Fantasy* or *Pokémon,* can achieve higher sales levels. Of course, these are all bestsellers; many titles will achieve sales levels that are a fraction of these numbers.

Sales for individual computer games and software are less on average than those for console video game titles. Some big-selling examples include: *Star Wars* titles for the Mac, some of which have sold a quarter of a million units in less than a year; Humongous Entertainment's *Pajama Sam,* which sold nearly 135,000 titles in the year of its release; and *Barbie Riding Club,* from Mattel, which sold more than 80,000 units, valued at $2 million, in just three months.

Studios that create animated entertainment properties, especially computer-generated productions, look at gaming as an important ancillary revenue stream, and design and produce game elements and animation along with the television series or film itself. The two media can share digital assets, which reduces costs and development time, allowing the game to be released near the show's debut. In addition, game developers who are involved early in the process can sometimes provide design or story input that positively affects the entertainment vehicle. Mainframe Entertainment is one studio that has tried to acquire interactive rights as well as television rights to properties it produces.

Video and computer game productions are becoming more like films, incorporating sophisticated animation and, on occasion, voice-overs by well-known actors. For example, Disney Interactive's videogames based on its film *The Lion King* featured all the original voice actors from the film, including James Earl Jones and Jeremy Irons. *Kingdom Hearts,* an action-oriented role-playing game starring Disney characters as well as new creations (a joint production for PlayStation 2 from SquareSoft and Disney Interactive), included star voices such as Haley Joel Osment.

At the same time, production and marketing budgets are rising, leading to a situation where only a few titles (5 percent for some companies) are profitable. That ratio makes it difficult for a developer to find a publisher for its titles, if they're not based on a hot license or a successful existing gaming franchise.

Another important trend in gaming is the rise of online, multiplayer titles, where gamers can compete against thousands or even millions of others in cyberspace. Some of these multiplayer titles are wholly for online use; the player downloads the software and passwords from the company Web site and logs onto the Web to play. Other multiplayer titles are a hybrid of console and online games, allowing individuals to play in the traditional

---

Exhibit 1.2

Snapshots of Media Sector Activity

Film

U.S. box office take (2001): $8.4 billion

Number of films released in the U.S. (2001): 482

Television

U.S. television households (2001): 105 million

Weekly hours of television watched, United States (2001): 52

Percentage of U.S. TV households with cable: 69%

Percentage of U.S. TV households with pay cable: 32.3%

Home Video/DVD

Percentage of U.S. TV households with VCRs (2002): 95%

Percentage of U.S. TV households with DVDs (2002): 35%

Home video and DVD cumulative revenues (2002): $20.6 billion

Percentage of revenues from sell-through: 60%

Percentage of revenues from rentals: 40%

Internet/Interactive Gaming

U.S. computer households (2001): 69.1 million

Percentage of U.S. computer households with Internet access (2001): 87%

Percentage of U.S. computer households with broadband access (2001): 12%

U.S. sales of computer and video-game software (2001): $6.35 billion

Percentage of sales from computer games: 28%

Percentage of sales from console games: 72%

Sources: MPAA, Nielsen Media Research, VSDA, U.S. Census, Jupiter Communications, IDSA

console manner, or against other players online. Some multiplayer games are being developed for wireless technologies as well.

DFC Intelligence estimated in 2001 that 114 million people would be playing online games by 2006, 23 million of them from consoles such as the Xbox. Even as of 2002, according to DFC, top online games can generate revenues of more than $100 million each.

2
Personnel

It is important to plan personnel needs carefully. Quality and customer service (including timely delivery of a finished product) will suffer if staffing and freelance support aren't adequate. On the other hand, assigning too many people to a project will break the budget, as will improper planning for their efficient use.

TOTAL PERSONNEL REQUIREMENTS

Total staffing requirements for an animation project range from one person or a very small team to a cast of hundreds, depending on the style, complexity, and length of the project, its budget, and its schedule. There are no "average" staffing levels.

Thirty artists and animators worked on *Waking Life* (Fox Searchlight, 2001), a feature starring sixty actors who filmed live-action scenes that were then animated using a proprietary technique. Another film, *Final Fantasy* (Sony, 2001), required two hundred CG artists and animators (from twenty countries), as well as thirty programmers. A traditionally animated German movie, *Werner: Volles Rooäää!!!* (Trickcompany, 1999) featured eleven hundred scenes. At the peak of production, four hundred animators were working in Germany and another two hundred and fifty in Vietnam. Background keys and one hundred CGI scenes created through motion-capture technology were outsourced to contract studios around the world.

A prime-time television series can utilize a staff of about one hundred for a season's worth of shows (twenty-four to twenty-six episodes). Personnel might include ten directors and five to twenty-five writers, with each lead writer and director responsible for two episodes per season. Groups of four or five writers work on each installment under the guidance of the lead.

A daytime animated series for children usually has a lower budget and a smaller staff. Each episode of a U.K. production, *Bill & Ben* (Cosgrove Hall), had four animators assigned to it as of 2003, while the CGI series *The Adventures of Jimmy Neutron: Boy Genius* (Nickelodeon) was completed by a team of thirty animators, a small staff for such a series.

Direct-to-home video productions often are completed on a low budget by a bare-bones roster of personnel. Others require staffing similar to that of a television episode, while some rival feature films in terms of quality and human resource requirements. An example of the last is DreamWorks's *Joseph: King of Dreams,* which was produced by a staff of nearly five hundred artists and animators around the world. Many of the personnel who worked on the sequel had also been involved with the original feature film, *The Prince of Egypt.*

In general, animation projects intended for online distribution require few animators, especially compared to other types of production. In part this is because the vehicles are usually only a minute or two long and can be created relatively quickly using Flash animation. Budgetary concerns also dictate that producers keep staff levels and other costs low; Internet animation, on its own, rarely generates much revenue.

On the other hand, some Internet animation can be complex and require more resources. Dotcomix, an online animation specialist that is now out of business, created a real-time 3D version of Garry Trudeau's *Doonesbury* comic strip character Duke, which appeared on the Internet, as well as on live television. It needed a team of forty people to manipulate the character during broadcasts.

In the interactive game segment many companies use small teams to create each title; this is especially true for products such as educational computer software titles that feature simple animated sequences. United States producers of more complex videogames often utilize staffs of about 50, while Japanese producers historically have preferred to devote as many as 200 people to a single title. As of the early 2000s one of the largest Japanese gaming companies, Square, had 670 employees on staff to create its games, including the *Final Fantasy* franchise; U.S.–based id Software, creator of the *Doom* and *Quake* franchises, had only 17.

A Gametek title for Nintendo, *Robotech: Crystal Dreams,* listed 28 positions in its game credits (with some people assuming more than one position), including 12 on the art staff, 3 game designers, 6 voice actors, a producer, and the publisher's vice president of product development. Classic Gaming's *StarControl II* included 58 positions, 16 of which were voice actors and 6 artists. The game credits for DroidQuest's *Robot Odyssey* listed 30 positions, many of which overlapped. Five of the 30 were game designers; one handled game graphics and one oversaw title animation.

In general, staffing requirements for games are on the rise as titles become more filmlike in quality and budget.

JOB DESCRIPTIONS

Job titles and descriptions vary from production to production, depending on the nature of the project and the size of the staff. On smaller projects, where flexibility is critical, each member of the team takes on more responsiblities. Large productions tend to be segmented, with each person's job narrowly focused and each task completed by one person or team.

The responsibilities associated with various job titles differ as well, especially from one medium to another. An executive producer or director working on a television project has a somewhat different role than an executive producer on a film, for example.

Producers and Production Staff

Producers and their production staff are primarily responsible for the business decisions facing the production. They particularly focus on setting up a realistic schedule and budget and then ensuring that the production stays on track operationally and financially. They often have some say in creative affairs, especially those at the top of the credits, such as the executive producer and producer; in fact, on a television series the creator often assumes the role of executive producer and leads the creative process. Those lower in rank, such as associate producers or production assistants, tend to have little more than tangential contact with the creative side of a project.

The production team can include executive producers (usually the title given to those responsible for securing financing or selling the show, or the lead creative person), a producer or producers, senior producers, supervising producers, coproducers, line producers, associate producers, creative producers, production managers and assistant managers, production supervisors, production consultants, production coordinators, production accountants, production assistants, production secretaries, and producer's assistants, among others.

Exhibit 2.1

Potential List of Credits/Titles Involved in an Animation Production

3D workbook/layout supervisor
ADR mixer
Animation checker
Animation checking supervisor
Animation lead
Animation timer
Animator
Apprentices
Art director
Artistic coordinator
Assistant animator
Assistant background painter
Assistant director
Assistant editor
Assistant layout artist
Assistant production manager
Assistant publicist
Associate producer
Audio visual engineer
Background painter
Background supervisor
Blue sketch artist
Camera operator
Camera supervisor
Casting assistant
Casting coordinator
Casting director
CG/CGI artist
CG/CGI supervisor
Character designer
Character modeler
Character sculptor
Chief technical director
Cleanup assistant
Cleanup breakdown artist
Cleanup inbetweener
Cleanup supervisor
Color model mark-up artist
Color model mark-up supervisor
Color scanner
Color styling supervisor
Color stylist
Compositing supervisor
Compositor
Conductor
Coproducer
Cosupervising sound editor
Dialogue director
Dialogue editor
Dialogue scripter
Digital painter
Directing animator
Director
Editor
Effects animator
Effects assistant animator
Effects breakdown artist

Effects designer
Effects editor
Effects inbetweener
Effects supervisor
Effects/prop modeler
Environmental modeler
Executive producer
Final check supervisor
Final checker
Foley artist
Foley supervisor
Game artist
Game engine designer
Game programmer
Hardware consultant
Ink-and-paint artist
Ink-and-paint mark-up artist
Ink-and-paint mark-up supervisor
Ink-and-paint supervisor
Key animator
Key cleanup assistant
Layout artist
Lead character modeler
Lead effects animator
Lead effects/prop modeler
Lead environmental modeler
Lead key cleanup artist
Lead programmer
Lead rigger
Lead technical animator
Lead technical director
Licensing assistant
Licensing director
Licensing manager
Lighting artist
Lighting supervisor
Line art scanner
Line producer
Location designer
Lyricist
Marketing assistant
Marketing director
Marketing manager
Messenger
Mixer
Music copyist/proofer
Music editor
Music producer
Music researcher
Musicians
Orchestrator
Overseas supervisor
Postproduction coordinator
Postproduction supervisor
Producer
Producer's assistant
Production accountant

Production assistant
Production consultant
Production coordinator
Production designer
Production manager
Production secretary
Production supervisor
Programmer
Programming supervisor
Projectionist
Publicist
Renderer
Rendering supervisor
Rerecording mixers
Rigger
Rotoscope artists
Rough inbetweener
Scanning supervisor
Scene planner
Scene planning supervisor
Score recorder/mixer
Script coordinator
Scriptwriter
Secretary
Senior technical director
Sequence/episode director
Software consultant
Software researcher
Song coach
Song producer
Sound designer
Sound mixer
Sound supervisor
Story consultant
Story designer
Story editor
Storyboard artist
Storyboard cleanup artist
Storyboard supervisor
Supervising animator
Supervising director
Supervising sound editor
Surface lead animator
Systems administration manager
Systems administrator
Technical animator
Technical director
Texture painter
Underscore composer
Visual development artists
Visual effects supervisor
Vocal coach
Voice cast—lead and supporting
Workbook artist
Workbook/layout supervisor

Note: Titles, credits, and total staff vary depending on medium, budget, and other factors. This is not an exhaustive list.

They are responsible for tasks such as tracking the project's progress, maintaining schedules, monitoring actual-versus-budgeted expenditures, routing, and trafficking. Their main purpose is to aid the director in achieving his or her vision, while keeping the property financially feasible.

If the purchaser of the production is known in advance—that is, if a studio, game publisher, or network is involved in the early stages of production—an executive from the buyer company oversees the production. This is usually a vice president of development or product development (the latter in the case of games), but the title can vary, depending on the nature of the buyer company and of the production.

The Director and the Creative Team

The director envisions the finished property and oversees the creative tasks that make the idea a reality. In film the director's role parallels that of a live-action director, in that both lead the overall creative development of the film. In television, especially on shows for children, some of the directorial and visionary duties often are assumed by the network executives assigned to the show, which leaves the director with less decision-making power and responsibility. Creator-led television shows are becoming more common, however, especially on cable networks; in this scenario the director's role is more akin to that of a movie director.

Film projects are more complicated than television or other types of animation production, and take longer to complete. On big-budget features, therefore, the director's job is often broken down into smaller components. The director leads the overall project, but is assisted by codirectors, each responsible for certain tasks. One may oversee development and editing, and another layout and animation, for example. The specific assignments depend on the needs of the project. Similarly, on episodic television projects, the series director may be assisted by a group of directors—their titles vary—responsible for individual episodes.

Other creatives that can be part of the directors' unit include the associate director, assistant director, supervising director, sequence or episode directors, and director's assistants. Again, names, titles, and responsibilities vary, depending on the size and type of production.

Underlying property owners often are involved as creative consultants; some have a broader role, voicing characters or writing scripts. Since they are the creators of the concept, some directors work closely with them. In other cases, however, their credit may be primarily honorary.

Writers and Script

Writers, of course, are an important link in the creative chain. Their work contributes critically to the success or failure of a given show, and may even be the primary factor. A well-written script can overcome poor animation or an unappealing production design, but the reverse is rarely true. In fact, in prime-time television the writer is often the executive producer of the episode he or she writes, since the script is the main reason a network executive purchases an episode. There are often a dozen writers on a prime-time series; they take turns serving as the lead writer, with each assuming this role a couple of episodes per season, assisted by the rest of the writing staff.

Writers tend to wield less power in children's animation than in prime-time network fare. In fact, the people who create the scripts often have little input into how their story is produced on a children's or daytime series. As noted, this may not be the case on a creator-driven, cable-distributed show where the writer is often the creator, the executive producer, and the driving creative force, much as would occur in prime time.

In film there may be several rounds of writers. One writes the original screenplay, which is then revised by additional writers who have expertise in one aspect of scriptwriting, such as plotting or dialogue. Other personnel involved in script development for all types of animation can include story editors, story consultants, and script coordinators.

Casting and Voices

Casting directors, supported by casting coordinators or assistants, are responsible for finding the best people to voice the lead and secondary roles, given the production's budgetary constraints. They must find a balance between the actor most suited to the role, the optimal use of financial resources, and the value of marquee names for marketing purposes. The voice talent, including the principal and supporting cast, are essential to the production. Whether stars or voice acting specialists, their performances combine with those of the animators (and the words of the writers) to create living characters on the screen.

While big-name actors are expensive, they can contribute to the success of the property from a marketing standpoint and are considered almost essential for feature films. Audience members may attend a film they otherwise wouldn't, just because a certain actor voices a lead role; these actors are also valuable in promoting the film, since they generate much more publicity than other behind-the-scenes actors and animators.

Using well-known names is increasingly common on prime-time and even on daytime TV episodes, as well as films; Disney's series *Hercules* featured nearly 170 voices in its first couple of seasons, including James Woods in a starring role. Stars also are increasingly involved in direct-to-video productions, Internet episodic series, and game titles.

Despite the increased visibility of name-brand actors in animation, most of the work is still done by a pool of about one hundred actors that specialize in animation and other voice-over work.

Recording directors, dialogue directors, voice directors, and vocal coaches are among those who can be brought into productions to capture the spoken script and to help the actors enhance their performances. If the voice talent includes children, producers hire staff teachers or child welfare specialists as well.

Music and Songs

Animated productions need music in addition to dialogue, both as background to set a mood and, especially in film, as part of sequences that move the plot forward. (Most films have a half-dozen scenes built around songs.) Sound tracks can include original music and songs, utilize lesser-known existing music, or incorporate popular or nostalgic hits.

Song creation and rights acquisition for music begins during preproduction. Composers must write key songs early in the process so animators can create visuals against the songs. The music is edited and added to the animation during postproduction, along with sound effects.

Some of those involved creating or procuring songs include composers, conductors, studio musicians, lyricists, music researchers, music editors, song coaches, song producers, orchestrators or arrangers, and proofreaders. Music editing and other music-related functions are often completed by subcontractors rather than staffers, but there can be exceptions to this rule if the music is an important aspect of a production.

The Animation Team

A production's lead director may also serve as the animation director, depending on the nature of the production and the director's experience. But producers often bring in a separate animation director, especially for films. The animation director is responsible for leading the animation team and ensuring that the animation is well-acted, of high quality, and captures the director's vision for the production.

Some members of the art and animation team are involved primarily during preproduction and others during production; some are needed throughout the entire process. (See chapter 3 for more on the stages of animation production.) Designers are active mainly during development and preproduction, when they create the look of the characters, props, and backgrounds or environments. During preproduction, storyboard supervisors, storyboard artists, and storyboard cleanup artists draw the sketched sequences (a sort of "visual script") showing the key poses of the action for each scene throughout the production. Other art, visual, and design positions involved during development and/or preproduction include: the art director and artistic coordinator; visual development or conceptual artists; production, location, special effects, and character designers; color stylists; background painters; maquette or sculpture makers; and CGI artists.

During production layout artists use the storyboards to draw the main ("key") frames in each scene, plotting out composition, perspective, camera angles, lighting, textures, values, and how the characters should move. This process adds more detail to the storyboard artist's vision and creates a blueprint from which the animator can work. Background artists and painters then take over, creating the backgrounds—in detail and with color—on which the characters will be set in motion.

The animators take the character designs and add personality and life to them through their choice of expressions and body language, essentially acting the role. The key animator creates the main poses; on films each key animator typically is assigned one main or a few minor characters to work on throughout the production, which enhances consistency from scene to scene. Sometimes other arrangements make more sense, however. On *Rocky and Bullwinkle* (Universal, 2000), a live-action film with four animated characters, animators were assigned by sequence rather than by character, attending frequent meetings with the other animators to maintain consistency. In stop-motion, too, animators are often assigned scenes, working on all the characters that appear in that sequence.

While character animators specialize in creating a performance for a character or characters, effects animators are responsible for giving movement to all noncharacter elements. This includes objects such as furniture, as well as explosions or rain, lighting and shadows, props, tones, and essentially anything that moves that's not a character. The visual effects department includes visual effects supervisors, animators, assistant animators, breakdown artists, lighting supervisors, lighting animators, and inbetweeners, all responsible solely for effects.

Once key animators are finished with a scene it goes to a team of cleanup artists who create the neatly lined final image that will be seen on the screen, using the key animator's sketches for reference. Cleanup artists must maintain the emotions and attitudes that comes through in the key animator's sketches, while adding details that make the character stylistically consistent through the production.

When cleaned-up key poses are finished, inbetweeners take over. These animators create the movement that connects each key pose, ensuring the character moves smoothly. Finally, ink-and-paint—the stage when color is added to the final drawings—occurs. The ink-and-paint department includes ink-and-paint artists, color stylists, color model mark-up artists, and paint mark-up artists; many of the department staff can perform several of these tasks.

Others on the animation team can include the background painting team (including digital background artists), animation checkers (who check the final product as well as various steps along the way), scanners, scene planners, animation timers, compositors (who put all the elements together for final output), and supervisors (who oversee teams of animators, inbetweeners and/or ink-and-paint artists on a given sequence).

In CG productions animators must have the same artistic talent required of 2D animators, as well as the technical expertise and math skills needed to plot the characters in the computer. On many 2D-animated series CG animators are responsible for effects, props, and backgrounds, since series in the 2000s often feature 2D characters on a 3D CGI background.

Additional positions that relate to the 3D process include set builders, riggers (who define characters' kinematics, or skeletal makeup and movement), modelers, surface animators or "skinners" (responsible for muscles and skin), rendering specialists, and touch-up artists (who specialize in software programs such as Photoshop or Inferno).

Overseas supervisors act as the liaison between the project's producers and overseas studios, which on television productions often handle at least ink-and-paint duties, and sometimes the entire production process, from key framing through ink-and-paint. Overseas supervisors must be familiar with every aspect of animation creation and must be able to convey humor and personality to people from cultures that might be unfamiliar with American- or European-style themes and entertainment, even acting out character parts for them. The overseas supervisor acts as the producer's and director's representative as the project goes through the subcontracting studio, and is charged with catching and resolving problems early. On *Beavis and Butt-Head Do America,* for which animation production was done in Korea, MTV hired six overseas supervisors and consultants as well as a background layout supervisor.

Technical Staff

On a 2D production the technical staff primarily plays a support role, helping to design and maintain the computer systems and software needed to complete the project. Technical directors serve as a link between the technicians and engineers that report to them and the director, artists, and animators. They help the two groups, who use differing terminology and sometimes have different objectives, to communicate with each other and resolve issues.

On CG productions the basic animation process requires technical expertise, and animators typically require lots of support from the technical crew, not only to problem-solve and keep systems in running order but to help create new software or plug-ins to help the animators achieve their creative objectives.

Technical crews can be large on a complex 3D production. There were, for example, more technical directors (90) than animators (60) in the 250-strong crew that worked on Pixar's *Toy Story 2* over a three-year span. (Other productions may need just a few technical staffers.)

The technical crew's general responsibilities include R&D, troubleshooting, general systems administration (including information systems), as well as technical direction. In addition to the technical director the crew can include animation software engineers, roto artists, and technical assistants, among others.

Postproduction

Once production is finished the project moves into postproduction. Many of the postproduction personnel involved with animation are employed by outside firms or are independent contractors; but in some cases a production may hire a few integral postproduction people. The postproduction supervisor is generally a staffer who may have a crew, depending on the nature of the project.

Sound and music, final editing, title sequences, and possibly retakes, are all part of the postproduction process. Stock and original music and sound effects are added and edited, with music editors, dialogue editors, sound supervisors, sound designers, mixers, ADR supervisors (who oversee rerecording and the integration of new dialogue), sound editors, and sound engineers among those involved during this process. Recording directors and voice talent may be called back during postproduction for retakes.

Editors responsible for the visual look of the production (some of whom are also involved during preproduction), include lead editors (responsible for sound and visuals) and their assistants and/or apprentices, and picture editors.

For live-action films that contain CG effects or animation, adding the effects is a task that is part of the postproduction process. The CGI supervisor and CGI effects animators, who typically are employees of an outside animation house and not hired by the production, start their assignment once live production has wrapped, and finish up the work just prior to the release of the film.

Film labs and video duplication facilities are also brought in as the final step of the postproduction phase.

Business Personnel

In addition to the people devoted to creating the production there are several business-related staffers hired during an animation project. These personnel are not involved with the production creatively, but offer support essential to the success of the property. They may be independent contractors, work for an outside company, or be on the staff of the production company, network, or studio. Full-time staffers may handle business duties for many productions within the studio.

Business affairs and legal departments advise on the acquisition and clearance of rights; negotiate contracts from employment agreements to partnership deals; register copyrights and trademarks; register films with the Motion Picture Association of America; monitor payments, credits, and marketing materials for compliance with contract provisions; work with unions; develop studio policies with regard to compensation, hiring, and other procedures; help artists from other countries complete the paperwork that allows them to take the job; check the script for legal problems, such as trademark violations; and perform numerous other legal and business activities.

Accountants and other financial personnel assist the production staff in tracking the flow of funds. The production staff itself is responsible for day-to-day financial and budgetary decisions and monitoring, but staff members are supported by people outside the production who handle accounts payable and receivable, keep records for tax and financial reporting purposes, and/or make sure cash is available as needed. Production accountants, whose cost is attributed to the production itself, work in conjunction with corporate or external accounting staffs.

Marketing and promotions directors and their staffs must stay informed about the progress of the production, as well as any changes in scheduling, creative elements, or key credits. The more information they have, the better they'll be able to create promotions, advertising, and other marketing initiatives that make sense, and sell the property to potential marketing partners. While marketers have little or no input into the production itself, they are important to its success, in that they help bring in money and generate awareness. Marketing personnel can be on the network's, studio's, or producer's staff, or can be employees of independent marketing agencies retained by the production, network, or studio.

Personnel responsible for ancillary activities, particularly licensing executives, are involved in a similar manner as marketers. They must be kept apprised of all the creative and scheduling developments associated with the property in order to be able to pitch it to retailers and licensees. Licensing executives are increasingly brought in during the development stage, not to have any substantive creative input, but to make suggestions that will enhance the property's licenseability (without affecting the director's vision). A property with merchandising potential tends to be more attractive to potential investors and partners. Licensing executives and their staffs may be employees at the larger production houses, or of the distributor, network, or studio, or they may be independent agents hired by the production.

Publicity personnel, who can be staffers, members of retained firms, or independent contractors, coordinate publicity, such as newspaper and magazine articles and reviews, aimed at fans at the time of the property's release. Earlier in the production process they release information to excite potential trade partners—such as theater owners, licensing partners and retailers, or video distributors—about the project. Like other members of the promotional and marketing team, publicists must be kept informed about any important changes to the production, as well as any information that might be newsworthy.

Productions also need administrative and secretarial staffs to keep the production moving forward and to assist creative and production personnel as needed. Many of the key executives in the production, including producers and directors, have full-time administrative assistants dedicated to their clerical needs. These assistants allow the executives to stay focused on the production. Additional adminstrative personnel may be assigned to a particular department or to the production as a whole, or may be employees of the production company, studio, or network and shared by multiple productions.

The human resources department is in charge of keeping track of paperwork regarding hiring, pay, benefits, and termination. Final hiring decisions are usually made by directors or producers, but human resources may screen candidates or assist in other ways, including with training. Some productions use their studio's recruiting department to seek out appropriate

Exhibit 2.2

Sample Credit Lists for Animated Films in Different Styles

2D/Live-action feature film (animation portion only)

1 story designer/department head, 1 layout/workbook designer/department head, 1 background designer/department head, 1 cleanup designer/department head, 1 CGI effects designer, 1 2D effects designer, 1 2D effects co-department head, 1 computer graphics designer/department head, 1 outsourcing department head, 1 2D/3D animation check department head, 1 scanning department head, 1 ink-and-paint department head, 1 final scene planning department head, 1 color compositing department head, 1 final check department head, 1 character designer, 1 location designer, 1 character sculptor, 7 scene planners/final scene planners, 1 animation production manager, 1 head of animation production, 1 cleanup supervisor, 1 production manager, 1 layout supervisor, 2 effects supervisors, 2 scene planning compositors, 2 artist casting directors, 6 color compositors, 11 color modelists/paint mark-up/registration artists, 15 CGI animators, 15 technical supervisors, 6 supervising animators, 4 lead animators, 39 animators, 16 visual development artists, 10 cleanup leads/keys, 20 effects animators, 15 digital effects animators/artists, 10 2D/3D animation checkers, 5 final checkers, 16 workbook/layout artists, 9 digital backgound artists, 50 voice actors.

3D feature film

1 director, 1 producer, 2 screenplay writers, 1 editor, 2 production designers, 1 composer, 2 executive producers, 1 associate producer, 1 production supervisor, 1 production office coordinator, 1 scheduling coordinator, 1 postproduction supervisor, 1 senior manager of editorial/postproduction, 2 casting directors, 1 associate casting director, 1 additional ADR voice casting director, 3 additional screenplay material contributors, 2 script coordinators, 4 original story writers, 1 story supervisor, 3 additional story material contributors, 1 story manager, 1 development story supervisor, 15 story artists, 7 additional storyboarding artists, 1 story consultant, 1 story coordinator, 1 lighting supervisor, 1 lighting manager, 1 lighting coordinator, 2 camera department managers, 1 camera supervisor, 2 simulation/effects supervisors, 1 simulation/effects manager, 6 sequence supervisors, 15 simulation/effects artists, 3 simulation/effects coordinators, 4 additional effects coordinators, 8 CG painters, 1 modeling supervisor, 1 modeling manager, 3 lead modeling artists, 34 modeling artists, 1 modeling coordinator, 2 supervising animators, 1 animation manager, 2 directing animators, 13 character-development artists, 48 animators, 1 fix animator, 11 software team leads, 39 software engineers, 1 layout supervisor, 1 layout manager, 1 lead layout artist, 1 senior layout artist, 3 sequence leads, 10 layout artists, 2 layout technical support people, 7 additional layout artists, 1 editorial manager, 2 second film editors, 3 additional editors, 1 editorial coordinator, 2 art directors, 1 art department manager, 1 shading supervisor, 1 shading manager, 2 lead shading artists, 22 shading artists, 1 shading coordinator, 1 modeling/shading fix coordinator, 1 set dressing supervisor, 12 production artists, 1 character designer, 2 additional character designers, 2 sculptors, 15 visual development artists, 1 main title design/animation direction, 1 main title animator, 1 end title designer, 2 orchestrators, 2 music supervisors, 1 music production manager, 1 music production coordinator, 2 music editors, 1 music recorder/mixer, 2 sound designers, 1 dialogue recordist, 2 additional dialogue recordists, 1 original dialogue mixer, 2 rerecording mixers, 1 mix technician, 1 rerecordist, 1 supervising sound editor, 1 temp sound editor, 3 sound effects editors, 1 ADR editor, 2 Foley artists, 2 Foley mixers, 1 Foley editor, 1 supervising technical director, 53 voice actors.

2D feature film

1 director, 2 producers, 1 scriptwriter, 1 screen story writer, 1 camera supervisor, 1 editor, 1 production designer, 1 music/conductor, 1 executive producer, 1 associate producer, 4 production associates, 5 scene planners, 1 production manager, 1 story department head, 1 computer graphics department head, 1 layout/workbook department head, 1 background department head, 1 cleanup department head, 1 effects department head, 1 scene planning department head, 1 animation check department head, 1 subcontractor production head, 1 color model supervisor, 1 scanning supervisor, 1 ink-and-paint supervisor, 1 final check supervisor, 1 final scene planning supervisor, 1 postproduction supervisor, 3 digital specialists, 2 animatic production specialists, 1 casting director, 1 associate casting director, 5 artistic casting/development people, 7 storyboard artists, 6 additional story contributors, 7 color stylists, 3 color modelists, 1 camera operator, 6 technology supervisors, 12 technology engineers, 8 technology operations people, 17

_____

Exhibit 2.2
_____

2D feature film (Continued)

CGI animators, 17 technical directors, 1 head of animation, 11 supervising animators, 37 animators, 16 additional animators, 7 visual development/character designers, 8 cleanup leads, 12 cleanup keys, 14 effects animators, 5 digital effects artists, 11 animation checkers, 2 workbook designers, 5 layout artists, 11 workbook designers, 1 lead bluesketch artist, 1 bluesketch artist, 12 background artists, 1 digital background artist, 6 character designers assigned to lead character, 1 artistic coordinator, 1 art director, 1 character sculptor, 1 orchestra, 2 electronic music score programmers, 3 orchestrators, 3 music score producers, 1 music editor, 1 music score recorder/mixer, 2 music consultants, 1 sound designer, 2 principal dialogue editors, 1 production sound editor, 2 rerecording mixers, 2 digital playback operators, 1 supervising sound editor, 1 supervising sound editor, 1 supervising dialogue editor, 1 sound effects editor, 2 ADR mixers, 2 Foley artists, 1 Foley engineer, 1 Foley mixer, 1 Foley editor, 1 consultant, 29 voice actors.

Stop-motion/puppetry feature film

1 executive director, 2 directors, 3 producers, 1 scriptwriter, 2 directors of photography, 2 editors, 1 executive art director, 1 music/conductor/orchestrator, 1 executive producer, 5 executive coproducers, 2 line producers, 5 production coordinators, 1 production team manager, 1 second unit director, 1 dialogue director, 2 casting directors, 2 script editors, 1 cameraman, 3 visual effects producers, 1 visual effects supervisor, 10 2D-effects operators, 13 3D-effects operators, 7 animators, 14 key animators, 4 Animo compositors, 1 animatic compositor, 1 2D computer animator, 19 puppet sculptors, 1 puppet facial articulation person, 4 puppet armature people, 4 puppet makeup people, 2 puppet character developers, 2 layout artists, 1 background artist, 2 background painters, 1 motion control operator, 1 supervising editor, 2 editors, 1 2D-art director, 1 executive set designer, 2 storyboard artists, 2 costume designers, 1 end titles/opticals (company), 1 title lettering, 1 orchestra, 1 choir, 1 orchestra leader, 1 music supervisor, 1 engineer, 1 sound designer, 1 sound supervisor, 1 dialogue recorder, 2 rerecording mixers, 1 sound editor, 2 Foley artists, 1 Foley rerecording mixer, 1 technical director, 5 research/historical advisors, 9 technical consultants, 52 voice actors.

Note: Some credits may overlap, with one person performing more than one task.

_____

animators and other staff; independent productions, or those being completed in smaller studios, usually don't have this luxury and depend on their production and directorial staffs to recruit and hire. (Some hire independent recruiters to handle these tasks for them.)

Gaming

Gaming productions employ many people with the same titles and responsibilities as television, film, or other types of animation projects, including 3D modelers, voice actors, sound designers, and character animators, although staffs are typically smaller than for a traditional animation production. In addition there are positions that are unique to the gaming industry; these include programmers (lead and assistant), testers, manual writers and online manual adaptors, and tutorial designers.

COMPENSATION

Compensation varies, depending on the job title, the experience and renown of the people involved, the budget of the production, and union regulations, if applicable. If a production is union, its compensation must be at or above guild-dictated minimum wage requirements; nonunion productions (which many animation productions are) may offer compensation below these levels. In many cases compensation packages are negotiable, especially for higher-ranking positions and during boom times for the industry.

Freelance animators are generally paid by the week or hour, or sometimes by the job for smaller productions. Staffers are paid an annual salary, which stays constant, no matter what they're working on at a given time. Staffers can be part of a studio's full-time employee roster and assigned to a given production, or they may be hired just for the duration of the production.

Unionized animators in California, New York, San Francisco, and Orlando are governed by the International Alliance of Theatrical Stage Employees (IATSE); those in Los Angeles belong to IATSE Motion Picture Screen Cartoonists Local 389. Animation personnel who are hired for work on union productions must join the union within a set time after being hired.

IATSE's minimum wages, which are published on the organization's Web site (www.mpsc839.org), include $1,475.77 per week for key animators; $1,283.28 for animators, background artists, and model designers; $1,227.80 for assistant key animators; $1,091.40 for assistant animators, backgrounders, and model designers; $1,203.24 for sheet timers; $1,135.64 for scene planners; and $905.68 for inkers. All told, 67 titles are listed.

Actual salaries vary widely, depending on a number of factors. A salary survey compiled by IATSE in the late 1990s found that the annual salaries of staff writers ranged from $59,300 to $175,500; producers from $57,600 to $750,000; directors from $62,400 to $351,000; sheet timers from $70,200 to $130,000; model designers from $39,000 to $109,200; color stylists from $52,000 to $98,800; character animators from $54,600 to $338,000; effects animators from $52,000 to $274,000; inbetweeners from $39,300 to $61,100; and animation checkers from $48,400 to $67,600, to name a few. It should be noted that average salaries vary from year to year, due to supply and demand, and that individual salaries can fall outside these ranges.

Salaries vary from country to country as well. Korean animators, for instance, are paid about a third what an animator in North America would receive. In the United Kingdom, where animators are covered by the Broadcasting Entertainment Cinematograph and Theater Union (BECTU), producers, directors, and production designers cannot be paid less than £644 ($1,060) per forty-hour week; art directors, production managers, and editors not less than £570 ($939); key animators not less than £606 ($998); computer animators not less than £549 ($904); rendering artists not less than £450 ($741); and production assistants not less than £389 ($641). All told, 56 titles are listed on BECTU's wage list.

Most people working on an animation production in the United States, if they're union, are covered by IATSE, but a few may be members of other unions. Writers, for example, can be part of the Writer's Guild of America (WGA) East or West (although writers specializing in animation frequently are members of IATSE instead), while virtually all voice-over actors are covered by either the Screen Actors Guild (SAG) or the Association of Federated Television and Radio Actors (AFTRA) and musicians by the American Federation of Musicians (AFM). These unions have their own minimums that must be followed if the production has a contract with the union. Most animation productions work with SAG or AFTRA, since the majority of voice actors are members.

Live-action productions usually offer better compensation than animated projects. The time of day in which a television show runs also affects animators' and other animation staffers' compensation. For example, a prime-time animation script might command $20,000 or more for a writer, while a daytime children's episode would be more likely to be valued at around $7,500.

Stars doing voice-over work, particularly for television, often agree to work for the same scale as the voice specialist actors, but many negotiate a higher payment, especially in film. Actors on long-running and successful television shows such as *The Simpsons* also have bargaining power and can increase their salaries to far above scale. An average television production using noncelebrity actors might pay $15,000 for thirty hours of voice work; that budget easily could double (or more) if celebrity talent is involved.

Other workers associated with an animated production are paid by the job, rather than earn a weekly salary. Composers usually receive a flat fee that is subject to negotiation. For a feature film the payment might range from $10,000 to $250,000, depending on how widely the movie is distributed. The fee can include composition, production, and recording of the music; alternatively, there migh be separate fees for each of those components. If the studio handles the producing and recording responsibilities, the composer might receive a fee for the composition only. Music contracts are traditionally structured as work-for-hire, since the studio wants to own all facets of the property and be able to exploit it fully. Composers share in future income from the song, however. All of these types of payments with outside contractors are negotiable.

Exhibit 2.3

Annual Salary Ranges for Selected Animation Positions

Position	Range
Producers	$57,600–$750,000
Directors	$62,400–$351,000
Key/character animators	$54,600–$338,000
Inbetweeners	$39,300–$61,100
Background painters	$48,900–$169,000
Storyboard artists	$78,000–$190,000
Cleanup artists	$41,300–$104,000

Note: Salaries are a matter of negotiation and can fall outside these ranges. Weekly union minimums are often higher than these amounts, but averages factor in nonunion work and the fact that many animators have time off between jobs.

Sources: SkillsNet, MPSC/IATSE, BECTU

Credits

Employees or contractors on animated productions can earn other forms of compensation in addition to cash payments. Credit is one of them. Most unions have minimum requirements for credits, which apply to primary and secondary distribution channels, as well as, in some cases, advertising and marketing materials. Creative- and production-team personnel can negotiate credits that are more prominent than dictated in the minimum requirements.

There are several elements associated with credit that the producer and its employees must negotiate. One is what the credit will say (e.g., what title will define the employee's work). This can be tricky when various titles (executive producer, coproducer, coexecutive producer, supervising producer, producer, line producer, assistant producer, associate producer, and so on) have no clear-cut role definition. Credits associated with animation functions, such as character animator, key animator, or effects animator, are relatively straightforward, although job descriptions can evolve over time. Animation directors, for example, used to be responsible mainly for the sheet timing function, but now are more analogous to a live-action director and want their credit to reflect that.

Credits are granted to consultants and associated parties as well. They might receive recognition through phrases such as "in association with," "thanks to," or "special material by," or they may be credited as executive producers. Sometimes the owners of the underlying property on which a production is based will get an executive producer credit, while other times they might be termed a "creative consultant," depending on the extent of their participation.

Credit negotiations also include the topic of placement. Some credits run during the main titles and others in the end credits. Participants also negotiate the placement of their credit vis à vis those of other personnel, as well as the size or even the typeface and color, if they have significant negotiating clout. In addition, the issue of whether credits extend to ancillary entertainment products (e.g., the person must be named visibly in the home video version as well as the original film or television show) and licensed merchandise, as well as advertising and other marketing materials, is also negotiable. Some of these extended credit rights tend to be difficult to achieve in animation, however.

Most contracts require the producers to pay a penalty if credit provisions are ignored or incorrect. They also must correct the mistake in future forms of the film, such as on home video. Creative staffers whose credit rights were violated are usually contractually barred from preventing the production from being distributed, however.

Back-End Participation and Residuals

Many personnel involved in live-action productions—actors, writers, directors, and producers, for example—receive residuals (small payments each time a show airs or film is shown). Animators almost never receive residuals; some directors, producers, and writers on animation projects might, if they have a strong negotiating position, but this is rare industrywide. (The WGA's Animation Writers Caucus is working to gain more residuals for animation specialists.)

Voice actors, who are members of SAG or AFTRA, receive residuals in most cases. Their initial payment most commonly covers two airings; any distribution after that requires additional compensation. Exceptions include dubbing from a foreign language, which does not require payment of residuals, although if a production is changed so much in translation that it is essentially a new script, voice-over actors may try to gain residual rights. Such was the case in 2000 with a *Digimon* episode, where SAG supported a group of actors who argued that the script of one episode had been changed so much that it did not fall under the category of dubbing.

Some of those involved in an animation production may negotiate back-end participation in the property in addition to their upfront fee, which entitles them to receive a cut of the royalties or fees from primary and secondary distribution channels and from ancillaries, depending on the results of the negotiations. Back-end participation usually is limited to personnel who are intimately involved in the creation or financing of the property and who are high-ranking in terms of credit (e.g., executive producers or lead writers might get participation, but line producers would not). In prime-time and some daytime television, where executive producers have a lot of creative input, they may share as much as 25 percent of the adjusted gross proceeds (revenues minus distribution expenses, production costs, and other payments) from all areas of exploitation on the series. (Adjusted gross proceeds are often far lower than the actual gross, so this term must be accurately defined and agreed upon during negotiations.)

Composers get a share of publishing royalties from sound tracks, live recordings, and sales of sheet music, in addition to their fees for composition and recording. Their share is about 50 percent for mechanical licensing (use on a sound track or other recording), with the studio retaining the remainder.

Benefits

Many animation productions, if they go on for a significant period of time, offer their employees benefits such as health insurance. Freelancers do not receive such perks, particularly if they're on a project for a short time.

It should be noted that in addition to benefits producers must also factor in additional costs associated with compensation as they develop their budgets. These include employers' contributions to their employees' taxes; various other federal, state, and possibly city taxes; payroll fees; FICA (social security); unemployment insurance; and possibly workman's compensation.

Other Compensation

Certain intangibles can be a form of compensation, and spur an animator or other participant to join a production despite less-than-desired monetary rewards. Creative control is one of these. An animator who gets creative control over all or part of a project (as tends to be the case for cinematic sequences in video games, for example) might be willing to join a production, despite low pay. While the monetary compensation is less than for other projects, the creative control can be attractive to animators, who rarely get such power in this collaborative art form where networks or studio executives make most of the decisions. Similarly, creators of a television show might opt to take their property to a network that will allow them to retain creative control, rather than to a network that will pay them significantly more, but with a loss of power.

Support from a studio may be another valuable element that could be considered compensation. A creator or other participant in a property may be willing to take less salary or a lower up-front payment in return for back-end participation if they feel the studio or network will back the production strongly in terms of marketing and promotion, boosting its chances of success.

HIRING

Producers and directors, assisted by casting directors, recruiters, and/or human resources executives, are responsible for hiring personnel for a given production. In some cases staffers are selected from among a studio's or production company's full-time roster; this tends to be the case during boom times, when studios are more likely to have a large group of full-timers with long-duration employment contracts. (See chapter 13 for more on how studios hire their employees.)

During slower times in the business most of the animation and other personnel on a project come from the ranks of freelancers. Using freelancers allows the producer to put together the best team for the project, while keeping studio overhead low. On the other hand, the producer faces the risk that the best person for a given position might not be available at the time of the project. Freelancers move from project to project and are likely to be working on another production when the call comes. Keeping good people on staff is expensive but ensures that those people will be available when needed.

During the animation boom of the mid- to late 1990s some star animators began to be represented by agents, something that was almost unheard of in animation. Although the boom ended by the early 2000s, some of the top animation artists (including lead animators, story editors, and background artists), as well as producers, directors, and writers specializing in animation, continue to be represented by agents, who take a 10 percent to 15 percent commission on all the animator's fees and salaries. A producer may end up negotiating with the prospective staffers' representatives rather than the animators themselves, which can make negotiations more difficult and raise costs. This is mainly just an option of the top echelon, however; most animators are unagented.

Employment Contracts

When animation is booming and good animators are hard to find, or if an individual animator is considered critical to the success of the production, a producer might offer an employment contract. This strategy ensures that the production will be able to keep key members of the staff on board as long as they're needed. If no employment contract exists, either party can end the relationship at will. The latter scenario is usually acceptable to the producer, especially in lean times, but key staffers who cannot be replaced easily might represent an exception to the rule.

The employment contract outlines what services the animator will provide, when the contract ends and whether there are options for continuation, what the employee will earn (including increases, bonuses, and nonsalary compensation, if any), what the employee's credit will be, and to whom the employee reports. These contracts are most often work-for-hire arrangements; employees don't retain any ownership of the properties on which they work. Contracts also outline financial penalties employees must pay if they violate the contract, and requires them to work exclusively for the employer, at least during work hours. Employment contracts may either allow or disallow freelance work during off hours; normally such outside projects are tolerated, but that depends on the specifics of the relationship between the two partners.

3
Budgeting

Creating a budget for an entertainment property is a difficult process, but it must be done accurately and realistically if a studio or producer is to gain financing and ultimately make money on its proprietary projects and coproductions.

AVERAGE BUDGETS

Each animation property is unique, and budgets vary widely, depending on project characteristics, deadline schedules, required staff size, and many other factors. Despite this variation, however, it is instructive to take a look at examples of animation budgets from various sectors. Any budget that is far out of line from the "average" for similar productions will have a difficult time attracting financing or buyers.

Film

According to the Motion Picture Association of America (MPAA), the average production cost for a live-action or animated feature film in 2001 was $47.7 million, excluding marketing costs, down 13 percent from $54.8 million in 2000. These figures incorporate everything up to the delivery of the negative, including production costs, studio overhead, and capitalized interest.

Exhibit 3.1

Budget Ranges for Animation in Various Media

Media	Range
Film, feature-length	$4 million–$150 million
Television, children's half-hour	$200,000–$800,000
Video/DVD originals	$60,000–$25 million
Interactive console games	$500,000–$20 million
Internet short	$1,000–$45,000

Note: Some properties may fall outside these ranges.

Costs for individual films can diverge significantly from this norm; a single sequence in one animated movie could have a budget of $300,000 while another could reach $2.5 million, an eightfold difference.

Animated films sometimes come in at or slightly above the average; the 2D/3D animated release *Titan A.E.* (Fox, 2000) cost an estimated $65 million, as did *Ice Age* (Fox, 2002). *Toy Story* (Disney/Pixar, 1995), *Antz* (Dream-Works, 1998), and *A Bug's Life* (Disney/Pixar, 1998) reportedly all had budgets in the $40 million to $80 million range. Yet, others veer far from the mean. *Final Fantasy: The Spirits Within* (Sony, 2001), for example, had a final budget estimated at between $115 and $140 million, while Disney's tentpole releases in the early 2000s typically exceeded $100 million and could go as high as $200 million, as was reported to be the case with *Dinosaur* (2000).

Meanwhile, the lower end of the spectrum included *The Powerpuff Girls Movie* (Warner Brothers, 2002), which cost an estimated $11 million, and *Waking Life* (Fox Searchlight, 2001), which came in at about $10 million. (It should be noted that it's difficult to get accurate cost estimates on individual pictures—film studios consider that information proprietary—so the figures in this analysis come from a variety of business and entertainment trade magazines.)

Reported budgets for CG-animated features (such as *Final Fantasy* or *Dinosaur*) can be misleading, because they often include the company's start-up costs for a new or improved CG studio, or the costs of developing proprietary software or purchasing additional hardware. That was the case with Disney's *Dinosaur*, for which the studio built a 3D studio. Overall, the costs of doing 3D CGI productions have come down, and total budgets can be less than those for 2D feature films, as of 2002.

The majority of live-action films incorporate substantial amounts of special effects. Their budgets vary. Industry reports estimated the production cost of *The Lord of the Rings:The Fellowship of the Ring* (New Line, 2001) at $60 million; *Harry Potter and the Sorcerer's Stone* (Warner Brothers, 2001) at $150 million; and *Star Wars: Episode I—The Phantom Menace* (Fox, 1999) at $120 million.

Films made by studios or producers outside the United States tend to have budgets lower than those produced and distributed by the major Hollywood studios. Spanish animation house BRB's *Romeo and Juliet* (2002), coproduced with Cattleya of Italy, reportedly cost $4.6 million; German studio Hahn Films and Trickcompany's Werner films (1990, 1996, 1999) each came in at less than $6 million; Italian producer Mondo's *Turandot* (2003) was budgeted at $15 million; and German/Dutch studio Greenlight reportedly produced *Simsala Grimm* (2002) for $30 million.

Budgets for independent films in the United States are similar to those in Europe; some come in at less than $10 million, although they typically end up with very limited distribution and are not seen by many people, at least in theaters. Once budgets exceed $10 million the active involvement of the financiers grows. Because of this, some producers choose to produce low-budget pictures for creative and control reasons, even if it means sacrificing viewership.

IMAX and other large-format film productions tend to have average production costs lower than feature films, ranging between $5 million and $20 million. But this varies, and will probably rise as the format becomes more successful and as more high-budget films target this distribution channel. An increasing number of films are being reformatted for IMAX theaters, rather than being created specifically for them—when Disney's *Beauty and the Beast* was reformatted for IMAX theaters animators created six extra minutes of footage—in which case the reformatting cost is much less than the budget for a new film.

Television

Budgets for animated television series depend on what type of animation style is used, as well as the complexity of the design and other factors. In general, most range from $200,000 to $800,000 per half-hour episode, with the bulk falling into the $300,000 to $350,000 range.

Flash-produced television shows tend to have relatively low budgets, while 3D CGI shows tend to be on the higher end. Traditional 2D animation falls somewhere in the middle. As of 2001 producers estimated CG TV budgets were about 10 percent higher than 2D budgets on average, although that differential is decreasing over time. *Princess Natasha,* a TV series developed in Flash by Rumpus, a toy company and producer/distributor of Internet entertainment, was budgeted at $185,000 per episode. There is significant budgetary overlap among animation styles, however, especially since many shows contain elements of more than one style, such as 2D characters combined with 3D backgrounds, or stop-motion mixed with 3D CG animation.

Typically, television series are produced at a lower quality than films, with less detail and fewer frames per second, and therefore tend to cost less per minute. Animated shows for children, aired in daytime slots, tend to be less detailed and less costly than prime-time animated programming. The latter often are budgeted in the $500,000 to $1 million-plus-per-episode range, almost double that of the average daytime series.

The budget figures cited here exclude marketing-related and other expenses that do not contribute directly to the production. BKN's *The Roswell Conspiracies* (1999–2000) had a production budget of $18.7 million for forty half-hour episodes (or $470,000 per episode); the company expected to spend an additional $2 million for marketing and promotions in the first season alone.

Home Video/DVD Productions

As with all animated projects, budgets for original home video productions depend on the style and quality of the animation. Even more than in other animation media, however, there are significant variations in quality from one home video original to another, with some rivalling film quality and others resembling a poorly made television show.

Feature-length productions created for home-video or DVD distribution typically cost less to produce than a theatrical feature film; budgets tend to be more in line with television productions on a per-minute basis. But the range is wide. Some direct-to-video features are budgeted between $5 million and $25 million; franchise-based features from major studios such as Disney can be significantly higher than these levels; and true independent projects are more likely in the $200,000 to $500,000 range.

The original *VeggieTales* video production (Big Idea, 1993), a half-hour episode, cost $60,000; nine years later the initial episode in the studio's second video series, *3-2-1 Penguins!* (2002), cost between $700,000 and $1 million. Both are 3D CGI series, although the latter is more sophisticated in its design and animation. Another 3D-animated Christian property, *Honk If*

You're Special, from Treetop Studios, reportedly had a budget of $1 million for a half hour.

Gaming

In some cases, development and production costs for interactive games, particularly console titles, rival those of feature films. Production budgets for video games in the mid-1990s usually fell in the range of $500,000 to $2 million per game, but as of the early 2000s average budgets rose from $1 million to $15 million, with tentpole titles often budgeted between $10 million and $20 million. Not only have the average costs of producing interactive games risen, but the discrepancy between the costs of the big, highly promoted titles and the small, niche titles is much more. (As with any animation vehicle, not all budgets fall within the average.)

In addition to the production costs associated with any form of animation, gaming developers must pay for the authoring tools required to make the game. These investments can add up if a company wants to create titles for several platforms, each requiring its own fee. On the other hand, some of the development and other production costs can be amortized over several titles if the same game is marketed for a number of different console systems.

As in the discussions of the other entertainment segments, these budgetary figures do not include marketing expenditures. As production budgets for high-profile gaming titles rival those of feature films, so do the marketing costs that support their release, with many backed by promotional programs valued at between $5 million and $10 million.

Internet

As of 2002 the bulk of Internet animation is produced using Macromedia's Flash software. Flash productions often cost between $1,000 and $2,000 per minute, but can be as high as $4,000 to $10,000 per minute or more. (Each episode of a webisodic series is typically one to two minutes long.) One series, *Night Knight* on www.djungo.com, was budgeted at $3,500 to $4,000 per 30-second episode; *Avenue Amy* on www.oxygen.com was budgeted at $15,000 per minute. (That series also aired on the Oxygen cable network.)

PRODUCTION PHASES

The four phases involved in creating animation—development, preproduction, production, and postproduction—all involve significant time and personnel. The amount of resources devoted to each phase varies depending on the job.

Development

The development phase, during which funding is secured and the creative attributes of the property finalized, can range from a year or two to many years. In addition to creating the concept (story line, character development, visual development, style, format, and length) and the materials needed to sell the concept (outlines, treatments, style guides, drawings, conceptual paintings, bibles, film scripts, pilots or pilot scripts), the development stage is when the producers generate a budget, seek financing, and negotiate financing deals, as well as develop proprietary software, acquire rights, and start putting together a production team.

Producers may never recoup funds poured into development. All the resources spent during this phase are speculative, since a distribution deal is rarely in place. It's important to develop a saleable presentation, but it's best to do it on as low a budget as possible. Therefore, freelancers complete much of the work during this stage, although some of the production's key staff are on board (such as the producer, writer, and director).

The more time spent on development—while being cognizant of the costs—the less chance of extensive and expensive changes later in the production process. A single sequence sent back to an overseas studio for a fix, for example, could as much as double the cost of production on that scene. A thorough and complete analysis of the property during development can prevent many of these problems.

In some cases ancillary departments or publicists are brought in during this phase, both to give their input on how to make the property as attractive as possible to the trade and consumers and to gather information to help them in their selling efforts.

When all the key elements of the production are in place the producer creates a production plan that is then used to develop the budget. The production plan itemizes all the labor and supplies required, attaches costs to each, and analyzes the time needed for each task and how to best schedule the production. The goal is to maximize quality and minimize costs. A lot of give-and-take occurs during this process, as the producers try to come up with a plan that balances the creative team's desire to achieve their vision and the purchaser's and/or partners' need to stay within budgetary constraints.

Once the production plan is finalized the producers can come up with a bottom-line budget figure.

The development of the plan is a complicated process that involves:

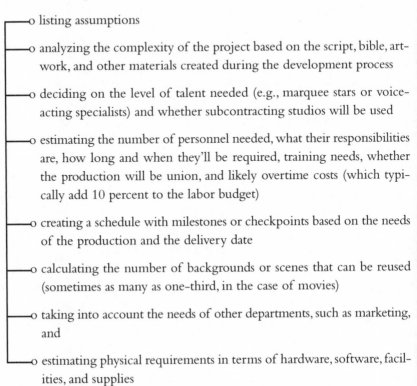

- listing assumptions

- analyzing the complexity of the project based on the script, bible, artwork, and other materials created during the development process

- deciding on the level of talent needed (e.g., marquee stars or voice-acting specialists) and whether subcontracting studios will be used

- estimating the number of personnel needed, what their responsibilities are, how long and when they'll be required, training needs, whether the production will be union, and likely overtime costs (which typically add 10 percent to the labor budget)

- creating a schedule with milestones or checkpoints based on the needs of the production and the delivery date

- calculating the number of backgrounds or scenes that can be reused (sometimes as many as one-third, in the case of movies)

- taking into account the needs of other departments, such as marketing, and

- estimating physical requirements in terms of hardware, software, facilities, and supplies

The process is like a big puzzle, with the producer deciding how many pieces are needed and what they should look like, and then putting them all together. Some of the creative characteristics of the property finalized earlier in the development process may need to be changed at this point due to budgetary considerations.

During subsequent production phases, producers may alter various items within this plan—for example, labor for one task may take longer than expected, so other departments are squeezed to make up for it—but the bottom-line budget remains the same.

Preproduction

Once development is complete and financing set, the preproduction phase begins. (A purchaser/distributor is often involved at this point, but preproduction can begin before distribution is in place, as long as financing from other sources is adequate.)

Preproduction involves tasks such as finalizing the script; creating detailed character and environment designs based on the specifications agreed upon during development and recording them in a style guide; doing background paintings and background keys; completing color modeling and color guides; building maquettes; designing props; and building 3D modeling and environments and creating the model pack.

Another key part of the preproduction process is the recording of the voice-over audio track; time budgeted for voice recording may include time for coaching and rehearsals. (Some scenes may need to be rerecorded in post-production, due to script changes or subpar performances.) Animators use the track to create the animation. They also videotape the performance, to capture body language used by the actors and sometimes their physical features.

Once the design and voice track are in place, storyboarding begins. On film projects production may begin before storyboarding is complete. But the storyboarding process can unearth many problems in the overall story line at relatively low cost, so it's best if storyboarders can complete all scenes before production begins. Once the storyboards are finished, animation timers take over, after which a story reel or animatic is put together. This step ensures that everyone can see how the production is shaping up, as well as giving licensing and marketing staffs a chance to view the production and sometimes use a copy as a sales tool.

Once executives sign off on the animatic, the production is slugged (the time each scene should take is calculated in terms of number of frames required). Exposure sheets (text-based guides to the action in each scene) follow, and include all details of the story and action, from visual effects to camera angles. These are used as reference for the animators.

The composer, music supervisor, producer, and director discuss the musical needs of the project during preproduction. The composer can begin to develop songs, if any, and the processes of hiring musicians and/or obtaining music rights begins. If a character will sing a song, it must be completed and recorded before animation of that sequence can begin.

Title scenes for television series are also finalized during preproduction.

As with development, the more precise and well-thought-out the work in the preproduction phase, the less likely the production will be to incur over-budget costs during production. For example, creating a complete visual style guide can be expensive and time-consuming, but a good style guide will prevent problems further down the line.

Production

After preproduction comes the production phase, which includes background painting, key framing, inbetweening, and ink-and-paint, among other tasks. For TV and direct-to-video projects, some or all of this phase is frequently done offshore, which saves money but adds time to the overall schedule. On 2D television series and home video projects, the preproduction and production phases are essentially separate, with the latter following the former (although there may be a slight overlap). In film the process is more circular, with revisions being made as production occurs and with scenes sometimes moving from production back into preproduction. In film the script is often revised during production, for example, requiring some scenes to go back into preproduction.

Animators working in 3D animation and gaming also use a back-and-forth process, completing many tasks historically associated with production during preproduction. For example, when creating the main model pack (like the character design in 2D), a preproduction task, 3D animators often complete some of the key framing, traditionally a production task. Conversely, the 3D production process will sometimes unearth technological needs that must be resolved, taking a scene back into preproduction. And since producers and directors can review dailies in CG, just as they can in live action, scenes can be revised immediately, creating more of a continuous or rolling editing process. By the time the animation is finished the editing is nearly done as well. (In part because of this interrelated process, 3D animation is rarely sent overseas during production, despite the fact that more studios in Asia and elsewhere are set up for 3D.)

The production phase for a 2D television series often takes between nine months and a year, ideally being completed a few months prior to delivery and the airdate. Cinar and Shanghai Animation Film Studio's *Simon in the Land of Chalk Drawings* went into production in September 2001 and finished in May 2002, with a delivery to the Teletoon network for a fall 2002 premiere. But some series, especially digital ones, can take as little as one to three weeks per episode, although that's shorter than the norm. For a 2D film the production process often takes between eighteen months and two years; various challenges during the process can lengthen that period significantly.

While an entire TV series can be delivered before the premiere date of the first episode, production on later episodes often occurs during the season, with each show delivered prior to its own air date. This is more common in a show's later seasons, once the production company and the network have established a good working relationship.

The production stage begins with the creation of the workbook, which essentially blocks out all the instructions for the animators, based on the materials developed during preproduction. The editorial department is an important link in the production phase, because it creates and maintains the story reel, which is updated throughout production and shows how the entire work is proceeding toward its final form. Once scene layouts are created based on the workbook, actual animation begins, including key framing, scene scanning, approvals, inbetweening, cleanup layout and animation, visual effects, final background painting, animation checking, ink-and-paint, color and paint mark-up, final checking, and compositing. As noted, the process varies somewhat between 2D and 3D production, and among TV, film, and interactive gaming.

If licensing, publicity, and marketing executives are involved in the project, they should be kept informed of progress periodically during the production phase. They also may need marketing materials, scenes, character drawings, or other information from the production in order to begin their selling process.

Postproduction

After production wraps on a scene, it enters the postproduction phase. This stage includes the music premix and final mix; sound effects design and sound editing; picture editing; rough cut; color correction; retakes and rerecording sessions, if necessary; title and credit approval; negative cutting; creating textless versions for foreign markets; quality control; and video duplication or film processing. Postproduction is the final phase in the animation process, and the time allotted for it is often squeezed, if other phases run long.

The director and the lead producers oversee the process with the help of a postproduction supervisor. Many of the tasks are sent out to contractors such as editing facilities, sound houses, and film labs. All of these outside partners need to be informed when schedules or specs change; if not, the producers will face late fees or perhaps lose their scheduled slot at the postproduction house.

In a live-action film, special effects, including animation, take place during the postproduction phase. When location or studio filming takes longer than expected, the time allotted for postproduction is reduced to keep the project on schedule, which means special effects houses have to do their job in a short, labor-intensive period. In some cases time is so short and the work so complex that additional effects houses have to be brought in to assist in order for the project to be completed on time.

Final delivery of the production to the buyer or partners should include the final script; release print, negative, and interpositive (or other final output forms); the music and effects tracks, music cue sheets, song lyrics, and score; and any other information that's due under the obligations of the contract.

SCHEDULING ISSUES

All four phases of the animation production process are interrelated. The amount of time and money devoted to one phase affects the resources that can be earmarked for the other stages and influences the overall budget. If there are problems during the production phase that put the project behind schedule, postproduction houses might feel the pinch; overtime costs, late fees, or unavailability of postproduction facilities later might make actual costs exceed budgeted targets. Conversely, trying to save too much time and money during the development or preproduction phases (in other words, giving short shrift to planning while devoting more funds to production) can cause problems later that put the project over budget.

While making too many changes to the schedule during production will incur additional expenses, it is important to remain flexible. One extreme example of flexibility is the Comedy Central series *South Park*. Writers complete the script for each episode only a few days before its air date so they can incorporate timely events. That means production, done through an efficient computer animation process, is completed in a much shorter time than other shows, allowing the director to make changes at the last minute. The series is produced in a just-in-time manner, at a pace of one show per week.

It should be noted that throughout the entire production process executives from networks, studios, coproduction partners, investors, and anyone else involved with the production are brought in to provide input and approve milestones. (The participation of each is worked out during the deal-making process—see chapter 8.) Checkpoints typically include the script; character, location, and prop design; color keys; painted backgrounds or CG environments; voice casting; selection of songs, composers, and vocalists; story reels; credits; and final film. (There may be other checkpoints as well.) Promotional materials are also subject to approvals.

BUDGET COMPONENTS

The first step in creating a budget is to break down the project into its components and estimate the costs associated with each. This process requires flexibility. There may be trade-offs necessary to achieve a balance between

---

Exhibit 3.2

The Basic Phases of the Animation Production Process

Development

    Assign or retain writer, director, producer, and core business team

    Develop script

    Create character and location designs, choose animation style

    Begin thinking about budgeting and scheduling

    Start talking to marketing, publicity, merchandising, and distribution partners

    Test and develop software

    Recruit production, editing, casting, and other teams needed during preproduction

    Configure and set up administrative and production systems

    Finalize bible

    Hire songwriters

    Finalize budget, schedule, and production plan

    Receive notes/approvals from buyer/partners on creative and financial aspects put together so far

Preproduction

    Revise green-lit script

    Hire staff needed for production

    Set up facilities and equipment and complete testing of systems

    Create storyboards

    Put together story reel and exposure sheets

    Select subcontracting studio, if any

    Complete 3D modeling, surfaces, and rigging, if applicable

    Complete casting, rehearsal, and voice track recording

    Complete legal review of script and storyboards

    Create visual style guide or model packages

    Clear music rights

    Hire recording facility

    Create title sequence

    Receive buyer/partner notes/approvals

Production

    Create workbook

    Prepare sequencing

    Complete layout

    Complete rough animation

    Complete scene planning and scanning

    Complete cleanup

    Complete effects

    Complete background painting

    Complete animation check

    Complete color styling, mark-up, and approval

    Complete ink-and-paint

    Approve color

Exhibit 3.2

Production (Continued)

    Create output

    Lock voice track

    Hire postproduction facilities

    Have meetings with ancillary, marketing, PR, and other allied groups

    Receive approvals and notes from buyers/partners

Postproduction

    Complete video transfer

    Complete off-line editing

    Complete retakes

    Complete color correction

    Cut negatives

    Create textless version for international markets

    Complete quality-control process

    Complete trailer

    Complete sound and music spotting

    Record score and songs

    Complete music, effects, dialogue premix and mix

    Complete final sound mix

    Receive final approvals

    Screen for ancillary and marketing groups

    Deliver final output

Note: Some tasks may shift depending on whether production is 2D, 3D, or stop-motion, and whether production is for television, film, home video, or another medium. This list is not exhaustive.

---

the ultimate desired quality and financial constraints. For example, design might be simplified or the number of characters reduced if the original vision costs so much that acquiring financing would be impossible.

Complexity

One of the main factors behind how many personnel hours are needed to complete a project is its complexity. The number of characters and how they interrelate, the number of sets, the number of special effects, the sophistication of backgrounds and character designs, the amount of music and sound effects, the number of layers in the animation, etc., all play into how many people the production must hire and for how long.

Some animated projects, of course, can be very complex, especially in the film sector. The 90-minute film *The Prince of Egypt* (DreamWorks, 1998) featured 1,192 shots, including many special effects. One scene depicted a 16,000-person crowd. In another DreamWorks film, *Antz* (1998), 500 of the 1,200 shots in the film (42 percent) were crowd shots; one scene portrayed 60,000 insects.

Designers created twenty-four sets for the film *Monsters, Inc.,* which contained 1,500 shots. That film also contained fifty monsters, many of which had textures, clothing, and hair that required a painstaking animation process. Even with sophisticated computer animation programs, it took a reported seventeen minutes to animate one second of output featuring clothing, and ten minutes per second to create the hair on the main monster, Sully.

Special effects such as rain, lightning, and the like add to the complexity of a project. *Titan A.E.,* a 2D/3D-animated film, incorporated 110 complex visual effects shots, which took a relatively short fifty-eight days to complete. All told, 80 percent of the film contains some sort of animated effects; the film contained 509 3D shots and 950 that combined 2D characters and 3D effects.

Television production is often less complicated than feature film production, but some projects are more complex than others. Television is also put through a faster-paced schedule than film. Each 21-minute episode of Mainframe Entertainment's series *Reboot* included 31,500 frames that animators and artists had to design, build, and render (reusing digital assets where possible), all in three weeks per episode. This workload translated to a schedule of 10,000 frames per week.

Labor

One of the main components of an animation budget, typically accounting for 25 percent to 50 percent of the total, is labor. Animation is not a simple process, nor is it quickly accomplished. Labor costs are a function of the number of people involved and how much time each spends on the project.

It took 180 people (all working together at peak times) two years to complete production on the stop-motion film *Chicken Run,* at a pace of 90 seconds per week. The roster included 22 animators and 10 assistants. (The two years doesn't include the development phase, which added another one and a half years). The 2D film *Waking Life* required 250 hours of labor for each minute seen on screen. A two-minute 3D short based on the children's book *Little Miss Spider* took six months to animate, with the crew reaching 15 people at peak times. It takes on average over nine months to finish one season's worth (22 episodes) of an animated show for prime time. An interactive game production can keep its staff busy for 18 to 24 months on one title. The computer game *Exile,* part of the *Myst* franchise, took approximately 90,000 work hours to complete, according to producers.

A video game production might require as many as 50 people to bring it to completion, including animators as well as programmers, screenwriters, graphic designers, musicians, and others. Warner Brothers' *The Road to El Dorado* (2000), most of which was traditionally animated, required close to 500 people in total (working in 30 countries) for more than four and a half years, while Disney's *Atlantis:The Lost Empire* had 350 animators, artists, and technicians on the job at the peak of production. In general, CG projects require fewer people than traditional cel-style animation. For example, a film such as DreamWorks' *Shrek* involved about 200 people, while Disney's 2D movie *Tarzan* required about double that.

One prime time animation production had a payroll per week of more than $250,000 at one point during production; the labor cost is likely to have translated to anywhere from 20 percent to 33 percent of the per-episode budget for that series. These large numbers also indicate how costly it is to have to do retakes or add more hours than expected.

Producers need to think about the organizational structure of the production (in other words, how people will be used, how they will interact, and to whom they will report). The goal is to maximize both quality and cost-effectiveness. CG television episodes are often set up in teams, with each team of a dozen or so assigned to a single episode for six to eight weeks. On some films there might be six (or more) lead animators, each with their team, responsible for one character; others might segment their lead animators and teams by sequence rather than by character.

The main considerations when estimating labor requirements include the number of people involved, how long each will be needed, how they can be utilized most efficiently, and their compensation. But producers must also look at training needs, especially on films and video game productions. These types of projects often require long-term training, not just to teach animators how to use proprietary software packages or plug-ins, but also to make sure the team is up to speed on character design and other elements essential to the production's look and feel. This type of training is ongoing throughout the production; new animators who come to the project as workload increases need to go through the same training process as those who came on board early. Aardman Animations, producer of *Chicken Run,* required its animators to go through a six-month training process.

Budgets must include not only hourly salary compensation for each employee, but all benefit and tax costs associated with each hour worked. These "fringe" costs can add up to 30 percent over the base pay.

Physical/Technical Setup

Another significant component of the budget is related to the software, hardware, and facilities needed to complete the project. Some productions, as noted, require the development of proprietary software or plug-ins, the purchase or construction of new facilities such as a studio or stage, or other infrastructure improvements. In addition, there must be enough work stations to keep production moving, and all necessary off-the-shelf software must be in-house and installed by the project's start date. Producers need to budget a certain amount of time for setup and troubleshooting by the technical staff during the development phase, as well as building in flexibility later in the process, so that the glitches that inevitably come up do not derail the schedule or break the bank.

The amount spent on computer hardware, software, and facilities varies drastically. Warner reportedly spent $60 million on *Quest for Camelot* before animation production began, while an independent producer estimated he needed a relatively low $400,000 worth of hardware and software to make his movie. The purchase of equipment prior to a production can add 50 percent to the total budget.

These improvements are often charged to the production for which they were created—the preferred method, if it doesn't make the budget too high to secure financing—but it is possible to amortize them over several productions if the studio acting as the producer has other shows in the pipeline. The cost of investing in these improvements in software, hardware, and facilities may take years to fully recoup, but they can generate significant savings in time and money during the production process.

Sometimes expansion or improvements must occur during the production itself, as the team discovers inadequacies that slow the process. Aardman Animations began *Chicken Run* on 60,000 square feet of stage space. As the stop-motion production grew to more than 30 animation units, each with its own set, the studio realized it needed an additional 40,000 square feet. It initially intended to to have 12 units shooting and 12 in preparation at any given time, but had to increase that if it was to stay on a 90-second-per-day schedule.

Rights Acquisition

There are two types of rights that contribute to the cost of a production. The first is the payment to the underlying rights holder of the property on which the production is based, if any. Producers must find and pay the rights holder, whether a book author, a comic book creator, a songwriter, a publisher, another television producer, or an independent creator. The underlying rights holder receives an option payment that gives the producer the exclusive right, for a given period of time, to develop an animation production based on his or her property.

Once the producers, or a purchaser such as a studio or network, greenlights the property the producers pay the underlying rights holder another fee (the "exercise price"). The amount of the exercise price is negotiated up front and is often stated as a percentage of the production budget. (The option price is commonly about 10 percent of the expected exercise price, although that depends on the specifics of the negotiations.) Each time the option is renewed, so the producer can continue the development process, another payment is due (usually equivalent to 5 percent of the expected exercise price, or about half the amount of the original option). In dollar terms, options can range from a few thousand dollars for a deal involving low-budget production or a relatively unknown property, up into the six or seven figures for a bigger deal, such as a feature film based on a well-known children's book.

In addition to the exercise price underlying rights holders may get a percentage of back-end revenues, depending on their negotiating clout, or a percentage of the production budget for the project. The latter can vary from 1 percent to 5 percent or more, with 5 percent being the most common. (Underlying property owners may also contribute financially or creatively to the production, becoming executive producers and/or retaining an ownership stake—see chapter 8.)

Options usually give producers a short period (often one to two years) to develop the property into an entertainment production, with a chance to renew. An alternative is for the producer to purchase the property outright, paying a bigger upfront payment in return for a longer time to develop the property and no later exercise fee. The purchaser could obtain the rights in perpetuity or the rights could revert to the underlying rights holder after a substantial period, such as five years. The underlying rights holder may still receive profit participation in the production once it is developed; all those details are subject to negotiation.

In 1999 the itsy bitsy Entertainment Company won film, television, and merchandising rights to *Eloise* for nearly $4 million, according to published reports. The company later signed an option with a film producer to develop a live-action feature. For rights to a children's book for a film only a producer might pay $70,000 for an option, applied against a payment of $700,000 if the film gets made; if the same producer were to make an outright purchase, it might pay $250,000, which would be the payment whether or not the film is ever approved.

The second group of rights involves the use of existing creative elements in the production. Primary among these is the use of songs or music; others may include graphic elements, dialogue clips, or other content.

Fees for the use of music in an animation production (known as a synchronization license) depends on the type of project (film, television, home video, Internet, gaming) and the size of its potential audience, as well as the length of the clip, how it's used in the film (is it an integral element?), and the number of times it's used. For a film a synchronization license might range from $2,500 or less for an independent film without wide distribution, to $15,000 to $40,000 for a high-profile film from a major studio (or higher if the song is a major component of the production). Smaller fees (such as 20 percent of the initial cost) might apply to a second use of a song within the same production. Quotes for the use of music vary depending on whether there will be a sound track album; if so, the up-front fee might be lower to account for the future income from royalties on sound track sales. The right to use a song on a sound track is known as a mechanical license.

Other types of elements in an animated production that may require permissions, fees, and/or licenses include the portrayal of trademarked brands, likenesses of celebrities, and any other existing content. Fees vary significantly and can include up-front payments, royalties, or a combination of the two.

It can be time consuming and expensive to research ownership and negotiate fees for many of these existing rights, on top of the up-front fee and royalty costs for the rights themselves. Much of this research occurs during the development phase, since prohibitively high costs or the inability to find a rights holder may dictate that a desired element be removed from the production.

A third rights category applies specifically to the gaming sector. Game developers and publishers must not only acquire licenses, likeness rights, trademarks, and music as any animation producer would, but they must also acquire the technological tools they need to produce games for various platforms and the right to use the console-maker's name.

Here's how it works, using Nintendo as an example. Publishers approach Nintendo for a license. They must sign a nondisclosure agreement, which allows them to receive the programming and development information to produce a prototype for the platform they desire. Once the prototype is approved, Nintendo may offer the publisher a three-year, nonexclusive license to use its trademarks, copyrights, patents, and other rights in conjunction with the approved games throughout the Western Hemisphere. Nintendo agrees to manufacture the game discs with packaging, instruction booklet, and various inserts. The licensee/publisher must purchase at least 3,000 discs from Nintendo within 90 days and then can order more at a minimum of

300 at a time. The cost to the publisher is $10.40 for single finished discs and $9.00 per single disc in bulk.

Meanwhile, the developer of the game must become a Nintendo-authorized developer. It can approach Nintendo, either having a relationship with an authorized licensee already in place or independently. If Nintendo approves the developer's application it sends a nondisclosure agreement for signature. The developer then receives software programming specs for the platform and earns the ability to purchase software development tools. The developer has rights only to develop and not to manufacture or market. Unless it has an agreement with an official licensee, it's developing the game on spec in the hope that either Nintendo or an authorized licensee will want to publish the game in the future. Developers pay Nintendo $10,000 to $20,000 per title, on average, for the development tools and information.

Other Costs

Another component of animation budgets consists of physical supplies needed to complete the project. These can include everything from acetate for traditionally animated projects, to computer disks or other backup media, furniture, paper and stationery, DSL or other high-speed transmission fees, wrap parties, janitorial services, research materials, and art supplies. Other costs include catering, travel, short-term equipment rentals, shipping, phone usage, petty cash, transportation, and gifts for actors, as well as expenses for insurance, accounting, legal fees, and copyright and trademark registration.

Fees to outside companies also add to the budget. Creating original music includes costs such as fees for composition and lyrics, salaries for musicians, and time at recording facilities. Music can account for about 5 percent of the total budget; using a great deal of original music or popular songs would push the proportion higher, while a bare-bones soundtrack of little-known music could make it significantly less.

Postproduction facilities for sound, editing, and other tasks are rented by the hour, half day, week, or month, with rates typically negotiated between the postproduction studio and the producer. While most postproduction houses have rate cards, the negotiated rates are often at least 10 percent less than the rate card.

Overhead

Some studio overhead is included in an animation project's budget, with total annual overhead amortized over all productions in a year. Each production and studio has its own methods of accounting for direct and indirect costs. Allocated overhead costs could include salaries of shared employees such as accountants, legal staff, administrative personnel, etc., as well as utilities, general computer maintenance, rent or mortgage expenses, and shared supplies or furniture.

The size of the studio has a bearing on the amount of overhead charged to a given production. Large studios have higher total overhead costs than smaller studios, which tend to be leaner operations where most expenses can be directly linked to specific productions. While larger studios have more productions to share in overhead costs, the total figure per production is usually higher than for a project produced in a smaller production house.

Overruns and Contingencies

The producer's goal is to set the production budget at a realistic level and to monitor the production process to ensure that actual expenses do not exceed those budgeted. This will ensure that enough money is available to pay for costs during production and increase the chances of profitability. Despite the best-laid plans, however, producers often exceed their budgets. This sometimes occurs due to misplanning, but virtually innumerable unforeseen glitches—computer failures, illnesses, approval holdups, and the like—can and do occur on even the most efficiently run productions.

Therefore, most producers add a contingency fund equal to 5 percent to 10 percent of the budget (or sometimes 5 percent to 10 percent of selected items only); in rare cases the contingency could be as high as 15 percent. This may not be enough to cover actual overruns; Square's *Final Fantasy: The Spirits Within* (Sony, 2001) ultimately cost nearly double the budgeted amount, according to industry estimates.

Circumstances beyond the production's control can affect costs and scheduling significantly. On DreamWorks's *Shrek* the development and pre-production processes were well underway—including much of the voice-over work—when actor Chris Farley, who was the original voice of the main character, died. He was replaced by Mike Myers. The change and the holdup in production reportedly added $34 million to the film's cost. Another glitch occurred when Myers didn't like his original recording work and convinced the producers to allow him to rerecord it. Animators thus had to redo many of the character's gestures and mouth movements to fit the new rendition. The rerecording and new animation together added $4 million and three months to the process.

Studios and networks may penalize producers whose actual costs come in over budget (including the contingency). They might not allow the producer to receive back-end participation until they recoup both the cost overruns and an additional amount equaling 100 percent of those overruns, for example, or delay the payment of up-front fees due to the producer, transferring those fees to cover the over-budget costs instead. Some studios reduce the producer's participation points for each preagreed-upon spending increment over the budget.

Scheduling

Scheduling each member of the team for maximum efficiency is a complicated task, but, if done well, it can help keep costs in control.

As noted, many of the tasks that occur during the production process overlap. In fact, some preproduction and production tasks occur simultaneously, especially on 3D productions and films, while some postproduction tasks can start before production is finished. On a feature where preproduction is scheduled to take 60 weeks, production 110 weeks, and postproduction 20 weeks, the total production process could be completed in 125 weeks due to the overlap in tasks.

The best way to figure out schedules and overlaps is to plot each department's schedule on a Gantt chart. Across the top of the grid is the number and/or start date of each week during the production, and down the left side is each task or department. Each square on the grid is shaded to represent weeks where the relevant department will be busy, and left unshaded if the department will be inactive. This analysis provides a map of overlapping bars that will clearly show where the action is scheduled to happen, as well as ensuring that all the production details can be fit into the overall time frame. Similar charts can be used to plot the weeks individuals within each department should be hired and when their work will end.

Keeping Costs Down

Once producers have compiled all relevant budget figures they look at the total to determine if it is realistic in terms of securing financing. A television series that comes in far above $350,000 per episode would be difficult to fund, for example, unless there was something very special about it or the producers were able to generate significant funding internally.

If the producer deems the total budget figure too high, it looks for places to cut. Sacrificing quality is one possibility, such as simplifying the design or reducing the number of characters. But there are other means of keeping

Exhibit 3.3

Budget Template

Above-the-Line Expenses:

Direct costs: personnel and other expenses related to the development and writing of the script, including fees for rights; personnel and other expenses related to the producers and their team; personnel and other expenses related to the directors and their team; personnel and other expenses related to casting, cast, dialogue, rehearsal, and recording.

Below-the-Line Expenses:

Indirect costs, divided into the following categories:

Preproduction

Includes: salaries, supplies, and other expenses related to lower-level production staff, visual development and model design costs, storyboarding, song composition and production, preediting, and shipping prior to production.

Production

Includes: salaries, supplies, and other expenses related to layout, animation, scanning, scene planning, cleanup, effects, backgrounds, preliminary and final animation checking, ink-and-paint, camera, subcontractors, 3D character and environmental modeling, design, props and surfaces, workbook, lighting, rendering, compositing, technical direction, hardware and software, and systems administration and miscellaneous fees such as furniture, insurance, janitorial services, research materials, etc.

Postproduction

Includes: salaries, supplies, vendor fees, and other expenses related to postproduction staff, video processing and editing, film stock and lab, titles, music and sound, and screenings.

Other

Includes: overhead (an allocation of studio overhead costs), publicity, and a contingency fund (stated as a percentage of the budget).

---

costs down that producers can look at before they resort to changing the creator's vision or the property's inherent characteristics.

One technique that saves a significant amount of money is to send all or most of the production phase to one or more overseas—often Asian—studios. Work is subcontracted out for most 2D television series as of the early 2000s, but it is increasingly an option for 2D films, 3D television series, and other formats and vehicles. Disney subcontracted animation production on *The Tigger Movie* to Asian studios, for example.

Producing a project in South Korea, one of the more expensive subcontracting regions, can reduce a production budget by as much as 30 percent, compared to doing the work in Europe or North America, while sending it to India could reduce the budget to as little as one-tenth what it would be in the United States, Canada, or France. Of course cost is not the only factor that dictates the choice of a subcontracting studio; quality, expertise, and other elements play into the decision.

Although many overseas studios are beginning to offer postproduction services, most producers prefer to keep postproduction activities, such as compositing or editing, in-house, or to send them out to a nearby studio. Since postproduction is the last step before the project is completed, doing post tasks in-house or nearby gives the producer more control.

Many studios keep costs down by maintaining a small full-time staff and using freelancers wherever possible. Freelancers are hired on an as-needed basis, which allows the studio to link personnel directly to the production and spend only as much on labor as is required to complete the project. When the online animation studio and destination site Icebox (which has become a content provider only as of the early 2000s) was trying to cut costs, it estimated that moving its in-house production to freelancers and outside Flash animation houses would cut production costs in half. Its internally produced *Zombie College* series cost $30,000 per episode, while *Queer Duck,* an outsourced series, came in at about $15,000.

Technology-related decisions can also lead to lower costs. Computer animation has come into its own over the last decade, largely as a means of cutting costs, and is now used almost exclusively for most aspects of both 2D and 3D production. The time and personnel savings are great, given equal quality. On the other hand, the computer also allows for increased capabilities, leading producers to try to break boundaries with ever more complex animation. So budgets remain high, although viewers end up with more sophistication for the money.

Software and hardware choices play into the total budget picture. Motion-capture can be a cost-effective means of doing 3D CGI productions, for example, and producers may look at this technology as an option, depending on the nature of the production. (It works well for human and humanoid characters—especially when real people are being depicted, such as athletes in a sports-related video game—but not as well for four-legged creatures or those that move in a nonhumanlike fashion.) Mo-cap cuts production time, especially for projects with many characters.

Porchlight Entertainment's *Jay Jay the Jet Plane* is one television series produced using motion-capture technology. Although the studio had to spend $1 million up front to set up a mo-cap studio, the technique sped up production and decreased per-episode costs. Porchlight is able to produce a high volume of animation each day, 11 minutes on average. Studios have used motion-capture for cost-effective film effects as well, such as to create the armies in *The Patriot* (Columbia, 2000).

Another way studios can reduce costs is to share digital assets from one production to another. Sharing digital assets—such as using files from a television series to produce a film based on it, or creating a video game at the same time as a film or TV series—significantly decreases development and preproduction costs. File sharing shouldn't be done to the extent that it prevents originality, however.

Setting up a flexible organizational structure also can reduce costs. Increasingly, animators involved with a production are asked to perform multiple tasks, pitching in where needed, rather than being segmented into a certain department. The use of computers for many elements of the production process enables the animator to perform more tasks, which in turn allows flexibility in staffing and ensures that no personnel are underemployed at any given time. The production team behind *Beavis and Butt-Head Do America* (Paramount, 1996) utilized a team of ten directors; they animated many of the film's thirty-two sequences themselves.

THE BUDGET

Based on the production plan created at the end of the development process, the producers can put together a budget that includes all the components noted above. Most develop two budgets: 1) a detailed document that outlines each component down to its most minute level, assigning each a number for accounting purposes (the list of numbered categories is known as the "chart of accounts"), and 2) a summary budget that gathers the details into several large categories, such as script development, storyboard, layout, animation, character modeling, subcontractors, scanning, postproduction, etc.

Budgets are divided into two sections, above the line and below the line. Above the line refers to direct costs of the production. When they are subtracted from revenues, the result is gross profit. Below-the-line costs are considered indirect; when they are subtracted from gross profit, the result is net profit. In general, costs related to the script, the producer's and director's teams, and voice recording (including casting) are direct; all others are indirect. Below-the-line costs can be further categorized as preproduction, production, and postproduction.

The last cost to be listed is the overhead allocation, which is calculated using a different formula in each studio but is typically either a percentage of the budget or, if multiple productions are in process at a studio, a portion of overhead appropriate for the size of this production versus the others. For example, if three similarly budgeted projects are produced in a single studio in a year, each might be allocated one-third of studio overhead costs. Finally, the contingency fund completes the budget.

Elements of each of the budget components listed throughout this chapter are typically scattered throughout the budget. For example, labor costs related to each employee are placed in the appropriate section; costs related to the producer's salary and benefits are above the line, while those related to the storyboard artist are below the line, in the storyboard line item under preproduction. The same is true of supplies, hardware, and other costs.

4

Distribution

Each type of animation medium—film, television, Internet, interactive gaming, and home video/DVD—is characterized by a unique distribution structure.

TELEVISION

Even with the increased importance of international distribution for a given property, the United States continues to be the largest and potentially most lucrative television market in the world.

The U.S. Market

Potential customers for animated programming in the United States include national broadcast, cable, and satellite television networks, local-market stations, and public television stations.

Broadcast and Cable Networks The traditional method of selling to U.S. broadcast or cable networks has been to license 13 or 26 episodes (a half-year's or a year's worth of shows) for a flat fee per episode, which gives the customer the right to air each show twice. In the 1980s, licenses for a

---
Exhibit 4.1

Selected Film and TV License Fee Ranges, by Territory, 2000-2002

North America

    TV (children's half hour), per episode: $500–$300,000

    Film, feature length: $1,000–$10,000,000

Europe

    TV (children's half hour), per episode: $50–$35,000

    Film, feature length: $200–$1,000,000

Asia/Pacific

    TV (children's half hour), per episode: $150–$18,000

    Film, feature length: $300–$900,000

Latin America

    TV (children's half hour), per episode: $80–$15,000

    Film, feature length: $100–$350,000

Note: License fees vary by budget, economic conditions, population size, and many other factors.

Sources: Hollywood Reporter, C21 Media.

---

half-hour show in the United States were usually in the $275,000 to $325,000 per-episode range, enough to cover or nearly cover the production cost. Secondary sales windows (such as reruns to a cable network), sales to international territories, and ancillary products then put the production in the black.

The environment changed in the late 1990s and early 2000s. License fees shrank to $30,000 to $50,000 for the typical 26-minute 2D-animated show, which covered only one-sixth of the cost of an average half hour ($250,000 to $400,000); networks even began asking producers to cut their budgets as a prerequisite to acquisition. That situation continues, meaning that the portion of the production budget left uncovered by the license fee (known as the deficit) must be generated through other means, such as international presales, coproduction partnerships, or other financing.

C21 Media, a European publisher and research company, estimated that in the early 2000s U.S. networks' license fees for a children's half hour (live action or animated) ranged from $35,000 to $100,000, PBS's from $2,000 to $10,000, and basic cable channels' from $7,500 to $35,000. In Canada, English national networks commanded $10,000 to $12,000, English regional networks $500 to $1,000, French networks $3,500 to $4,000, and French cable channels $2,000 to $3,000.

Networks are increasingly becoming coproducers and cofinancers in the shows they air as a means of gaining exclusivity and creative control. They purchase an ownership stake or full ownership in the property, rather than simply licensing the rights to air the show. As stake holders they also receive revenues from international and secondary TV sales, home video, merchandising, and other ancillaries.

Many networks acquire series and concepts from sister companies within the same corporate family, some purchase or invest in shows from independent producers (although this is becoming less frequent on the broadcast networks), and some generate their own ideas or purchase concepts outright, becoming the sole proprietor and major financial beneficiary of the program. Most use a combination of these methods. A series still can end up on a network through a traditional acquisition strategy, but this is less common than it used to be.

In the early 2000s a trend developed in which broadcast and cable networks allied with individual program producers and/or distributors to fill entire blocks of programming. The networks leased out key time periods, such as Saturday mornings, to a content provider that could program the whole block. As of 2003 Discovery Communications supplied NBC's Saturday morning children's block, while Nickelodeon did the same for CBS, Canadian studio Nelvana for PBS, and 4Kids Entertainment for Fox. The same situation has occurred to a lesser degree in cable.

The 4Kids/Fox example, a four-year pact valued at over $100 million, began in 2002. 4Kids paid Fox $25 million per year to lease the space, with the option to pay $10.3 million of the annual fee in the form of stock. It supplied the programming, sold the advertising, and controlled any ancillary product or marketing activity, retaining all ancillary and advertising revenues that accrued from the block. 4Kids believed those income streams would cover the annual fee and allow the company to make a profit on the deal.

Analysts valued the other block programming deals mentioned above at far less than this agreement. The Discovery/NBC pact, a three-year partnership covering three Saturday morning hours, cost Discovery $5 million to $6 million per year; it retained all advertising revenue from the block.

The lowering of license fees has hurt children's daytime programming more than prime-time fare. Even after the prime-time animation boom of the late 1990s ended, the programs that have been successful in the evening hours have continued to generate license fees high enough to cover their budgets, which are significantly higher than those for daytime series. In 2001, *The Simpsons* received a license fee of $1.8 million per episode, and *King of the Hill* $1.5 million. These types of fees depend on a proven track record, however; Fox licensed *Futurama* the same year for $950,000, which covered about two-thirds of that show's budget.

The total number of networks is on the rise, with new cable, digital, and satellite networks being launched and more households able to receive satellite and digital television transmissions. Digital and satellite audiences are still small compared to broadcast and cable networks in the early 2000s; AT&T Broadband's introduction of Nicktoons TV in 2002 attracted about 14 million customers in the United States, compared to 86 million households for the Nickelodeon cable network. Meanwhile, new niche-oriented cable channels continue to start up; in late 2002 ADV Films announced its intention to launch a 24-hour cable channel devoted to anime programs.

The growth in channels results in more points of entry for animated programming, as well as additional windows for secondary sales (such as when Cartoon Network purchased cable rights for the entire 72-episode package of *Futurama* after the program had been cancelled from the Fox broadcast network). An emerging trend is for shows to run nearly simultaneously on two channels, such as premiering on a pay cable channel and then airing later the same week on a cable or broadcast network.

Syndication   Syndication is the act of selling a program to individual stations one by one (giving each an exclusive in its own market) until the roster of stations is large enough to make it worthwhile for an advertiser to consider buying time on the show. Stations can pay the syndicator for the show in cash, enter into a "barter" deal, or agree to some combination of the two; the last option is the most common and the first option the least common.

In a barter agreement the acquiring station donates time during the show, usually reserved for local advertising sold by the station, to the syndicator, which then seeks national advertisers to fill that time. The syndicator can offer advertisers a nearly U.S.-wide reach during those minutes, whereas the station could only offer its own local audience.

The split of available advertiser minutes during a barter-syndicated show is usually fifty-fifty (although the percentages can vary), meaning that the syndicator can sell half the time during the show as a national buy and the station can sell the rest to advertisers in its own market. Each retains the revenues for the ads it sells.

Stations are usually contractually required to promote the show a certain number of times per day at specified times of day, since the ratings depend on the show being marketed adequately. The syndicator, meanwhile, guarantees the advertiser a certain rating and level of national coverage, and/or number of top markets. Advertisers normally will not consider buying time on a program unless it has at least 65 percent to 85 percent coverage, but this depends on the advertiser and the show. (The greater the clearance, the higher the advertising rates charged.) If the syndicator is unable to achieve these milestones it must make up the difference between the promised and actual numbers, either through make-good advertising (that is, additional free ads) in a show with similar demographics, or by giving cash back, with the first option more common.

Each syndication deal outlines a specified time period (usually a year or a half-year for a first-run show and several years for reruns) and number of episodes (such as 13 or 26) as well as an agreed-upon number of airings during that period (usually two for a first-run show). It also dictates the time of day in which the show must run.

The syndicator compensates its program suppliers (e.g., animation houses) by giving them a percentage of the net national advertising receipts received for their program. From total net receipts, defined as actual receipts minus advertising agency commissions, which are usually around 15 percent, the barter syndicator deducts a percentage as a distribution fee. The cut is about 30 percent to 35 percent if the syndicator distributes the show as well as sells advertising, and around 10 percent if the program supplier physically distributes the show and the syndication company handles advertising sales only.

The syndication market for children's television programming changed drastically starting in the mid- to late 1990s. In the 2000s it is virtually impossible to garner a national audience for a children's show through syndication. The launch in 1995 of two new networks, the WB and UPN, each formed from stations that had been unaffiliated with any network, reduced the number of independent stations to which syndicated programming could be sold. The new networks were part of entertainment conglomerates (Time Warner, now merged with AOL, and Viacom, respectively), which could supply them with programming. Horizon Media, a media-buying company that researches the television market, estimated that syndication accounted for 21.1 percent of all gross ratings points for children's programming in 1994, just prior to the launch of the WB and UPN networks, but fell to virtually no share by the end of 2000.

As a result of this market contraction, most companies that previously specialized in sales of children's programming through syndication got out of the business. In 2000 BKN, formerly one of the leading kids' syndicators, moved out of syndication and became a content provider. It had tried to sell a program block under the BKN Kids Networks brand, but could not gain adequate coverage or ratings through syndication—due to lack of stations and strong competition from broadcast and especially cable networks—and ended up discontinuing the effort after two years. One of BKN's highly promoted shows, *Monster Rancher,* attracted only a 0.1 rating among children and 33 percent U.S. household coverage.

Despite the difficulty of syndicating children's programming, there are still a few producers that opt for this method of distribution. In 2002 animation studio Wild Brain began distributing its children's series *Poochini* to the United States through syndication, retaining The Television Syndication Company (TVS) as its partner. *Poochini,* which was coproduced with EM.TV of Germany, had been launched successfully in several international territories, which enhanced TVS's ability to sell it in the United States.

In many cases producers choose syndication as the distribution method of last resort. Even if not the optimum alternative, however, syndication can benefit children's properties by giving them a track record that can lead to a network sale. This was the path taken by 4Kids Entertainment with *Pokémon* in the U.S. market. Yet, the *Pokémon* experience also illustrates the challenges of this distribution alternative. Despite hit-level ratings in syndication, stations—many of which were affiliated with the WB or UPN—began to air the show in lower-viewership time periods because their sister and parent companies were supplying programs for the better slots. Based on the program's successful history, 4Kids signed a deal with the WB. For the first season the show ran weekly on the WB and daily in syndication, then it went to six days a week on the WB and left syndication completely.

When children's syndication deals do occur the partners are becoming more flexible and the deals more creative. Station groups (which consist of several stations around the country owned by a single national company) might negotiate a percentage of net profits from the series overall, or a cut of merchandising revenues, in return for airing a show. Or a station or station group might ask for some type of bonus compensation for placing the show on its schedule in a desired time period. BKN had been offering 10 percent of licensing, merchandising, home video, and international sales from its programming block to stations, pooling the income and splitting it among its customers.

There is still a robust syndication market for prime-time programming—this is how *Star Trek* programs have been distributed, for example—although few of these shows, as of 2002, are animated. Second-run or off-network syndication, in which shows that have already aired on a network are sold for additional airings through syndication, is also a viable technique for series that have several seasons' worth of episodes available to sell. Programs such as *The Simpsons* and *King of the Hill* earn significant revenues from repeats distributed through syndication to local U.S. television stations. *King of the Hill* earned a total of $3 million per episode from its launch in second-run syndication, with 22 Fox-owned stations accounting for half of that.

Public Television   Selling to public television stations is an alternative to broadcast, cable, and syndicated distribution, particularly for children's programs with an educational bent. In fact, some of the most successful programs for preschool children, both in terms of audience size and merchandising revenues, have come from the realm of PBS, including *Barney, Teletubbies,* and, of course, *Sesame Street.* Animated programs that have aired on PBS stations include Cinar's *Arthur* and Scholastic Entertainment's *The Magic School Bus.*

The Public Broadcasting System (PBS) buys programming and offers it to its 349 stations. They are not required to air the shows distributed to them by PBS, but most do. Having a program offered through PBS's National Program Service (NPS) is analogous to a commercial network deal, although, unlike the networks, PBS stations can air the program any time they wish during the week it's offered. (PBS also provides fully funded programs through its PBS Plus service, in addition to the programs it distributes through NPS.)

PBS often contributes financially to productions it distributes to its members, while corporate underwriters, individual public television stations, the producers, and nonprofit groups contribute the rest of the budget. A typical split might be 40 percent from PBS, another 30 percent from the Corporation for Public Broadcasting (a funder of public television programs), 15 percent from corporate grants, 10 percent from government grants and nonprofit programs, and 5 percent from foundation grants. PBS does not accept commercials, although it offers time before and after a show for promotional spots from the underwriters. Increasingly, PBS takes a percentage of ancillary revenues, such as from merchandising and home video, related to the programs it funds and airs.

Many producers find more success pitching their shows to local public television stations, who may finance and air a series locally, contribute partial funding, and/or sponsor it for national distribution, than directly to PBS. These stations can also help assist the producer with outreach requirements, fundraising, and other elements of PBS distribution.

Another option for getting programming on public television stations is through a program provider other than PBS that specializes in distributing shows through a system that's analogous to syndication in the commercial market. Companies such as American Public Television (APTV) sell programs to public television stations on an individual basis in an attempt to conglomerate a national audience. Children's series on APTV's roster as of this writing include *Redwall* and *The Big Comfy Couch*. These programs achieve a fraction of the coverage PBS offers. In addition, while stations air PBS programs during the same week, if not on the same day, stations who acquire programs through APTV can air them at any time within a specified period. This makes national promotions or marketing difficult.

International Television Distribution

As in the United States, international broadcasters traditionally have purchased programming through a license fee. International sales for U.S. (and other) companies are usually handled by international distributors or foreign sales agents (which also distribute films, home video, and sometimes other media); most companies take a distribution fee of 10 percent to 40 percent, with 25 percent being average. The larger studios have their own international television distribution arms.

Jim Henson Productions hired Salsa Distribution, a subsidiary of European producer TV-Loonland, as its exclusive Latin American distributor. Salsa sold several of its series in 2002 to MVS Television, a pan-Latin cable service based in Mexico. At the time Salsa represented more than six thousand hours of programming from TV-Loonland companies and other producers.

License fees vary by country, depending on the number of TV households, competition among a nation's broadcasters for programming, relative acquisition budgets, the desirability of a program, and other factors. They also differ from broadcaster to broadcaster within the same territory. In the late 1990s Canadian cable network Teletoon paid license fees of $2,300 to $4,000 for Canadian product and $3,000 to $5,000 for shows from the United States, Europe, and Australia. Its license fees were far lower than those paid by its children's programming rival YTV; the latter had 75 percent more viewers than Teletoon, as well as a programming budget close to ten times the size of Teletoon's.

There is no standard license fee for U.S. children's programs aired abroad. The sale of an animated half-hour show might bring in as little as $200 or $300 per episode in the Middle East, between $5,000 and $15,000 in one of the primary television markets in Europe or Latin America, $1,000 to $5,000 in Australia, and up to $20,000 in Japan, according to program suppliers and *The Hollywood Reporter*. Each fee is subject to negotiation.

C21 Media estimates the average nonfeature programming hour (including those originating in all territories) can generate license fees of $200 to $6,500 in Africa, with South Africa on the high end of that range, and $300 to $1,500 in the Middle East, with Syria on the low end and Israel on the high. In Australia and Asia a children's half hour can generate as low as $160 in Sri Lanka and as high as $18,000 in Japan; in Europe as low as $50 in Malta and as high as $35,000 in the United Kingdom; and in Latin America as low as $80 in the Dominican Republic and as high as $5,000 in Brazil, with pan-American deals ranging from $2,500 to $5,000.

In the early 2000s television license fees were declining abroad, as they were in the United States. In 2001 alone, fees paid for U.S. programs abroad dropped 5 percent to 10 percent in some countries, due in part to lower network advertising revenues, which reduced the license fees networks were willing to pay for programming. Increased competition also played a role in the decline; broadcasters in some countries were finding they could get higher ratings from local programs than from more expensive U.S. shows. Because of the changing landscape, international networks have begun to dictate prices to U.S. program suppliers rather than having to negotiate, as in the past.

In some developing television markets license fees continue to rise as economies improve, networks are privatized, and competition grows. In Eastern Europe, for example, average license fees were as high as $1,500 per episode for a half-hour children's program in 2000, compared to just $200 or $300 a year or two earlier.

As in the United States, international television networks increasingly desire to secure programming early in the production process and to retain rights in that programming to enhance revenues. As a result, many networks are becoming coproduction or cofinancing partners in shows, providing up-front financing in return for the right to air the programming in their home territory, as well as a stake in back-end revenues.

In 2001 Teletoon reportedly spent $600,000 (15 percent) of its $4 million programming budget on coproductions, investing a total of $8.5 million in shows for current and future years. France's pay channel Canal J devoted 60 percent of its programming budget to acquisitions and 40 percent to coproductions. In one year it invested $1.3 million in 46 hours of animation, contributing 15 percent to 20 percent of most budgets. Also in 2001, French broadcaster La Cinquième spent $2.3 million on animation coproductions, versus $670,000 on animation acquisitions. Several networks, including Spain's pay-TV network Sogecable, have set up production arms to develop their own and coproduced programming.

The Australian Broadcasting Corporation (ABC), purchases home video and merchandising rights along with TV rights when it can, and sometimes acts as the Australian licensing agent for the property in all categories of merchandise. Many networks are starting to ask for a share in merchandising and home video, along with their participation in distribution, especially in presales situations.

When German broadcaster RTL acquires programming, it looks for long license terms and all rights within its territory. When it acquires audio, video, merchandising, and online rights, it not only makes money on the back end, but can make its advertisers happy and increase its own ad revenues by offering cross-media buys.

Original programming is most often sold on a show-by-show basis, while library content is sold in packages (as is the case in the United States). In some cases programming deals involve both new and library offerings. In 2002 German programming provider EM.TV agreed to sell three hours of daily programming to SF DRS, the Swiss national broadcaster. The three-year deal, which first appeared on air in 2003, included more than 1,700 episodes to be broadcast under EM.TV's Junior brand, as well as 675 30-second interstitials featuring animated spokescharacters.

Content suppliers' distribution strategies vary from country to country. Canadian animation house Nelvana's broadcast sales in the Asia-Pacific region in 2002 illustrate how market entries can differ, depending on the show and the territory. In Japan, Nelvana sold its series *Rolie Polie Olie* to a satellite channel, ATX, and *Pecola* to a leading broadcaster, TV Tokyo. In Australia it licensed *Medabots* and several other shows to both the pay-TV network Foxtel and the broadcaster Network Ten. In New Zealand, among other deals, Nelvana sold several series to the niche broadcaster Maori TV.

As cable and pay-TV networks have expanded to build a regional or even worldwide reach, some producers have sold shows to one purchaser on a multiterritory basis. Singapore-based animation house Peach Blossom Media sold 26 episodes of its series *The Tomato Twins* to Nickelodeon for distribution across Asia, for example. For the most part, however, global and regional broadcasters have separate acquisition and programming executives in each region, and their strategies differ from nation to nation. Content providers might sell a show to The Disney Channel, Cartoon Network, or MTV for the United Kingdom only; this deal does not guarantee expansion into other markets in which the network operates, including the United States.

In fact, regional channels have succeeded by localizing their content and tailoring their schedules to national tastes. This segmentation extends to promotional IDs and bumpers—which are individualized for each country, while maintaining a consistent brand image on a worldwide basis—as well as to programming.

FILM

Unlike the fragmented television distribution business, the global film market is dominated by the Hollywood studios, which not only produce and finance films but also control their distribution in the United States and abroad. It is very difficult to get an independently produced film into the theatrical marketplace on a widespread, worldwide basis without partnering with one of the studios' distribution arms, although it can be done by going through an independent distributor.

Distribution Basics

Film producers have several means of distributing films. For widest distribution, they must ally with a major studio, although this can mean giving up significant rights. Studios often get involved early in the production, financing all or much of the film's development and production budget and handling distribution. In return they receive all rights (including the copyright) and control all creative, marketing, and distribution decision making. Studio-distributed films tend to be the ones with the widest audiences, and filmmakers can benefit financially (although their cut comes after the recoupment of expenses and can be far less than expected). But they do lose control.

Although this template describes the most common route to theatrical distribution, producers have some alternatives to this strategy. Major film studios and independent distributors (such as Lion's Gate) can simply distribute a film, controlling marketing and distribution but not production. The studio tends to get involved only after it sees the completed film; funding comes from elsewhere. In this case the domestic distributor or studio takes an approximately 35 percent cut of gross distribution revenues (all deals are negotiable), and deducts expenses before remitting the remainder to the producer.

Another option is for the distributor (either independent or one of the studios) to sign on to distribute the production before completion; their distribution cut is higher in this case, because they are assuming more risk and because their involvement provides the additional benefit of allowing the producer to gain financing. The producer can bring the signed distribution agreement (including the fact that the studio will pay an advance upon delivery of the completed negative) to a bank as collateral for a loan. This type of deal is known as a negative pickup. In a negative pickup, the distributor receives the distribution rights, usually in all media, for a given length of time or even in perpetuity. (It's in the producer's best interest to negotiate automatic options based on performance milestones, rather than granting perpetual rights; the rights can then revert to the producer if the distributor stops actively marketing the film.)

As these examples show, distributors or studios can license films at various points during the production process. They can get involved while the film is still being financed, during production, or after the film is finished. The timing depends on who the producer and distributor are and their past relationship, if any, as well as the nature of the film and the creative personnel. The more elements there are that seem to point toward success, the more likely the distributor is to pick up the film early in the process; the more unknown quantities, the likelier it is the distributor will sign on for a film only after it has seen the completed version. An early pickup gives the distributor more creative input into the film and its marketing, both of which help it reduce its risk, as well as a better financial deal and an ownership stake.

Some distributors and studios also come on board as coproducers, which leads to a level of involvement somewhere between owning all rights and simply distributing a film. The studio provides financing, has creative input, and shares in the back-end revenues, as well as being able to oversee distribution and marketing, but does not have full control. The financial deals for these types of arrangements vary significantly. (See chapter 8).

Generally a producer signs one distribution deal for the United States and Canada (both are included in the "domestic" market) and another for other territories with a foreign sales agent, also called an international distributor. Deals with the major studios usually cover the whole world; the studios may use local distributors in certain countries where they don't have operations. (See the next section for more on international distribution.) Studios usually cross-collateralize revenues from each territory, meaning revenues from all over the world go toward recouping expenses (rather than tying recoupment to each territory), before producers or other partners see any profit. In this case the producers will have to wait longer to receive payment.

Distributors often do not make money from theatrical releases alone; feature films are important because they generate awareness—which drives future sales of home videos and other secondary distribution—but at a high cost and rarely at a profit. Therefore, most distributors, both domestic and foreign, want distribution rights to all media, from theatrical and home video to merchandising and sound tracks. Typically, producers will grant theatrical, television, and home video rights, and retain the rest.

Sometimes a producer licenses a distributor for all rights, after which the distributor sublicenses or sells off the rights in which it is uninterested, taking a cut of any royalties or sales. A home video distributor might buy all rights and sell off theatrical, television, and ancillaries, retaining home video distribution for itself.

Distributors tend to want deals ranging from ten years to forever, while a filmmaker will want a one- to three-year deal. The result is a often a contract dictating automatic renewals, as long as the distributor's performance exceeds preagreed levels. That way, if the distributor is aggressively marketing the film it will be allowed to continue, but, if not, the rights revert to the producer.

Distributors pay the costs associated with physically distributing a film, including prints, advertising, and shipping, then are reimbursed through a deduction from the gross amount remitted to the producer. These deductions should be capped, either as a percentage of the gross revenues (such as 10 percent) or as a dollar amount.

The average new feature film cost studios $31.01 million in domestic print and advertising (P&A) in 2001, according to the Motion Picture Association of America (MPAA), with 88 percent of that going to advertising and 12 percent to prints. On the other hand, the costs for an independent film distributed on the art-house circuit can be less than $1 million, since these releases require fewer prints and are supported by less-expensive local advertising. The producer consults with the distributor on the creation of television, print, Internet, and in-theater advertising, including trailers, or at least retains approval rights, and the two agree beforehand on a marketing budget (which, if significant, helps the distributor sell the film to exhibitors).

Some independent producers that aren't able to secure a traditional distribution deal from a studio or distributor opt for a "rent a system" arrangement. A studio or other theatrical distribution company distributes the film to theaters for a fee—a percentage of gross (usually 17.5 percent, or half the traditional 35 percent), a flat fee, or a combination of the two—but does not handle the cost of prints and advertising, as is usual in a distribution deal. The producer is responsible for these costs.

In general, distributors are unlikely to become involved early in the process with a film from a small independent producer. Independents must finance and produce the film without any distribution presale money, then try to find distribution at the Sundance Film Festival or other markets where independent films are sold. Just a small percentage of the companies pitching their projects at film festivals succeed in securing distribution.

Some independents prefer to avoid the studio system because they're unwilling to lose creative control and ownership, even if it means no one will see their film. Some companies try to self-distribute, as animator Bill Plympton did with his compilation film *Mondo Plympton,* a difficult route in which distribution costs far outweigh the cost of production. Others look for alternative distribution outside of theaters, such as home video or the Internet.

In some cases distributors/studios and production companies sign agreements that cover several films. These deals usually include some sort of financing on the part of the studio. One example was a $250-million deal between DreamWorks and Aardman Animations, in which DreamWorks agreed to distribute and help finance five stop-motion animated films Aardman produced. *Chicken Run* was the first release under this partnership.

International Distribution

U.S.-made feature films released in the United States by one of the Hollywood studios are usually distributed throughout the world by the same studio, or one of its joint venture partners overseas (such as United International Pictures [UIP], a venture between Universal and Paramount that finances and distributes independent and indigenous films as well as studio releases). There are also independent distributors in each region that distribute films from the local market, the United States, and elsewhere. Local distributors include Shochiku and Gaga in Japan, Aurum in Spain, Cheongoram in Korea, Roadshow in Australia, and Filmauro and Medusa in Italy. The distribution fee for foreign rights normally falls in the range of 20 percent to 25 percent of gross receipts; as with the domestic market, expenses are deducted.

Some distributors acquire rights to a wide range of territories, servicing those where they have offices and sublicensing local distributors in territories where they don't have expertise. This adds another layer of distribution fees, so most producers ask for a cap on total fees.

Presales into foreign territories can be a means of acquiring financing, similar to a negative pickup deal in the United States. (The percentage of the budget that can be achieved this way is falling, as international distributors are waiting to see finished films before they commit.) All the distributors involved essentially become partners, or cofinancers, in the production and receive a percentage of revenues from the film (but no ownership or creative control). Several distributors in different territories collectively can contribute 50 percent of a production budget. These types of agreements, known as split-rights deals, grew in popularity in the mid-1990s, viewed as a viable financing option by Hollywood studios and independents alike. If the advances are received upon delivery of the negative, the promised funds can help secure a bank loan; any advances paid upon contract signing can go immediately toward production expenses.

For the U.S.–based studios, the international rollout schedule has been compressed in recent years. The studios used to release films internationally six months or longer after their domestic premiere, but now they can debut just a few weeks after or even at the same time as their U.S. debut. Dream-Works's *The Prince of Egypt* was released simultaneously in most territories around the world in 1998.

With the rise of the Internet and global broadcast media, news of films travels the world quickly. It makes sense for studios to take advantage of existing awareness from global media and marketing campaigns by releasing films across markets in quick succession. At the same time, prime moviegoing periods and holidays vary from country to country, which affects the best release date for a given territory. Other factors also have an impact on release schedules; for example, studios sometimes introduce films fairly early in Singapore and Malaysia in the hopes of reducing piracy. Time needed for dubbing can also affect the release schedule.

Disney staggers its release of animated films around the world, opening around Thanksgiving in the United States, in the following summer in Asia and Latin America, and in Europe in the fall (in the United Kingdom in October and the rest of Europe in November), a year after the film's domestic release. This schedule takes into account holidays and peak filmgoing periods in each territory, as well as allowing the studio more time for dubbing into thirty-plus languages.

As with international distribution of television shows, license fees for films are negotiated and vary, depending on the movie's characteristics, its budget, and the country. Territories with smaller movie-going audiences tend to pay lower fees than those with larger movie crowds.

According to *The Hollywood Reporter,* an independent producer in 2002 could expect license fees ranging from $5,000 to $60,000 per country in Europe, for a film budgeted at between $750,000 and $1 million, with Greece and Portugal at the low end and France and the United Kingdom at the high. In the Asia/Pacific region, for a film with the same budget, fees ran from $5,000 to $50,000, with Indonesia, Singapore, the Philippines, and Malaysia at the low end and Japan at the high. Latin American license fees could be as low as $5,000 in most countries and as much as $30,000 in Mexico, while Eastern Europe ranged from as low as $2,000 in the countries of the former Yugoslavia to as high as $15,000 in Russia, the Czech Republic/Slovakia, and Hungary. For an indie film with a higher budget, such as $6 million to $12 million, license fees could be as high as $900,000 in Japan and as low as $25,000 in Greece. All of these are significantly lower than in the recent past.

Films distributed internationally must be tailored to each market. The localization can be limited to adding subtitles, but often includes dubbing and editing, especially when it comes to animated films. On Disney's *Tarzan,* musician Phil Collins rerecorded his songs in French, Italian, German, and two Spanish dialects; local singers were used in other dubbed versions. The film was also dubbed into thirty-five different languages, including Bahasa Malay in Malaysia (usually a subtitle territory), the most ever for a Disney film.

Foreign movies are also distributed in the U.S. market, of course. Most international films are brought in by independent or art-house distributors, with Disney affiliate Miramax one of the leaders in this segment. Disney finalized an agreement with the leading Japanese animated film producer, Studio Ghibli (known for films such as *Princess Mononoke* and *Spirited Away*) and contributed 10 percent of the production budgets of the films under the agreement, while Ghibli's corporate parent Tokuma Shoten and Japanese television network NTV also contributed financing. Disney's deal included the right to distribute in all worldwide markets outside Japan; Miramax handled the U.S. release.

Secondary Markets

A significant portion of a film's total revenue can come from secondary sales channels that occur after domestic and international theatrical distribution. These include sales to IMAX theaters, home video/DVD, pay-TV channels, cable networks, broadcast networks, and eventually local stations. These sales can be a significant contributor to overall revenues. Lucasfilm and 20th Century Fox's *Star Wars: Episode I—The Phantom Menace* reportedly generated $150 million in worldwide broadcast and pay-TV distribution and $500 million in home video/DVD sales (versus $431 million in U.S. box office and another $491 million worldwide). Sales of a film's home video release can exceed its gross box-office take, especially for movies that did not meet box-office expectations.

As noted in chapter 1, IMAX and other large-format screens are a growing opportunity for feature films. The cost of reformatting a film for IMAX can be high, with extended shots or new scenes requiring additional animation. *Shrek,* for example, cost $10 million to transfer; IMAX covered these costs. The rerendering and rerecording of Disney's *Fantasia 2000* took five months to complete, but the film brought in nearly $50 million in IMAX theaters.

Television sales windows start with the high-end outlets (those with smaller audiences made up of subscribers who pay a fee to receive the channel) and continue through the most mainstream, free broadcast networks and stations. A similar series of television windows is available in each country around the world, although the significance of each opportunity varies, depending on the television distribution structure of that country. Once all the first-run options have been exploited, the film can be sold for second runs in each window; these can be exclusive or nonexclusive, long-term or short-term, and are often sold in packages (with the price of each film in the package negotiated separately).

In many cases a film from an independent producer sold to a cable network will get more exposure on cable than it did in theaters, where it may have been limited to festivals or art houses. These deals can be lucrative, with license fees sometimes reaching 40 percent of the film's budget (with wide variation from deal to deal). The distributor, if there is one, takes a fee that has traditionally ranged between 15 percent and 35 percent. Payments are often tied to theatrical performance, with bumps in fees at certain milestones as audiences grow, especially if the network has taken on the film prior to or early in its theatrical release. The length of the deal is normally between a year and eighteen months, with a cap on the number of times the film can be shown.

As is the case with first-run television series, TV outlets around the world are paying lower license fees to air theatrical films, with prices dropping 20 percent to 40 percent annually in some markets during the early 2000s. At that time *The Hollywood Reporter* estimated that the "typical" price paid for a U.S. feature film grossing more than $100 million at the domestic box office ranged from $4,500 from a terrestrial broadcaster in Thailand, on the low end of the market, to $8 million or so in Germany, on the high end. Prices vary drastically within each market, however, depending on the specifics of the film and the negotiations.

Developing markets offer a strong opportunity; Disney's Buena Vista International Television sold a group of Disney and Pixar animated films, called the Classic Treasures package, to Poland's Telewizja Polska. The deal marked an expansion of the company's previous activity in this country, where it had distributed some of its television series.

Short Films

Many independent studios as well as the majors make short films as a way to promote themselves, show off new styles or concepts, or to keep staffers busy during down times and satisfy them creatively. Short films are not lucrative in and of themselves, but they may lead to a character becoming popular enough to warrant a longer production being made.

Short films often gain theatrical exposure only at film festivals, but can appear in mainstream theaters as prefeature entertainment. Theatrical shorts are usually produced by the same company that produces or distributes the film; it is rare for independent studios to garner distribution this way. Warner Brothers, Disney, and Pixar have shown short films prior to their features.

While it is difficult to secure theatrical distribution for short films, the number of nontheatrical markets for this sort of entertainment is growing. Broadcasters and cable networks worldwide are looking for short films that fit with their brand image to air as interstitials between programming. The Internet also offers many opportunities for distribution of short films, especially shorts of 1 to 5 minutes, whether on the producer's own site (usually a promotional rather than money-making enterprise), an entertainment destination site, or a corporate site.

THE INTERNET

In the late 1990s many animation companies had high hopes for the Internet. The rosy profit scenarios have not come to be, however, and few entertainments-themed Internet companies remain in business, at least as pure-play Internet operations. Yet the Internet remains an important distribution channel for new animation properties trying to gain an audience, as a convergent marketing tool to support on-screen animation properties and, sometimes, as an ancillary revenue stream that plays into a property's total profit picture.

The exposure generated by an animated property over the Internet can be meaningful, at least for productions targeted toward a niche audience that frequents particular online sites. UGO Networks, an online content provider aimed at 18- to 34-year-old males, attracted 8.9 million unique visitors through five hundred affiliate sites in January 2002, ranking it among the top ten entertainment-related Internet sites for that month.

Destination Sites

Destination portals—sites that specialize in animation or entertainment—are one possible outlet for Internet animation. A leading example of this type of site is AtomFilms.com, operated by AtomShockwave since Atom's merger with Internet gaming and software provider Shockwave.com in 2000. As of 2002 the two sites together had 10 million content plays per month.

While AtomFilms features a wide variety of content, other destinations

---
Exhibit 4.2

Internet Distribution Models

Destination sites

- Sites generate revenue from advertising
- Content providers generate revenue from fee per download (sometimes with advance) and/or percentage of advertising revenue

Syndication

Exclusive:

- Syndicators/distributors generate fee per episode, often covering production budget; may also generate revenues per download
- Content providers share revenue with syndicator

Nonexclusive:

- Syndicators/distributors generate small fee per episode from each site, plus revenues from selling advertising on entire network
- Content providers share revenue from syndication fees and/or advertising

Incubator model

- Distributors generate revenue through options (and deals from exercise of options) for TV, film, or other off-line entertainment, taking a distribution fee
- Content providers generate revenue from options and deals, less distributor's fee

Ancillaries

- Distributors generate revenue from sales of properties for DVDs, licensed merchandise, or other ancillary products, usually through a licensing royalty (including guaranteed minimums and advances)
- Content providers share revenues from licensing deals, often a fifty-fifty split of royalties

Pay-per-view and subscriptions

- Sites generate revenue from user fee per download or view, or from annual or monthly user subscription fee to site
- Content providers share revenues from both sources of income

Combination model

- Sites/distributors generate revenue from a mix of some or all the methods listed above
- Content providers share in revenue through a combination of percentage shares and fees per use or download

Note: This list summarizes the most common methods for distribution and payment. Specifics of individual deals vary widely and are still evolving.

---

have focused on a single subject with a reachable and avid target audience. DistantCorners.com, for example, positioned itself as a specialist in horror, science fiction, and fantasy, with original animation being part of its content offerings, along with news items, merchandise, streaming video, and chat areas.

Most destination sites originally were founded on an advertising-supported business model. They hoped to generate audiences large enough to attract advertisers, who would spend to have their advertising featured on the site. They would be attracted, it was hoped, by the Internet's ability to allow them to monitor the effectiveness of their ads and collect information and feedback from potential customers.

Some sites generate income from advertising, although this revenue stream usually cannot, on its own, support them. AtomFilms continues to offer advertising, including short, TV-style commercials playing before its films, which have generated click-through rates as high as 30 percent. (A click-through rate measures the percentage of people who view an ad and then click on it to receive more information. Clicking typically transfers them to the advertiser's Web site.)

One animation house, Spumco, set up an Internet site to distribute its own and other studios' productions. It experimented with advertising and sponsorship methods outside of traditional banner advertising, including inking a sponsorship deal with retailer Tower Records for its series *The Goddamn George Liquor Show*. Tower sponsored an episode in which the main character took viewers to the Tower Web site and encouraged them to purchase CDs to help fund future episodes of the series. Spumco received a percentage of profits on sales at the Tower site if the customers clicked directly from Spumco. The promotion also incorporated desktop animations that popped up randomly on Tower.com, directing browsers to Spumco and telling them they'd be able to see additional animations when they came back to Tower's Web address.

Most of the animation destinations in business at the peak of the Internet boom went out of business or changed their business model before significant ad revenues were recorded. Current business models revolve around generating revenues through a combination of sources: sponsorship, advertising, syndication, e-commerce, and ancillary products and entertainment.

Syndication

Many former destination sites have evolved into content providers, while others positioned themselves as such from the beginning. MediaTrip and Urban Entertainment are among the companies that have used syndication as a key element in their business models; companies such as UGO Networks and Mondo Media benefit from multiple income streams but rely most heavily on syndication sales.

There are two primary syndication methods. The first involves selling a property or properties to many Web sites on a nonexclusive basis, creating a network of affiliated Web sites and receiving a fee—or revenue-sharing, often in a fifty-fifty split—per download or page view. Some distributors then pitch advertisers on the strength of the cumulative viewership, generating additional revenues from advertising. Brilliant Digital Entertainment distributed 20,000 3D-animated movies per day to individuals through 150 online sites in early 2001. Its advertising, at the time, generated rates of between $3 and $10 per thousand viewers.

The second method of syndication consists of selling a property or properties to a corporate or entertainment site on an exclusive basis. The purchaser handles advertising sales, if any, while the content provider reaps a fee that is higher than in a nonexclusive deal. Compensation is negotiated on a case-by-case basis, but often is centered around a royalty or fee per viewer, download, or page view, sometimes with an additional up-front fee or advance against royalties. Although it's difficult to state an average advance, payments between a few hundred dollars and $8,000 are not uncommon. In some deals the exclusive purchaser may pay the series' production fee as full compensation.

Mondo Media's model has utilized both syndication and advertising. It licensed its series *Thugs on Film* exclusively to BBC America for use on its online site as well as on air. It also has syndicated content nonexclusively to 30 affiliate partners, including Real Networks, Netscape, and Lycos, with a total audience as high as 100 million users. Mondo charged each of its affiliates $500 per nonexclusive weekly episode and has sold advertising to companies such as Priceline.com and Altoids; its 12-second advertisements were priced at between $50 and $75 per thousand viewers in 2001. Each episode of *Thugs on Film* reportedly cost $15,000 to produce and generated $60,000 through a combination of syndication fees and ad sales.

AtomFilms is a destination site, but it also syndicates content to affiliates and exclusive partners. An example of the latter was an agreement cemented in 2000 with Volkswagen of America, through Volkswagen's advertising agency, Arnold Communications. Atom sold the company sixty short films to be shown on VW.com over a six-month period. The sale was part of a larger promotional deal in which the car maker sponsored a live tour AtomFilms organized to support two of its filmmakers (whose short film featured a VW bus).

Most syndication-model Internet distributors air their programs on their own sites as well as their affiliates'. For example, 8Legged.com aired its 8-minute animated episode *Deep Fried, Live!* on its own site and, in syndication, to sites such as CampChaos.com, Humor.com, and WeaselCircus.com. The goal is not to make money from the proprietary site, but to use it as a promotional tool to show potential partners the animation that's available.

Companies involved in the syndication model often distribute both their own content and content acquired from outside creators. In many cases, they initially distribute episodes for free, in the hopes they can prove the property's success and enter into a paid deal later.

The Incubator Model

As television networks and film producers recognize the ability of the Internet to act as an "incubator" for potential new content, more sites are taking this approach to their business. For example, nibblebox.com has funded short films by student animators, as well as mentoring them and offering distribution. It takes the best of these efforts and pitches them to television networks.

Many sites are hoping to tie down TV or film deals on behalf of the filmmakers whose work they distribute. This type of deal is still rare, however, and not lucrative enough to be a stand-alone business model. But an incubator strategy can be one of many revenue streams for animators whose work is on the Web. As noted in chapter 1, MediaTrip's *Gary the Rat* and Urban Entertainment's *Undercover Brother* are two examples of this model. The latter reportedly earned $2 million from Imagine Entertainment, which developed the webisodic series into a film.

A number of organizations have launched online film festivals to help increase exposure for online animation and other productions, both to the end user/audience and to industry executives, who might pick up one of the ideas for development in mainstream media. Some of the festival sponsors have included Macromedia, Marvel Comics, Cartoon Network, and the Sci Fi Channel.

Ancillaries

Selling Internet-origin properties to outside companies for use in off-line products, services, and entertainment vehicles is another possible distribution channel and revenue stream. While not representing a viable standalone business model, the sale of DVDs, home videos, sound tracks, and licensed products can become a strong revenue stream for some properties. AtomFilms has released DVDs featuring entertainment available on its site, as well as licensing its content to airlines for in-flight programming. Its creators receive a percentage of the revenues that come in from these and other sales.

Most Web-based entertainment does not have nearly enough exposure to attract a significant number of licensees or establish a widespread licensed merchandise program of the sort that characterizes a successful television series. Yet small efforts encompassing just a few products targeted to the core audience and sold on the Web site can be viable. In fact, this relatively small amount of income can go a long way toward recouping production costs for Flash animation.

Stan Lee Media (SLM), a now-defunct Web site operator that featured original online series, created its own comic books based on *The Backstreet Project*. It sold more than 50,000 units at $10 each on the site, mostly to young girls who were fans of the music group on which the property was based. SLM also agreed to a promotional alliance with Burger King, valued at $50 million worth of exposure, and a subsidiary rights deal with Venture Soft of Japan, which brought in $5 million. These deals were not enough to sustain the company, however, and it ceased operations in 2001.

Shockwave.com received over one thousand orders for 10-inch dolls tied to the series *Radiskill and Devil Doll* (which aired on Shockwave before its merger with AtomFilms) at $11.95 each, while Rumpus.com offered toys tied to several of its properties, including the 38-minute *Herschel Hopper, New York Rabbit*. Ancillary products and services help promote the content and the sites on which they appear, as well as bring in some revenue.

A few online-origin properties can succeed in mainstream merchandise channels. Mondo's *Happy Tree Friends* was the focus of a 2003 deal with retailer Hot Topic. The chain sold a variety of merchandise, including apparel, featuring characters from the series in its mall-based stores. The property appealed to the chain's customers, mainly teens and young women.

Pay-Per-View and Subscriptions

A few online entertainment distributors have experimented with paid distribution. Comedy Central made online episodes of *South Park* and *Dr. Katz: Professional Therapist* available for downloading on SightSound.com. A two-day rental of one episode cost $2.50; customers could purchase an episode, giving them unlimited use, for $4.95.

IG Studios also experimented with pay-per-view, offering a 24-hour, video-on-demand, Internet event to support *Blood: The Last Vampire* on sputnik7.com. The promotion occurred on the same day the production became available on DVD and VHS. The tactic was intended to boost awareness as much as generate income.

Icebox.com, a former destination site turned content provider, made its entire animation library available in 2001 on a pay-per-view basis through a deal with AllCharge, a payment-solutions company. Visitors to the Icebox on-demand site could download one episode for free and subsequent episodes at 25 cents apiece, for unlimited viewing during a 24-hour period.

Some companies have considered implementing subscription systems for their Web sites, charging a monthly fee for unlimited usage, similar to a basic cable or online service system. So far this has not happened; research shows that, to date, consumers are not willing to pay for Web entertainment.

How Online Distribution Deals Work   In general, when content providers or creators sign a deal with a distributor they receive a small up-front fee and/or a percentage of all the income from any future deals, both online and off-. For example, they might earn a small fee or a percentage of income each time a customer downloads their content through one of the affiliates in a syndication network, a percentage of advertising income generated from the series, and/or a percentage of each home video or licensed item sold.

In some cases the distributor might fund the production as well as distribute it. If this is the case, then compensation, financing, and distribution are all tied into a package, as they would be in any other sector of the entertainment industry. (Deal making is discussed further in chapter 8.)

HOME VIDEO

Compensation for a home video distribution deal is normally based on a royalty (a percentage of each dollar amount sold) or fee (flat fee per unit sold), rather than a percentage of the production budget as in television or film. Home video can be lucrative; many productions budgeted in the $200,000 to $300,000 range earn 25 percent to 100 percent profit on top of the break-even point. (Home video distributors often want the right to sell original projects to broadcasters as well as video rights.)

Home video distributors acquire productions—both made-for-video projects and properties from other media for which video is a secondary distribution channel—to sell in their home territory. For a straight distribution deal, payment often takes the form of an advance against royalties, with royalties usually being somewhere around 10 percent to 25 percent of the wholesale price of the video, with 20 percent the most common cut. Rights are often granted in perpetuity. The distributor bears the distribution expenses, including manufacturing, marketing, and advertising.

Some distributors are willing to enter into a fifty-fifty net deal in lieu of a royalty agreement, which means that the distributor deducts distribution expenses from gross revenues first, then splits the remainder in half between the producer and itself. This type of deal tends to be more lucrative for the producer if sales are high, while a royalty tends to be better if sales are low.

Distributors often help finance home video productions, similar to a television coproduction or cofinancing deal, or a negative pickup or presale deal in film. The advance against royalties—often paid in installments, with part up front, part upon delivery of the final production, and part at a third milestone in between—is used to fund the production, acquire further financing, or secure a loan.

One unique aspect of video distribution is the existence of the sell-through and rental portions of the market. Sell-through, which represents the most common segment for chidren's animation projects, means the products are priced to allow consumers to purchase them. Rental tapes or discs are priced higher; the video store purchases a few copies, which are rented over and over to consumers. Distributors often share in the stores' rental income and split the revenues with the producer at an agreed-upon percentage. Animated feature films can be aimed at the rental market, but typically family films will be priced for sell-through. (The royalty paid by the distributor on sell-through videos may be reduced to 10 percent to 15 percent.) Some of the copies become available for rental, but sales are the primary revenue source.

The major studios have their own video distribution arms, which handle their theater- and television-based titles, their original products, and offerings from other producers or studios. Rights owners can sign a video distribution deal with one of the majors, or with an independent distributor such as LIVE Home Entertainment.

Some independents specialize in children's product or have divisions or labels that focus on children's titles. In 2002 Ventura Distribution started a children's and family label under which it acquired titles and developed its own. Like other distributors, Ventura offers video content providers several services, including home video sales in the United States and abroad, manufacturing, marketing, and various creative services.

While the bulk of videos are sold in video specialist chains such as Blockbuster, independent video stores, and mass merchants such as Wal-Mart, some niche titles are sold in other channels. Anime videos have traditionally been distributed through comic book specialty shops and specialty catalogs, for example, although the increased popularity of the genre has led to expansion into traditional video outlets. Religious or inspirational videos are often sold primarily through Christian bookstores, at least initially. Big Idea Productions launched *VeggieTales* in the Christian market and stayed there exclusively for three years before moving into mass channels. As of the early 2000s Big Idea had sold about half of its videos in mass channels.

Home video deals can encompass entire libraries of product or just one production. In 2000 Entertainment Rights received a $500,000 advance from Universal Pictures Video UK to distribute its home videos, including Barbie titles, in Britain.

INTERACTIVE GAMING

There are a number of ways for interactive gaming products, whether on computer media or console cartridges, to reach consumers' hands. Essentially, developers create the games; publishers manufacture and market the games, design and produce the packaging, and own the inventory; and distributors get the games into retailers' hands. Most of the larger interactive gaming companies, such as Electronic Arts or Infogrames, are involved in more than one of these areas.

Distribution is one of the main per-unit expenses associated with a game title. Distributors (or affiliate labels) can take a cut as high as 60 percent to 70 percent of the net sales price. The distributor sells the merchandise on consignment to the retailer, who can return it if it doesn't sell.

Since distribution, marketing, and development costs are high on video games, publishers must sell many units to break even. They bear most of the financial risk. Publishers usually fund the cost of developing the game through a fee to the developer or an advance against royalties. The developers' royalty, if they receive one, ranges from 5 percent to 20 percent of the publisher's net revenue, with 10 percent being common. (All distribution deals are negotiable, and the ranges mentioned are only yardsticks.)

Distribution in the gaming industry can take a number of forms. Co-publisher arrangements, which are usually exclusive, occur when a small publisher forms a joint venture with a larger publisher or affiliate label. The two companies share expenses and risks associated with developing content, producing inventory, and marketing and selling the games. After the venture has recouped all expenses the partners split any further revenues.

This type of deal works best if both parties bring equally valued resources (e.g., financial resources, distribution expertise, or creative services) to the table.

Another method of distribution is an affiliate-label strategy. Large distributors/developers/publishers or medium-size independent labels distribute the titles of smaller publishers along with their own. Sometimes the titles are cobranded with both the publisher's and the distribution label's brands, or they may be marketed under the publisher's label only. The distributor/affiliate label advises the publisher on packaging and marketing, and sells to retailers, sometimes directly, but more often through a national distributor. The affiliate label takes a 60 percent to 70 percent distribution fee (higher than a typical distributor's cut, as outlined below), and an additional 3 percent to 9 percent for marketing, some of which which goes into a co-op advertising fund that supports retailer promotions and advertising. The affiliate label keeps 5 percent to 20 percent of sales in reserve to cover future returns. The affiliate-label strategy is expensive for publishers, but it might be the only option for a small or new publisher. Warner Brothers Interactive Entertainment signed an affiliate label agreement with Electronic Arts for Looney Toons games in early 2003.

Exhibit 4.3

Partners Involved in an Interactive Game Title

Developer

Creates the game. Generates income through a fee from the publisher and sometimes further participation in revenues.

Publisher

Publishes and markets the game. Usually finances the developer's work. Generates income from sales of the games, less distribution fees.

Distributor

Sells the game to retailers. Generates income by deducting a distribution fee from sales. Some publishers and distributors sell games through copublishing or affiliate label relationships in addition to straight distribution deals.

Console/Platform Maker

Authorizes rights to publishers (licensees) and developers (official developers) to use the game maker's name and create products for its platforms. Sells game development tools to developer and packaging/disks to publisher (which equates to a fee per unit produced).

Intellectual Property Rightsholder

Licenses the rights to create games based on existing properties. Usually licenses the publisher but can license a developer; both must be approved. Generates royalty on each unit sold, with guaranteed minimums and advances.

Note: Some companies serve in more than one of these roles.

Another distribution method is selling to retailers through a national distributor. The distributor typically takes a 40 percent to 50 percent discount off the suggested retail price plus additional co-op or promotional fees (taken as an additional percentage) to support its marketing efforts with retailers. Expenses are deducted before the publisher's portion is remitted. Deals with national distributors are nonexclusive and leave more operational and administrative costs with the publisher than the affiliate-label or copublisher strategies discussed above. The publisher is also responsible for consumer marketing. A national distributor may not be able to reach all accounts where video games are sold, leaving the publisher to sell directly to unserviced channels or find another distributor to fill in the blanks. (Some large industry players, such as Electronic Arts, are able to sell directly to retailers, without the involvement of a national distributor.)

To distribute internationally, publishers use national distributors (some of which are also publishers and developers) in each country or region around the world; many of these can cover multiple territories. NewKidCo, a United States–based publisher of children's video game titles, aligned with Ubi Soft in a multiyear deal that allows Ubi Soft to publish its titles in Europe, Australia/New Zealand and South Africa. Many U.S.- and Japan-based publishers, as well as some in Europe, are global organizations; due to high development costs, it doesn't make sense for companies to sell to only one region. Most major players have worldwide or close-to-worldwide marketing and distribution capabilities.

TIMING OF DISTRIBUTION WINDOWS

One question producers need to ask when looking at the total distribution picture for their properties is how the various windows will be timed to maximize their profitability and not cannibalize each other. Once a studio knows where its property will originate—in television, as a video game, or as an Internet webisodic, for example—it must take a look at the best way for the property to roll out to a wider audience.

In some cases the decision is dependent on factors outside the company's control. Creating a television series or film takes time, and it is hard to plan for variables that arise in the process of putting together a deal, acquiring financing, producing the vehicle, and so on. Market conditions (e.g., the economy and the competitive landscape) and characteristics (e.g., what times of year are best for distributing a certain entertainment product) also play into timing decisions, as does the property's inherent lifespan. A property that becomes hot and is likely to burn itself out quickly will roll out faster than one that the producers believe can have a long and profitable future. A combination of strategic thinking and flexibility are needed to determine the best schedule.

5

Ancillaries

Many properties generate additional revenue streams through ancillary products and entertainment. T-shirts based on webisodic series, original videos tied to a television show, books spurred by a home video production, video games from a movie, action figures related to a video game, comic books inspired by a television franchise, and sound track CDs associated with a film are all examples of ancillaries. Some are content-driven while others feature logos or graphics. Most entertainment sectors can serve either as core or ancillary categories; for example, a property could start on home video, making that the core entertainment, or it could extend into home video from television or film.

A popular toy line can generate over $500 million in retail sales in a year, translating to approximately $25 million in royalty income for the core property's producers and other rights holders to share. In addition to this potentially large financial gain, ancillary products generate awareness for the core property; seeing an animation-based toy on a shelf at a Target store reminds consumers about the property, reinforcing the marketing message delivered through advertising and other promotional techniques.

Television and/or film distribution alone can't bring in enough guaranteed income to cover production budgets, much less allow for marketing and profit generation. Producers and coproduction partners look toward ancillaries as an important part of their financial stake in the property, and each wants to retain as many ancillary rights as possible. The importance of ancillary categories is illustrated by the British preschool series *Bob the Builder* (HIT Entertainment), which attributed 76 percent of its revenues to merchandising in 2001, the licensing effort's best year.

It should be remembered, however, that ancillary revenues are not guaranteed. The success of licensed products, for example, depends on many factors, including the popularity of the core entertainment vehicle and its spin-offs, the length of time the franchise endures, an appropriate marriage of product and property, whether or not the property lends itself to merchandise at all, and whether the target audience for the property is likely to buy entertainment-themed merchandise.

Another point often forgotten is that when there are several rights holders involved in a single property, each wanting a share of licensing and other ancillary revenues, the income flowing back to each partner is likely to be small. In addition, the total pool of money is not as large as many believe, except for the biggest blockbusters; revenues for most ancillary products are based on a small royalty payment for each unit sold.

METHODS OF EXPANDING INTO ANCILLARY CATEGORIES

There are several ways owners of entertainment properties can expand their franchises into ancillary categories. The primary method is licensing, where the rights holder (the licensor) authorizes a manufacturer or service provider (the licensee) to create and/or market products or services in return for a royalty. All the elements of the deal, including compensation, are negotiable, but royalties generally are 5 percent to 12 percent of the manufacturer's sale price to retailers. Most agreements require the licensee to pay the licensor a minimum guaranteed royalty based on sales forecasts—the guarantee can run from a few hundred to millions of dollars—with a portion of that due upfront as an advance. Animation houses often use licensing agents to handle their licensing activity; agents take an average commission of 35 percent to 40 percent of all licensing revenues.

In some categories, such as home video or music sound tracks, property owners can work with a distributor. The distributor acquires the rights to format existing content into the new medium (e.g., a CD or DVD), manufacture the physical products, and sell them to stores or direct to consumers. In return they take a distribution fee and remit the remaining revenues to the licensor or pay a royalty on each unit sold. (See chapter 3 for more on home video distribution.)

Some property owners choose to set up joint ventures with allied companies rather than following a licensing or distribution strategy. In a joint venture, both parties contribute to the partnership financially, creatively, and strategically, and both share in any profits on a fifty-fifty or other equitable basis. For the rights holder a joint venture is more expensive up front than working with licensees or distributors, but it allows more control as well as the potential for a greater share of profits.

Large animation companies, particularly those that belong to entertainment conglomerates, often opt to keep their ancillary licensing and distribution deals within the corporate family. For example, the bulk of Nickelodeon's publishing is done with Simon & Schuster and its films and videos are distributed by Paramount, both sister companies within the Viacom family.

On rare occasions entertainment studios will decide to manufacture and/or distribute ancillary products themselves. For example, they might commission a company to make T-shirts based on one of their properties, pay for the shirts up front rather than through a licensing deal (meaning they assume ownership of the inventory, which is not the case in licensing), then sell the T-shirts on their Web site.

This strategy mainly occurs when quantities are small and distribution is narrow, or if the entertainment company has a division with expertise in that category. Animation house Curious Pictures, for example, has a toy division, Curious Toys. Some animation houses have brought video and/or computer game production in-house in order to take advantage of synergies between the creation of the core entertainment and the ancillary game or video. Yet overseeing an in-house department for an ancillary product such as an interactive game can be expensive, requiring the hiring of artists, designers, programmers, producers, and writers dedicated to gaming.

MAJOR ANCILLARY CATEGORIES

The major ancillary categories, each of which has its own mode of operation, are discussed below.

Home Video/DVD

Home video and DVD can be considered vehicles for original productions, secondary distribution channels for films and television shows, or ancillary product categories. (Home video and DVD distribution are discussed in detail in chapter 4).

As a secondary distribution channel, films tend to do better than television shows in the video format. Consumers rarely want to see TV programs on their VCRs or DVD players when they've seen the original and possibly several repeats on broadcast and cable. Cult television shows, including foreign and nostalgic programs, can do well in video if they are not widely distributed elsewhere. In 1999 Rhino Records released 12 episodes of the 1980s series *Transformers* on video and DVD; consumers reportedly purchased close to 800,000 units. A growing number of current series do well on DVD, where an entire season of television shows, along with extras, can be released on a single disc. *The Simpsons* is one animated series that has been introduced successfully on DVD. In fact, the advent of DVD has increased the market for TV-based products. Consumers have responded to having a whole season on one disc, along with extras such as interviews with actors.

Films often do well on video and, lately, on DVD, even surpassing their box-office grosses. DreamWorks's *Shrek* sold 2.5 million DVDs and 4.5 million VHS cassettes in its first three days on the market in 2001. Together their sales totaled $420 million (20 million units) after two months of U.S. availability. *Shrek*'s U.S. box-office total was $267.7 million and the worldwide gross $481.9 million. The same success can be had for classic films. Japan's Pioneer Entertainment released the anime movie *Akira* on DVD after restoring it at a cost of $1 million, and it hit the number-one spot on U.S. bestseller lists.

Several producers in the children's market have created original videos based on existing franchises. These types of productions can be considered ancillary, since they are extending an existing brand by creating new content for a different format. Original videos, whether based on an existing franchise or, more rarely, completely original, are put together financially as any original production would be. (This process is discussed in chapter 8.)

The major studios produce and distribute home video and DVDs through in-house divisions. Smaller companies can self-produce new video projects (sometimes sending the actual animation production to an overseas studio) or put them together through coproductions, but nearly always must look to a large studio or an independent distributor to manufacture the cassettes or disks and distribute them to stores. On occasion producers license an independent company to create, produce, and distribute videos and DVDs. This route is uncommon for an animation studio, which would normally want to be more involved with the production, but a smaller creator may not have the resources or expertise to enter this market without a licensee.

Interactive Software

Interactive software is an increasingly important revenue source for animation rights holders. For a property targeted toward teen boys, this category easily can account for 50 percent or more of all ancillary activity and rival the core property when it comes to sales and viewership. Software is also an effective way to increase awareness of the franchise, particularly among teen and young adult males.

The marriage between the two industries makes sense. In 2001 the trade magazine *Variety* estimated that interactive games collectively contributed over $1 billion in revenues to the major Hollywood studios. Meanwhile, from the point of view of the game makers, titles that are tied to popular licenses, including animation, tend to sell well and come with a ready-made story line and characters.

Most often deals between animation property owners and game publishers or developers are achieved through licensing, although joint ventures or other partnership structures are possible. The Hollywood studios maintain interactive gaming divisions and produce titles based on their own properties in-house or through interdivisional licensing deals.

There are many parties involved in the creation of a video game based on an animation property. First there is the licensor, who grants the rights and dictates how the characters can look, how they will be used, and other guidelines for game creation. Second there is the developer, who creates the game within the parameters set forth by the licensor. Third there is the publisher, who manufactures and markets the games. The fourth party is the distributor, who sells the games to stores. Finally, the fifth partner is the maker of the console or other hardware on which the game will be played (e.g., Nintendo or Sony), which licenses the publisher and the developer and provides the tools they need to develop and create the game. (See chapter 4 for more on interactive titles and how they're distributed.)

Some licensing deals in the gaming world encompass many different platforms (e.g., PlayStation 2 or Xbox), maximizing developers' and publishers' profit potential and creating marketing synergies that enhance overall sales. But not all developers or publishers are set up to create games for all platforms, since the cost of entry can be steep. So licensors must sometimes grant several licenses to ensure their property appears in every possible format. (Licensing a different company for each platform maximizes up-front revenues for the licensor, but most property owners feel this strategy doesn't benefit the overall franchise.)

Where possible, licensors in the early 2000s prefer to grant as many platforms as they can to one licensee. This was the theory behind a deal between licensor Jim Henson Interactive, creator and former owner of *The Muppet Show,* and TDK Mediactive. Their three-year, renewable licensing agreement allowed TDK to develop and publish games featuring *Muppet Show* characters in PS One, PS2, Xbox, Nintendo GameCube, Game Boy Advance, and all computer platforms.

As was noted earlier, digital assets, particularly from 3D CGI productions, can often be shared between the producer of the core entertainment and the developers of the related interactive games. In fact, creating assets specifically for the games is sometimes done simultaneously with the film or television show itself, allowing both to come to market at the same time, reducing production expenses and enhancing the development of story and characters for both. Games are rarely just interactive versions of the original; they include new story lines and sometimes new characters that serve to expand the world established in the original entertainment property.

Publishing

Book and comic book publishing are not usually the top ancillary categories in terms of revenue, dwarfed by such categories as home video, interactive games, and toys. But books and comic books are important. They generate awareness with the target audience; provide a means to extend story lines, backstory, environments, and character development beyond the core entertainment property; and enhance the brand's image, in some cases, by strengthening its association with literacy and education.

Licensed books based on animation properties, especially popular television franchises, frequently reach the children's best-seller lists produced by the *New York Times, Publishers Weekly,* and others. In the early 2000s, *Bob the Builder, Dora the Explorer,* and *SpongeBob SquarePants* were among the television shows to have translated into best-selling book series. Typical formats, depending on the age of the consumer and the nature of the property, include board books, original novels, novelizations (for films), story books, and nonfiction books, such as a joke book based on the humor in *Shrek* or a book on dinosaurs under the *Jurassic Park* brand.

Property owners take this category seriously when it comes to approving products, since publishing, more than most other categories, reflects on the show and its content. The quality-control process can be more complicated for publishing than for other licensed goods, where the design of the property—but none of the story or other content—appears on the merchandise. The marriage of entertainment and books is so important in terms of content that creative personnel associated with the entertainment property, such as writers or producers, are often credited as authors of the books.

Many of the larger book publishers are affiliated with Hollywood studios: HarperCollins with Fox, Simon & Schuster with Paramount, Hyperion with Disney, and Little Brown with Warner Brothers, among others. Corporate objectives encourage synergy between the various divisions, which leads to a lot of tie-in publishing activity between corporately related companies. Even independent or midsize animation houses, such as HIT Entertainment in the United Kingdom and Corus/Nelvana in Canada, own or are affiliated with book-publishing arms. Not only does this give them control over publishing based on their properties, but it also serves as a source of properties with the potential to be translated into animation.

Comic book publishing is a small but viable category for a few properties. While many comic book characters and story lines have inspired successful entertainment vehicles (*Spider-Man, Batman, Men in Black,* to name just a few), franchises seldom travel in the other direction. Comic book readers tend to favor properties that originate in that genre. Exceptions include anime and science fiction, which often find success as graphic novels (comic books that are produced in paperback form and sold in book shops).

Interactive game properties also make their way into comic books; the two media have a similar target audience comprised of male preteens, teens, and young adults. *Dragon's Lair* is an interactive game franchise (with characters created by animator Don Bluth) that was introduced in 1983 and accumulated $107 million in sales in 20 years. Its licensor, Dragon's Lair LLC, signed a four-year license agreement with MV Creations to create a comic book series and related products.

Magazines are a rare tie-in product, but can work for classic franchises or brands encompassing multiple characters. Both Nickelodeon and Cartoon Network publish magazines that support their rosters of characters and shows; Nickelodeon's sells over 1 million copies per issue. Tie-in magazines tend to be more popular in other countries than in the United States, particularly in the United Kingdom, where most popular children's properties can be found on the newsstand in magazine form.

A few animation properties are licensed for syndicated newspaper comic strips, generating a small fee per newspaper for each comic strip released. In 2000 Speed Racer Enterprises granted a newspaper syndication company called Comicfx the rights to produce a daily comic strip based on the classic Japanese cartoon *Speed Racer.* A *Pokémon* comic strip was distributed to newspapers through Creators Syndicate.

Musical Sound Tracks

Many film producers and executives from other entertainment sectors take sound track sales into account when they plan the music for a film. Incorporating musical acts that are popular with young adults, teens, and pre-teens—the primary purchasers of CDs—can enhance sales of the sound track album even among those who haven't seen the film. Warner Brothers' *Quest for Camelot* sound track sold well beyond the film's short run at the box office, for example. The marketing synergies also can work the other way around; having a popular singer play an important role in the sound track can bring people into theaters who might not otherwise see the film.

In addition to sound tracks, some licensors have authorized original music CDs that feature well-known artists who perform songs inspired by, but that do not appear in, the film or TV series. In 2000, for instance, an alternative rock album called *Heroes and Villains* was tied to the Cartoon Network series *The Powerpuff Girls,* while a *Lion King* album at the time of the film's release featured African-inspired music.

When a licensor does a music deal with a major label (such as EMI), the label licenses the rights to manufacture and market a CD (or, increasingly, a downloadable digital file). In deals with independent artists the label usually retains ownership rights to any new songs or arrangements on it. Music labels give the artists an advance, often in the hundreds of millions, which goes toward the costs of recording, touring, and producing a music video. (The video alone can cost anywhere from $5,000 to $1.5 million, with most falling in the $50,000 to $150,000 range.) Royalties (of about $.75 per unit on average) go first toward recouping the advance, so the artists often have to wait a long time until they receive additional royalties. (Some never earn out the advance.)

Independent labels and those that are working with an animation studio or other licensor rather than an individual artist often negotiate deals that are far more favorable toward the licensor than is the norm in the industry. However, since royalties are often shared by a number of parties (the licensor, who commissioned the song, the artist, composer, and lyricist, other investors or coproducers), this category is more for promotional purposes than a lucrative sideline, unless the sound track CD becomes a big hit.

When well-known artists or already-existing songs or music are incorporated into an animation sound track, licensors must be sure to acquire all the rights needed to feature those songs on the sound track CD as well as in the film itself. To include a song in a sound track requires a synchronization license (with payments negotiated with the music publisher). Putting the same song on the sound track CD requires an additional mechanical license to the publisher of 8 cents per unit for a song 5 minutes or less and 1.55 cents for every minute after that (as of 2002). Both types of music licenses require approval from the artist, songwriter, music publisher, and/or record label as well. Only when the producers commission original music on a work-for-hire basis do they automatically own all rights for its use in the production as well as ancillary products.

Some partnerships for music-based products are long-term and broad-based. For example, in 2002 4Kids Entertainment, a U.S. television production and distribution company, partnered in a joint venture with Cherry Lane, a music publisher. Cherry Lane planned to market products based on the master recordings and compositions from several of 4Kids's television series, including *Teenage Mutant Ninja Turtles, Yu-Gi-Oh!,* and *Cubix.* In return for the exclusive right to administer these music properties, Cherry Lane received 50 percent of 4Kids's interest. The deal was an expansion of the two company's previous partnership for *Pokémon*-related music.

Children's musical albums and music videos are other music-related opportunities for animation properties, although both are relatively small and are viable for just a fraction of entertainment-based songs.

While most sound track activity historically has been associated with feature films and, to a lesser extent, television, one growing area of activity is comprised of sound tracks based on electronic games. Electro Source, a distributor of video games including Square Co.'s titles, signed an agreement with TokyoPop Soundtrax in 2000 to distribute sound track CDs from Square's games, starting with *Parasite Eve II* and *Final Fantasy IX.* Similarly, in 2002 Microsoft Game Studios licensed producer Nile Rodgers to distribute and market sound tracks based on its Xbox game *Halo: Combat Evolved.* As video game productions become more complex and filmlike, they incorporate original and existing music that appeals to preteen and teenage fans, so sound tracks are becoming an important ancillary product in this sector.

Toys

Toys are the primary licensed product category for most children's animation projects, with action figures, dolls, and board games among the strong items, depending on the property. For some children's properties, especially action figure–driven TV shows for boys such as *Teenage Mutant Ninja Turtles,* toys can account for more than 50 percent of all associated licensed merchandise sales.

Toys are often one of the first licenses granted for an animation property. Their product development and manufacturing require long lead times; therefore, if toys are to come to market at the same time or prior to other licensed products, the licensor must sign a licensee early. In addition, the primary (or "master") toy licensee tends to advertise its product line heavily, which also promotes the show and other licensed items. So the existence of a powerful toy company on a roster of licensees helps attract other manufacturers to the property. Finally, because the sales potential of toys is relatively strong, toy licensees' advances and guaranteed royalties tend to be one of the highest of all the partners, which is a financial boon to the licensor and/or producer. In the case of television, these funds can go toward future production or help recoup production monies already spent. Because of the unpredictable nature of licensing, these funds are rarely incorporated into the property's financing structure directly, although the existence of a strong toy licensee can help attract investors and partners.

Because of consolidation in the toy industry, just a handful of companies are able to assume the role of master licensee, with Mattel and Hasbro leading the pack. Because of the expense of developing a toy line, and since most major toy companies operate on a global basis, master toy deals often cover the entire world, or most of it. If a property already has a toy licensee in a certain region before it is introduced in other territories, that region is excluded from future global toy deals. For example, most Japanese properties that become hits in the United States already have a successful toy program in Japan and the rest of Asia, so the master toy licensee can only acquire rights for the territories not yet accounted for. This has been true of properties such as *Pokémon* and *Medabots*.

Some animation-based toy lines are narrowly focused, unlike the wide-ranging, global deals typical of children's television or film properties. A licensor of a new, relatively unknown television program might, for example, self-distribute toys, or sign a licensee for a small range of collectible toys for sale over the Internet. This technique allows the licensor to test the market, gauging demand and soliciting qualitative feedback. Such information allows it to decide whether to proceed with a larger licensing effort and helps it build a track record so it will be more attractive to potential licensees. Cartoon Network chose to test a dozen products based on its new series *Samurai Jack* in 2001, with sales initially limited to its Web site.

Exhibit 5.1

Summary of Methods for Ancillary Media Extension

Method of Extension	Relevant Media	Pros	Cons
Licensing	Merchandise	Inexpensive upfront	Lack of control
	Home video	Steady royaltiy potential	Potential for low profit margin
	Sound tracks	Benefit from manufacturer's expertise	
	Interactive		
	Premiums		
	Publishing		
Distribution	Home video	Little expertise needed	Distribution fee cuts into profits
	Sound tracks	Sometimes no other way to enter market	Lack of control
	Interactive	Benefit from distributor's expertise	
	Internet		
	Film		
	Television		
Joint Venture	Home video	Higher potential profit margins	Upfront investment required
	Interactive	More control over strategy	Need expertise
	Publishing		Need compatible partners
In-house	Premiums	Higher profit margin potential	Need facilities, expertise
	Limited-edition toys	Control over strategy	Expensive upfront
	Home video		
	Television		
	Film		

Note: Expansion methods vary depending on category, expertise of licensor/animation house, objectives, and other factors.

Licensors of properties meant for an adult audience interested in toys for their collectible value may sign a smaller licensee that specializes in collectibles. 20th Century Fox licensed a small company known for metal robot toys as the licensee for its series *Futurama*, while a video game series, *Dragon's Lair*, inspired an action figure line marketed by a toy and collectible company called AnJon.

Other Licensed Products

Toys, publishing, interactive games, and home video/DVD are considered the four primary categories for most youth-targeted, animation-based licensing programs. But the number of possible products is almost limitless, depending on the nature of the property and its audience. The licensing trade publication *The Licensing Letter* identifies seventeen broad categories of licensed merchandise, with gifts, apparel, stationery, and foods and beverages among them.

Some properties, such as *Pokémon,* can extend into virtually all product categories, while others are appropriate for just a few opportunities, if any at all. Each program is different. Cartoon Network's *The Powerpuff Girls* reportedly generated well over $500 million in retail sales, mainly focused on products for girls (although the show itself was popular with both genders). *Bob the Builder,* distributed and licensed by HIT Entertainment and seen on Nickelodeon in the United States, focused on preschool toys and other products for preschoolers. The risqué German film property *Werner,* which had sold 11 million comic books in Germany as of the early 2000s, extended into adult-targeted products such as sound track CDs, T-shirts, mugs, and even condoms and cigars.

It is always important to listen to consumers rather than try to impose a program that makes sense to the licensor and its licensees. Nickelodeon started licensing *SpongeBob SquarePants* into children's categories such as books and water toys. But it soon discovered that college-aged males were watching the show in large numbers and were buying merchandise. This information led Nickelodeon to alter its program to focus on products this group would like, such as soap-on-a-rope and other novelty items that fit the show's themes. Once this strategy proved successful, the licensor began expanding again into a wider consumer base, including children. By the beginning of 2003 total *SpongeBob* retail sales had reached $750 million and have continued to grow.

Television and film producers take merchandising into account during the property's development stage. While ancillary product concerns do not dictate how creative decisions are made—the quality of the show itself is primary—a studio's merchandising personnel are often on hand to make suggestions to enhance licensing potential without taking anything away from the producer's and director's vision. An animation studio's licensing executive might encourage producers to modify the design of a vehicle or weapon so it's more "toyetic," add colors to the show's palette that would make products more appealing to customers, or alter story lines slightly to strengthen the play pattern. But none of these changes would occur if they harmed the integrity of the show.

Licensors must make many strategic and tactical decisions when creating and implementing a licensing strategy. They include: the timing of product introduction and rollout in each country where the property is released, which categories of product and individual items make sense for the property, how many and which licensees to sign in order to maximize revenues in the short and long term, whether licensees or retailers should have exclusive or nonexclusive rights, and in which types of stores the licensed products should be sold. All of these choices impact not only revenue potential but the show's image and its on-air success and duration. Too many products on store shelves too early can shorten the life of the licensing program and, more importantly, the franchise itself.

In some cases a single licensing deal can involve rights for many properties owned by a single licensor. Applause, a marketer of plush toys and gifts sold through specialty stores, signed an agreement that allowed it to market a wide range of exclusive products for many Nickelodeon franchises including *Rugrats, Blue's Clues,* and *SpongeBob SquarePants.* It has similar agreements with other large licensors of multiple animation properties, including Universal Studios, 20th Century Fox, and Disney.

Entertainment-based products increasingly debut at just one chain of stores, through exclusive promotional/licensing deals. These arrangements can be long-term or last for one to six months at the product launch, and can involve one or a few products or a full slate. DIC Entertainment signed an exclusive with Toys 'Я' Us in conjunction with the premiere of its animated history series, *Liberty's Kids,* distributed on public television. Toys 'Я' Us agreed to develop, manufacture, and sell toys, accessories, party goods, apparel, and school supplies for a three-year period, with merchandise introduced in spring of 2003.

Animation Art and Collectibles

There is a sizable collector market for animation art. This sector is not a big focus for most animation studios, but does bring in revenue and keep avid fans happy. The main focus in this business is selling original animation cels, both signed and unsigned, through galleries specializing in animation art. Some collectors are interested in other artifacts related to an animated film as well, such as preliminary production drawings, paintings of characters and backgrounds, pencil, rough, and cleanup drawings, storyboards, model sheets, concept art, layouts, and maquettes.

In addition some galleries, in conjunction with the studios, sell high-quality reproductions such as limited-edition serigraph prints of cels—limited editions from the DreamWorks film *The Prince of Egypt* have commanded prices of $3,000—although these types of products aren't as in-demand as cels or other material actually used in a production. The rarity of original cels, however, has created a desire for other items.

Original cels are becoming even rarer, now that a large proportion of production is done digitally. As a result, the definition of "animation art" has broadened to include digital printouts from the production. Some studios create a single "animation cel" for each frame from their digital files that then can be sold as unique animation art. Many studios back up their files on film for archiving purposes—so they'll have the film, in case digital files are damaged or misplaced—and can create a limited amount of animation art for sale to collectors during this process.

Most of the major studios have allied with online auction houses such as Yahoo! and eBay to oversee online auctions of unique props and other material used in film or television production. Disney Auctions on eBay is one example.

Animation art and collectibles represent a truly ancillary business; it is not budgeted for or relied upon as other merchandising activity can be. The business is normally handled by a member of the licensing department or by the licensing agent, especially for smaller animation houses; larger studios that do a big business in this area may have a small dedicated animation art department or staffers focused on this category.

Some galleries that are authorized dealers of animation art include American Royal Arts, Cartoon Factory, and Animation USA. Most are licensed by the studio to distribute animation art, either exclusively, nonexclusively, or

---

Exhibit 5.2

Common Ancillary Product Categories for Selected Animation Properties

Preschool Children's TV Show

Plush toys, board books, bath books, bath toys, home videos, wooden toys, electronic learning toys, other educational toys, apparel, layette and bedding, room decor

Family/Children's Film

Wide range of products including toys, games, apparel, backpacks, foods, home videos/DVDs, sound tracks, books (novelizations, "making of," novelty books, original novels, etc.), video and computer games, greeting cards, school supplies, bedding, room decor, shoes, collectibles, Christmas ornaments, magnets, novelties, shampoo, lunch boxes, sporting goods, wrapping paper, Halloween costumes, computer accessories, etc.

Action-Themed Video Game

Action figures, T-shirts, novelties, comic books, sound tracks.

Note: Many other categories are possible, depending on the specifics of the property; not all properties will lend themselves to these categories.

Exhibit 5.3

Potential Ancillary Entertainment Vehicles

Mall-based tours of live shows

In-school live shows

Theatrical plays

Theatrical musicals

Concerts

Film festivals showcasing a property

IMAX films

Theme park attractions

Ice shows

Museum exhibits, traveling and permanent

Interactive attractions

Note: Ancillary entertainment is defined as a secondary entertainment vehicle based on or inspired by the original property. Films, television, or other entertainment vehicles can be considered ancillary, if based on an existing property.

exclusively within their geographic region. Other galleries operate in the secondary market (distributing cels that previously have been owned by someone outside the studio) and are not official distributors or licensees.

Entertainment

New entertainment vehicles based on an animation franchise are sometimes considered ancillary, since they come after the original. But many of these productions dwarf their predecessors in terms of revenues from distribution and merchandising.

Even when the "ancillary" entertainment is not the biggest component of the franchise, it still can bring in significant profit. The film based on the *Tomb Raider* video game, for example, generated a box office total of over $130 million in the United States. The five titles in the original series of games sold 25 million units. Meanwhile, a 1995 film inspired by the *Mortal Kombat* video game franchise generated $70 million, less than 2 percent of the franchise's total revenues over its lifetime of $4 billion-plus, but still a nice addition to the business.

"Ancillary" entertainment vehicles are developed and financed in much the same way as an original production, with the producer of the original often acting as a producer, coproducer, or executive producer of the second entertainment vehicle or, at a minimum, participating in the revenue streams. In some cases a studio might license another company to produce, market, and distribute the entertainment, reaping some of the financial rewards but not participating much creatively outside of approvals. Such might be the case for a mall-based live touring show (popular for preschool animation properties) or a theatrical play. Most television or film producers don't have much expertise in these areas.

6

Marketing and Promotions

Producers spend millions of dollars creating television series, interactive games, films, and other animated entertainment. But if these vehicles are not marketed adequately, especially in today's crowded landscape, they'll usually fail, and all the investment will have been in vain. For that reason animation producers, distributors, and allied companies spend millions or even tens of millions of dollars on marketing efforts to support their high-profile releases. Investment in advertising and promotions can equal or even exceed the amount put into the production itself.

There are two major tiers of marketing: trade campaigns and consumer campaigns. First, content providers must market the property to the trade; that is, the gatekeepers that stand between the producer and the consumer, such as theater owners, networks, and retailers, as well as potential production, marketing, and ancillary product partners. Once a production gets closer to its release date the studio and its partners must market it to consumers, so they will be excited to see or purchase it when it becomes available.

Since marketing is a critical component of a property's success, producers begin discussing advertising and promotional strategies early in the production process, even during development. A solid marketing plan can help secure financial and coproduction partners, not to mention networks, licensees, and other allied companies. In addition, marketing initiatives may require extra footage for use in both trade and consumer campaigns (such as for television commercials); it often is more cost-effective to provide the necessary animation during the production process than to create it later.

For large studio productions initial marketing meetings may involve as many as fifty people, including the producers and various creative, marketing, and support personnel. The animators themselves often want to know how their characters will be used in advertising. They have a vested interest in ensuring that the property succeeds, but they also want to make certain no advertising or marketing tactics will violate the integrity of the property or their work.

While the highest-profile marketing campaigns involve big-studio releases of films, television shows, or franchise-based videos, lesser-known animation properties also benefit from promotional activity. LuminetIK, a 3D animation and effects house, licensed a Generation X–targeted superhero character, *Alex,* to Queench, a manufacturer of bottled water, in 2002. Queench expected to use the character in all of its promotions, events, and advertising, making the character an integral part of the brand identification. In this case the marketer was looking for a character that would appeal to its target consumer group but was not overexposed and therefore could be associated closely with its own brand. For LuminetIK the deal brought in revenues and helped build awareness for the character with the appropriate audience.

Marketing strategies vary depending on the type of entertainment product being supported. Promotional activity surrounding an Internet-only property would be far less than for a TV series based on an established book or comic book. Yet the traditional rules are changing. Some direct-to-video sequels benefit from as much promotional support as films, while video releases of features sometimes receive more marketing support than the theatrical releases on which they were based. DreamWorks heavily promoted the video release of *Spirit: Stallion of the Cimarron,* attracting more marketing partners than for its *Shrek* video, even though the latter generated more than three times the domestic box office that *Spirit* did.

TRADE MARKETING

Trade marketing supports studios or producers in pitching their properties to potential production, financial, distribution, and ancillary product partners. (The process of pitching is discussed in chapter 7.) Animation houses also market themselves and their properties on an ongoing basis, so that the industry and potential partners are aware of them and more open to a meeting when they come to call in the future. This nonspecific, or "image," marketing leads to contacts and inquiries that may result in future alliances or business partnerships.

Not only must the core entertainment property be marketed to the trade, so must ancillary products, secondary entertainment vehicles, and all aspects of the franchise.

Trade Shows and Conventions

One method of increasing exposure for an animation studio and specific properties is to attend and exhibit at the major trade shows attended by animation executives and others allied with the animation industry. There are many relevant trade shows. For television they include MIPCOM and MIP-TV, both focusing on the global production and distribution market, and NATPE, for syndication. For film there are similar opportunities, such as the American Film Market (AFM) and MIFED in Europe.

There are also trade conventions for other types of entertainment vehicles and ancillary products, which animation producers often attend if their properties have relevance in these industries. A few include the Video Software Dealers Association (VSDA) show for the home video and DVD market, the Electronic Entertainment Expo (E3) and Comdex for interactive gaming, and the Licensing Show for licensed properties, among many others.

Gatherings focusing specifically on the animation business include SIG-GRAPH, for special effects, and the World Animation Celebration (WAC). (A list of trade shows of interest to the animation and allied industries appears in appendix 2.)

Producers can take their own booths at relevant shows and conventions, or be represented at their distributors' or production partners' booths. Even if they decide not to exhibit, most studios send representatives to all or most of these fairs, to have meetings and walk the floor. Trade shows and conventions are gathering places for entertainment executives, convenient centers for networking, pitch meetings, licensee and promotional partner summits, and coproduction partner updates. They also feature opportunities for education, either through seminars or by taking an informal look at what competitors are up to.

Film Festivals

For independent film producers, whether of feature-length or short movies, film festivals are a means to market properties to potential distributors. Some also increase exposure among fans, especially avid moviegoers that can generate word-of-mouth publicity. For example, the Sundance Film Festival is primarily a trade gathering, but many fans congregate there, and publicity about the event further boosts awareness for the films screened. Gaining recognition from distribution executives, however, is usually the primary objective for being included in a film festival.

Acquisitions and development executives attend festivals to look for films to purchase or distribute, and this may be the most effective way for independent producers to make sure people who have the power to get their films distributed actually see them. It would be difficult for many independent producers to gain access to these executives any other way. Some festivals, such as Spike and Mike's Sick and Twisted Festival of Animation and Spike and Mike's (classic) Festival of Animation (which tour art-house theaters around the country), are more for fans, while others, such as the World Animation Celebration or the ASIFA-Hollywood Anifest, are more for the trade.

The Annecy Festival is probably the best-known festival focusing exclusively on animation, going on since 1960. Like many other festivals geared toward the trade, it combines a film market (the International Animated Film Market for Movies and Television, or MIFA) with the festival. The World Animation Celebration, which has been running off and on since 1975 and, as of 2002, is an annual event, is another animation-centric festival featuring a conference and networking events.

With the advent of the Internet as a potential distribution channel for entertainment fare, a number of companies have launched online film festivals. Although potential partners and the public can view these entertainment vehicles online any time, a well-publicized film festival draws attention to a site and its films, attracting first-time or infrequent users. Online festivals also may help bring in advertisers or sponsors. Some festivals exhibit online-origin films in a theatrical setting, while others are online-only events.

Examples of film festivals spotlighting Internet animation have included the Yahoo! Internet Life Online Film Festival, the Virtual Film Festival (a

Swedish national festival) and the World Animation Internet Animation Competition. (See appendix 2 for a list of festivals.)

Associations

Joining an association is a way for animation executives and creative personnel to make contacts, as well as keep up with industry trends and what their competitors are doing. Knowing what's going on helps executives formulate marketing plans, and creatives come up with new ideas that will stand out from the competition. Contacts made through professional associations can lead to future deals, while attendance at meetings keeps a studio's name familiar among colleagues and potential partners. Groups such as the International Animated Film Association (ASIFA), which has affiliates around the world, and Women in Animation are just a few examples.

There are also regional organizations around the globe, such as the Association of Indian Producers of Animation (AIPA) and the Association of Spanish Animation Producers (AEPA), which were launched to promote the local industry to potential customers around the world, as well as serving as a venue where regional companies can network with one another. (A list of animation trade groups and associations is given in appendix 2.)

Advertising

Advertising is another method of reaching potential trade partners. Regular advertising, whether property-specific or general, keeps a studio's name in the minds of distributors, licensees, or other targeted groups, causing them to think of the studio when new business opportunities come up. Advertising individual properties is a way to generate interest among companies the producers might not otherwise consider approaching. Advertising current projects and achievements also helps strengthen the studio's reputation in the eyes of colleagues, possibly leading to new relationships in the future.

Some of the events or themes touted in advertisements could include events (such as inviting the industry to a screening), recent awards, the availability of a property for distribution, the existence of a strong roster of licensees attached to a merchandising program, and so on.

Some advertising is simply image-building, not meant to promote an individual property or initiative but rather to spread the word about the company and its strengths, services, and accomplishments. Many studios opt not to run this sort of advertising because they cannot justify the expense; it cannot be tied to any particular revenue-generating project and its effectiveness is difficult to track. In addition, a regular schedule of property-based ads with specific objectives also acts as an image-building tool, making more general advertising unnecessary. The companies who are best known in the industry tend to have a regular advertising program of some sort in place.

There are numerous trade publications in which animation studios can advertise, depending on the nature of their message and who they want to reach. Prior to the major television markets, such as MIPCOM, many producers and distributors run ads touting their show offerings and booth numbers in publications such as *Variety* or *The Hollywood Reporter.* Companies trying to get the word out about new properties available for licensing take out ads in one of the trades specializing in that business, such as *Kidscreen* or *License!* Video distributors wanting to alert retailers of a new release can do so in *Video Store News* or *Video Business.*

The animation trades, including *Animation Magazine,* are potential vehicles for ads. Local newspapers in the studio's home city are also possibilities for advertising, but are less frequently used, except in the L.A. area. Even then, most animation studios focus on trade publications for business-themed advertising.

Costs depend on the frequency (rates are reduced for advertisers with multiple insertions in a year), the size of the ad, and whether spot color or full-color printing is used, as well as the nature of the magazine, who its target audience is, and how many subscribers and readers it has. An ad in the *AWN Spotlight,* a "Special Announcement" e-mail sent out by the online magazine *Animation World Network* to 28,000 animation professionals, costs a flat fee of $995. The base rate for a full-page, black-and-white ad in *Variety* in 2003 was $6,950; full-color was an additional $5,450. Each publication has a rate card (often available online) detailing costs and deadlines.

Most studios include a trade component in their advertising budgets for a specific property; some also have an annual advertising budget for general use that is considered part of studio overhead.

Public Relations

Public relations is an important and cost-effective way for a studio to promote itself and its properties. Like trade advertising, most publicity efforts are focused on specific objectives or initiatives, but a regular publicity program helps reinforce the studio's name, properties, and positive attributes in potential partners' minds.

One of the main publicity techniques available to animation houses is a media release (also known as a news or press release), a one- to two-page announcement of news. Media are sent to a targeted group of publications (and possibly broadcasters), including the animation trades and specific outlets that target the audience for which the message is intended. For example, a press release about the launch of a merchandising program or an initial roster of licensees would be more effective in one of the licensing trades, which licensees and retailers read, than in the entertainment industry trades, which a few licensing executives receive, but which are mainly geared toward producers and others involved in the creation of entertainment.

Another publicity tool is a media kit. These are packets of information that contain recent media releases, a one- or two-page background sheet about the company's history, fact sheets about the company and/or some of its key properties, biographies of executives and/or key creative personnel, and images such as screen shots or head shots. Publicists periodically send media kits out to their entire roster of media contacts, and include them with media releases to new contacts. They also place them in the press room at trade shows.

Other publicity tools include submitting productions for awards, such as Oscars or ASIFA-Hollywood's Annies (for animation), which can then be promoted to the trade and consumer press; holding press conferences; and hosting events such as parties at trade shows, holiday get-togethers on the studio premises, and screenings of new or award-winning properties. All serve to maintain a high profile for the studio.

The ultimate goal of trade publicity is to get the company's name into business publications to which the desired audience subscribes. When corporate executives are interviewed by the trade press the exposure boosts the profile of the studio. Regular publicity mailings to journalists will keep the executives and the producer or animation house in reporters' minds, and they will begin to call when working on stories where the studio might be able to contribute.

While publicity has the advantage of being inexpensive compared to advertising, it has the disadvantage that the studio can't control it. The studio can keep a rein on what publicity messages it releases, but it can't have a final say over how publications or broadcast news sources use the information. In general, however, the adage "any publicity is good publicity" holds true, because it keeps the studio name in people's minds.

The cost of publicity programs varies depending on whether the studio handles the effort in-house or hires a public relations firm, as well as how many publicity initiatives the studio undertakes over a given period of time. Retaining a public relations company can be expensive (retainers can run several thousand dollars per month, with additional costs for specific initiatives), but the cost can be recouped in increased exposure, especially if the studio lacks media contacts or public relations expertise.

Trade Components in Consumer Marketing

While consumer marketing efforts are targeted toward the viewer or end user of the entertainment vehicle or product, rather than the gatekeepers, most consumer efforts include some components aimed at the trade. Unlike the trade marketing tactics outlined above that are meant to preview a property to the trade prior to its consumer introduction, these types of marketing initiatives are intended to support the consumer marketing efforts. Studios want to generate enthusiasm among retailers, movie theaters, or other venues where consumers purchase or interact with the product.

A marketing campaign to support a video release would contain elements to excite employees of the video distributor and retail chains, as well as video buyers/renters. A consumer promotion might include an in-store display contest that offers prizes to the store whose employees develop the best display. The studio would provide signage or other materials through its distributor, which employees could enhance with objects of their own choice. Each store would send pictures of the display to the distributor or studio for judging. The winning store might receive premiums, a pizza party, or some other prize. This tactic would result in big and unique displays in stores throughout the country, raising the profile of the new video and possibly spurring sales and rentals.

CONSUMER MARKETING

Consumer-marketing campaigns for major film, television, video game, or home video releases are often multifaceted, multipartner programs. Other times initiatives can be narrower in scope. The choice depends on the marketing budget, the timing of the promotion, and the financial expectations of the property, as well as the objectives for the campaign.

Many marketing programs are set up to support a brand-new production or product, but they can also occur at various times during a property's life. In addition to studio- or producer-led promotions, partners such as licensees, distributors, or networks may arrange their own efforts, which can be backed by the studio, financially or otherwise.

<u>Exhibit 6.1</u>

Consumer Marketing Elements to Support an Animation Property

Advertising	Nonprofit overlays
Character appearances	On-pack coupons
Contests	Packaging messages
Copackaging	Personal appearances by creative personnel
Cross-couponing	
Cross-merchandising	Posters
Direct mail	Press functions
Discounts	Product inserts
Educational marketing	Product placement
Endorsements	Purchase-with-purchase premiums
Exclusive or limited-edition products	Rebates
Fan events	Sampling
Fan visits to production facilities	Signage
Free premiums	Sponsorship
In-store display materials	Sweepstakes
Internet components	Tours
Licensed products	

Consumer-Marketing Elements

While each marketing campaign is unique, depending on the partners' objectives, the characteristics of the property, and the target audience, most include one or more of the elements described below.

Personal Interaction   Producers want their audiences to feel more connected with their properties, and marketing campaigns often feature components that give consumers a chance to interact personally with the property in some way. They might incorporate contests where the winner receives a trip to the studio where the animation is produced or the opportunity to be a guest voice or be animated into an episode. Nickelodeon and Cartoon Network are among the companies that have used these devices to strengthen the bond between their viewers and their programming and brands.

Live events also serve to connect the fans and the animation:

To mark the tenth anniversary of *The Simpsons* in 2000, 20th Century Fox held a Global Fanfest, a three-day event attended by two thousand winners of a *Simpsons* trivia contest.

o DC Comics and Warner Brothers Consumer Products created an auto racing event to support their classic property *Superman;* a driver in each racing circuit, including NASCAR, CART, the National Hot Rod Association, and the World of Outlaws, drove a car with *Superman* graphics. Kmart sold replica die-cast cars and limited-edition comics tied to the event.

o When Stan Lee Media launched its online series based on the Backstreet Boys music group, it held an event at the Hard Rock Live outlet at Universal Studios in Orlando. The first episode debuted at the event, which marked the kickoff of the series.

o With each new *VeggieTales* video release, Big Idea Productions sent out kits to Christian-product retailers that explained how to hold *VeggieTales* big-screen premieres at churches or local theaters. For the 2000 release, *The Story of Esther,* a half million people in 48 states attended these events. Big Idea believes the kits helped quadruple first-day sales of its new video releases.

Advertising   Some entertainment vehicles can benefit from consumer advertising. Films rely on local newspaper ads and glossy entertainment magazines, while video releases utilize ads in entertainment, parenting, and family-oriented publications. Computer and video game releases are advertised in magazines that target gamers. Films and videos are advertised on television, as are television programs, at least on the networks where they appear. Manufacturers advertise licensed merchandise and interactive games on television as well, although the Federal Communications Commission has dictated that products based on a show can't be advertised during episodes of that series.

In the case of animation and animation-related products, Nickelodeon and Cartoon Network air much of the supporting broadcast advertising. In fact, as of the early 2000s Nickelodeon reaped more than 50 percent of all dollars spent on television advertising for children. Overall, an increasing portion of TV advertising to support animation is being devoted to cable. Some studios, especially those that have cable networks in the corporate family, devote a quarter to a third of individual properties' advertising budgets to cable television, where there is more flexibility about when ads run, more dayparts from which to choose, and more opportunities for on-air event programming.

Outside of television and print, direct-response advertising, both via mail and the Internet, is another potential channel for marketing messages. Interactive game maker Activision is among the marketers that has utilized e-mail to promote its games. In 2001 it supported one of its *Star Trek* titles by sending two e-mail marketing messages to fifteen thousand known *Star Trek* fans in the company's database of registered users.

Ad messages can also appear on flyers distributed with the packaging of products associated with a franchise; for example, an interactive game title's box could include a brochure advertising an upcoming film or other licensed merchandise based on the same characters.

The Motion Picture Association of America (MPAA) estimated that for the average film released in 2001 studios spent their advertising dollars on the following media: 25.4 percent on network television, 16.9 percent on spot TV, 13.1 percent on newspapers, 5.1 percent on trailers, 1.3 percent on the Internet, 20.2 percent on other media (such as magazines, radio, comic books, billboards, busses, and so on), and 17.9 percent on nonmedia (such as promotions).

The Hollywood Reporter categorizes advertising spending differently—for example, separating some segments into their own categories, while the MPAA groups them together—but its figures also demonstrate how film distributors use a number of different advertising vehicles to get the message out. The publication estimated that distributors cumulatively spent $2.7 billion on film advertising in 2001. Spending by advertising segment was as follows: 35.4 percent to network television, 5.9 percent to syndicated TV, 12.7 percent to cable, 12.8 percent to spot TV in local markets, 28.7 percent to newspapers, 1.9 percent to outdoor media, 1.5 percent to radio, and 1.2 percent to magazines.

The Hollywood Reporter noted that in 2000 *Shrek*'s total media expense (the amount paid for print space and broadcast time, excluding the creative costs of developing advertising) totaled $57 million. That was the equivalent of 21.3 percent of its domestic box office total of $267.7 million. *Monsters, Inc.,* released the same year, had $41.5 million in media expense, equalling 17.3 percent of the $239.5 million it generated at the box office.

While television and print account for the bulk of entertainment advertising, other media can be effective. Golden Books Family Entertainment, now part of Classic Media, promoted video releases of classic *Felix* and *Underdog* television episodes in 20 U.S. markets with radio promotions. They featured giveaways of *Underdog* and *Felix* merchandise and provided a link with the stations' Web sites. Golden also ran in-theater advertising on 800 domestic screens during family films, reaching 6 million theatergoers.

The Internet accounts for a small portion of total advertising for films and other entertainment vehicles, but studios, producers, and distributors are using it to reach targeted audiences of avid fans. Amazon.com reportedly took in $1 million per month on film advertising in the early 2000s. There is often an Internet component connected to mainstream advertising or promotional events as well; ads send consumers to the Web site where they can get more information, enter contests, etc. A 2000 report by Cyber Dialogue (now Fulcrum Analytics) estimated that 31 percent of people who logged onto film-related Web sites see more movies than those who don't visit the sites; they also directly connected their decision to see certain films to information gleaned from the Internet.

When entertainment vehicles are based on an interactive property, as is often the case, the Internet component gains importance as a means of reaching fans. Sony, the distributor of *Final Fantasy: The Spirits Within,* based on a video game, promoted it on the Web portal Lycos in 2001, spending an estimated $150,000.

Contests   Games, contests, and sweepstakes are among the most commonly utilized promotional elements. They get customers excited about the property; give the studio and its partners something to promote widely in advertising, on packaging, and online; and allow the studio or partner to capture the names of potential customers and track the promotion's effectiveness.

Contests can take many forms. When Nelvana supplied CBS with its Saturday morning kids' programming in 1998, it oversaw a national sweepstakes involving Toys 'Я' Us. Twenty-five local CBS affiliates conducted their own write-and-win contests in association with the promotion, as well as implementing events and on-air programming tie-ins. The effort was supported by cable television ads in ten markets and a Web component.

To support *DragonTales* on PBS, Sesame Workshop and Mott's signed a deal for a six-month promotion that included an instant-win game featured on 70 million product packages. The grand prize was a theme party for fifty guests, with the show's character Cassie hosting. Five collectible animation cels served as first prizes, while lesser prizes included 10,000 *DragonTales* books.

Premiums   Premiums can be distributed on or in a product package, at a retail location, or in response to write-in requests or box-top promotions. They may be free to consumers; available for free with a purchase of another product (e.g., in a McDonald's Happy Meal); or meant for purchase at a discount (such as a book that retails for $3.50 being made available for $1.99 if a consumer sends in two boxtops with payment), either with or without another purchase. How they are distributed depends on a variety of factors, including the objectives of the promotion and the premium cost.

Licensees who market retail products often supply premiums in their category as well. If no retail licensees make an item similar to the one desired for a promotion, then producers or licensors can custom order from a specialist company. Premiums can include just about any item that has value to the customer, from inexpensive plastic figurines to more costly items such as limited-edition prints or cels. Premiums may or may not be character- or property-identified, but usually are in the case of animation.

To promote its online role-playing game *Everquest,* Sony Online Entertainment created a promotion in which fans who purchased any Gateway PC with an Intel Pentium 4 processor received free online gameplay. Consumers could take advantage of the promotion at sites tied to both *Everquest* and Gateway, as well as at Gateway's stores and toll-free phone line. The promotion was intended to help Gateway sell more PCs and Pentium more chips, while increasing customer sampling of the game.

This sort of sampling is important because it can create long-term fans. Offering *DragonTales* books through a juice-box promotion, for example, may turn children into regular viewers of the television show. Id Software offered customers free downloads of its *Doom* software to get them to try the game; once samplers became fans, the company sold them upgrades. *Doom* generated $100 million in revenue (through 2002), after giving away 15 million downloads of the first-generation game.

Licensing   Licensed merchandise, in and of itself, promotes an animated property to potential fans as they wander store aisles, see a neighbor with a *SpongeBob* T-shirt, or hang *Winnie the Pooh* curtains in their child's room. In addition there can be synergies between licensed products and other promotional activity. Licensees can provide products to promotional partners for use as premiums, as noted above, supply merchandise for use as contest prizes, or cross-promote their products with those of other licensees and distributors.

One promotion, created for the Disney/Pixar film *Monsters, Inc.,* counted Pepsi, Frito-Lay, Hasbro, and Sony among the partners. Hasbro supplied *Monsters, Inc.* toys to consumers for $5.00 off the retail price if they redeemed proofs of purchase from marked Frito-Lay or Pepsi products. At the same time, a consumer sweepstakes offered $100 worth of Hasbro's toys, as well as a Sony PlayStation video game tied to the film, as prizes.

Product Placement   Product placement is when a company's brands are featured in an entertainment vehicle, lending the property a sense of realism and giving the marketer added exposure among its target consumers. A character might wear Nike shoes or drink a can of a Coca-Cola-brand soda in a film or television series. The marketer sometimes pays for the placement, but this is not universal; it often becomes a promotional partner as well.

In animation, of course, the placement would involve a cartoon depiction of the product. This practice is relatively rare in animated films and television, but occurs with growing frequency in video games and online entertainment. Sony's *Cool Boarders* video game includes a product placement for Burton Snow Boards; Burton gave away copies of the game when it promoted its own merchandise at events at ski areas. Similarly, the Ford Focus automobile is featured in a game called *DJ Fu,* which is available on AtomShockwave.com. Ford believed the presence of its brand in the game was an effective way to convey its marketing message to an attractive consumer group. A CGI Film called *Foodfight,* produced by Threshold Digital Labs, utilized over 40 branded spokescharacters, none of which paid any fee to be in the movie.

Internet Components   As of the early 2000s virtually all promotions include the Internet in some way. The Web can serve as a mechanism for entering a contest or as a location consumers can consult for further information. Many promotions include a dedicated site set up specifically for the promotion, which may have its own Web address (URL) or reside on an area within one of the partners' sites. There are always links to all the partners' sites in any case.

The Internet is an effective promotional tool because it allows the partners to track results and capture names for their future database-driven marketing efforts. It also gives consumers exposure to the property and the partners' marketing message in an additional channel and allows them to more personally interact with the property.

When Kellogg's tied in with Disney's film *Atlantis: The Lost Empire* in 2001 it created a dedicated minisite within its corporate Web presence that featured *Atlantis*-themed games and e-cards, an offer for an *Atlantis* CD-ROM game with four Kellogg's proofs of purchase, and other promotional offers tied to the film. It also marketed *Atlantis* cereal in grocery stores.

The Jim Henson Company promoted its series *Farscape,* which airs on the Sci Fi Channel, through a CD-ROM giveway. The disk featured footage and character profiles from the series, in the hopes that recipients would then tune in to the cable network to watch the show. The CD-ROM contained a code allowing the user access to a dedicated Web site, but they had to watch a particular episode to get that code.

Sponsorship   Sponsorship is another way for outside partners to get involved in promoting animation. A company might sponsor a live event, a mall tour, a film festival, or a premiere, for example, expanding its awareness among members of a coveted demographic group and helping to finance the event. (A sponsorship fee for an Internet show or mall tour could finance the entire production.) Television or Internet programming can be sponsored online or on-air as well. Tower Records sponsored one of Spumco's online series, while Kix is the corporate sponsor for Scholastic's *Clifford* on PBS.

Public Relations   Public relations plays an important role in consumer marketing efforts, just as it does in programs targeting the trade. Magazine, newspaper, television, or Internet coverage of the developments surrounding a property, whether focused on creative angles, profiles of key personnel, local ties, or even marketing initiatives, helps keep the property in consumers' minds so they're primed to view it when it debuts.

The basic tools used in public relations efforts to consumers are the same as those for the trade, with media kits, press releases, and backgrounders serving as the foundation of any program. As with trade efforts, the publicity information must be targeted to publications and broadcast vehicles that reach the intended audience, in this case the end-users of the property (that is, the fans). The message conveyed in the publicity must also be relevant to those end-users.

Partners

Many types of companies can partner with producers of animation properties. For children's animation, toy companies, cereal makers, fast-food chains, and retailers are frequent allies, but nearly any company can be a partner if the fit is right.

T-Mobile, a wireless company, tied in with *Monsters, Inc.* for a seven-week promotion in the United Kingdom that offered daily "monster" prizes of about $1.5 million, distributed through a lottery for new customers on its wireless portal. Ramada Inns tied in with the classic 1970s stop-motion cartoon *Mr. Bill,* made famous through appearances on *Saturday Night Live.* Heinz allied with *Shrek* to promote a million bottles of its EZ Squirt Blastin' Green ketchup. Local cable operators supported some of Sony Wonder's animated series, such as *MegaBabies,* backing the promotion with advertising and air time, and bringing in their own partners. (Sony Wonder has since been purchased by TV-Loonland.) The lettuce brand Foxy got involved with Golden Books Family Entertainment, now part of Classic Media, supporting its *Pat the Bunny* videos by offering licensed merchandise in a sweepstakes promoted on the lettuce wrapper.

Some promotional partners are companies that are also involved in the production or financing of the property, such as a broadcast network, a licensee, or an investor. General Mills's Kix brand is a promotional partner for the Scholastic television series *Clifford;* it also underwrites the PBS series. But there are many cases when outside partners sign on for a promotion without any financial or other interest in the property; fast-food and retail chains fall into this realm. Wendy's has been an outside partner for *Clifford.*

Choosing a partner involves evaluating several criteria. What does the partner bring to the table in terms of financial resources or in-kind contributions? Does it have similar objectives and a similar target audience as the studio does? Does it have a track record of success with similar promotional efforts? Does its brand fit well with the property in terms of image? All of these and other factors play into the decision of which partner or partners to choose.

The more partners, the more exposure. For the video and DVD release of *Ice Age* in 2001, 20th Century Fox created a campaign involving fourteen partners, including restaurant chains Applebee's, Carl's Jr., Hardee's, and Papa John's; retailers Bloomingdale's and Chevron; hotelier Day's Inn; food and beverage marketers Coca-Cola, Cold Stone Creamery, Dole, Ian's/ Fran's Frozen Foods, Langer's, and Van De Kamps; software marketer Microsoft; the National Hockey League; and direct-response marketer Val Pak. All these partners contributed to a campaign valued at more than $85 million, with $40 million of that in advertising and the rest in promotional activities. The effort generated more than 8 billion consumer impressions.

At the same time, a greater number of partners leads to more complexity and an increased need to communicate freely and work together to create a program that benefits all of them.

Exclusivity

Partners gain exclusive rights to utilize the property promotionally within their category (e.g., only one retailer and/or one fast-food chain is able to ally with a single property) for a certain period of time. (Note that, in the *Ice Age* example above, exclusivity among restaurants was broken down narrowly, Papa John's being the exclusive pizza restaurant, for example.) The trend in the 2000s is for many partners to work together to promote the same property—to achieve maximum exposure—but with each having exclusivity within its own line of business.

Many promotional partners look for other elements of exclusivity that will allow them to offer something no other company can. This desire is particularly important for retailers who want to differentiate themselves from their competition by having a product that can't be purchased anywhere else. This exclusivity may extend to all products based on a given property, or may be limited to one or a few exclusive products.

Mervyn's department stores, a division of Target Corporation, tied in exclusively with Warner Brothers's *Frosty the Snowman* during the 2001 holiday season. The chain's advertising linked its own spokesperson with an animated Frosty. Mervyn's outlets offered their first 700 customers on a particular day a free Frosty bobblehead doll. The chain also sold 18 Frosty-licensed items, which were promoted with signage throughout the aisles.

Integration

Multipartner promotions or marketing campaigns, as well as simpler efforts, contain several disparate promotional elements. Most licensors try wherever possible to integrate all these elements. Each partner and promotional component puts forth a similar message and property positioning, while every effort is made to drive customers back and forth through cross-couponing, cross-promotional messages, or Web site links. A producer of a television show, for example, would bring together the broadcaster, exclusive retailer, video distributor, book publisher, and various licensees, as well as any outside promotional partners, early in the process. They would help define the promotional strategy and come up with ideas on how they can work with each other. The broadcaster's ads for the show could drive people to the Web site; the Web site could capture names from a contest, to be shared with all the partners; contest prizes could be plush toys supplied by a licensee; the plush toy's packaging could include a coupon for a dollar off a book purchase; and the book could have a message on its cover driving readers back to the show.

Disney integrates promotions among several of its brands and divisions

Exhibit 6.2

Potential Consumer-Marketing Partners for Animation Properties

Entertainment Partners

Book publishers
Cable networks
Cable systems
Film distributors
Film studios
Home video distributors
Movie theater chains
Music labels
Software publishers
Television networks
Theme parks

Retail Outlets

Book stores
Catalogs
Department stores
Drug and grocery chains
E-commerce sites
Fast-food chains
Gas stations
Hotels
Mass-market chains
Music stores
Specialty stores
Video stores

Media Partners

Internet service providers
Local television stations
Magazines
Newspapers
Online services
Radio stations
Web sites

Consumer Goods Partners

Apparel companies
Beverage marketers
Candy makers
Cereal makers
Consumer electronics marketers
Food marketers
Footwear companies
Health and beauty marketers

where possible, as do other vertically integrated multimedia companies. For instance, it offered redeemable certificates for free *Monsters, Inc.* movie tickets inside Disney/Pixar three-packs containing *Toy Story, Toy Story 2,* and *A Bug's Life* in VHS or DVD format. It also signed a $1.5 million deal with Toys " Я " Us in 2001 that allowed the toy chain to gain exposure on Disney's television programming, magazines, Radio Disney, and the corporate Web site.

Exposure

Promotional activity involving partners can generate many more consumer impressions, and in more venues, than marketing efforts involving the entertainment producer alone:

- o Kraft offered an instant-win game in support of Nickelodeon, as part of an ongoing relationship between the two companies that started in the mid-1990s, on 30 million packages of Oscar Mayer Lunchables; a simultaneous premium offer of *Rugrats* stickers on Jell-O Yogurt packages added 2.1 million impressions to the mix.

- o When Minute Maid, a division of Coca-Cola, joined with Cartoon Network during the 2000 back-to-school season, 130 million Hi-C multipacks featured graphics of animated characters from Cartoon Network shows. A Kellogg's promotion with the same network involved 40 million boxes of cereals, waffles, toaster pastries, and snacks.

- o For the release of the effects-laden made-for-video film *Casper: A Spirited Beginning,* Fox Home Video generated an estimated 2 billion impressions from its promotional activity, which translated to consumer sales of 1.2 million videos in a week.

- o Colgate-Palmolive offered books and videos tied to Scholastic's *The Magic School Bus,* promoting the effort in newspaper advertising inserts received by more than 55 million households.

Marketing Support Materials

All consumer and trade elements outlined here require various marketing materials. Many partners supply their own signage and other support (approved by the licensor), while the licensor or animation house contributes other print or broadcast materials. Some of this promotional information must be tailored to a specific use, while others (e.g., a fact sheet) may work in many situations. Being able to repurpose the material is important when it comes to property graphics, especially animation; it is expensive to create new material for each commercial or live event where an animated clip is required.

Many producers create additional animation during the production process, either specifically, such as for a commercial that has already been written and storyboarded, or generically, such as scenes that can be used later for as-yet-unknown purposes. It makes sense to have the animators, while they are under contract to the production, create additional footage for a commercial, DVD, or CD-ROM press kit, for example. In addition, producers sometimes document some of the behind-the-scenes work that goes on during the production process, which can come in handy in future publicity efforts.

With CG animation, digital files can be used later, repurposed for TV, games, online usage, print, or publicity. While this is a cost-effective strategy, there still may be times when new footage is required, as in a commercial that shows the animated characters interacting with the advertiser's product or service directly.

Timing

There are many timing issues that studios must take into account when creating an advertising and promotional strategy. A film property generally launches its consumer marketing efforts two weeks to a month prior to its theatrical debut, and they run an additional two weeks to a month after the premiere. But there are exceptions. Some marketers may want to begin promoting the film early by teasing it on Web sites aimed at potential fans or by trying other tactics to generate prerelease buzz.

A television show, on the other hand, is normally not promoted heavily until its second season, except on the network where it will air, which wants to increase viewership. Most partners don't want to get involved until the show is established and there's less chance of cancellation. They may ignore this policy if the show is based on a recognized property such as a book, in which case they might be willing to enter into a promotion to support the premiere.

Some promotional partnerships are multiyear efforts. In 1999 Warner Brothers and General Motors' Chevrolet division launched a four-year deal allowing GM to use the *Looney Tunes, Batman,* and other Warner Brothers properties to promote the Venture minivan and other brands (such as the Monte Carlo and OnStar) in commercials and promotions. Coupons, music CDs, and product discounts, as well as live events, were among the elements featured during the promotional period.

Fast food tie-ins, on the other hand, rotate every four to six weeks. Restaurant chains' main objective for entering into a marketing partnership is to continuously offer something new to keep their customers coming back; they also appreciate the added awareness that the tie-in brings to the company. In 2001, 4Kids Entertainment partnered with Burger King in a typical effort. A five-week promotion offered ten robot premiums based on 4Kids's series *Cubix;* five of them were components of a larger robot, which was meant to encourage customers to return to the restaurant to collect all five pieces.

Most tie-ins center around the release of new entertainment vehicles, whether films, videos, TV series, or other media. Some, however, support an ongoing franchise. A promotion might make sense simply because there's a good fit between the property and product, such as Homer Simpson and Pentium (a Pentium chip in the famously dim-witted character's brain made him smart). Another frequent timing choice is to link a promotional effort to an anniversary. When Nickelodeon's *Rugrats* celebrated its tenth anniversary in 2001 the network brought in companies such as ConAgra, Nabisco, Pepsi-Cola, and Embassy Suites for a promotion valued at $15 million.

Animation companies and their tie-in partners have different timing needs. Most corporate partners plan their promotions a year and a half in advance, while entertainment companies want the flexibility to put a promotion together (or alter it) right up until the release. Compounding this problem is the fact that entertainment release schedules are unpredictable. Partners have a set schedule for promotions that cannot be changed easily, so a release date being pushed up or pulled back wreaks havoc on the partners' plans. When Warner Brothers' *Quest for Camelot* release was delayed from fall 1997 to summer 1998 some promotional plans were already in place, resulting in a costly scramble to change them.

Geography

Another strategic element involved in putting together a promotional strategy is the geographic scope and rollout. Is the promotion for North America or the United States only? In which international countries is the promotion viable and when should it expand into those territories? In most cases the answers to these questions are based on where and when the entertainment vehicle will be released. The distribution decision-making process drives any promotional action, not the other way around.

Producers must consider how to tailor the promotion to different countries. The studio or licensor wants to put forth the same marketing message on a global basis, yet must localize the promotion so that it succeeds in all territories. Language and cultural differences may require not only translation but a rethinking of the message and associated promotional details. Local consumers in each country shop in different types of stores, have different tastes in products, embrace certain types of premiums over others, are governed by different laws regarding promotional activity, and accept or respond to different advertising and promotional messages and vehicles.

Panregional or even global promotions are increasingly possible, but they, too, must be tailored to local markets. Warner Brothers and Cartoon Network created a promotion with the global retailer Ahold throughout nine Latin American countries. The effort supported *The Powerpuff Girls,* called *Las Chicas Superpoderosas* in South and Central America. The main message of the promotion, tied to the "super" theme (super prizes, super brands, super sales), was the same throughout the region, but specific elements varied. For example, a different Ahold-owned retail chain was involved in each country: Disco in Argentina, Santa Isabel in Chile and Peru, Más por Menos in Costa Rica, and Paiz in Honduras and Guatemala. There were shopping rewards integrated into every promotion, but the grand prizes varied from country to country, depending on tastes and incomes.

Demographics

As noted earlier, all successful promotions begin by targeting the appropriate demographic and/or psychographic group, whether children, teens, preteens, or adults, or some subsegment, such as girls six-to-ten, college-age males, or fans of interactive gaming. Both the producer and the partners must want to reach the same audience.

Some properties appeal to a wide range of customers. The Fox film *Ice Age* was not only appropriate for children and their parents to see together, but incorporated elements that appealed to both. Unusually, the film also appealed to teens, a group that tends not to see films their younger siblings or their parents like. Fox targeted all of these groups in its advertising and promotions, both together and separately. In the online and offline gaming worlds, it targeted teens with a message focusing on the property's humor. For families, it took a more traditional promotional path involving deals with Burger King, supermarket chains Ralph's and Safeway, Target, and Langer juices.

Tracking Results

It can be difficult to track the results of promotional techniques. While it is almost certain that advertising and publicity increase attendance, viewership, and sales, it is hard to know exactly what spurred additional fans to come to the property.

One method of tracking promotional effectiveness is to include some sort of measurable direct-response element or giveaway. A studio or partner can measure the number of coupons redeemed, the number of contest entries, the number of people who logged on to a dedicated Web site, or the number of premiums given away or sold.

Producers can also measure success indirectly. They can gauge viewership, sales, attendance, or store traffic during the promotional period versus a period of similar length when no promotion is going on, or versus a promotional period involving other properties. In the case of film attendance or video releases, producers can compare opening attendance or first-weekend sales with those of similar products. These measurements do not prove directly that a promotion was a success, but they provide anecdotal evidence.

MARKETING COSTS

Marketing campaigns to support animated properties can be costly. As noted earlier, according to the MPAA, studios spent an average of $27.28 million on advertising for each film released in 2001, in addition to $47.7 million in production and $3.73 million in prints. Many studios spend far more than that to market their films, especially animated fare with family appeal and ancillary potential. Activity supporting high-profile examples of these types of properties easily can be valued at upwards of $50 million.

Trade publications estimated that Disney's promotional activity surrounding the film *Mulan* in 1998 totaled more than $100 million, with partners including McDonald's, Nestlé USA, and Eastman Kodak. For *Atlantis: The Lost Empire* in 2001, support was estimated at $150 million, with $50 million of that in advertising spending by the partners. The total effort generated an estimated 3.5 billion impressions (the number of people who saw the message multiplied by the number of times they saw it). Sony's effects-laden film *Godzilla* (1998) benefited from a tie-in with Taco Bell that had an estimated value of $25 million; the property had other promotional partners as well. The promotion was considered successful, even though the film didn't meet box-office expectations.

Significant marketing expenditures are not limited to films. Microsoft, Sony, and Nintendo tend to spend $200 million to $500 million on a global basis to market new game hardware and the software titles that accompany those releases. High-profile individual titles might receive between $3 million to $20 million in support; Nintendo spent an estimated $10 million on a title tied to *Star Wars: Episode I—The Phantom Menace*. Mattel and Artisan's promotional campaign for the original home video production *Barbie in The*

Nutcracker was valued at $9 million and included a McDonald's tie-in and a broadcast TV special.

It can be difficult to attach a cost to a promotional effort, particularly when multiple partners are involved. When a trade publication states a tie-in's value at $50 million, that does not mean that $50 million in cash changes hands. Promotions are "valued" at the amount the studio would spend on advertising to achieve the same number of impressions as the promotion generates. Some of the total figure does translate to actual expenditures, with much of that devoted to advertising and licensing fees.

A quick-service restaurant or other tie-in partner usually must pay a licensing fee to tie in with an animated property. But its payment may also incorporate in-kind donations of goods or services. It might be responsible for printing placemats, signage, or food bags with property-themed artwork, for example, or for mentioning the promotion in its already-scheduled advertising. The costs of these contributions are usually incremental; that is, the company has to print placemats and run advertising with or without the tie-in, so the costs linked directly to the promotion are only those on top of what would be done anyway.

FRANCHISE MARKETING

An increasing number of entertainment releases in all media are based on ongoing franchises. Producers and partners often are more willing to devote significant funds to support these types of properties, since they believe the built-in recognition that already exists, before any tie-in activity, reduces their risk.

For the producer, any promotional activity supporting one component of a franchise—a new TV series, a film, a book—supports the entire franchise. A franchise-based video game and the promotional support surrounding it, for example, help drive sales for comic books and viewership for the related TV series, even if no marketing dollars are devoted specifically to either of those venues.

Franchise marketing tends to be different from the type of "event marketing" strategy that would surround a one-time occurrence such as a stand-alone film. Too much hype can shorten the life of the property, even though it may increase sales and audience size during a short window. While releases of new entertainment incarnations represent a viable time to promote the franchise, the needs of any specific component must be balanced by the needs of the overall franchise.

Exhibit 6.3

Checklist for Choosing a Marketing Partner

Partners target complementary audience/consumers

Partners have complementary objectives for brand/property/promotion

Time frame works for both parties

Partners have complementary brand images

Product/service and property make sense together

Partners bring equitable and complementary strengths to the deal

Partners each get something of equitable value from the deal

Partners are honest with each other and work well together

Partners bring additional exposure to the property and vice versa

---

One of the reasons franchise marketing and franchise development have become so important is that it is much easier for a new entertainment property to gain distribution if it is based on a known quantity. A direct-to-home-video release will have a difficult time securing shelf space at the store unless it is based on a franchise that consumers will recognize as they peruse titles in-store. Also, the promise of long-term revenue streams helps offset the costs and decrease the risks associated with any single promotion within an overall franchise.

Franchise marketing also makes sense in that ongoing properties tend to have a more or less measurable core audience, as indicated by sales of past products, for example. While the fan base is likely to build with each incarnation of the franchise, the existence of that avid existing market makes it easier to predict how many purchasers there might be for videos or licensed merchandise.

That core audience becomes the focus of promotional activity any time a new production based on the franchise is introduced. When Warner Brothers released *Scooby-Doo* as a live-action/animated film in 2002 it began by promoting it in conjunction with the classic animated series running on Cartoon Network. The network is also a primary channel for promoting other facets of the franchise, such as a live touring show that visited malls around the United States in the early 2000s.

Because franchise marketing has become so important, studios large and small develop new films, TV series, Internet properties, and videos with the idea that they will represent the launch of an ongoing, multifaceted "brand." Nickelodeon's *Jimmy Neutron: Boy Genius* is a good example of the franchise-marketing mindset. In late 2000 the network introduced the characters in on-air interstitials and in short films on its Web site. The following year it ran a two-minute minisegment starring the character, as well as clips from the upcoming movie, on Nickelodeon's sister network CBS, just after CBS aired Nickelodon's *Rugrats* film. This occurred a month before the premiere of the *Jimmy Neutron* feature in December 2001. The following September Nickelodeon began to air a television series based on the property. All of these vehicles were supported by promotions by Nickelodeon and its outside partners.

7

Pitching a Property

Pitching is the main method of generating interest from partners, studios, distributors, and financial backers in an animation concept or property. The pitch varies, depending on who is being pitched; networks and studios are interested in the creative aspects of the entertainment, while investors or ancillary partners are interested more in financial potential. (When it comes closer to decision-making time studios will be interested in budgets and financial potential, of course, but the initial pitch is focused on the creative attributes.)

Depending on the situation, producers pitch to major studios, networks, distributors, or Internet companies. Licensing executives pitch to manufacturers and retailers. Marketing executives pitch to tie-in companies such as fast-food chains as well as media and retailers. Distributors pitch to theater chains, networks, and retail stores. Independent concept creators pitch to animation houses that could produce the entertainment vehicle; that studio then takes over pitch duties to secure other potential partners.

Other more general trade marketing activities, as discussed in chapter 6, set the stage for the pitch. These efforts, such as PR or attending conventions, raise awareness among industry executives about the studio and its properties. More generally they lead to contacts that might open doors for future pitches.

Preparing a pitch is time-consuming and often expensive, especially given the relatively small chance that a given concept or property will make it on the air, onto theater screens, or into retail stores. Television networks, film distributors, and other partners take on more risk when they sign an animation property rather than live action. Animation takes a long time to complete and buyers often must make their decision before seeing any finished episodes or sequences. By the time the property is complete, it may not turn out exactly as expected or market conditions may have changed. In the case of television, it is difficult and costly to cancel the series early in its run, unlike live-action.

For these reasons it is important to spend adequate time and money to prepare a pitch presentation that accurately represents the property and serves as a persuasive sales tool.

RESEARCH AND FIRST CONTACT

One key to preparing an effective pitch is to know what the customer wants in terms of the style and content of the property. For television the seller must find out what the network's brand image is, what the holes are in its schedule, and what it's looking for to fill those holes. The goal is to provide a show that satisfies a need, helps the customer stand out from the competition, and yet fits within its overall programming niche. The same is true for film studios, video distributors, and Internet sites. Each has a defined image and wants to stay true to that while seeking properties that are unique in the marketplace and will generate interest from consumers.

This is not to say that property creators should research buyers' needs and then create a property they think will make them happy. During creation the emphasis should be on developing an entertainment vehicle that is funny or dramatic and has a good story line, interesting characters, and an appropriate setup. The property should be something the creator is passionate about, not one that was created simply to fill a perceived need in the marketplace. Even if an example of the latter manages to make it through the production and distribution processes, it will almost never succeed with consumers.

The best research techniques are to watch the networks, browse the video stores, read the trade magazines, and study the companies' Web sites. The more that's known about the company, the better it can be determined if there's a fit between the property and the buyer. Some Web sites also explain the pitch process and feature downloadable submission forms that represent the first step in contacting the company. They also often incorporate a list of executive contact information, so the seller can determine the best person to pitch. Since Web sites are not always up-to-date, it's worth a follow-up call to verify the information.

Phone calls to the customer's development or acquisitions office can also be an effective mode of research. Sellers can find out not only who to send materials to, but what to include in the proposal and what form it should take. They can explain their property in a sentence or two (no more) and see if it's something the customer would consider at all, saving time and money over the long run. Similarly, if a buyer is interested in the concept and calls the seller in for a meeting, a call beforehand can determine exactly what should be included in the live pitch.

In some cases it may be difficult for an unknown producer to get through to someone at the buyer's company, but in most cases studio executives want to pass along information on the submission and pitch process, since it makes their jobs easier if the sellers know what they want and in what form.

In most instances sellers will have to send a proposal to the customer before securing a meeting for a live pitch. (Those who have a relationship with the seller may be able to skip this step and do the prepitching by phone.) The proposal allows the buyers to screen out concepts that are definitely not right for them and to call in only those creators who have a real chance to convince them to purchase the property.

Who to pitch at each company varies depending on the type of pitch and the buyer. At a television network or film studio the appropriate person is usually an executive in charge of development or vice president of development, but could be an acquisitions, programming, creative, or current executive. These executives are responsible for deciding which concepts are worth developing, and for developing them to the point where the studio gives it the green light. Some development executives stay with their acquisitions through production, but in many cases the properties are passed along to a production executive once they get the go-ahead. (The production executive is often the person responsible for green-lighting and who works with the development executives during the development process.) Development executives usually are assisted by junior executives and a staff, and producers' first contact with the company is most commonly with one of these employees.

At a distributor a producer might pitch an acquisitions executive or a vice president of distribution. At a home video company the appropriate department might be program development, marketing, or acquisitions. At a manufacturer it might be the director of licensing, a vice president of product development or brand management, or the president. At a publisher it would likely be an acquisitions editor. At one of the vertically integrated film studios the development department typically handles acquisitions in all media. The only way to know for sure who to contact is to call or e-mail the company and ask.

Even before deciding which specific buyers to pitch, sellers must determine what kind of company they should start with. This choice depends on the overall strategy for the property. Producers could pitch a new animation concept intended for all media to one of the majors, since they can handle distribution from initial entertainment to ancillaries, as well as provide funding. Other sellers might opt to start slowly, pitching an idea first to a publishing company or a video distributor as a direct-to-video project in the hope that this step will help the property build a sales history, or to an independent animation house that can help develop the property. The sell-

---

Exhibit 7.1
List of Potential Customers/Partners an Animation House Might Pitch

Agents/reps

Book publishers

Cofinancing partners

Comic book publishers

Coproduction partners

Home video distributors

Independent film distributors

Independent television stations (for syndication)

Interactive game developers

Interactive game distributors

Interactive game publishers

Licensing partners (manufacturers)

Live tour companies

Music labels

Networks

Outside investors

Promotional partners

Retailers

Studios

Syndication companies

Toy companies

Note: Pitches vary depending on the customer being pitched.

---

ers or their partners could approach one of the major studios later, or work with independent distributors in each medium.

TAILORING THE PITCH

Pitches will differ for a television network or a studio, an Internet destination site or a game developer, a financier or a licensing partner. Each has unique needs reflected in the proposal, the live pitch meeting, and any supporting materials. A surprising number of sellers use a boilerplate pitch and standardized presentation materials, but this is a nearly surefire way to fail. Potential buyers can tell if the sellers have done their research and don't like to hear pitches that are mass-produced.

The timing of the pitch also must be tailored to the customer. Within the television industry some buyers want to see the property in its very early stages of development, while others are interested only after other partners are in line and at least partial funding is in place. Similarly, in film some studios want to get involved in financing and the creative aspects of a movie as well as distribution and should be pitched early, while others want to wait until a film is finished before evaluating whether they want to distribute it. Interactive partners often want to get involved during the initial stages of production so they can take advantage of cost-effective synergies between animation and interactive game development.

A studio can start prepitching licensing and marketing partners fairly early in the property's life, even before preproduction. The actual sale occurs much later, however; manufacturers and marketers most often want to wait until distribution and financial partners are in place and until sample footage and completed scripts are available before they make a decision. In television many licensing partners won't consider a TV property until it has had at least one season of success on the air. So the early work in spreading the word about a property to the licensing community is really intended to set the stage for the subsequent sales effort.

Tailoring a pitch does not mean compromising the original vision for the property. Rather than altering a concept's essence to make it fit a buyer's needs, most producers would opt to approach a more appropriate buyer instead. Some customers are just not right for a particular property, demographically, stylistically, thematically, or on other levels.

The types of information included in a proposal or pitch differ depending on who is being pitched. To a network the pitch is about the property itself. Many sellers focus on aspects such as marketing and ancillary potential rather than on the creative aspects of the entertainment, but buyers for network television are more interested in whether the show will entertain their viewers. To a licensee or marketing partner, on the other hand, sales potential is paramount. The characteristics of the property are important, too, because they give the buyers a sense of whether customers will embrace it, but the business plans are where the focus should be.

THE WRITTEN PROPOSAL

Most buyers want to see a written proposal before agreeing to meet with a seller, unless they have a preexisting relationship with that seller. Some customers have preprinted submission forms (usually available online) that buyers can fill out and send or e-mail in. The desired information varies, but can include format (length, number of episodes, target audience, animation style), a synopsis of the concept in a few sentences, and any information on budgeting and financing already acquired. Some also want a resume of the producers' or creators' experience.

Some ask for additional details, but in general this is a brief, to-the-point document that contains only enough information for the buyer to do the initial screening and weed out those properties it knows are not right. Similarly, a proposal generated by the seller should be brief, conveying the essence of the property but not going into too much detail about either creative or marketing aspects.

Similarly, the process of contacting licensees, marketing partners, financial investors, and others often starts with a written proposal or sales sheet summarizing the property, with a focus on the details most important to the buyer. No matter what information is included in the proposal, brevity is important in these early stages.

In cases where the buyer and seller have an existing relationship, a phone call or meeting may start the relationship; there is often no need to send a written document in advance. In most situations, however, a short written proposal or summary document is a useful, or even necessary prequel to the live contact.

THE LIVE PITCH

Once the buyer and seller have arranged a meeting, the seller must prepare for the live pitch. The first step is to know every detail about the property.

Not all this knowledge—in fact, very little of it—will make its way into the pitch presentation, but the seller nevertheless should possess an intimate familiarity with every aspect of the concept. During the pitch sellers should be able to answer any questions that might come up, as well as to exhibit a deep passion about and understanding of the series, film, or other vehicle.

It is important to be able to describe the property succinctly in one or two sentences. (This summary is called a "logline.") Producers or creators who know their property well sometimes have a hard time describing it without including every detail. Explaining too much dilutes the main message and confuses the buyers. The pitch presenters should be able to sum up the essence of the property in a sentence or two; if they can't, it usually means they're unprepared or that the property itself is not well enough defined.

The core pitch should be brief and to the point, focusing on the premise, the main and secondary characters (both good and evil), the environment in which they live, and the story (and backstory, if important to the setup). Without going into too much detail about individual episodes the creator should be able to explain the proposed development of the story across one hundred episodes. The presenter should describe the style of animation and details such as episode length. Some artwork to show the main characters, either separately or in an action scene, supplements the presentation and gives buyers a complete sense of both the verbal and visual sides of the concept. For films the pitch focuses on the story, with character development and other facts being integrated into the storytelling.

Although potential buyers have different preferences as to how long a pitch should take, a rule of thumb for a television series is for the main presentation to take less than five minutes, leaving 10 to 15 minutes for further discussion if interest is piqued. (A pitch presentation for a film or direct-to-video feature for which the story is significantly more complex will be longer, perhaps 20 minutes for the main pitch.) Executives are busy and do not grant time for pitches lightly; it is important to make the most of the time allotted, so that both parties are satisifed with the results.

The pitch itself should be entertaining. The buyer should be able to get a sense of how funny or involving the story is, and the best way to convey that is to put that humor or dramatic impact into the pitch. It can be effective to act out characters, use different voices, and do anything else that gives a sense of what it would be like to watch the show. Storyboards or images to accompany the presentation may help the buyers connect the story and images, but the storytelling is the most important aspect of the pitch.

Many creators type out their presentations and practice reading them aloud to get a sense of timing and become adept at delivering them. But buyers say it's hard for them to get excited about a property from a prepared speech. Having the printed presentation handy ensures the sellers won't forget key points, but the presentation itself should come from the heart and not from a piece of paper. The more personality-driven the pitch, the better.

While sellers must must have a handle on every detail about their concept, they also must remain flexible. Buyers who are looking to acquire the property early in its life span want to be able develop it to suit their needs. Creators have a lot of emotion and energy invested in their show and are sometimes unwilling to make any changes—and if too many alterations are demanded the buyer and seller probably are not a good fit—but being too immoveable about the details is often a deal-breaker. This flexibility not only indicates that the property can be tailored more closely to the buyer's needs but also shows the buyer that the seller will be easy to work with.

It should be noted, however, that to be flexible is not to be wishy-washy. All the details about the property should be set—the style, number, and length of episodes, etc.—even if they may be changed later. Sellers should walk into the room with a distinct vision rather than a need to please.

When pitching to potential business partners rather than creative partners, the facts about the property are more important than entertainment value. Financiers or ancillary product makers want to hear about budgets, funding, sales potential, marketing plans, distribution deals, multimedia opportunities, global intentions, and revenue history. They need the creative details and a sense of what the show is like, but their focus is on future income or other business objectives. Therefore, the pitch will be tailored to those aspects of the property, as will written backup materials.

Most pitches, of course, do not lead to a deal; a single network hears hundreds of pitches each year, and other potential customers, from licensees to investors, see a similarly high number of proposals cross their desks. Customers pass on concepts for any number of reasons; a "no" does not necessarily reflect poorly on the property itself and shouldn't be interpreted as a reason to give up. If given the opportunity, creators can learn a lot by asking potential customers why they decided against the property. If there was a weakness to the presentation, sellers can apply that knowledge to the next pitch.

It is also worth mentioning that it can take a while—months or even years—for creators to hear a final decision about their pitch. If they sense interest from a buyer, but no definite answer has been forthcoming, they should keep in touch, although without becoming a bother. While a friendly ongoing relationship may not help the current property succeed, it may open the door for future pitches.

Each potential customer has its own view of what constitutes a good pitch. Some prefer simplicity, while others are impressed by sophisticated presentations with lots of bells and whistles. There is no single right or wrong way to pitch, as long as the presenter clearly and concisely conveys the essence of the property and its benefits to the customer.

PITCH MATERIALS

In addition to the initial proposal, creators or producers need to prepare a number of materials. Some support the live pitch while others serve as leave-behinds that give buyers a reference to jog their memories as they ponder their decision. Written materials can provide additional detail that can't be covered in the live presentation. Exactly what materials are left depends on the company making the presentation, the characteristics of the property, and the desires of the customer.

Support materials could include a "minibible," outlining all the key elements of the property's creative development—a treatment or a pilot script, a list of future episodes that illustrate the long-term story arc, a sheet showing character designs and/or descriptions, a fact sheet listing the specs of the property, budgeting and funding information, and a marketing sell sheet with information on licensing and promotional potential. Not all of these are necessary for all buyers; in fact, leaving too much or the wrong information can overwhelm the buyer and, more importantly, dilute the impact of the property.

As for visuals, it is essential to have some graphics that at a minimum illustrate the look of the characters, since animation is a visual medium. This is especially true in television; in film the story takes precedence. Some presenters bring preliminary background paintings, character designs, scenes showing the characters in action within their environment, or a short animation sample on a CD-ROM or Web site. As with text, the simpler the presentation the better. And whatever artwork the seller uses should be of high quality. A poorly animated sample or rough sketches will not necessarily allow the executive to visualize the final version and may be more harmful than helpful.

Sellers thinking of creating a clip to use during the presentation or to leave behind should ask a representative of the buyer, before the meeting, if the executive wants to see a sample and, if so, whether they prefer a VHS tape, a DVD, or a CD-ROM version.

Many sellers choose to set up a Web site to feature the written and visual details about their property. With a laptop computer the presenter can show the animation during the live pitch, and leave behind the Web address (URL) and password so the customer can look in more detail when time permits. In addition to animation clips a Web site can contain all types of information the customer might want to see in order to make a decision, including spec scripts, online webisodic series tied to the property, detailed character or premise descriptions, episode synopses, history of the seller's company, resumes of the creators, and so on. While the live presentation remains short and to the point, the Web site allows sellers to post as much information as they want and potential customers to follow up, in as much or as little detail as they like, without being overburdened by paperwork. In addition, the same site can be used for all buyers, whether business or creative partners.

Essentially, the types of materials used during the pitch or left behind do not matter as much as whether the vision of the property and/or its business potential comes through. If a storyboard and/or prototype maquettes will help sell the property to a network, creators should use them. But they should avoid adding information or fancy presentation materials that take away from a focus on the basic concept and story. If the buyers want more information they can ask for it.

It's important to put any leave-behind materials into as convenient a format as possible. Executives want to be able to write on the proposal, separate the pages, pass sections along to colleagues, and easily file all the materials. They don't want to have to return anything to the seller. Large boards are inconvenient; fancy bound proposals are unnecessary. This is another reason the Web is gaining favor; buyers can gather information on an as-desired basis and print out and file only what they need keep.

REPRESENTATION

There are differences of opinion on whether the seller of a property needs representation before going into a pitch meeting. Many artists and creators are leery of pitching their properties at all, because they are afraid the potential buyers will steal their idea. If this is the case, property owners may feel better if they go in with the support of a lawyer or agent.

Studios both large and small normally have ongoing legal counsel, either in-house or on retainer, and often business representation such as agents or managers, who they can utilize during the pitch process. Most independent creators do not have such representation and must hire an agent, or more likely an attorney, on a temporary basis.

It should be noted that copyright law protects the creative expression of an idea (the words, the story lines, the look of the characters), not the idea itself. The best way to protect an idea before pitching it is to develop it adequately and, as an extra protection, register the presentation with the U.S. Copyright Office. (See chapter 13 for more on copyright.)

Sellers may ask potential buyers to sign a confidentiality agreement before the presentation. Some buyers may agree to do so but many will not. This is because a similar idea could already be in development or because a buyer might sign a different property later, only to discover that the original creator views the other property as a knockoff. Many creators have felt that buyers have ripped off their ideas, when in fact that may not have been the case at all. Buyers' attorneys often recommend that their clients not sign confidentiality agreements, in the hopes of preventing lawsuits they consider frivolous. Some even require the seller to sign a paper saying they won't bring such a suit.

Some studios and networks (such as the Kid's WB!) do not accept unsolicited submissions. They only will look at pitches from agents that they've worked with before or, occasionally, from agentless creators—perhaps because of a recent split with their rep—with whom they've had a relationship. In this case sellers won't get in the door unless they have retained an agent familiar to the buyer. Other studios or networks are open to—or even encourage—unagented first-timers, which they believe keeps their content fresh. Examples include MTV and several other cable networks.

The three primary types of representation available to animation property owners are agents, managers, and attorneys. Agents act as a creator's representative in setting up and delivering pitches. They can present a property alone or with the creator present; if a buyer is interested it will want to meet the seller before making a final decision, but the agent may handle the initial pitch. Agents most often take a cut of 10 percent to 15 percent of any options or purchase agreements that are signed while they are representing the seller; some ask for a cut of the back end as well. Agents sometimes counsel their clients on legal matters or help them manage their businesses, but their primary objective is sales.

Attorneys, on the other hand, do not represent the client in its sales efforts, but rather assist them on contract negotiation, rights and intellectual property matters, nondisclosure agreements, contracts, and other topics that relate to the pitch and development processes. Creators or producers can retain an attorney for a long-term alliance, or hire one on an hourly basis. The latter is a good option for creators who are worried about protecting their properties during presentations but can't afford an ongoing relationship. Hourly rates usually start at two hundred dollars per hour and go well above that, while most monthly retainers are in the thousands of dollars. A few attorneys might work on a percentage of revenues (such as 5 percent), but this is rare in animation.

As their name suggests, managers manage the careers of actors and other creative personnel. They normally don't act as sales reps or agents, and many people in the entertainment industry use both agents and managers, as their duties complement each other. Managers are usually paid 15 percent to 45 percent of any income that comes in during their tenure, with 20 percent being a common split. Actors and musicians are more likely to have managers than most creative personnel involved with animation, where traditional management deals are rare.

Sellers that decide to pitch their properties without representation will need to secure assistance—an agent, an attorney, or both—once a studio or other partner shows interest in the property. They shouldn't try to negotiate options, purchase agreements, financial or distribution partnerships, or any other type of contract without legal assistance from an attorney specializing in entertainment deals.

Many creators are on tight budgets and can't afford high-priced representation. They can take advantage of a few low-cost alternatives. California Lawyers for the Arts, for example, is a nonprofit group that provides legal help to independent studios and freelancers, while associations such as ASIFA or Women in Animation may be able to recommend lawyers who are their members and specialize in working with solo creators.

NETWORKING

It can be difficult for creators and studios who lack a previous relationship with a buyer to cold-call that buyer to set up a meeting. While they can submit their proposals, it can be a challenge to stand out, especially if the buyer has working alliances with other sellers. To develop a relationship that can lead to a foot in the door, studio executives and creators must put themselves in a position to meet the right people.

As noted in chapter 6, exhibiting at markets and trade conventions is a primary way to expose properties and the seller's company to potential buyers. The L.A. Screenings, an annual event that allows sellers from around the world to reach U.S. buyers of TV properties, and MIPCOM, a convention held in France each year that serves a similar purpose for the global television market, are two examples of important trade conventions. Film festivals, both traditional and online, put properties in front of studios and independent distributors.

Attending these events—whether a film or TV gathering, licensing convention, toy fair, or video/DVD market—is important, even for independents who cannot afford to exhibit or do not have a completed property ready to submit. By walking the show aisles sellers can approach booths to find out more about each company and get a sense of whether they are an appropriate target for a given property. They can ask who the appropriate development executives are and sometimes even show materials to those executives, or someone who has influence with them. Leaving take-away materials will usually not lead to a direct callback (although it's possible), but it helps support the seller's overall campaign to increase the buyer's familiarity with the property and the seller's company.

Any of the techniques discussed in chapter 6 can raise the profile of the seller and its property or properties and pave the way for a meeting with an appropriate buyer when the time comes to pitch.

TIMING

A pitch can occur at any time during the development or production process. Properties can be pitched at the concept stage and at any point thereafter, all the way through to a finished product. The decision on when to pitch depends on when success is most likely and how much financial backing the producers have. Sometimes the pitch process starts with the concept and moves forward continuously as the property is being produced, until the seller finally succeeds in placing the property with the right partners.

Pitches to secure financing usually come up front, as do distribution pitches if distribution is an integral part of the property's funding scheme. On the other end of the scale are ancillary and marketing pitches; preselling activity can go on throughout the production process, but the final pitch usually doesn't occur until the property is complete or nearly complete. (If the ancillary company is providing funding as a part of the deal, the pitch would occur early.)

While pitching can occur throughout the year, it generally falls into certain time periods, depending on the nature of the industry being pitched. Studios work seasonally, as do licensed product manufacturers, home video producers, and other partners. Television shows can start any time throughout the year, but most premiere in spring or fall. Toys, home videos, and video games are sold to retailers in the spring, with the bulk of consumer sales falling in the Christmas holiday season; pitches to manufacturers must take this schedule into account. The bulk of tentpole movies are released in late spring and late November, although premieres are spread throughout the year. All of these factors determine when development or other relevant executives are most interested in hearing a pitch.

Pitching takes time. Preparing the presentation, waiting for a response, following up with further meetings, negotiating a satisfactory preliminary agreement, and repitching after hearing "no" all combine to create a long process. It's important to remember to build this time into the overall scheduling plans for the property.

WHAT HAPPENS NEXT

Once buyers become interested in a concept or more developed property they can either purchase an option or make an offer to acquire the property outright. An option, which is the most common alternative, is when the buyer pays the seller for the exclusive right to develop the property during a defined period, usually a year, giving them time to hone the property and make a decision on whether to greenlight it. The buyer and seller negotiate the exercise price, or the price they'll pay if they decide to produce, usually stated as a percentage of the per episode or total production budget. This percentage is often in the 2.5 percent to 5 percent range for an unproven concept from an outside creator, but can vary significantly.

A percentage of the expected exercise price is paid upfront as the option price. The option is often equivalent to 10 percent of the expected purchase or exercise price, but stated in dollars. If the option is renewed to give the buyer more time to develop the property another fee (often equal to 5 percent of the expected exercise price, or half the option) is due. If the buyer decides not to produce the project and not to renew the option all rights revert to the seller. The partners often negotiate a series of exercise prices for different formats (such as TV or film) if the final form of the property isn't known; the option will be a flat fee. Options and exercise prices vary depending on the relative negotiating power of the buyer and seller.

Exhibit 7.2

10 Tips for Pitching Success

1. Research the customer's needs
2. Ascertain the correct person to pitch
3. Prepare a proposal that excites the customer about a future pitch
4. Focus on main elements of interest to the customer—keep it short
5. Prepare backup materials to customer's specifications
6. Have Web site or more materials available upon request
7. Show enthusiasm and passion for the property
8. Be professional in presentation
9. Create art reference that properly shows the property—no rough sketches
10. Keep in touch if there's preliminary interest, but don't pester

---

When the buyer purchases an option, it and the seller negotiate up front all the contract points that will occur if and when the option is exercised. This process is costly for both parties, since there are no guarantees that the property will be produced. After a year or two of development the seller could be back to square one and the buyer can have spent a significant amount on development that won't be recouped.

An option alone does not bring much financial gain to the property owner. Depending on the nature of the property, an option could be as low as a few thousand dollars, although it could be into the tens or hundreds of thousands of dollars for a well-established franchise being developed for a new entertainment vehicle. The buyer assumes the further costs of development, although the seller may be involved to various degrees, depending on the nature of their agreement.

Generally the business affairs department takes over the negotiation once both parties agree to pursue an option agreement. First the lawyers for the buyer and seller create a short-form contract (or deal memo) that summarizes the key points of the agreement (fees, compensation, back-end royalties, length of the option period, length of the deal after the option is exercised, credits, services provided, ownership, and exercise price), then a long-form contract that contains all the details. The full contract can take three to nine months from the beginning of negotiations to signing. In most cases development doesn't begin until all parties sign the agreement, but on a project where speed is of the essence development could begin once the short-form agreement is complete.

Many factors can derail the property's progress between the signing of the option deal and the time when the option is exercised. The buyer might have a difficult time assembling a creative and business team, setting up distribution, or putting together financing, or the two partners might disagree on the creative development of the property. A champion of the property, such as the development executive who acquired it, might leave the buyer's company, putting the process in jeopardy. Even if the process is smooth, the development process for animation can take about two years, with significant variation from property to property.

8

Financing and Deal Making

Once producers put together a budget for their proprietary project, their next step is to obtain financing either through internal funding or by pitching various partners that can contribute funds. Major studios and networks can fully fund some of their productions each year, whether developed in-house or acquired. Universal Pictures Visual Programming produced and financed its 3D series *Sitting Ducks,* based on a British art property, greenlighting it before it even tried to sell it to broadcasters. The company felt strongly about the brand and wanted to keep all the rights to the property.

Most producers, however, cannot fund their own projects. They need to assemble a complex package in which distribution partners, investors, coproduction studios, and other sources combine resources to finance the show. Each provides some sort of contribution, whether up-front financing, reduced fees, distribution, or in-kind services. In return each receives

Exhibit 8.1

Elements of a Coproduction Deal

Element	Possible Contributions/Inputs	Possible Rewards/Outputs
Distribution/Ancillaries	Expertise	Territorial Rights
	Connections with territorial distribution partners	Category distribution rights
Creative Services	Fee reductions	Work flow to the studio
	Expertise in various production tasks	Additional credentials/experience
Money/Compensation	Up-front investment	Fees for production work
	Distribution or ancillary advances	Share of worldwide back-end
	Government subsidies/tax breaks	Profits from territorial exploitation
		Credits
Rights and Ownership	Underlying property	Partial or total copyright ownership
		Territorial representation

Note: Elements are interrelated and overlapping. Deals place a value on inputs and distribute outputs equitably.

something of value in proportion to its contribution. The return can be in the form of the right to exploit the property through distribution or ancillary categories in a certain geographic region, reaping the financial gain, or it can be a share of the property's overall revenues. There are many possible variations on this structure and there are no "average" or "typical" deals.

Participating in an animated property is risky for financial partners. Not all animation properties generate a profit. Others may result in a small income, of which the multiple stakeholders each see a tiny share. All the partners should be aware that, while their contribution may have the potential to make them a lot of money, this financial gain—or even the recoupment of their investment—is not guaranteed.

This chapter takes a look at some of the possible structures of animation deals in different media. The first section, which covers television, is the most detailed. Many of the elements that come to bear on a television deal also apply to deals in other media. The sections on film, video, the Internet, and interactive properties that follow examine elements that are specific to each of those industries. But the basic components of the deal—distribution, financing, services, etc.—are similar to what is outlined in the section on deal making in the television market.

TELEVISION

Most television packages include one or more broadcast partners and one or more coproduction partners. More complex agreements can bring in other contributors, such as investors, banks, international distributors, licensing agents, toy companies, home video companies, interactive software publishers, creators of underlying properties, and book or comic book publishers. All of these partners want to recoup their costs and generate a profit; the more revenue streams there are, the better the chance of doing so.

Most partners join a production either as cofinancing or coproduction partners. Cofinancing is when investors contribute money up front in exchange for certain rights, such as distribution or merchandising, in a given territory. They are not involved in the creation of the production. Coproduction is when the partner contributes services, such as character and visual development; script, storyboarding or other preproduction services; animation production; or postproduction services. These contributions are provided at a reduced fee, often in combination with some cash financing.

Elements of a Deal

Each partner's contribution, and what each wants as a reward or payment, are mostly measured in financial terms, although the deal can satisfy nonfinancial objectives for a partner as well. There are no average payments or deal structures when it comes to putting together a financial package for a television series. But there are certain key elements that must be considered when entering into any deal; these are discussed below. All are interrelated.

Distribution and Ancillaries

A television property, like any form of animation, needs distribution to succeed. Therefore, securing global broadcast distribution as early as possible is a key element of any television production deal. In addition, distribution agreements bring in monetary rewards in the form of advances. These advances can account for a large proportion of the financing needed to produce the show. International television presales, when deals from several countries are combined, can cover as much as 90 percent of a series' production budget, although the percentage is usually more like 30 percent to 50 percent. U.S. distribution, if secured, can bring in about 20 percent of production costs for a children's show.

Networks around the world are more often becoming involved in television shows as cofinancing or coproduction partners, rather than signing on, once a production is completed, as pure distributors. They want to receive the exclusive right to air the show in their territory, creative input to ensure that the series will succeed with their audience, and/or financial gain through geographic ancillary rights sales or a share in overall revenues. To gain these benefits they become partners up front, funding a portion of the production budget. Some broadcasters have animation houses as subsidiaries and are able to enter the partnership as coproducers, but most are strictly cofinancing partners. TF1 in France, the BBC in the United Kingdom, and the ABC in Australia are some of the networks involved as partners in television productions.

Distribution is so important that in some cases the selection of an animation studio as a partner is due more to its ability to bring in a broadcast sale with a network in its territory than to any financing or services it provides. Most of these partners make other contributions as well, but their relationship with a broadcaster is a key benefit.

Ancillary entertainment and product categories represent another way to bring in funding and expand awareness. Preselling rights to home video, licensed merchandise, sound tracks, publishing, interactive games, online entertainment, and films can generate additional revenue streams and sometimes advances that can go directly toward production costs. The ancillary-product distributor becomes a cofinancing partner in return for distribution rights in its category (and sometimes other participation).

Toy licensee Playmates helped finance the *Teenage Mutant Ninja Turtles* TV series in the 1980s in return for the exclusive rights to market what turned out to be a multibillion-dollar toy line. Some manufacturing companies, especially in the toy industry, will fund up to 30 percent of the budget in return for these rights. Licensing agencies, which represent animation companies in their merchandising activity, are becoming coproduction partners as well, taking a financial stake in return for licensing rights and advising the producers on how to make the property more merchandisable.

It is important not to include future royalty streams from ancillaries as part of the financing picture for the property, except in terms of profit potential. Many things can happen to affect ancillary businesses and the revenue streams they bring in, and producers cannot count on them to pay for production costs. Yet, even if ancillary potential does not directly contribute financing, its presence is still a boon to a production. Many partners want to receive a share of merchandising royalties and other ancillary income and will be more likely to become involved in a production if it has ancillary potential. In addition, licensing and other ancillaries are valued because they help market the property itself, enhancing its chances for overall success.

The division of distribution and ancillary rights, and of the revenue participation from these businesses, can be complex, and varies from production to production. When German broadcaster RTL agreed to air Igel Media's *Oggy and the Cockroaches* in Germany, Austria, and Switzerland, it negotiated a 30 percent share of merchandising revenues in that region. Mike Young Productions retained all international TV distribution and merchandising rights, except sound tracks, when it coproduced a show with MTV; the network retained domestic distribution rights. On another show, which MYP coproduced with the U.K.-based Just Group and the Chinese studio DCDC, MYP retained only theatrical and some ancillary rights, which it later sold to a U.S. studio.

Merchandising can play a role in syndication deals as well. Raven Moon Entertainment, producer of *Gina D's Kids Club,* was looking for exposure for its half-hour preschool comedy and music series. It offered network television affiliates and independent stations its series at no cost in 2002. Stations reserved 100 percent of the commercial airtime and, if they aired the series for two years, they received a share, divided among all the stations, of 15 percent of gross profits on ancillary products.

Creative Services   Contributions to a production can take the form of creative, production, or licensing and marketing services at any stage from development through postproduction. Often, these services are provided at a lower-than-usual cost, which reduces the size of the budget and therefore contributes to funding. This is called a "soft" contribution, as opposed to a "hard" or cash contribution.

In a simple deal, a service provider supplying all the animation production could cut 50 percent from the cost of its services. It would receive a production fee equal to half the work's value and contribute the rest. In return it could get a 50 percent participation of back-end revenues, although usually its share will be lower. Or it could receive a recoupment of 110 percent to 120 percent of its soft investment from early revenues (in other words, the amount it contributed in services, plus 10 percent to 20 percent), after which it would get a smaller equity share. As will be noted throughout this chapter, there are any number of potential configurations for reimbursement.

Sometimes the division of labor is natural, given the expertise of the partners. United States, Canadian, or European animation houses tend to have more expertise in developing series and scripts, while Asian studios are more suited to animation production (although many are expanding into preproduction and postproduction services). At least one coproduction partner often comes from Asia, since sending production overseas for production can reduce a show's budget by 20 percent or more. Asian producers reduce their fees further in order to become coproducers, although this traditionally has given them distribution and ancillary rights in their own territories that have been difficult to exploit. Asian houses are starting to contribute cash in addition to reduced-fee services, which allows them to gain meaningful distribution rights or back-end participation.

When studios' expertise overlaps and their objectives for entering the coproduction are similar, dividing the creative work among the coproduction partners can be difficult. While they're interested in future financial rewards, they also want to keep work flowing into the studio, and being involved in coproductions allows them to do this. Meanwhile, other partners might need to handle a certain amount of the service work in order for the entire project to benefit from government subsidies and tax breaks. Therefore, the work has to be divided so that studios' objectives are met, costs are minimized, and government subsidies maximized. This can be a complex negotiation.

Creative control is another thorny issue. Most of the key partners want a say in the final look, feel, and content of a project. They may have unique concerns when it comes to censorship issues, audience tastes, and cultural sensitivities. All the partners want the property to have global appeal and yet retain a coherent vision and unique qualities that make it stand out from the competition.

The underlying rights holders or creators desire creative control and input as well. They may or may not be able to retain this control, depending on their negotiating clout. If the underlying rights holder is the proprietor of an ongoing, successful property, such as a comic book that is being developed into television, or if it has production expertise, it may well be involved in the creation and approval of all aspects of the property.

The more parties involved in the physical production and creative approval of a property, the more complicated the entire process will be. Broadcast schedules in each region vary and all the partners have to work together to ensure they meet global delivery schedules. Coproductions tend to take longer than solely financed productions to begin with, due to the various levels of approvals and the added layers of communication among the partners. Extra time must be built into the schedule to allow all parties to make their contribution and still have the project delivered when promised.

The main creative elements to be negotiated include: Who will have ultimate creative control at each stage of production (e.g., script, storyboard, design, final version)? Who will have creative input at each stage? Who will be doing the physical production at each point in the process (e.g., visual design, ink-and-paint, sound effects)? It should be noted that the partner or partners handling pre- and postproduction have most of the de facto creative control. Significant financing partners might have consultation rights, such as being sent storyboards and animatics for comment.

Money   Although the partners can make various contributions to a production, financial contributions tend to correspond most directly with financial rewards. The greater the percentage of the budget covered, the greater the share in total revenues. When major entertainment conglomerates finance a production in its entirety, they want not only production and distribution rights but also total ownership and creative control. They also want the lion's share of financial gain. The studios may agree to a small royalty stream to the creator and/or originating studio, but only after they deduct costs and distribution fees.

As noted above, cofinancing can come from broadcasters, other distribution partners, merchandisers, and coproducing studios. It can also be sourced from governmental funds, nonprofit organizations, and for-profit funds that specialize in animation or entertainment. In 2002 Happy Life, a Swedish producer, entered into a coproduction deal with the Berlin Animation Fund (BAF) for an animated series it created called *Microphonies,* which was budgeted at over 55 million Swedish krone ($99 million). Sesame Workshop financed a Korean version of *Sesame Street* (including five years of production, a radio program, and outreach) with a combination of $4 million from the U.S. Agency of Independent Development (USAID) and $3 million from a Korean corporate sponsor, Sanlam. Organizations such as UNICEF, The Advertising Council, and the Environmental Protection Agency have also provided financing for animated series that promote ideas they support.

Sometimes financial contributions come from outside investors that have nothing to do with animation production, distribution, or marketing. Carrington Productions International, a U.K. company, was an equity investor in entertainment coproductions, including animation. Its mission was to provide 15 percent to 35 percent of the budget for international coproductions initiated in the United Kingdom (although it sometimes provided 100 percent funding), in return for an equity stake. It spent $20 million on animation from 1994 to 1999. (That year it was folded into Entertainment Rights, a U.K. entertainment company.) Companies such as Carrington make their investment decisions based purely on the show's business plan; their sole objective is to reap a return on their investment.

Some production and distribution companies have set strategies dictating what percentage of a show's budget they'll fund; the proportion is often related to coproduction regulations in their country. Other companies take varying stakes from production to production. U.K.-based HIT Entertainment, for example, might cofinance 10 percent or 12 percent of a budget, usually through distribution guarantees, if a producer approaches HIT for financing after other partners are already in place. But if HIT wants to control a franchise's destiny and is able to get involved early in the process, it might fund 100 percent of the budget. HIT is involved with coproductions as well, at various financial levels and with varying amounts of creative input.

Bank loans are another option, but they're rare in television. Some producers use advances from international presales to secure a loan to cover the production deficit, but most TV productions prefer to find 100 percent of the funds without borrowing. A coproduction partner may look to its own internal funds (beyond what it has already contributed) to cover the last unaccounted-for 5 percent of a budget, rather than attempting to get a bank loan for the rest.

Once enough partners and investors are on board to cover the entire budget, negotiations begin on how to value each of their inputs and allow them a chance to recoup their investment and receive a proportionate share of revenues. As might be imagined, this is a complex process and is interrelated with

---

Exhibit 8.2

Sources of Funding to Cover a Proprietary Property's Production Budget

Ancillary product advances

Bank loans

Distribution advances

Domestic license fees

External investors

Fee reductions

For-profit funds

Government subsidies and tax incentives

Internally generated funds from production partners

International license fees

Investments from distribution partners

Nonprofit organizations

Note: All of these funding sources apply to animation properties in any medium.

the other elements discussed in this section. (See the section below on deal making for more on the overall negotiation process.) There are many ways returns can be structured; they grow increasingly complicated as more partners become involved.

A partner's financial reward may come in many forms. Those involved in distribution might secure the financial income that comes from selling the property to broadcasters, home video companies, and/or merchandise licensees in their own territory. Other participants (and distribution partners) may receive a cut of worldwide or regional profits for the property as a whole. Some receive a combination of these configurations.

A creator or licensor that brings a new, unexploited concept to a production studio might receive 1 percent to 5 percent (with 5 percent being more common) of the production budget for each episode produced based on its concept. Creators or licensors of a property already established in another medium may receive a small share of back-end revenues as well, and may maintain an ownership stake in the new property. Some partners receive revenues without maintaining an ownership stake, while others own part or all of the copyright as well as earning income.

In addition to the division and definition of revenues, the partners must negotiate the timing and order in which all shareholders are paid. Financial investors or major studios often want to recoup their investment before other partners begin sharing in profits. Pure investors, who are assuming much of the risk, usually get paid back first (even before the recoupment of production expenses). They may get a higher-percentage share until they recoup their investment, followed by a smaller ongoing share thereafter. Or they could be paid back until they receive the amount they invested in the production plus a premium (anywhere between 10 percent and 100 percent), and then receive a small (or no) percentage thereafter.

If a partner receives compensation based only on its exploitation activities in its own territory, its revenue stream may be separate and no payback ranking would be necessary. But if multiple partners share in territorial or worldwide revenue streams, they're paid back through a complicated scheme that allows those who invested the most to earn a profit first. The lower the partner ranks, the less profit potential it will have, unless the property is a blockbuster. The low-ranking partner may be included in earlier revenue streams, but with a very small participation until other partners recoup.

Sometimes the partners' compensation and profit are cross-collateralized. That means that all income from any source—from merchandising, to home video, to distribution—goes to the primary investors (including a major studio) first, before any other partners are paid. In a noncross-collateralized structure, each partner's payment comes from a certain revenue stream. When expenses directly related to that stream are paid off the partner starts receiving revenues.

The negotiations regarding payment percentages, rankings, and timing are tricky, especially if a large number of partners is involved. Simply valuing everyone's contribution equitably can be complicated. For example, U.S. studios tend to charge more than European studios for the same preproduction services; each studio wants their contribution to lead to fair compensation. It is also difficult to place a value on an idea, such as a concept created by an unknown artist without a previous animation resume.

In international coproductions the negotiations must take currency fluctuations and tax implications into account. For projects involving a U.S. partner payments are often expressed in U.S. dollars. This puts the burden of risk on the non-U.S. partners, since European or Asian currencies easily can fluctuate 20 percent against the U.S. dollar over the course of a production. Coproduction partners solve this problem by setting an exchange rate up front and using that stable rate for all payment conversions during the course of the production, no matter what the actual rate is. This tactic spreads the risk more evenly.

Exhibit 8.3
Methods of Structuring Financial Compensation/Rewards/Return

Fees

For development, preproduction, production, and postproduction services (possibly reduced)

For underlying properties

Rights exploitation

Distribution fees from exploitation of territorial distribution rights in all media

Licensing commissions for selling territorial rights to ancillary products

Back-end participation

Participation in revenues from ancillaries and distribution in all media in a territory, after production expenses

Participation in revenues from ancillaries and distribution in all media on a worldwide basis, after production expenses

Investment return

Participation from some or all revenue streams until investment plus a premium is paid back (before or after production expenses, or a combination of both)

Note: Each partner is paid back for his or her investment through one or more of the methods listed above. Percentages sometimes change after production costs are recouped or as higher ranking partners are paid in full for an investment. Revenue streams may be cross-collateralized.

Each country has its own rules and regulations regarding taxes applied to animation production in general and international coproductions in particular. The partners must take all tax implications into account when negotiating a partnership. Each partner wants to minimize its own tax burden and will negotiate financial aspects of the partnership with that in mind. In addition, government funding can be related to tax implications, so these must be taken into account for the good of the production as a whole.

It should be noted that this discussion covers production expenses only. The partners will require additional financing to cover any marketing and promotion surrounding the property.

Rights and Ownership   The issue of rights and ownership is another element that plays into negotiations. Some companies come to the partnership with the ownership of the underlying rights as their main contribution. This input has significant value, of course, especially if the property is well known. These rights holders may or may not retain an ownership stake in the television property, although they are credited as being the copyright and/or trademark holders for the property on which it is based. Ownership of copyrights and trademarks in the show can fall to one owner or can be shared by two or more partners.

In a joint ownership, the partners should define each co-owner's stake clearly. (Equal joint ownership of copyright and trademarks is required by local law in certain countries.) Does each partner own certain elements of the property, or do both share in the property as a whole? The second alternative may cause problems down the road if the joint owners disagree on the property's strategic or creative direction. In any case, the partners usually grant one of the owners power of attorney to handle any copyright or trademark issues, including piracy and infringement, on behalf of all of them.

On the animated series *Marcelino Pan y Vino,* based on a classic live-action film from Spain, three coproducers divide ownership equally: Nippon Animation in Japan, VIP Toons in Spain, and TF1 in France. Similarly, Gullane Entertainment (now part of HIT Entertainment) and S4C International split the ownership of *Fireman Sam.*

Exploitation rights are another negotiable component of a coproduction deal, as was discussed under the section on distribution above. Some of the partners' main objective may be to reserve distribution and/or ancillary rights in various media within their territory. Their financial contribution is often intended to ensure that they control the exclusive right of exploiting the property in their categories; a share of worldwide rights on top of that may be a secondary desire.

MTV retained U.S. distribution rights for *Undergrads,* while Decode held the rights for the rest of the world, although the latter was required to offer the series first to global MTV channels before pitching it elsewhere. (The copyright for *Undergrads* is jointly owned by Decode and MTV.) In many cases the division of explotation rights is determined by language or proximity; on the book-based series *Dr. Dog,* coproducer Silver Lining Productions of the United States retained English-language rights for television and merchandising, while France Animation retained European rights.

In the case of television shows based on underlying properties several additional rights issues arise. Publishing and video game series are ongoing, changing entities, as are television series. Any deal linking the two must deal with the issue of who owns and can exploit new properties that are created after the date of the original deal. Will a television producer, for example, have the right to add characters created later for a video game title to its TV show? Or does the video game developer or publisher reserve those rights, granting the producer only the use of characters that existed at the time of the deal?

Similarly, merchandising activity often encompasses products tied both to the TV series and to the underlying property. Each has a somewhat different graphic look and often appeals to a slightly different consumer segment. Sometimes the underlying rights holder handles the original property, while the producer handles the TV characters and imagery. In other instances the TV studio handles all licensing, with the underlying rights holder receiving a share of royalties. Another option is for the underlying rights holder and the studio to split merchandising rights by category, with one handling publishing and the other nonpublishing categories, for example.

Government Support   Several countries offer subsidies or tax breaks to animators of shows that qualify as local content. Bringing in coproduction partners in these countries adds funding on top of those contributed by the partners themselves. Coproductions involving more than one studio that can earn these incentives are in an especially good position, which explains why there are so many Canadian-French alliances. Those two countries are among the most supportive of their domestic animation industries and have coproduction treaties with each other and with many other nations. Government funds can bring in 30 percent or more of the budget in some cases.

Governments that offer incentives require a certain percentage of the work to be done in that country (thus ensuring that the show qualifies as local content). In many cases the financial gain is such that it benefits the producers to keep production services in these countries, even if the actual cost is higher than it would be elsewhere, such as in Asia.

Local content requirements are based not so much on cultural factors as on ownership percentages and the use of local talent. In Canada, for example, a production gets credit for using Canadian directors, art directors, lead actors, camera operators, composers, editors, writers, and storyboard supervisors, with the key positions holding more weight; Canadians must fill a certain number of these slots for the production to qualify as Canadian and receive government support. (Key animation must be done locally, although inbetweening can be sent overseas.) In addition, 15 percent of the show's budget must come from Canadian sources; a license fee from a Canadian broadcaster alone usually does not meet the requirement. Canada has coproduction treaties with dozens of countries and is negotiating more.

The type and level of government support varies from country to country, with some subsidizing production and others offering tax breaks. In addition to Canada and France, some of the other countries offering incentives (at lower levels than Canada or France do) include Germany, China, Bangladesh, Malaysia, and Ireland, among many others. Some nations offer subsidies through individual states, territories, or provinces, as well as from the national government; Australia is one of these. Others offer no tax breaks or subsidies. In many cases the process of negotiating the often-changing rules and regulations can be complex, adding headaches to the coproduction and financing process.

An animation producer who can bring in funds to a property itself as well as additional support from its government and local broadcasters is a particularly attractive partner. The Toon Factory, a French company, is able to bring 50 percent funding to animation projects in which it is interested. Twenty percent of that is internally generated, with the remainder a combination of government support and money from a French broadcaster. The Toon Factory then seeks the rest of the funding from countries outside of France.

Credits   Another component of animation deal making is the granting of credit. This represents a relatively minor element of the negotiations. Yet, credit is part of the compensation package associated with participating in a property and is important to the partners.

There are few standard credits to describe the roles of coproduction and cofinancing partners. A company who may be assigned a credit ranging from executive producer to an "in association with" credit. The partners must negotiate the specific wording so that each partner's on-screen credit reflects its contribution, as well as the order in which the credits will appear.

Deal Making

Putting together a deal for a television series involves balancing the contributions from each of the categories listed above and disbursing rewards so that all the coproduction, cofinancing, and investment partners are satisfied. The objective is to minimize risk and maximize the chances of success for all partners, given their respective objectives, while fully financing the budget and enabling the property to be produced and distributed. Raising additional funds for the all-important marketing program can be part of the deal as well. Above all it is essential for all partners to feel they have a good chance of recouping their investment. To ensure this most partners want their compensation tied to multiple revenue streams; this complicates negotiations but makes it more likely each will prosper financially.

For a deal to work, no matter what its specifics, all partners should have common creative and financial goals. Each also should bring complementary contributions to the table, whether cash, distribution, production, or creative skills, licensing or marketing skills, or some combination of these.

The negotiation itself can take a year or more, with many stops and starts and substitutions among the major players. The partners must come to an agreement on the value of all parties' contributions, and then create a win-win division of revenues (while ensuring the payment of production expenses), credits, creative control, services, and ownership.

The final agreement should clarify each party's rights and responsibilities down to the smallest detail. Specific items include (but are not limited to): penalties for breach of contract or actions that affect the production, such as late delivery; timing of payments and production milestones; division of ownership and decision-making power; creative control and creative responsibilities; procedures in case of disputes; bank guarantees required to back up financial investments; whether revenue streams are cross-collateralized; what happens to the property if one or more of the parties leaves the partnership; and tax and other legal considerations. The producers must also define all the terms used in the agreement, particularly as they relate to financial terminology. What expenses are deducted from revenues to come up with "gross" or "net" profits, for example? This checklist is only a sampling of potential issues that may need to be incorporated into the final agreement.

A good contract not only tells the partners what is expected of them and what they can expect of their allies, but it serves to prevent future disagreements, which can be costly and long-running. A dispute between Disney and the Slesinger family, the underlying rights owner of *Winnie the Pooh,* had been in the U.S. courts for ten years and counting as of 2002. The Slesingers granted Disney U.S. and Canadian television, merchandising, and future media rights in 1961 in exchange for a percentage of gross revenues from *Pooh* entertainment and products worldwide. In the multibillion-dollar suit, which was dismissed in 2004, they were questioning whether Disney properly paid them for royalties owed.

In some cases partners (usually after developing a strong relationship) will agree to long-term coproduction alliances involving many properties. Mondo TV of Italy and Hahn Shin of China finalized an agreement in the early 2000s for the production of 200 TV episodes and a feature film, followed by 520 more episodes and 5 features from 2004 through 2008. Hahn Shin retained Asian rights to all the series, as well as some North American rights, and contributed 70 percent of the 405 billion lire ($226 million) total investment. (The deal was done before Italians switched to the euro as currency.)

Examples of Television Deals

Because each deal is unique and specifics vary so widely, it may be easiest to get a sense of the differences and similarities through examples. (All occurred from 1999 through 2003.)

- *Watership Down* was a Canada/United Kingdom/France coproduction, with production work taking place in all three countries. A German cofinancing partner contributed funding through the presale of certain German rights.

- Cinar of Canada (now known as Cookie Jar) agreed to a coproduction deal with Shanghai Animation Film Studio for 52 ten-minute episodes of an animated series called *Rumble & Growl.* A government agency, Telefilm Canada, helped facilitate the deal. Cinar retained international distribution rights, while Shanghai TV aired the show in China and handled animation production.

- BBC Worldwide and Ben Productions were the coproducers of the preschool stop-motion series *Bill & Ben.* Ben Productions consisted of a group of private investors that contributed a portion of the series' $3.2 million cost. BBC Worldwide was the distribution partner for all media worldwide.

o Cinar contributed $6 million of the $9 million budget for a 26 half-hour series, *The Country Mouse and City Mouse Adventures.* Partners Reader's Digest of the United States, France Animation, and Ravensburger of Germany collectively provided the rest of the financing; all four companies had creative input.

o Nelvana of Canada and TMO Film GmbH of Germany joined together for a series called *Ned's Newt.* Nelvana developed the property and oversaw scripting, storyboarding, design, art direction, and postproduction, as well as retaining worldwide merchandising rights and distribution outside Germany. TMO sold the series within Germany and contributed painting, compositing, and rendering services, in association with a Hungarian studio. The two partners split layout duties, while a Philippine studio did animation production.

o *Wilf the Witch's Dog* was a coproduction of Skryptonite of Scotland, RTV of Germany, Jade Animation of Hong Kong, Cine Cartoon of Australia, and Red Kite Productions of the United Kingdom. Jade handled distribution throughout the Asia/Pacific region, excluding Australia and New Zealand; RTV sold the series worldwide outside of Asia (except in the United Kingdom and Austria). Broadcaster ORF purchased the series in Germany.

o Broadway Video Enterprises of the United States and Cuppa Coffee Animation of Canada signed an exclusive deal for three animated children's properties, *Gordon Giraffe, Cinema Sue,* and *Ted's Bed.* Cuppa Coffee was responsible for production on all three, while Broadway managed all worldwide sales activity, including television, home video, theatrical distribution, and licensing and merchandising.

o Nelvana signed a deal with German television network RTV that gave the broadcaster television, home video, and merchandising subagent rights for 560 half hours of Nelvana's new series, along with episodes from its library of older series, in Germany, Eastern Europe, and Scandinavia. Nelvana received a nonrefundable advance of $10.25 million during the first year. A $22 million, three-year reciprocal distribution agreement was also part of the deal, wherein RTV would buy TV, merchandising, and home video rights to five Nelvana series per year. The two companies also agreed to coproduce at least two 26-episode series over a three-year period.

o *Laura's Star* was coproduced by ZDF Enterprises, a subsidiary of the broadcaster ZDF, and Baumhaus Medien, both in Germany. ZDF retained worldwide distribution rights while Baumhaus managed publishing activities (the show was based on a 1.7-million-unit-selling book). Cartoon-Film of Germany handled 2D animation.

o TV-Loonland held all worldwide rights for a CGI series, *Dragon's Rock,* except in Germany, where cofinancier Super RTL, the German broadcaster, secured the rights for twenty-one years. GUM Studios of Germany was a coproduction partner and handled animation production.

o *Hamilton Mattress* was a three-part series (a half hour per episode) of stop-frame animation. Link, in the United Kingdom, and Denmark's Egmont jointly handled worldwide television and home video rights, while Link reserved merchandising and Egmont publishing. (Link was a major licensing agency in the United Kingdom and is now part of Entertainment Rights. Egmont is a leading European children's publisher.) Harvest Films of the United Kingdom completed the animation production but was not a coproduction partner.

o Korean studio Ameko did a coproduction deal with DIC for *Super Duper Sumos,* in which it retained distribution and merchandising rights to the Korean market, with DIC handling the rest of the world. Ameko also oversaw animation production.

o Energee Entertainment of Australia sought $8 million for its series *The Magic Pudding* and ended up with twenty investors. Presales were secured from the ABC in Australia, Showtime in the United States, Ravensburger in Germany, and Luk in Spain, with deficit financing secured from the Berliner Bank. Gaffney International of Australia took worldwide licensing and merchandising rights, and HarperCollins signed a nine-book deal; Australian and worldwide theatrical distribution rights were part of the package as well.

o The Evangelical Lutheran Church in America (ELCA) tried to get its 1960s stop-motion series *Davey and Goliath* back on the air in the early 2000s. To fund production of 26 twelve-minute episodes it planned to raise $4 million from licensed merchandise and promotional licensing to companies such as Mountain Dew. The organization had granted home video rights in the late 1980s to Program Source, which had sold about 600,000 videos over a decade.

└─o When Nelvana Entertainment sold its Bookworm Bunch programming block, based on classic children's books, to PBS in 2000 it received a production commitment from the broadcaster estimated at $40 million, but no additional distribution fee. PBS essentially got to distribute the programming for free (aside from its production contribution), and received merchandising participation.

As these examples show, there are many routes to financing, producing, and selling an animated television series. Flexibility and a thinking-outside-the-box mentality are critical to success.

FILM

Film financing has much in common with television financing, especially in that each partner that invests in a project (with financing, distribution, services, concepts, etc.) must receive a reward package in which the profit potential is commensurate with the value of its input. Components to consider can be categorized along the same lines as for a television series, with cash, distribution, marketing and ancillaries, creative input and control, credits, and ownership among the key elements in the negotiation, and distribution and financing usually carrying the most weight.

The key difference between film and television deals is that the major Hollywood studios dominate theatrical distribution, not only in the United States but worldwide. In the most common scenario, a major vertically integrated studio such as Warner Brothers acquires worldwide rights to market and distribute the film, as well as ownership of the copyright, in return for funding the production. These rights commonly include merchandising and other ancillaries and go on in perpetuity, and the studio maintains creative control. While this arrangement favors the studio, it is often the only way a film can be distributed widely.

Because of the way studios account for films, they are rarely profitable on their own. Being a participant in "net profits" (as many producers and creators will be in the type of deal just described) may not mean much, since studios deduct distribution fees (around 30 percent to 35 percent of gross), interest, overhead, and other costs to come up with the net profit figure, which often ends up being a loss.

Studios don't always assume total control of a property. They often employ a mix of techniques to create their annual roster of films. They buy all rights to some projects, as outlined above, cofinance others (paying up front for the right to distribute the film worldwide, but not funding production), act as a coproducer for some (providing a portion of financing as well as distribution and production expertise), and simply distribute others (signing on after the film is complete). In the last scenario the studio maintains no ownership in the property.

Some studios form strategic relationships with established producers that encompass several films and spread the risk between the two parties. Disney's and Pixar's five-picture deal gave the two companies an equal share in profits; both contributed 50 percent of financing, with Pixar handling production and Disney managing distribution. Before the advent of this deal Disney financed the first *Toy Story* film and Pixar reaped 15 percent of the profits. The deal will end in 2005, as the two companies could not agree on terms for a renewal.

Disney and Vanguard Films inaugurated a strategic alliance in 2002 for a number of computer-animated feature films, starting with *Valiant*. The alliance was to give Vanguard enough funding to internally develop and fund its own animation projects, which would be distributed by Disney. The partners' goal was to make each film within two years at a cost below $40 million. Before approaching Disney, Vanguard secured some financing and had completed scripts and budgets, computer-graphics tests, and character and production designs in place, all of which helped sell the studio on the alliance.

Film producers who either cannot secure studio distribution or opt not to go through the studio system can work with an independent distribution company. Many of these companies are members of the American Film Marketing Association (AFMA). Independently distributed and produced films tend to result in less exposure, since they're exhibited mainly on the small art-house circuit, but may still be profitable, since their costs are so much less than a mainstream release. The distributors rarely add much financing, but the deals leave some or all creative control with the producers.

Producers that can secure financing independently, such as from internal operations or private investors, can go to an independent distributor or studio with a completed product. Fathom Studios was able to enter production on a 3D, CGI theatrical film, *Delgo*, with funds from three investment sources all connected to the company. Without having secured distribution, the studio was able to produce the film and planned to talk to the major studios about a distribution-only arrangement that allowed it to maintain creative control.

As in television, distribution presales from U.S. and international markets can help finance a film. Independent film producers without studio support can presell territorial rights to distributors around the world, pitching the executives at film festivals, trade shows, and film markets. It is rare that all presales taken together will cover the entire production cost—especially since only 10 percent of the license fee is forthcoming until the final product is delivered—but they can account for a significant portion. Bank loans (which can be acquired from selected institutions, such as the Union Bank of California, that specialize in entertainment-industry lending based on guaranteed presales) and/or financing from coproduction partners are needed to cover the rest.

An alternative type of presales is called split-rights financing. An independent producer first secures a domestic distributor who is willing to finance up to half the cost of production and allow the production entity to keep the copyright. Then the producer goes overseas for the rest of the money, approaching international distributors to become investors rather than simply acquiring distribution rights. The producer gives these distributors an interest in back-end revenues and therefore the potential for increased profits in addition to their distribution activities. Because of their stake in profits—and because they're guaranteed exclusive rights in their territory without entering into a bidding war—they're willing to invest more up front than they would in a straight presales deal. This decreases risk for the producer and allows it to retain ownership. Bank financing usually is still needed to fill the gap.

Another film-financing option for independents is to enter into a coproduction, allying with another company that can offer production services or expertise in addition to financing. The funds generated from the partnership can then be supplemented by distribution presales or split-rights financing. A coproduction deal may have other benefits aside from cash; when Lucasfilm and Anime World Osaka joined together in 2000 for an animated movie called *The Tiny Fairy Mirun,* Anime World contributed all of the $18.5 million budget, but the fact that George Lucas was credited as executive producer was a marketing coup for the film. The two companies split production duties.

Coproduction deals for independent films can involve multiple production and financing partners. One French film, *Le Château des Singes (A Monkey's Tale),* required 22 different sources of funds. The producers wanted to avoid bringing in any American partners so they could maintain creative control. Production was split between three studios, La Fabrique in France, Cologne Cartoon in Germany, and Keskemetfilm in Hungary.

Film production, coproduction, and distribution deals, like those for television, must clearly define the responsibilities and rights of each party, including how back-end revenues and ownership are divided, in what order the various investors/distributors are paid, and whether payments come before or after the recoupment of production costs. Recoupment for distribution partners is often segmented by country (unless a U.S. major studio is involved), with the U.S. distributor's investment paid back from revenues in the United States and the same for distributors in other countries. After all costs are accounted for there can then be a split of worldwide revenues among all the investors.

International distribution deals often give the distributor the right to sell the film in all media within its territory; it can sublicense those categories where it doesn't have expertise. Exceptions include instances where the producer has already signed a partner for worldwide distribution, such as a television network or home video distributor. Enoki Films of Japan represents animated television properties on a worldwide basis.

The granting of ancillary rights is an important negotiating point, since licensed products and videos can contribute significantly to a film's total profit picture. For example, from 1989 to 2002 Warner Brothers' *Batman* franchise, which began as a 1989 film, generated revenues of $2 billion, according to *The New York Times*. Of that 34 percent came from films, 29 percent from home videos (of films and TV episodes, as well as originals), 19 percent from licensing and merchandising, 10 percent from domestic television rights, and 8 percent from foreign rights.

HOME VIDEO

Financing of original home video productions, like television and film financing, is accomplished through coproduction arrangements, cofinancing deals including presales, and/or internally generated funds. (See chapter 4 for more on how home video distribution works.)

Studios that create original videos based on their existing franchises, such as Disney or Warner Brothers, fund their own productions of course. They also retain video rights for many of the films or television shows they distribute, as well as selling home videos for independent producers on a straight distribution basis.

For independent producers, presales from distribution can often be a key component of the financing scheme for the production. The deals work much as described in the section on films, except home video distribution companies take the place of film distribution companies. They can come on board for a finished production, taking a distribution fee but not being involved in the creation or financing of the project, or they can sign on early and help fund the project, retaining some ownership. Some take on worldwide distribution rights (often sublicensing distributors in other countries) while others handle distribution in their own territory only. In the latter case the producer signs separate distribution deals in each country where it wants the production to be available. As in other sectors of animation, a studio can retain a foreign sales agent to sell the property abroad for a commission.

In addition to distributors funding can come from other producers (through fee reductions or hard money), outside investors, or other parties.

ONLINE

Online productions can be funded by the producer/creator, who then distributes the property itself on its own Web site or signs a distribution deal with another site. In other cases the distributor or destination site pays for production. A distributor or site such as AtomFilms can also represent the property for distribution in other media, such as television, films, DVDs, sound tracks or airline screens. The producer or creator receives a share of advances and sometimes a small fee per download (in the case of distribution to other Web sites) or a royalty or revenue sharing on product sales (as in a DVD or video).

The budgets for online episodic series are low compared to budgets for other types of entertainment productions, of course. This increases the chance that the creator or studio can fund the project internally. At the same time, the chances of significant revenue streams from the property are remote, which makes it difficult for producers to attract outside funding, except through distributors that specialize in this business.

In the boom days of Web animation Internet producers often offered ownership stakes in their company to investors in return for financing, or as partial compensation for a distribution deal. These rights turned out to be valueless, as the companies' stock price plummeted. Ultimately many of the companies went out of business. While offering an ownership stake is still a possible financing option for Web entertainment, it is unlikely to be a major component of the deal.

Much of the most successful online entertainment as of the early 2000s appears on convergent sites tied to one of the major television networks, such as Nickelodeon or Cartoon Network. Online rights and funding for online productions are often key points in the negotiations surrounding a television series or film. Having a Web site with appealing content is an important marketing tool, making animation properties that work well on a site a desired commodity. The creator's compensation will include some sort of revenues related to the Web site, such as a fee per download or page view.

INTERACTIVE SOFTWARE

Most of the financing for interactive games is provided by the publisher, which serves a role somewhat analogous to that of a film studio. The developer is paid by the publisher for its work—this fee covers the actual production budget for the title—and sometimes receives a 5 percent to 15 percent royalty on net sales after the deduction of development costs; the developer is usually responsible for paying the console or computer maker for the authoring tools needed to create the game. The publisher also must pay the console maker for the right to be an official licensee and must purchase the physical disks from the console maker. The distributor (if an outside distributor is used) takes a significant commission on sales (see chapter 4) but, unlike in other forms of animation, usually doesn't provide any funding for the production. If a licensor (underlying rights holder) is involved, it takes a 10 percent (or so) share of net sales as a royalty; it may provide funding for the game, but this isn't standard.

There are exceptions to these rules. Sometimes publishers and distributors, or licensors and publishers, form joint ventures or other types of deals where they share in the up-front investment and in the revenues from the partnership. In many cases the larger interactive gaming companies are able to develop, publish, and distribute their titles internally, although they frequently work with independent developers.

The publisher owns the copyrights and trademarks for the titles. This ensures that, if a publisher has to terminate a deal with a developer halfway through production, it still can publish the title, with production completed by another outside developer or its own staff. (The contract dictates that the developer must hand over any source codes or necessary tools upon termination of the agreement.)

Developers with a significant track record of previous successes may have enough bargaining power to not only get a royalty payment but to secure minimum sales guarantees, guaranteed royalties, and marketing guarantees from the publisher. They may also be able to retain rights to approve the final games, as well as marketing materials. This amount of clout is unusual, however.

Exhibit 8.4

Checklist of Selected Elements in an Animation Partnership/Funding Deal

---

Description of each partner's contributions

Descriptions of each partner's compensation/return

Division of services

Definitions of terms, especially financial

Order of payment among partners

Division of ownership in intellectual property

Penalties for breach of contract

Timing of payments

Production milestones

Division of creative control

Credits and order of credits

Procedures in the case of disputes

Grounds for termination

What happens if one or more partners leaves the partnership

Tax and legal considerations

Warranties and guarantees

Options for future properties

Rights and ownership in new property elements created after the deal is negotiated

Notes: This checklist includes some of the many elements to consider when negotiating a deal. Some terms will be complex in their final form and there may be additional terms, depending on the specifics of the deal. Contracts should be negotiated and finalized by an attorney specializing in animation or entertainment.

One difference between the gaming industry and other forms of entertainment falls in the realm of intellectual property. Not only is there the issue of copyright ownership but also patent ownership of the technological tools being used in the creation of the property. (In addition to the tools licensed from Nintendo or other console makers developers have their own tools.) If proprietary, this technology distinguishes the developer from its competitors and represents a valuable asset. (Companies such as id Software have a nice ongoing business from licensing their technology to other developers and publishers in addition to revenues from games they create.) The developer therefore grants a nonexclusive or short-term license to the publisher for the proprietary tools or other preexisting works used to create the title, even when the publisher holds the copyright to the game itself.

PART II
CONTRACT WORK

9

Overview of Work-for-Hire Projects

While creating and retaining ownership in proprietary animation projects can be lucrative, it is also risky and expensive, especially in the early stages of development. On the other hand, contract or work-for-hire projects bring in predictable amounts of money, with the entire bill paid soon after the completion of production. While the upside potential is not as high as for proprietary properties, studios rely on the steady cash flow and the opportunity to keep staffers busy during lulls in proprietary work.

Some studios specialize in work-for-hire projects, while others balance a mix of contract and proprietary work. The latter strategy has gained frequency since the late 1990s as studios have sought to maintain more control over their destinies while still maintaining stable revenue streams from work-for-hire projects. In Asia, Philippine studio PASI attributed nearly 80 percent of its revenues in the late 1990s to service work, but in the early

2000s less than a quarter of its revenue streams came from that segment. The remainder was from properties in which the company had some ownership interest; coproductions comprised about half of the company's total workload.

The types of contract work available are varied. More companies from a diverse roster of industries are considering animation for use in their marketing, commercial, and online activities. Work-for-hire jobs can involve entertainment productions or corporate work, projects in all distribution channels, and the use of all styles of animation. While the number of opportunities are on the rise, however, so is the level of competition. Even solo entrepreneurs can satisfy many clients' needs with animation of high quality. Because of this crowded landscape, studios say that providing an ongoing and sophisticated level of service is an important factor behind success in the contract market.

In certain niches of the animation industry, such as special effects, commercial animation, and Flash animation for corporate Web sites, work-for-hire contracts are the norm; there is rarely any opportunity for animators to take an ownership stake in these types of productions.

COMMERCIAL ANIMATION

Animated spokescharacters represent one of the longest-standing and best-known uses of animation in commercials. A few famous faces include Tony the Tiger for Kellogg's Frosted Flakes, Punchy for Hawaiian Punch, the red, yellow, blue, and green candies for M&Ms, and the Hamburger Helper Hand for General Mills. Many of these characters have been in use for decades or are being brought back or modernized to appeal to contemporary consumers. The Pillsbury Doughboy has been reworked in 3D animation as a cost-effective alternative to the original puppetry.

Some of these characters become so popular they take on a life of their own. The 2D-animated quilters that appear in commercials for Georgia Pacific's Quilted Northern brand of tissue, animated by J. J. Sedelmaier, were integrated into product packaging after gaining a following on air. Characters such as the animated M&Ms have found their way into popular licensed product lines. (Most animation houses don't share in the royalty revenues from this merchandise.)

In addition to spokescharacters, 3D, 2D, and stop-motion animation have been used for all-animated commercials. The Quilted Northern spots mentioned above and AT&T spots, where the company's blue logo morphs into different shapes, are just two examples. This technique has grown in popularity as advertisers seek innovative graphic looks that will allow their products to stand out from the mass of competing brands advertised every day. A unique animation sequence can gain viewers' attention.

Not all commercial work is for television. Animation houses produce advertising spots for site-based media (e.g., kiosks in stores), movie theaters, and the Internet. On the Internet advertising opportunities include animated banners, interstitial spots, and webisodic series incorporating branded product placement. While Internet advertising hasn't taken off as once was hoped, advertisers such as BulkRegister.com, itself an Internet company, are among those advertising on the Web. BulkRegister.com's ad agency FMT Advertising commissioned Renegade Animation to produce a cartoon series that entertained while educating consumers on the site's domain-registration services.

Several corporate brands use animation as a marketing tool on their own sites. The Midol Web site featured an interactive game starring animated characters that battle "the menstruation monster." The game debuted on Alloy.com, a Web site for teen girls, and then was transferred to Midol's site in the hopes that girls would follow it there.

Animation houses contract with advertising agencies for commercial work—unless the client handles its advertising through an in-house department rather than an outside agency—and report to the agency's creative director. The advertiser has input into the creative direction of the ad, of course, but the agency takes the lead, hiring a producer (or assigning one of its staff producers), a director, and animation and postproduction houses during the development process. Animation studios send their invoices to and are paid by the agency.

In difficult economic times advertising industry billings tend to decline as corporations look for ways to cut costs. This contraction in turn affects advertising agencies and animation production houses. In March 2002, Industrial Light & Magic, one of the leading special effects houses for film and television, closed its thirteen-year-old, twenty-employee division focusing on commercials. The downturn in advertising led the company to conclude that it didn't need a standalone division for commercials when it couldn't keep its employees busy full time. The company planned to continue taking on commercial work through its main ILM operation, which specializes in entertainment effects. At the former division's peak commercials reportedly accounted for an estimated 25 percent of ILM's revenues.

In commercial animation the client owns the rights to all characters and other elements created by the animation house, even in instances when the animation supplier developed a character's look or designed other important creative elements. A rare exception would be when an animation studio creates a character in-house that is then picked up exclusively by a client for use in its advertising. Rights to this spokesperson, while closely identified with the brand, may revert to the creator when its association with the brand is over, and the creator receives a fee or royalty for its use. In general, however, clients protect their valuable trademarks and won't allow them to be diluted or threatened in any way, including by giving studios who work on the commercials a share in ownership.

LONG-FORM AND SHORT-FORM ENTERTAINMENT

While the entertainment industry offers opportunities for animation houses to retain ownership stakes in properties developed internally and by others, much animation work is still done on a contract basis. Producers of films, television programs, home video/DVD products, theme park rides, music videos, and the Internet all, at times, use outside studios on a for-hire basis to complete all or part of their animation.

Primarily for cost reasons, the bulk of contract animation for entertainment (especially 2D) is sent to overseas studios, particularly in Southeast Asia, China, and increasingly India. Although studios in the U.S., Canada, Europe, Japan, and Australia also perform contract work, especially for studios in their home countries, the Asian houses tend to provide lower-cost 2D services at a comparable level of quality. Asian service studios are also expanding the roster of services they offer; most have digital capabilities and some are getting into CGI, motion capture, or Flash animation.

A decade ago studios in the major animation-producing countries relied on Asian studios mainly for ink-and-paint services, but now they can go to the same houses for compositing, special effects, camera, coloration, and other postproduction tasks. Meanwhile, as traditional animation centers such as Korea and the Philippines have grown more sophisticated in the services they provide, other countries such as China and Vietnam have taken over the simpler, lower-cost duties. While some overseas studios continue to specialize in certain services, most are nearing full-service status, able to handle backgrounds, storyboards, layout, and postproduction as well as traditional contract services such as inbetweening or ink-and-paint.

Some larger studios have opted to source their contract work to North American or European houses instead of Asian facilities due to perceived quality issues; the challenges have sometimes been so great that working with the Asian studios turned out to be more expensive than working with houses closer to home because of retake charges due to misunderstandings. This is changing. Many Asian studios as of the 2000s can provide quality rivaling that offered by studios in Europe and North America, although communication still can be an issue.

In general, the North American and European studios handle pre- and post-production of television properties in-house or domestically and send the production phase to a service house. But the number and types of services contracted vary depending not only on the capabilities of the service provider but also on the needs of the production and how busy a studio is at a given time.

Some studios tend to give their service contracts to companies with which they are affiliated, such as subsidiaries or sibling companies. This strategy keeps all the revenues in the corporate family, although money changes hands between the divisions. IDT Media, a branch of a global telephone company, coproduced an animation property with Cartoon Pizza, a children's animation creator. It used its own subsidiary, Global Animation Studio, to do the animation production on a contract basis.

Contract work can give a new studio expertise that allows it to eventually create its own properties or take part in coproductions. Bazillion Pictures, which gained a name in commercial work for campaigns such as the animated smiley face in Wal-Mart advertising and the logo treatments in Northwest Airlines' in-flight entertainment, entered the proprietary production market in 2002 when it coproduced, with Good Friends Entertainment, an original video series for children called *Farkleberry Farm*.

The Internet has given rise to more opportunities to provide Flash animation services. Although Flash animation is relatively inexpensive and often can be completed in-house by the creator, many contract animation houses added Flash capabilities to their portfolio of services as the demand for Internet animation began to grow. They not only provide commercial work for corporations, as described earlier, but also produce entertainment on a contract basis.

Pileated Pictures created animated cartoon skits for a Web site tied to a 2002 MCA-released hip-hop music album. Shockwave and Brilliant Digital Entertainment both produce online music videos; Brilliant uses its proprietary Pulse 3D technology, while Shockwave combines MP3 files and Flash animation. Animator eStudio has created character design, animation, and storyboards for online episodic productions including *The Kellys* and *Gary the Rat*.

The types of animated entertainment on the Web are varied. Marvel began creating online animated trailers for some of its comic books in 2001, meant to appeal to customers who were familiar with the characters from video games, films, or television but had not been introduced to the company's roster of comic books. Several companies have created animated content for graphics-enhanced e-mail systems such as FunMail, while others are producing "cybercelebrities," animated spokescharacters that appear on the Web, often in real time. Real-time animation for television, which allows viewers to interact with animated characters, is another opportunity for contract studios. Possible Worlds created real-time animation for *Phred on Your Head,* the former spokescharacter for the Noggin cable channel.

DVD is a growing technology that has created a lot of opportunity for service work. In addition to the core entertainment, most DVDs include extras such as games and short original animations featuring characters from the film. Studios have discovered that these added-value features correlate with additional sales, so demand for animated extras is likely to stay strong. Studios often will look to outside companies to provide this content.

SPECIAL EFFECTS

Opportunities for special effects are growing as more effects are included in all types of live-action entertainment and commercials. At the same time the industry is cyclical and tends to rise and fall along with the economy and the fortunes of the entertainment and advertising industries. The number of films and commercials released in a year, along with the average budgets associated with them, determine the amount of work available for special effects houses. Competition also has become more intense as smaller companies have entered the market using off-the-shelf software.

In earlier days a few large companies provided the bulk of effects (a few giants, including ILM and Digital Domain, continue to dominate) using largely proprietary technology. Now even the majors use off-the-shelf packages, often in conjunction with unique, in-house-developed solutions. The two can be mixed and matched depending on the requirements of the job. Using off-the-shelf software allows a studio to maintain a flexible workforce; those using proprietary packages need to keep trained employees on board so they'll be available when needed.

The effects market is divided into three layers in terms of studio size. There are the few large studios, as noted above, which account for a significant percentage of film and commercial effects work. There are also small freelance operations that are able to provide sophisticated effects from home.

In the middle are the medium-size independent studios, which include Rhythm & Hues and Tippett Studios, among many others.

In such a competitive environment effects studios have diversified. Instead of focusing on one style of animation or type of customer, they try to provide everything from stop-motion, to 2D, to 3D-CGI and pitch clients in all segments, including entertainment and commercials, video games, music videos, and site-based and theme park work.

Virtually all top-grossing live-action films contain a large proportion of special effects shots. *Harry Potter and the Sorcerer's Stone* (Warner Brothers, 2001) featured 740 effects shots, while the same studio's 2001 release *Cats and Dogs* contained 750. Music videos, television shows, video game cinematics, commercials, and even Internet productions also feature a growing number of effects. Special effects are used not only to create fantasy situations but to recreate realistic live action, if it can be done more cost-effectively or safely with the computer. The effects in *Cats and Dogs,* mentioned above, primarily depicted realistic-looking animals. In the syndicated live-action television hour *Sheena,* a "digital stunt double" performed actions that were either dangerous or impossible for a human actor to achieve.

Animated work is enhanced with special effects as well. Of 560 shots in the Disney film *James and the Giant Peach* (1996), two-thirds involved some sort of effect, including compositing or CGI imagery. This is true of many CG-animated productions, as well as 2D/3D combinations. Sometimes these effects are animated by the same house doing the character animation and backgrounds, but complex shots can be farmed out on a contract basis.

It is becoming more common for several effects houses to work on a single project, especially in film. In a Sci Fi Channel production of the classic Frank Herbert story *Dune,* a company called Area 51 was the lead effects provider, but three other houses contributed effects. A dozen different facilities added effects shots to the film *Mission to Mars* (Touchstone Pictures, 2000).

Sometimes multiple studios are called in because productions get behind schedule and need the extra help so they can premiere on time. In other cases the producers may opt to use more than one studio because they feel each is best at a particular style or type of effect, or because the studio they prefer is too small to complete an entire job. They also can add studios to the project when specs change over the course of production; such was the case with *Dune,* where the plan was to have 250 special effects but 500 were in the final production. Small studios sometimes join together to pitch an effects job that is too big for one to handle alone but can be cost-effectively completed in partnership.

The proliferation of lower-cost software packages gives some customers the impression that budgets for special effects jobs should be reduced, an idea that fits in well with their desire to keep costs down. In reality, while computers and software are faster and cheaper, clients are demanding more sophisticated effects with each film or commercial, so the time and cost remain, at a minimum, the same. In addition, labor is a more significant component in the cost of creating special effects than hardware or software is, so the fact that the equipment's cost has come down does not necessarily mean total costs have declined.

While most houses are trying to diversify, as noted above, some houses, especially in certain segments of the industry, continue to specialize. For example, digital matte painting is most commonly completed by companies that focus on this niche, including Illusion Arts and Matte World Digital. (Digital matte painting is used when locations are fantasy-based or when it is too difficult or expensive to conduct a live shoot.) Motion capture has traditionally been another specialty, although many full-service houses are adding mo-cap capabilities.

DVD production is becoming an area of growth for some effects firms. Effects houses such as Cinesite are adding divisions to handle DVD mastering and authoring to better position themselves to take advantage of the opportunities in this fast-growing field.

The ownership of digital assets developed during the creation of special effects can be a point of contention between effects houses and their clients. In general, film or television studios and corporate customers maintain ownership of their trademarks and copyrights, but digital assets can sometimes be reused by the effects house on future jobs with other clients, thus reducing costs. Therefore, effects houses want to keep pieces of technology they develop that are not specific to the job. Studios also want to keep the assets so they can use another service company, if desired, to create further incarnations of the same property.

While special effects is and will remain primarily a work-for-hire domain, some studios are using downtime to develop proprietary entertainment properties utilizing the skills they've learned from special effects work. In addition, there are effects providers looking into developing equity stakes in productions for which they provide effects work. They believe it makes sense for them to have participation in back-end revenue streams when effects comprise a large portion of a film, especially when they contributed significantly to the creation and design of key CG characters. This type of arrangement also benefits the producers of the film, since effects providers will reduce their fees or reinvest part of their fee back into the production, making a financial as well as creative contribution. Additional investment is also possible, although most effects companies don't have the resources to commit a large financial stake upfront. While this strategy is still emerging, it is something that more houses are looking into and that some have successfully pursued.

GAMING

The interactive software and gaming industry has become a force in the entertainment industry. Major studios take their game divisions seriously and try to maximize synergies between the two. Creating interactive gaming requires many of the same skills as 3D animation, and animators increasingly go back and forth between the two disciplines as opportunity dictates.

According to Miller Freeman, a publishing company and trade show sponsor that managed the Game Developers Conference, about a hundred thousand people were employed in the game-development industry as of 1999, with almost a third of those being 3D animators and artists. Many animators find the games industry appealing, since artists tend to have more creative control when working on interactive titles than in other, more collaborative sectors of animation. Small teams of four or five artists can be assigned to an individual game title, with each being allowed a good deal of input.

The crossover potential is particularly great for those focusing on special effects for films, where the technology used to create the images is similar to that used in gaming. In some cases game companies can provide better compensation to animators than the entertainment industry, including perks and benefits, as well as offering technical challenges and more creative opportunities. For example, animators involved in special effects rarely get experience in storytelling, as those working in gaming do.

As technology improves games are becoming more like interactive films. Not only does creating gameplay and designing environments take similar skills to animating long-form entertainment, but animated minifilms, or cinematics, are inserted within the game environment as a way to explain new levels, reward players for achieving goals, and further the story line. Cinematics get longer and more sophisticated with each generation of game.

While most gameplay and design is done in-house by game developers and publishers, cinematics are often farmed out to 3D animation studios, some of which specialize in this type of work and others that are involved in special effects or other types of animation. Cinematics are labor-intensive, requiring many shots within short deadlines (e.g., one hundred shots in two or three months), but many animators like doing them, mainly because of the creative control they have. Cinematics are frequently sent off to small studios, with ten or fewer employees, because there is not enough profit to sustain larger companies in this type of work. In the mid-1990s most cinematics were 20- to 30-second clips; as of 2002 they could run as long as 5 minutes and were more realistic in style than in the past.

As in traditional animation, the rise of lower-cost and more sophisticated software and hardware has enabled independent animators and small animation houses to enter the gaming business, something that was impossible in the past because of the high investment cost. At the same time, some traditional animation houses that had sourced out their game development to specialists have brought those projects back in-house, as new hardware and software have allowed them to do the job cost-effectively.

Most studios work with outside developers on a for-hire basis to create games, even if they have in-house capabilities. Universal Interactive, for example, retained an independent game developer, Blue Tongue Software of Australia, to create interactive titles tied to its *Jurassic Park* franchise, which were released under a copublishing deal with Konami. Blue Tongue composed the music in-house and contracted with animation and 3D graphics house Act III for cinematics, including the opening sequence.

Many studios are starting to use motion-capture technology more often to animate interactive titles. Mo-cap reduces costs and is especially effective for sports games, where the athletes being depicted can participate in the animation process (e.g., making their patented basketball moves while wearing mo-cap equipment) for more in-game realism. EA Sports, a major sports-related game label and a division of Electronic Arts, is a frequent user of mo-cap technology.

While violent video games tend to be the most high-profile interactive titles, there are many styles and genres on the market. Some titles are for young children, with simple graphics and game play, and often some educational elements; examples would be the *Arthur* CD-ROM games and Disney's interactive storybooks. Others are for adults and are more focused on story than action. An example of the latter is the *Myst* franchise, one of the first successful interactive graphic adventures.

Other interactive segments include casino and arcade games, for which animated sequences often are created on a work-for-hire basis. DMA Animation of Texas did animation for a Betty Boop video slot machine at Bally's casinos, with approvals handled by Betty Boop's licensor, King Features.

CORPORATE OPPORTUNITIES

Aside from commercials, corporations and other nonentertainment-based clients, such as nonprofit organizations, use animation in various ways. They virtually always farm the the work out to external studios, since they don't have in-house animation capabilities.

The Internet is one area where animation and corporate messages go well together. In addition to the Web-based advertising and entertainment opportunities mentioned earlier, there are other applications for animation online in a corporate setting, particularly when it comes to online demonstrations. The American Boardsports Company, a manufacturer of sports equipment, has a Web site focusing on the sorts of extreme sports in which it specializes. The company uses Flash animation to show characters using its products, such as a sequence where an animated athlete rides a snowboard. Similarly, the Eddie Bauer Web site depicts its products in 3D animation that allows users to view them from all sides before purchasing. Lowes.com, the Web site of the home-improvement retail chain Lowe's, featured more than one hundred animated sequences on its Web site in 2002, each demonstrating home-repair instructions, such as how to build a deck.

The boundary between marketing and entertainment can be blurry. Games or animated episodes, for example, can help support a brand message and keep potential customers coming back to the Web site. Swedish milk producer Milko AB allowed customers to make their own music videos on its Web site in support of its Fjallfill brand. Each video included an animated version of Milko's cow logo, which moved and "sang" according to the customer's specifications, accompanied by a genre of music selected by the customer. The campaign gained popularity through word of mouth, and sales of the brand rose more than 20 percent in the first two months after the company inaugurated the effort.

Other corporate opportunities outside of commercials and the Internet include animation featured in corporate training videos, courtrooms, medical and science applications, architecture, and manufacturing. Demonstrating products or techniques, sometimes with "virtual instructors," livening up charts with movement, or gaining audiences' attention with entertaining sequences are all viable uses of animation.

Many companies use animation in the creation of premiums as well, such as giving consumers a free minicomputer game containing branded product placement to reinforce their brand message. The Gap has experimented with this technique, offering a computer game titled *Snow Day* in which animated children wear Gap clothing. The game was distributed in store as a free-with-purchase premium.

BROADCAST DESIGN

Broadcast design involves creating an on-air look for a broadcast or cable network that is recognizable as soon as viewers click to the channel. The design must be flexible because it will be seen in many permutations, yet it must consistently maintain and support the brand identity the network wants to associate with its name.

Broadcast design includes the creation of corporate and show-specific logos, promotional spots of various lengths, color schemes to identify the network, and opening sequences ("opens") for programming closely identified with the network, such as news or sports. It requires both graphic design and animation skills and encompases motion and still graphics, logos and text, and live and recorded voice-overs. Marketing and branding expertise are also essential components of the job.

Broadcast design houses—often specialists in this field, but sometimes also active in commercial work or special effects—work closely with the client in formulating a branding strategy, creating an on-air look that supports the brand positioning, and executing the individual elements that comprise the on-air visuals.

Broadcast design and animation firms also create opening sequences for films. Nexus Productions animated the title sequence for *Catch Me if You Can,* released in late 2002. The same company has done animation for the rock band U2's Pop Mart world tour, as well as television opens and graphics.

The design and redesign of Web sites also falls under the category of broadcast design. Some companies spend close to $350,000 to create or rebrand their corporate Web sites, especially those that are graphics-heavy. While Internet entertainment has not turned out to be a big opportunity for marketers of proprietary animation properties, the Internet represents a significant market for companies specializing in animation for broadcast design. Often Web-based branding or rebranding efforts involve convergent sites; the branding initiative ties together the look of the Web site with the look of the television network or other entertainment company that operates the site.

RIDES AND THEME PARKS

Theme parks represent another potential client base for animation houses, especially those involved in special effects. Many of the jobs involving these clients are rides that use large-format, stereoscopic 3D films as environments through which the ride travels. Theme and amusement parks also seek stand-alone films, which can serve as attractions themselves or can be used to entertain the people standing in line for a ride. Olive Jar Studios, before it became part of Red Sky Entertainment, produced 2D animated features of 15 minutes in length, intended to run continuously while people waited in line for Universal Studios Theme Parks rides. The films told the stories of the characters featured in the attractions.

Digital Domain worked on the *Terminator 2* 3D ride at Universal Studios, which was, at the time, the most complex and expensive animation ever done on a per-minute basis and the biggest 3D animated display ever, more than 160 feet wide. The cost of the film, for which Digital Domain created a digital 3D creature, was estimated at over $60 million.

At Paramount Theme Parks, another effects house, Blur Studio, created a 3D simulator ride based on *The 7th Portal*, an animated Web original created by now-defunct Stan Lee Media. Producing a stereoscopic 3D effect requires two cameras and double the amount of animation of a standard production; in this case, Blur completed more than fourteen thousand frames for the ride film. Projection systems vary somewhat from park to park, which complicates production even for experienced animation studios. This production was unusual in that it involved thirteen main characters in a 4-minute video, while most focus on one or a few characters.

DreamWorks and Universal Studios Theme Parks created a film called *Shrek 4D,* which featured the voices of Mike Myers, Eddie Murphy, Cameron Diaz, and John Lithgow, who provided voices for the original feature film on which the attraction is based. *Shrek 4D* opened at Universal parks in Hollywood, Orlando, and Japan in 2003. The 15-minute film told the story of what happened to the characters between the time period of the original film and that of the 2004 sequel. DreamWorks' subsidiary PDI, which produced the animation for the film, supplied the animation for the attraction as well.

POSTPRODUCTION

Postproduction traditionally has been handled by dedicated postproduction houses, who take over a project after the animation production is finished. Tasks such as telecine (a process that makes video look more like film), compositing, picture editing, sound track synchronization, color correction, and sound effects, as well as special effects in live-action productions, were passed to one or several postproduction houses after the production phase was complete.

Now that the computer is used for all aspects of the animation process, however, the tasks assigned to animation houses and postproduction houses increasingly overlap. The two groups have become competitors to a certain degree, offering many of the same services to their clients. In fact, animation houses often are able to complete the job with increased efficiency, since post tasks can be integrated into the production process. In the commercial sector agencies often look for houses that can do both animation and effects, as well as other postproduction tasks. As a result, postproduction houses are trying to reinvent themselves, adding services to replace those lost to the animation studios.

The growing competition and reduced need for some postproduction services has led to a consolidation in the "post" industry. The business historically was comprised of small shops, with many focused on a particular niche. Now, however, as clients are looking for full-service houses, these boutiques have had to ally with each other and with animation or effects houses, either through merging or forming partnerships.

Animation producers still look to outside postproduction houses for certain services. For example, audio tasks and sound effects are rarely handled in-house by the studio, but are sent to post houses that are expert in these functions. Sound effects represent one area that has grown in importance in animation production; sounds are increasingly layered and created to be as realistic as possible, unlike in the past when cartoony, stock sounds were the norm.

Similarly, producers more frequently commission original musical sound tracks for their productions, rather than relying on existing songs. This has long been the case in film, but it is starting to occur in television, especially in the case of creator-driven series on cable networks, and in the gaming industry. All of this increased sophistication in sound and music takes time and costs money, although technological advances have made the job easier, particularly when it comes to editing. Database management allows sound engineers and editors to store and retrieve archived sounds more easily; most music and sound are done digitally, although analog continues to have a place in some productions.

Animation producers who have a familiarity with the postproduction process will save time and money by being able to give instructions in such a way that the two parties can communicate effectively. Animation executives who understand postproduction will also realize the importance of getting the project to the post house on schedule; post often is viewed as a place to make up time, but, in fact, condensing the schedule during this phase can cause problems that will lead to a late delivery of the finished

Exhibit 9.1

Checklist of Potential Work-for-Hire Animation Projects

Commercial animation

Television commercials (30- and 60-second)

In-theater commercials

Internet commercials and banners

Home video trailers

Entertainment

Interstitials

Subcontracting for films, videos, and television series

Online entertainment for various clients

Motion graphics for e-mail

Real-time animation for live productions

DVD extras

Special effects

Films

Television

Video/DVD

Commercials

Effects for animated productions

Theme-park ride films

Gaming/software

Game development

Cinematics

Opening sequences

Casino games

Educational software

Interactive storybooks

Corporate

Web sites

Training

Demonstrations for sales purposes

Medical and science

Courtroom

Architecture

Manufacturing simulations

Animation in premiums (e.g., entertainment with product placement)

Broadcast design and titles

Overall branding

Program opens

Film opens

On-air IDs and logos

Titles

Other

Music videos

Concert background video

Postproduction tasks involving animation

product. (This is especially true with special effects in live-action productions.) Many post houses penalize their customers for shortening the time allotted; these penalties are written into their client contracts.

Animation professionals hired by post houses include 2D compositors, colorists, editors, CG artists, and those with experience in Web site, DVD, CD-ROM, and multimedia development. Several postproduction houses specialize in serving the animation industry; for example, Screenmusic, a sound and music design specialist, and Vitello Productions, which does music and picture editing, each attribute 90 percent to 95 percent of their work to projects completed for animation studios.

10

Personnel and Budgeting for Contract Work

In many respects, personnel requirements and budgetary issues related to work-for-hire projects are similar to those for proprietary productions. Salaries, types of jobs, and job descriptions are similar in each sector, for example, while the basic components of and methods of developing a budget are the same. (See chapter 2 for more on animation personnel and chapter 3 for more on budgeting. Both focus on proprietary projects, but much of the information applies to the contract sector as well.)

One key difference between work-for-hire and proprietary productions is that in the latter the producer must handle all aspects of the production, from accounting, to distribution, to financing. It must hire or retain accountants and marketers as well as storyboard artists and animators, not to mention worry about financing and distribution. In a work-for-hire situation the animation or effects house is responsible for only the animated or effects portion of the job. This difference means that budgeting and personnel decisions for a given project are narrower, focusing only on the services being handled by the studio.

PERSONNEL REQUIREMENTS

As with proprietary productions, personnel requirements for work-for-hire jobs vary depending on the nature of the project. Handling all the special effects for an entire film can occupy many or all of a studio's artists, while animating a character in a commercial may require a small team.

Film and Television Special Effects

Live-action films and television shows, whether emphasizing realism, fantasy, or a combination of the two, contain a large number of effects and require a large staff of effects animators. On Warner Brothers' film *Cats and Dogs* effects house Rhythm & Hues produced 450 shots using almost 200 technicians, animators, designers, sculptors, and compositors, representing a large percentage of the company's permanent staff. Similarly, *The Lord of the Rings: The Fellowship of the Ring* (New Line, 2001) featured close to 500 visual effects shots, about 90 percent of which were completed by WETA Digital. Like *Cats and Dogs, Fellowship* required more than 200 technicians and artists, including key frame animators, modelers, computer artists, digital paint artists, compositors, motion editors, and software engineers. In the early 2000s *A.I.* featured 200 effects shots, *Panic Room* 50, *The Time Machine* 249, and *Queen of the Damned* 114. *Star Wars: Episode I* featured effects in virtually every frame, for a total of 2,000 shots.

Most television series historically avoided using special effects—with certain exceptions, such as science fiction—due to the high cost, but that has changed. In some cases effects are more cost-effective than live-action, depending on the desired result: shows depicting extinct animals or other scenarios that are impossible to film and those containing photorealistic scenes that would put actors at risk are examples. Television series can feature 100 or 200 shots per episode, with 30 shots completed in three days often being a typical schedule for a series.

The Discovery Channel's *Land of the Mammoth* (2001) included 100 CG shots accounting for 23 minutes of the finished production. The work was completed by a team of eight in less than four months at London's Skaramoosh Design. On another Discovery Channel program, *When Dinosaurs Roamed America* (2001), a team of 20 animators completed 500 CG-animated effects. Because of delays during preproduction, Meteor Studios of Montreal had five and a half months to deliver the scenes, a very compressed schedule for that number of photorealistic shots.

Animated films and television shows contain special effects as well (e.g., rain, lightning, and gunfire), which can be sourced out but are almost always done by the same animation studio producing the character animation and environments.

Commercial Animation and Effects

Live-action commercials, like entertainment productions, employ a large number of special effects, particularly to create photorealistic situations that cannot occur in life (e.g., pigeons doing the wave at a sports stadium) or scenes that would be too expensive to film live (e.g., a truck driving on a hard-to-reach rocky peak in Utah). Animated effects are also used as a stylistic tool to make commercials stand out from their competitors.

The number of people involved in the production of a commercial varies, depending on how complex the animation or effects are. Including personnel from the agency, client, animation or effects studio, and postproduction house, as well as voice actors and musicians, the number can easily reach 30 people working over a three- or four-month period on a 30-second spot. The number of those devoted to animation varies. In 2000 a Kellogg's commercial done in 2D animation required three animators; an MCI Worldcom spot that combined animation and a live background took close to 40 animators including keys, assistants, and effects specialists.

One live-action spot with special effects had the following credits:

- o the advertising agency (which supplied the creative director, copywriter, art director, and producer)
- o a commercial production company (director, director of photography, head of production, executive producer, production manager, and producer for the live-action portions)
- o a post house (executive producer for postproduction, Flame artist)

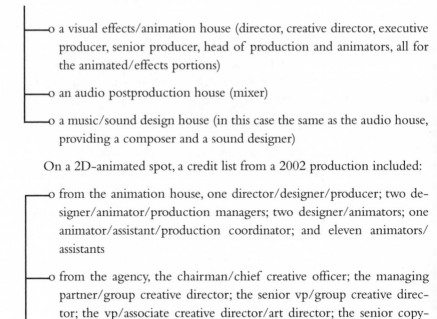

o a visual effects/animation house (director, creative director, executive producer, senior producer, head of production and animators, all for the animated/effects portions)

o an audio postproduction house (mixer)

o a music/sound design house (in this case the same as the audio house, providing a composer and a sound designer)

On a 2D-animated spot, a credit list from a 2002 production included:

o from the animation house, one director/designer/producer; two designer/animator/production managers; two designer/animators; one animator/assistant/production coordinator; and eleven animators/assistants

o from the agency, the chairman/chief creative officer; the managing partner/group creative director; the senior vp/group creative director; the vp/associate creative director/art director; the senior copywriter; the group head/senior executive producer; and the assistant producer

o from the visual effects house, two production managers and a technical director

o from the audio post and music/sound design house, two mixers, two production assistants, one composer/arranger, and one sound designer

As is evident from these rosters, personnel involved in commercial animation production must be flexible; many assume several roles at different times depending on the needs of the production.

The time required to produce a commercial varies depending on the project's specifications and the number of people assigned to it. The stop-motion animation Nissan "Toys" ad (animated for agency TBWA Chiat/Day by Will Vinton Studios in 1997), in which two dolls drive a toy car around the house on a date, involved a four-week shoot (including, as is the case on many productions, overtime) by five animators using six sets.

Another stop-motion spot, for Brisk Ice Tea, combined live-action filming, puppets, stop-frame animation, and CG animation. It took six months to complete, including six weeks to film the puppets. Background characters (a crowd of 40 puppets involved in a riot) were done in CG, with compositing by post house Quiet Man and stop-motion and CG animation by Loose Moose.

Gaming and Online Animation

Interactive titles range from multimillion-dollar video games whose budgets rival those of feature films to simple educational CD-ROMs. The latter might include a small team of animators working for a few weeks, while the former would require a bigger staff, albeit nowhere near the size for a similarly budgeted film.

The credits on *Barbie Pet Rescue,* a 3D-animated CD-ROM from Mattel, included a creative director, five game designers, four programmers, four 3D modelers, one writer, eight animators, one music composer, three sound editors, two producers, one project designer, and a game development company. Several of the tasks overlapped, with a single person performing several functions; for example, the creative director was also one of the game designers.

Another title, *Baby Smartronics,* a computer-based educational toy distributed by Fisher-Price, involved one creative director, one art director, one senior designer, one senior engineer, two programmers, one writer, six animators, two composers, one lead sound designer (also one of the composers) and three sound designers (including the other composer), one multimedia coordinator, one executive producer, one producer, one project manager, one educational consultant, and a project design and development company.

Even if a software title is not animation-driven, it still can incorporate a lot of animation. A *Monopoly* interactive computer game, which emulated the gameplay of the board game, contained more than 800 animations that pop up on screen to provide information and an entertaining break in gameplay. This type of project requires a small staff devoted to the animation portion.

While these types of educational CD-ROMs and Web site projects are simple, there are more advanced interactive projects, mainly in the video game sector. For example, a clay-animated adventure title, *The Neverhood,* produced by DreamWorks Interactive in 1996, contained more than 50,000 frames of animation. Such a title needs a large staff to complete the entire production. A company like DreamWorks might farm out some sequences to outside contractors, although it is likely much of the work would be kept in-house.

Interactive animation also extends to Web sites, including basic animations for a corporate site to webisodic entertainment for an entertainment-driven destination. Most of these projects are created in Flash animation and require small groups, or even a single animator, to complete. Using a more sophisticated 3D application could increase the size of the production team. In many cases, animation projects for Internet use are completed by in-house corporate Web designers, the entertainment companies running the site, or outside producers that own the property and license it to the site. In some cases, however, contract studios are hired to do the job. A corporation without an in-house animation team might hire a freelancer or contract with an animation studio, for example, although its Webmaster and staff may have the skills to do simple animation.

Exhibit 10.1
Sample Credit Lists for Work-for-Hire Animation Productions

2D all-animated commercial

1 agency producer, 1 art director/group creative director, 1 copywriter, 1 designer, 1 animation director/producer, 1 head animator/production manager, 5 animators/assistants, 1 executive producer of digital services, 1 lead compositor, 3 compositors/colorists, 1 composer, 1 sound producer, 1 mixer.

3D CGI commercial with live backgrounds

1 creative director/lead Henry artist*/on-set visual effects supervisor, 1 executive producer, 1 visual effects supervisor/on-set visual effects supervisor/Inferno artist, 1 Inferno artist, 4 Henry artists, 1 Mac graphics designer, 2 rotoscope artists, 4 CGI animators, 1 senior producer, 2 producers.

CG effects for live-action film (effects portion only)

2 visual effects supervisors, 2 visual effects producers, 1 visual effects editor, 1 additional visual effects editor, 1 associate visual effects supervisor, 1 visual effects production manager, 1 visual effects plate supervisor, 1 visual effects line producer, 1 visual effects match mover, 3 visual effects coordinators, 2 previsualization editors (8 companies for visual effects in total), 1 special effects supervisor, 2 special effects floor supervisors, 1 special effects workshop supervisor, 8 senior special effects technicians, 1 special effects modeler, 8 special effects modelers, 1 second unit special effects floor supervisor, 1 second unit special effects senior technician, 4 animatronic engineers, 1 supervising modeler, 1 senior modeler, 1 model unit supervisor, 1 model build unit coordinator, 1 model director of photography, 1 first assistant director of models, 2 model unit coordinators, 2 senior workshop technicians, 1 senior special effects technician, 2 senior modelers, 35 modelers, 4 model sculptors, 2 graphic artists, 1 3D-motion-control previs supervisor, 1 3D-motion-control previs, 3 sculptors, 4 key animatronic model designers, 17 animatronic model designers, 4 fabricators, 1 sculptor, 1 mold maker, 4 sculptor/modelers.

Note: Some credits may overlap, with one person performing more than one task.
*A Henry artist is a specialist on a type of digital visual effects machine.

Other Contract Animation

The variations on the types of animation projects that can be outsourced to animation houses on a work-for-hire basis range from music videos, corporate presentations, and training films to home video projects and cyberhosts. Some of these are simple, requiring one to a half-dozen animators, while others are complicated and rival the more complicated commercial spots, or even an entertainment or gaming production.

Compensation

Payment for animation personnel involved in contract work is similar to that for those producing proprietary projects. Most studios work on both contract and proprietary projects and use the same animators for both, which leads to equity in pay. (See chapter 2 for more detailed information on payment.) Animators on low-budget proprietary projects may take a cut in pay, however, if they believe in the project and are getting some nonfinancial benefit from working on it. In contract work all the costs are covered by the client, so animators usually don't reduce their salaries. Budgets differ from project to project, of course, but salaries are not often one of the elements that will be slashed to lower the budget. If small companies or independent freelancers want to secure a project that has a very small budget, however, they might think about receiving compensation below their usual rate.

Most studios use a combination of staffers and freelancers for contract projects, just as in entertainment, keeping a lean operation on a full-time basis and hiring more people as needed. Payment for staffers is on a salary basis, with the salary varying depending on the expertise and specialty of the worker. (Chapter 2 outlines some of the salary ranges typical of different animation positions.) Freelancers, who can comprise the bulk of the credits for an individual project during busy times for a studio, are paid by the hour or sometimes by the job.

BUDGETS

The basic components of a budget for a contract project, and the essentials of developing a budget, are the same as those used for a proprietary animation production (outlined in chapter 3). As noted earlier, the scope of a commercial, effects, or other work-for-hire job is usually narrower, since most studios are responsible for just one aspect of the production (animation only, special effects only, or just a few sequences of either of these), rather than for assembling and budgeting for the entire project.

The essentials are the same, however. Clients give their service studios as much detail as possible about the specifications of the projects. The studios then simultaneously work out a creative approach to the commercial or effects, including storyboards in some cases, and develop a budget to match their approach. They analyze the project and break it into its components, including how many animators and other personnel are needed and how many hours they will devote to the project, as well as any supplies, equipment rentals, software purchases, and other costs, including a contingency premium. (The budget then becomes the main basis for pricing the project; methods of pricing will be discussed in chapter 11.)

It's important to be realistic when estimating costs on a work-for-hire project, as in the proprietary world. Padding the project could cause a studio to lose the job, since its bid will be higher than those of its competitors; estimating too low might secure the job, but if actual expenses turn out to be higher than budgeted it will cause problems in both the short and long term. If the studio's contract with the client makes the studio responsible for overbudget costs, overruns would cut into the studio's profit or result in a loss. If the contract allows the studio to charge the client for overruns, the studio's profit margin will be safe but its relationship with the client will be harmed, and it won't be able to expect any repeat work.

When doing commercial spots the animation company works directly for the advertising agency's creative director (although it may have contact with the client on creative matters) and submits bids and invoices to the agency. Traditionally, advertising agencies have been paid a commission of 15 percent on production and media costs; in other words, they mark up all the actual costs associated with the animation studio, service houses, and other subcontractors. The 15 percent markup represents their profit.

Things have changed from this historic norm, however, with agency compensation sometimes based on a fixed hourly rate agreed upon before the project begins rather than on actual costs. When this is the case the agency must try even harder to keep expenses in check. As a result, animation companies' profit margins can take a hit as agencies look for lower bids. The actual costs that go into creating the budget remain the same; the only place to skim off the final bid is in the profit margin. Animation houses must then be even more vigilant during production to ensure that actual costs do not exceed budgeted forecasts.

According to an annual survey by the American Association of Advertising Agencies (AAAA), the average total production cost of a 30-second commercial (including live-action and animated spots) in 2000 was $332,000, versus $343,000 in 1999; 68 percent of all commercials were 30 seconds in length. The cost of animation used in commercials dropped 12 percent from 1999 to 2000, as animation houses' fees were lowered and budgets squeezed.

A yardstick for special effects budgets, whether for commercial or entertainment, has been that one minute of high-quality digital effects costs $1 million, on average, with photorealistic effects generally costing more than stylized. (Of course, actual budgets can deviate far from this average, depending on the specifications of the job.) Photorealism requires more rendering and shading than effects intended to look like effects, which requires more time. The 20 minutes of special effects that created the dragon Draco in the film *Dragonheart* (Universal, 1996) cost about $20 million.

As was noted in chapter 9, effects studios are relying mainly on off-the-shelf software instead of developing their own proprietary solutions, which is keeping costs down for individual films and for the industry overall. On the other hand, clients expect more and more in terms of effects, which keeps budgets on a par with historic averages (or even higher), albeit with more delivered for the money.

When budgets are tight, some studios are leery of green-lighting effects-heavy pictures, even though these tend to be the ones that generate top box office results. (The top five films of 2002 were *Spider-Man, Star Wars: Episode II, Harry Potter and the Chamber of Secrets, The Lord of the Rings: The Two Towers,* and *Signs,* all relying on a significant number of special effects; some featured effects shots in almost every frame.) Other producers will opt to use more crowd-pleasing special effects in their pictures, looking for ways to cut costs elsewhere. For example, they might use nonstar actors in key roles, transferring the money they would've paid a star to the effects budget instead.

Special effects can comprise a significant amount of the budget of effects-heavy films like those mentioned above, easily accounting for $5 million to $10 million of the production cost. Even modestly budgeted films have some special effects. One 2000 live-action film with a budget of $30 million spent an estimated $290,000 for special effects (including the creation of snow); $40,000 for visual effects (such as a background that was matted in digitally); and $50,000 for titles. All three together accounted for about 1 percent of the budget.

As a rule, studios tend to wait as long as possible to make assignments for effects production, shrinking the time allowed for this portion of the post-production process while not increasing the budget. It is better for the budget and the final result to bring in an effects company during development, however, since the effects vendor can help the producers maximize the results and minimize the budget if they're involved early.

FLEXIBILITY

The cyclical nature of the service animation industry, client budget cuts, and increased client demands have all contributed to the need for flexibility on the part of contract studios. As in any type of animation work, contingencies arise despite everyone's best efforts; the better a studio can deal with these emergencies, the more profit they'll earn and the more work they'll generate from satisfied clients.

On DreamWorks's film *Small Soldiers* (1998), which combined live-action and CG-animated toy soldiers, the original agreement with the effects house, ILM, called for 175 character shots. During the production that number grew to over 250 character shots, but with the same six-month deadline in place. All told, at the peak of production 90 ILM staffers were working on the film. These types of situations call for flexibility.

One method of maintaining this flexibility is to keep a lean operation and rely on freelancers for peak periods, as is discussed further in chapter 12. A midsize studio with 160 to 170 employees, for example, can usually take on jobs with as many as 150 shots, but when more than one project comes in at the same time, deadlines loom, or specifications change, it must hire freelance people to supplement its staff.

As touched on in chapter 9, another strategy that gives clients and contractors additional wiggle room in budgeting for special effects or other animation production is to hire several companies for a single large job rather

---

Exhibit 10.2

Budget Ranges for Selected Work-for-Hire Projects

Thirty-second commercial, live-action/animation combination: $250,000–$400,000

Animated effects in a live-action feature film: $300,000–$50 million

Animated interstitial for a corporate Web site: $1,000–$10,000

Note: These samples are guidelines only. Individual projects may fall far outside these ranges, depending on complexity.

---

than relying on just one effects house. Sometimes the clients drive this move as they look for ways to compress the effects schedule without breaking the budget. Other times the animation or effects houses take the initiative in banding together to bid for a single job. This allows them to secure contract work on projects they'd have no chance of winning alone.

11

Soliciting and Pricing Contract Work

To keep a steady stream of service work flowing into a studio, its executives must build and maintain a reputation as a high-quality, cost-effective provider of animation. One key element of this strategy is to implement an ongoing marketing program that introduces the studio's name in the marketplace, keeps it at the top of potential clients' minds, and encourages the flow of incoming projects and bids.

Once jobs start to find their way into the studio, studios must be able to create attractive concepts, put together realistic bids, and develop professional pitches. This not only helps the studio secure the project in question but also positions it as a reputable contractor over the long term. Word, both positive and negative, travels fast within the animation industry and within the industries that hire animators. Even if a studio doesn't end up being assigned a particular job, its professionalism will open doors for future opportunities.

A critical element of this professionalism is the bid preparation process. A bid must not only take into consideration the studio's costs and desired profit margin but also be fair to the client. Delivering a fair bid in a timely manner suggests that the studio possesses the ability to complete the job in much the same way.

CREATING AND MAINTAINING A PROFILE

Making sure potential clients know what services a studio provides, what projects it has completed successfully, and how it stands out from its competitors will spark those clients to think of the studio when projects become available. While studios can and do pitch their services aggressively on a one-to-one basis, they need to build a certain amount of name recognition in order for word of potential projects to reach them.

The steps animation houses can take to raise their profile among ad agency creative directors, special effects or technical directors, corporate clients, and other potential customers are much the same as those used by studios to market their proprietary productions to trade partners. (These are discussed in chapter 6.) But the message and the recipients of that message are different.

The choice of venue—whether a trade show, an association, or a magazine for advertising or publicity—should be tailored to the appropriate customer. For example, an ad in the trade publication *Advertising Age* or attendance at the trade show Siggraph will raise one's profile among those in a position to hire animation houses for commercials or effects, respectively; appearing at a film festival or home video convention, which is a key strategy for a proprietary property, would not do much for studios mining for contract work. The themes put forth in marketing materials should be tailored to these customers as well.

Some of the marketing materials used by studios going after contract work include:

- a demo "reel" (now most commonly distributed on CD-ROM rather than VHS tape)

- a list of past clients

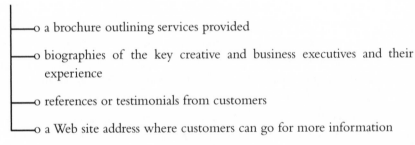

- a brochure outlining services provided
- biographies of the key creative and business executives and their experience
- references or testimonials from customers
- a Web site address where customers can go for more information

These materials can be distributed at trade shows, sent in mailings to a roster of potential customers, or made available in response to requests for information and bids.

The demo disk is an especially important tool. It contains three to five minutes' worth of short samples of past work (with the clients' permission). The disk is not meant to be encyclopedic; it is intended to represent the work the studio has produced, showing a variety of styles and content. While emphasizing diversity, it should also suggest the styles for which the studio is most known. The demo disk serves as a way to convey the studio's brand image and make it stand out from the competition.

Web sites have become an important tool in the marketing process. They allow a studio to post a comprehensive overview of the studio and its work and more fully portray its mission and focus. Potential customers can browse as much or as little of the site as they want. Written materials are useful because they provide a quick snapshot and introduction; the Web complements these by letting the client study the shop in depth before contacting it.

The Web also serves another valuable purpose. It allows potential clients to discover a studio without the studio making a first contact. Many clients that have animation projects in the works research the Internet, typing "animation studio" or another keyword into a search engine and browsing the sites of listings that are relevant. The clients can use this process to create a short list of studios to contact for a bid.

PITCHING AND SOLICITING BIDS

When an ad agency or other client needs to solicit bids for an animation project, it has several approaches at its disposal: search the Internet and call a short list of houses found there; call one or more animation reps with whom it has worked before and ask them to send information, including demo disks for studios it feels make a good fit with the parameters of the job; check its files for materials it has received by mail from new studios and contact those that seem appropriate; or call studios with which it has worked before and ask them to bid on the job. While all of these are used, the last option is the most common.

In some cases a client may approach only one studio for a bid, particularly if it has worked well with that house in the past. Or it might approach two to five different studios in a competitive bidding process. The latter route not only allows the client to compare the bids from a financial viewpoint but also lets them compare the creative approaches each studio will take on the project. According to a study by the AAAA, a group representing advertising agencies, 54 percent of 30-second commercials produced in 2000 were the result of bids from single companies, while the remaining 46 percent were multiple bid.

If the client has a good idea of what it's looking for in terms of animation, it will send storyboards to the studio or studios and have them bid on the creative elements as set forth in the boards. In other cases, however, the client might decide it wants to use animation but rely on the studio(s) for an injection of fresh ideas. In that case it will leave the creative approach open (within certain parameters) and let the bidding studios provide sketches or storyboards that explain how they would tackle the problem.

Either way, studios who are competing for the project should ask for as much information as possible from the client in order to create a bid that's realistic and tailored to its needs. Having a script or a treatment of a project may be enough to create a sketch of the vision and a rough final bid, especially for a repeat customer, but it leaves a lot to chance. Storyboards are the central reference for creating a pitch presentation, but any other reference material is helpful, from concept art to reference books. Of course, the more flexible the client is about the look of the project, the less information will be available up front.

Many studios are aggressive about pitching. Rather than waiting for storyboards or requests for bids to come to them, their account executives regularly call potential clients to see what projects they have coming up, positioning themselves to be asked to bid. In addition, if they get wind of an upcoming project through the industry grapevine or at an industry gathering, they take the initiative in approaching the client. Because of the intense competition for jobs, animation studios are spending significant time and money on pitching, creating expensive presentations, and bidding on more jobs. The studios spend these resources knowing there's no guarantee they'll end up with the assignment.

Some studios have the funds (and are willing to spend) to create sophisticated and expensive pitches, which raises the bar and the expense level for the whole industry. This is especially true when the industry is slow and requests for bids are rare. A presentation that summarizes the studio's vision for the project, complete with storyboards, design boards, and rough animation, can cost tens of thousands of dollars. (Of course, not all jobs are big enough to warrant this kind of upfront expenditure.)

Many studios devote 20 percent of their time to pitching and 80 percent to working on projects already secured. It's important to spend enough resources on the pitch process to ensure that work continues to come in, without sacrificing any projects already in-house. There is a limit, however. If a studio's expertise doesn't fit with a potential job in terms of style, for example, it would be a waste of time to dedicate financial and human resources to trying to secure the project. Some agencies send boards or requests for bids to a wide range of studios rather than narrowing the roster down to a short list of appropriate studios first. This haphazard approach results in some studios spending time pitching a job they have little chance of gaining or that doesn't fit well with its capabilities. Studios must learn to say no.

If the studio is assigned a project, it often can include the cost of the pitch in its fee to the client, within reason. With the amount of money spent on pitches rising, it is often not possible to pass along the entire amount. In fact, some animation houses do their pitches for free as an incentive to the client.

Pitching to existing or past clients is less expensive than going after new customers. The client already knows the studio's capabilities and can envision its ideas for the new job without a fancy or expensive presentation. At the same time, the studio's chance of winning the job is greater than for a brand-new client. A studio cannot rely on existing clients alone, however, and must pursue new customers if their projects are a good fit and the potential gain is worth the expense of pitching.

The title of the appropriate person to pitch at each client varies. At an ad agency the creative director is usually responsible for hiring animation houses. For films or television special effects the title might be technical director or special effects director. Houses wanting to create cinematics for a video game would approach a product development executive at the developer or publisher. The best way to find out exactly who to pitch is to call the company or check its Web site.

No matter how fabulous a studio's pitch presentation, sometimes factors beyond the studio's control play a role in the client's final decision. Existing relationships between clients and studios often determine who gets the final bid, for example; a network's sister animation company or a studio-owned effects house are favored if all other things are equal. Only when the fit between the client and the preferred studio is distinctly not right will other studios prevail. This situation is something to keep in mind when deciding whether to pitch a certain project to a client with such relationships in place.

As was noted in chapter 10, studios sometimes band together to bid for a commercial, special effects, or other contract project. Each handles certain parts of the job, but they bid as a team. A joint effort like this may help the studios win a job; together they can provide better, faster, and more cost-effective services than their competition. This strategy also helps spread the costs of the pitch itself and gives smaller studios a chance to participate in bigger projects they wouldn't be able to complete on their own.

PRICING

The process of setting a price for a bid takes place at the same time the creative brainstorming occurs, since the final price depends on the creative vision and its implementation. When a studio is preparing a bid for which it

---

Exhibit 11.1
Checklist of Marketing Techniques for Work-for-Hire Studios

Distribution of Marketing Materials

Demo disks

Client list

Biographies

Brochure or list of services

Web site (referenced on other materials)

Networking Opportunities

Trade shows and conventions for animation industry

Trade shows and conventions for client industries (advertising, special effects, corporate and professional)

Associations for animators and clients

Advertising and Publicity

Advertising in animation magazines

Advertising in client magazines (advertising, film, television, corporate)

Publicity campaigns targeting advertising and client publications

Events and parties

Press conferences

Contests and awards

---

has flexibility on the creative side, it will try to maximize the visual quality while minimizing price, finding the balance that offers the best value for the customer while meeting its needs creatively. Even when the specifications are set by the customer, there is some give-and-take as far as how to achieve the client's vision in a cost-effective manner.

There are two main ways to prepare a bid. A firm bid is when the animation house estimates the budget for the shoot, component by component, including a contingency, and marks up the total to add a profit margin, usually of 15 percent. That final number becomes the bid. Actual costs are then monitored to ensure the studio can charge that amount and still make a profit.

A preliminary bid outlining the costs and the markup usually is submitted first, so the client can approve each component and decide where it wants to cut if its budget dictates a lower price for animation. Once the elements are OK, the final cost becomes the bid and is the amount invoiced. If production expenses exceed the budget, the animation house usually must eat the costs at the expense of its profit margins. In certain cases the two parties may agree up front that the client or agency is responsible for a certain precentage of overruns.

Another option is to use a cost-plus-fixed-fee, or "cost-plus" method, where each component is billed separately to the agency (e.g., effects, postproduction, 2D graphics, 3D graphics, cel animation, CGI animation), at actual cost. The studio's profit margin is stated as a flat fee (usually calculated as 15 percent on top of expected costs) and remains constant even if costs change during production. The animation house must provide a complete accounting of all the actual costs to the agency or client at the end of the job; the cost of this accounting is added to the bill. This type of bid is used mainly when there is a chance the specs of the job will change over time, or if certain aspects of the production aren't set in stone at the time of the bid. (In the firm-bid method any changes in specifications will affect the bid, which has to be renegotiated to account for the changes.)

Firm bidding is more common than cost-plus. The AAAA survey mentioned earlier found that, in 2000, 97 percent of 30-second commercials (including live-action) were bid out as firm bids, while only 3 percent were cost-plus. In both methods there has to be a provision for how much of the final cost is due if the project is cancelled once production is under way.

An alternative to final bid or cost-plus pricing, used mostly in postproduction, broadcast design, or special effects, is to charge an hourly or daily rate. In postproduction, for example, tasks can be segmented by the type of machine used, with each associated with its own hourly rate that is predetermined based on a calculation of average costs.

In this type of hourly pricing the services of a broadcast design animator might be billed at $150 to $200 per hour or a Web designer's at $300 per hour. Rates may be set depending on the type of project as well; an effects house might charge $900 per day for a computer game, $800 for a network television show, $1,500 per day for film effects, $600 for cable show effects, etc. These rates are calculated based on animators' salaries, corporate overhead, and other factors; charging any lower than $600 per day for any task is usually unrealistic. Animation and effects companies usually mix and match many tools, depending on the job at hand, which makes it difficult to segment the tasks or charge an hourly or daily rate.

In some cases a studio will come in with a final bid (fixed, cost-plus, or an estimate of total hours) that is high, but the client prefers that studio's approach over its competitors', or has only solicited one bid. The client will follow up by divulging what its budget for animation is and ask if the studio can alter its bid to work within that budget. If the studio cannot or chooses not to cut its price, the client can select one of the other bidders, or send out further requests for proposals.

During slow times many studios are willing to include some free services in their bids as an incentive for the client to select them for the job.

Before submission, the final bid, as calculated based on expected costs and time, needs to be weighed against what others in the market would be able to charge. Studios want to get the job and therefore are careful not to overprice—they are competing against other studios and, while money is not the only factor in customers' decision-making process, it's an important one—yet they also need a profit from each job so they can cover overhead and stay in business.

One problem that makes the pricing process even more difficult is that many companies tend to underbid, either due to inexperience or deliberately in order to get the job at any cost. In the latter case they know their estimates are too low and that they will either have to charge the customer for the overages later or use the job as a loss leader (a low-priced job that can be followed by profitable jobs later). Larger firms with many projects in the hopper can bid jobs at or below cost, letting more profitable projects assume more of the burden. This puts pressure on smaller shops, for which each job has to pull its own weight.

Even if all the bids are honest and realistic, the intensity of competition for each job leads bidders to cut margins as thinly as possible in the hope that their bid will be low enough to secure the project.

Exhibit 11.2
Pricing Methods for Work-for-Hire Projects

Fixed bid:

> Estimate expenses for the job in advance. Submit to client for approval of expenses. Total the approved list and add a markup (15 percent on average) for profit to determine the flat fee for the job. In advance, negotiate what happens in the case of overruns; the studio will usually have responsibility for over-budget costs unless they're due to changes in specs by client, but this varies.

Cost plus fixed fee:

> Costs are estimated up front for forecasting purposes, but client is billed for actual costs at the end of the job. (Accounting fees for creating an itemized list of expenses are included as one of the costs.) Studio adds a flat fee (usually equivalent to 15 percent of expected expenses), which remains constant even as expenses change. This method is used when there's a good chance costs will change or if specifications aren't finalized at the time of the bid.

Hourly or daily rates:

> Each task is billed at a flat rate for each personnel hour or personnel day required to complete the job. Rates are preset and calculated based on the studio's average direct, indirect, and overhead costs associated with the task. This procedure is most common for postproduction tasks, but may be used in other cases. In most animation and effects jobs, the tasks can't be separated easily and the amount of work done per day varies depending on complexity, so an hourly or daily rate is impractical.

ANIMATION REPS

Some houses involved in service work retain animation reps or agents to help them sell themselves to potential clients. (Many have their own full-time account executives to perform these duties.) Most reps focus on one region of the country, developing contacts with ad agencies and other clients in that area. Therefore, most studios will use several reps, such as one responsible for each coast and one for the Midwest. Some animation representatives or agents have offices throughout the country and can handle clients on a national basis, while some smaller firms have allied with others around the United States to form a national network. Reps are also located in major cities outside the United States.

Generally, agents who represent studios are called reps and pitch to potential clients, while those who represent individual animation artists are called agents and pitch to studios. But the names are interchangeable and both essentially perform the same duties. Commissions for this work vary, but range between 10 percent and 40 percent, with 10 percent to 15 percent being the most common. A 40 percent commission suggests that the rep performs additional duties, such as helping the animator or studio manage a career or business strategy, in addition to selling.

Some animation houses utilize commercial production houses (those that produce live-action commercials) to serve as their representatives. For example, Psyop, a New York city–based design-and-animation firm, used MTV Commercials to represent it in the United States for spot work. The relationship also gave the studio the opportunity to work with MTV Commercials directors, something that wouldn't have been possible under a traditional rep structure.

Some reps specialize in interactive content, music videos, or other sectors of the contract animation business, while others focus on commercials or special effects in one or all media. Many agents are positioned to provide full-service representation.

PART III
THE COMPANY

12

Overhead and Funding

Whether doing proprietary productions or work-for-hire projects, studios accrue certain costs that cannot be attributed to any specific job and therefore fall into the category of overhead. These include everything from general office supplies to accounting software to staff personnel assigned to a particular project. A portion of overhead is allocated to contract project bids and included in proprietary budgets.

Cash flow from operations is not necessarily stable, due to the ups and downs of the animation business, but overhead costs continue to accumulate each month, whether projects are in production or not. A studio's goal is for monthly cash flow to be high enough to sustain continuing operations and, if not, to have a cash reserve big enough to cover expenses when work is scarce.

In some cases studios seek outside financing to help cover cash deficits. They also look toward outside sources of funding when they want to invest in future growth. Adequate financing is especially necessary at the beginning of a studio's life, when there are few cash reserves and little cash flow to cover expenses. In fact, expenses are usually higher during the early phases of a company's life, when it is spending heavily on equipment, software, supplies, furniture, facilities, and other one-time expenditures. A studio must have adequate financing available at its launch to cover both early overhead costs, while operations are ramping up, and start-up investments. There are many examples of studios that failed within the first few years because cash was generated more slowly than expected and there was not enough money put away to sustain them in the meantime. Lack of financing is one of the leading reasons for failure in a studio's early years.

START-UP COSTS

Start-up costs can be significant, depending on the size and specifics of the studio. Mondo Media, an online entertainment company, spent more than $10 million on sales staff and infrastructure in its first year or so in business; HIT Entertainment launched its HOT Animation subsidiary in the United Kingdom at an estimated cost of $3.5 million in 1998. Toonz Animation India opened a new facility for $2 million in 1999.

The costs don't have to be that high, however. Many small 3D gaming and effects operations have started their digital studios for $250,000 to $300,000, which includes hardware and other equipment; initial overhead costs, including the founders' salaries and rent; and support staff including accountants and attorneys. (These studios often seek more financing, as much as $1 million to $2 million, soon after they launch, to cover early overhead expenses beyond the costs directly attributed to the start-up.) Small studios working on a shoestring have launched effects businesses for as little as $40,000.

If a company has signed contracts with clients in hand upon its launch, its revenues may be enough early on to reduce the amount of financing it needs. But for most studios it takes a while to generate client relationships and paying jobs, especially when the focus is on proprietary projects. In addition, early projects may be done at a low profit margin as the company tries to prove itself. This means it will need adequate funding to cover facilities, hardware, software, staff, and miscellaneous business expenses until revenues build.

Facilities

Small companies, with a few staffers working on PCs or Macs, won't need much studio space initially. When determining facilities requirements, however, these studios should think about whether they want to include room for expansion according to their business plan. In addition, they may need to plan space where freelancers can work when they come in for short periods during peak production times.

Most companies need more room on an ongoing basis than these small studios do. Foundation Imaging, a special effects and postproduction house, needed room for motion-capture and green-screen stages as well as animation, compositing, editing, and audio postproduction equipment. It opted for a 22,000-square-foot space. India's Colorland, a 3D animation studio, opened with a 60,000-square-foot facility for its staff of 330.

Nickelodeon built a 72,000-square-foot animation studio for its Nicktoons division in 1999 after announcing a $350 million financial commitment to animation and a production schedule of 600 episodes over five years. The studio was intended to house between 300 and 400 employees and included a recording facility, 175 work stations, 25 editing and screening rooms, three Avid-equipped editing suites, a theater with 80 seats, and an animation archive. Studios of this size can be expensive; Pixar's headquarters in Silicon Valley cost $88 million.

Equipment and Supplies

Software, hardware, and other equipment needs are dependent on the number of people planned for the studio in the short and long term, both permanent and temporary, as well as the types of animation to be produced and number of services offered.

Hardware In general, costs of computers and work stations are coming down and low-priced machines are becoming sophisticated enough for many high-quality animation applications. But the amount spent on hardware for an animation studio varies greatly. Some companies doing sophisticated 3D effects for films might spend $30,000 on each Silicon Graphics (SGI) work station, while a small video game developer might work on off-the-shelf PCs running Windows NT or Mac G4s, with each unit costing $2,000 to $3,000. The animation in the film *Waking Life* was produced on G4s; Pixar uses SGI work stations for its 3D-animated films and purchased 250 addition machines in 2001 for $7.5 million. Dream-Works's film *Spirit: Stallion of the Cimarron,* a 2D film, required more than 200 Linux-based work stations and servers to complete.

The average motion-capture system is priced at around $100,000 as of the early 2000s, with some lower-cost versions falling in the $20,000 to $80,000 range. Ink-and-paint stations run between $15,000 and $120,000, while video equipment to view progress on commercials combining live-action and animation might cost as much as $250,000 per unit.

While these examples represent just a small sampling of the equipment a studio might need—and the rapidly fluctuating prices associated with them—they show how quickly costs can mount up when a company tries to assemble a several-work-station studio or a hundred-PC render farm for CG animation. A full CG studio might require spending $2 million to $3 million on hardware, with each seat ranging from $10,000 to $15,000, as of the early 2000s.

These investments are not limited to the start-up phase either; studios have to keep up with the latest technology in order to stay competitive, and often want to expand with the purchase of additional equipment. China's Hong Ying animation studio, which had 1,200 employees in three locations as of the late 1990s, added 3D production capabilities to its 2D setup, requiring the purchase of 180 SGI work stations.

Sometimes the need for expansion comes suddenly as a result of one big job, rather than through a planned strategic move. When DreamWorks was producing *Shrek* for a 2001 release, it had to order over 40 additional Hewlett-Packard computers just four months before the film's scheduled release.

Software   According to the research firm Frost & Sullivan, high-end animation software for gaming, television, film, and modeling can retail for over $14,000, while low-end animation programs for personal computers, often used in corporate, training, and Internet applications, can cost as little as $89.

A few examples illustrate the variation in animation/effects software prices. (It should be noted that prices change constantly and vary depending on the retail outlet; these examples illustrate the variation in software costs rather than serving as a reference to actual prices. In addition, large studios may received discounted or wholesale prices, while smaller studios would usually pay retail.) As of early 2003:

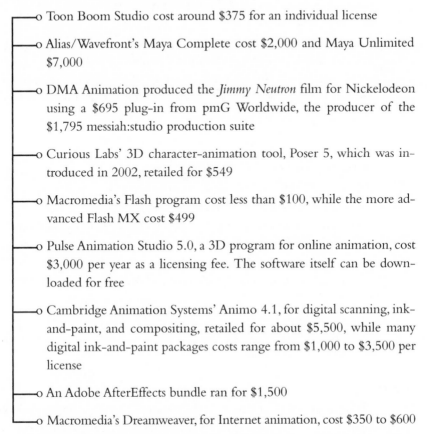

- Toon Boom Studio cost around $375 for an individual license

- Alias/Wavefront's Maya Complete cost $2,000 and Maya Unlimited $7,000

- DMA Animation produced the *Jimmy Neutron* film for Nickelodeon using a $695 plug-in from pmG Worldwide, the producer of the $1,795 messiah:studio production suite

- Curious Labs' 3D character-animation tool, Poser 5, which was introduced in 2002, retailed for $549

- Macromedia's Flash program cost less than $100, while the more advanced Flash MX cost $499

- Pulse Animation Studio 5.0, a 3D program for online animation, cost $3,000 per year as a licensing fee. The software itself can be downloaded for free

- Cambridge Animation Systems' Animo 4.1, for digital scanning, ink-and-paint, and compositing, retailed for about $5,500, while many digital ink-and-paint packages costs range from $1,000 to $3,500 per license

- An Adobe AfterEffects bundle ran for $1,500

- Macromedia's Dreamweaver, for Internet animation, cost $350 to $600

As these examples show, the costs add up when a studio starts buying everything it needs, including some of these packages and many others, to be a full-service animation provider. In addition, some companies, especially those involved in feature films, special effects, and gaming, develop their own unique software packages or plug-ins, which can cost millions of dollars. (These are often counted as part of the direct cost of a given production if they're developed in response to a need that arises during the project.) Disney created proprietary packages for *Atlantis, Tarzan,* and *Dinosaur,* which were used in combination with off-the-shelf software, including Alias/Wavefront's Maya and Pixar's RenderMan. Most studios rely primarily on off-the-shelf packages, however, which are flexible, reasonably priced, and don't require additional training.

In many cases studios will ultimately end up selling licenses for their proprietary packages to the industry as a way to recoup costs and add another revenue stream. This is what Pixar has done with RenderMan, now an industry standard for 3D animation. D'Ocon, an animation studio in Spain, spent eight years and $6 million developing a software system that it then offered to other animators.

In addition to software used to create animation or effects, studios need other packages in order to run their business. These include design and word processing, financial and accounting, and tracking and filing systems. Often, these are the same off-the-shelf packages that other businesses use, but in some cases they may be industry-specific.

Other Equipment, Supplies, and Services   While software and hardware comprise the bulk of equipment expenditures for start-up animation studios, they must invest in other equipment and supplies as well. These include paper and pens, backup disks or other media, desks, chairs and tables, office decor, lockers, break room equipment, assorted office supplies such as file folders, supplies dedicated to animation (such as celluloid for traditional 2D work), stationery and business cards, reference books and materials, shipping supplies, and any number of other items. Other start-up expenses involve services, such as the design of a logo and marketing materials, or the creation of a corporate Web site.

Labor

The third major component of the start-up cost, after facilities and equipment, is labor. As noted in chapter 2, labor is the largest single cost associated with any animation production. Where possible, labor hours are billed to clients or expensed directly against a proprietary project, but there are many labor hours that can't be linked directly to a specific project and therefore fall under overhead. This includes all permanent staff during down times, as well as support staff such as accountants and office managers. In addition, start-up financing has to cover all labor costs in the company's early months, until cash flow grows to a point where it can cover salaries, benefits, training, and related expenses.

The total number of employees at a studio can range from a few on up. Some boutique studios maintain a staff of just 4 to 10 people; small indies often operate with a complement of 35 to 60 full-time staffers; midsize to large independents frequently have employees numbering into the hundreds; and a handful of majors have over a thousand employees. Pentamedia, a 3D animation house in India, has 1,800 people on staff.

Exhibit 12.1
Checklist of Start-Up Costs

Accounting fees

Animation supplies

Break room equipment

Computer accessories and peripherals

Computer backup media

Facilities (rent or purchase) for office space, stages, etc.

Freelance costs

Furniture

Hardware/workstations

Legal fees

Marketing costs for brochures and advertising

Office supplies (pens, folders, etc.)

Phone/fax/e-mail/high-speed access

Printing costs for business cards and stationery

Shipping supplies and accounts

Software (animation and general office) including licenses

Start-up labor costs (salaries, benefits, taxes)

Systems setup costs

Utilities

Web site design and launch

Note: A studio may need to cover expenses beyond this list. Studios need reserves to cover expenses until operating cash flow can sustain them, which is usually at least six months to a year.

Most studios streamline their operations by keeping a small full-time staff and then bulking up with freelancers when work is heavy. As noted, this keeps overhead down and allows the studio to survive in lean times without losing the few critical people it keeps on staff. On the other hand, it means the studio has to hire from the pool of freelancers that's available at the time; while freelancers can be loyal to certain clients, they will take appropriate jobs wherever they find them in order to survive and may not be available when a favored customer calls.

Studios do what they can to keep a network of freelancers available when they need them. Dallas animation and design studio ReelFX Creative Studios keeps 16 staffers on the permanent payroll, supplementing them with a network of 80 animators worldwide, which it calls the Globally Networked Animation Team (GNAT). All are networked on the Web, allowing them to work from home on an as-needed basis.

Although the percentages vary, many studios—whether their full-time staff is 50 or 200—keep about half the number of people on staff permanently that they need during peak times. That is, a studio with 80 full-time staffers expands to 160 or more when the studio is operating at full capacity. The percentage of freelancers on board at busy times may be higher for very small firms and lower for very large. Larger firms tend to have slightly less drastic ups and downs in work flow, allowing them to handle the higher overhead. They also are more likely to have proprietary systems that make it beneficial to keep a fully trained staff on board even during lean times.

How permanent staff is configured depends on the studio, the services offered, and the average work flow. Some studios have staffers dedicated to certain clients, styles, or business segments; about a third of Will Vinton Studios' 100 to 200 employees in the early 2000s were devoted to commercial work. Others, especially smaller studios, try to maximize flexibility by moving animators from job to job and task to task.

The number of employees at a studio and their job descriptions may change as a company alters its strategic direction. When one 3D animation and effects house, Tigar Hare Studios, decided to move into more character animation, it added an executive producer, a character animation director, and a vice president of business development to its full-time roster. Similarly, a move toward using overseas studios for production tasks changes the configuration and number of employees needed at the domestic studio. One studio cut 19 animators, colorists, and digital artists (out of a total of 160 employees) when it began to outsource some of its animation production to Asian studios, leading to cost savings of nearly 50 percent. On the other hand, video game publisher Electronic Arts anounced in 2003 that it would build a studio in Los Angeles ultimately staffed by 500 people. This included 200 employees from other facilities and 300 new hires.

Exhibit 12.2

Permanent Staff Sizes for Animation Studios

Small studio: 4–10 people

Medium studio: 30–60 people

Large studio: 100–1,000-plus people

Note: This list represents a common breakdown. Many studios have total employees outside these ranges. At peak times the addition of freelancers may double the roster.

ONGOING OVERHEAD COSTS

As noted, overhead costs are ongoing expenses that are not directly attributable to a specific animation project. They include indirect labor, facilities maintenance (e.g. rent and upkeep), supplies, utilities, communication costs, and travel. Burdensome overhead costs are often a major contributor to the financial problems that lead animation studios to shut their doors.

Even the large studios have tried to cut overhead. While they used to have many full-time animators on board, for example, they let hundreds of their permanent staffers go in the early 2000s, opting to use freelancers instead.

FUNDING THE OPERATION

A studio needs funding to launch its operation, to maintain it on an ongoing basis, and to help finance growth. Funding for ongoing costs, direct and indirect, comes mainly from internal sources (cash flow and reserves), while start-up and expansion financing usually comes from a combination of internal funds and external investment. Any cost requiring a large up-front investment that the studio can't recoup right away is a candidate for external funding.

Internal Revenue Streams

Studios have a number of revenue streams and are looking for ways to increase that number. Those that do work-for-hire projects have steady income, albeit

---

Exhibit 12.3

Funding Sources for Start-Up, Growth, or Expansion

Internal Sources
> Ongoing operations
> Cash reserves
> Founders' contributions

External Sources
> Outside minority investors
> Allied minority investors (e.g., distributors or other synergistic companies)
> Majority investors, allied or outside
> Outright sale of studio to another party in return for funds
> Bank loans
> Bond sales
> Stock sales

---

with low margins and little potential for growth from fees for those jobs. Studios that participate in proprietary projects and coproductions, for which they either own all or part of the copyright, may reap a portion of several revenue streams associated with a given production. As noted in chapter 8, primary and secondary distribution channels, both international and domestic and in all media, as well as global ancillary products, can all bring in revenue to a studio in the form of advances and royalties.

It should be noted that any of these streams alone does not account for a significant amount of money. For example, the pool of royalties from a single licensing deal can be fairly small to begin with; after taking out agency commissions and sharing the income with all the other partners that have a stake, the final amount to the studio can be minimal. This is why studios look to create as many revenue streams as possible, so the cumulative total will be of significance.

Studios that own copyrights can receive additional revenues when third parties create new entertainment or media vehicles based on their underlying rights. Options, funds from exercised options, and royalties on future exploitation of these secondary entertainment vehicles all represent potential income streams. Other studios have set up lucrative side businesses that take advantage of their areas of expertise, such as acting as a licensing agent for outside properties or repping other studios for commercial work, which bring in revenues from commissions or fees.

Marketing and promotions are another source of revenue for proprietary properties. They mainly are intended to raise awareness for the property, and therefore indirectly boost revenues by increasing distribution and sales of core and ancillary products. But they also can bring in revenues directly. For example, a tie-in partner using a character in a consumer promotion pays the owner of that character a fee, which can be in the tens of thousands of dollars or even higher, depending on the popularity of the property.

As noted earlier, some studios generate income by selling technology. Id Software, creator of the video game franchise *Doom,* generated annual revenues of $20 million with a staff of just 15 to 20 employees in the early 2000s. This figure was a combination of sales of its games and 3D game engine licensing fees.

During a studio's start-up phase "internal funding" usually refers to the partners' personal bank balances. The first products of the Baby Einstein Company, which creates educational videos for infants, were produced in the creator's basement using her savings account. She brought the first video to market with almost no advertising or marketing support and, through word of mouth, earned $100,000, which she was able to parlay into four more videos. As of the early 2000s the franchise had sold more than 1.5 million video units.

External Funding Sources

There are several sources of external funding. They include attracting outside investors; being purchased by a larger company, which brings in an infusion of cash from the sale and possibly other financing; selling stock to the public; and securing a loan from a bank or other source.

Investors and Partners   Financial partners or investors receive an equity share in the company in return for adding funds to the studio's reserves. Investors may be silent partners, offering financial support but not dealing in the day-to-day operations of the firm. Or they may be knowledgeable about running a business and bring expertise as well as funds. Founders of animation studios tend to be well-versed in the creation and production of animation, but may need some help on the business side. Even silent partners closely monitor studio operations, and especially results, to ensure the security of their investment.

When bringing in a financial partner it is critical to define the roles of the investor and of the existing owners. The contract should spell out the details of who has ultimate decision-making power on creative, strategic, and financial issues; what each partner's role will be on a day-to-day operational basis; what each partner's financial interest (ownership) in the company will be; and what happens financially, operationally, and equitywise if one of the partners chooses to leave. As a rule, investors' control, particularly over strategic and financial issues, grows as their share rises. An investor with a 50.1 percent or more ownership stake is the de facto head of the company.

Most creators who start their own studios want to maintain strategic, operational, and financial control, even if they acknowledge their need for someone with business expertise to move the company forward. Therefore, if possible, they want to accept only as much funding as will ensure that their stake remains at 50.1 percent or more. The founders' proportion could be less if several partners are involved in the venture; as long as their share is greater than any other partner, they'll be able to maintain control. Id Software's founder owned 40 percent of the company, which gave him ultimate creative and financial control, since his two manager-partners jointly owned 50 percent of the operation.

The desire to maintain total control and 100 percent ownership may prevent success. An infusion of outside funds is often necessary to get the operation through the start-up phase and/or finance growth. While having partners often leads to wrangling over strategy and can be difficult on the ego at times, it may be the best or only way for a company to prosper, especially in the case of a smaller studio.

Potential investors can include companies that have a synergistic relationship with the studio. IMAX, the large-screen theater distribution company, owns 19 percent of 3D animation studio Mainframe Entertainment, whose help it intended to enlist to boost its 3D animation offerings. Hahn Film, a German entertainment company, sold a 25 percent stake to Constantin Film AG, a leading German film distributor. The deal not only gave Hahn increased distribution clout but also brought in funds so the company could more than quadruple its average film budgets to between $20 million and $30 million per film.

It can be risky for a studio to rely on a single investor for the bulk of its external funding. Glassworks, a U.K. postproduction house, counted video game publisher Eidos Interactive as a main financial backer. When Eidos pulled out of the partnership in 2000 the young company had to scramble to find another backer quickly so it could survive.

Sometimes investors can be financial institutions or other parties without entertainment-business expertise, in which case the interest is purely financial. Spanish studio BRB Internacional wanted to expand into new businesses and international markets in 2001, so it offered a 25 percent stake in the company to Portugal's Banco Espirito Santo de Investimento. Selling this one-quarter stake brought in significant funding without forcing management to reliquish decision-making control. Similarly, CinéGroupe in 2001 wanted to boost its production slate and move into more multimedia production, so it went to Québec's Société Générale de Financement for $14 million in equity capital to help it achieve these goals.

Banks and venture capitalists are uncommon partners in animation studios, however. They're looking for a large return (often at least ten times the amount of the investment) in a relatively short period of time (such as three to five years), something that is rarely possible in animation. In the late 1990s venture capitalists were willing to fund animation houses that provided content for online and off-line entertainment. But those investments proved to be bad risks; in many cases there was no return, as the content companies were unable to turn a profit before failing.

Mergers   An alternative to the partnership and investment relationships described above, which allow studio founders to remain majority owners, is to be bought or merged into a larger company. This was the case when the British entertainment broadcaster and distributor Granada International bought 75 percent of the U.K. animation company Cosgrove Hall Films in 2000. Such a deal causes the founders to lose majority ownership and ultimate control over decision making, although they may ostensibly have control over the studio's daily operations.

Studios generally consider this option only when the founders are ready to leave the company or let someone else take over its management, or when so much cash is needed that selling a minority ownership isn't enough to keep the company in business. In a few cases, it is simply viewed as the best way for the studio to achieve future growth, either because of the financial resources or the synergies the deal brings.

Such acquisitions or mergers can take several forms. The purchase may essentially involve the company's assets rather than its continuing operations, in which case the acquired company goes out of business and its assets, including intellectual properties, are transferred to the purchaser. (Company executives may join the acquiring company or not.) Or the acquired company can become a division of the parent, keeping its own staff and executives but being under the parent's control. It may assume the name of the parent company or keep its original name. While the acquisition allows the purchased studio to continue operations as usual, even under the same name and with the same staff, the acquiring company controls the purse strings and therefore ultimate decision-making power. In many cases the founders of the acquired company end up leaving because their vision and strategies don't match that of the new parent.

If a studio's management agrees to a merger as a way to raise funds, it must be certain that the acquiring company's vision for the future of its new subsidiary is in line with that of the founders. In addition, and most importantly, the founders must realize that they are giving up control of their own studio, and if the parent and subsidiary management disagree on issues in the future the parent will prevail.

Studio management must also feel that the merger meets their objectives as well as those of the acquiring company. Janex International, which designs, manufactures, and sells children's products, wanted to expand into the children's entertainment and education industry. It did so by acquiring Bright Anvil Studios, a 2D and 3D animation company whose clients included DreamWorks, Disney, Sony, and Warner Brothers in 2001. Janex got a controlling interest in the company, while Anvil received shares of Janex stock plus $500,000 in working capital and $150,000 in funds for production.

THQ, a gaming publisher, bought Rainbow Studios, a Phoenix-based animation and game developer, in 2002. The acquisition helped THQ internally develop more game titles, while providing Rainbow with funds that it would never be able to generate through its own operations. French producer Carrère purchased 51 percent of French animation house Les Armateurs in the early 2000s; that deal gave Les Armateurs over $70,000 in new capitalization, as well as marketing, distribution, and operational synergies. Les Armateurs's films are budgeted at between $5 million and $15 million each.

Nelvana's decision to allow itself to be purchased by Corus Entertainment was not an easy one, according to executives. But Corus owned Canadian broadcast channels, giving Nelvana more reliable domestic outlets for its programming. It also fit with Nelvana's recent strategy, which was to vertically integrate; it had purchased publishing companies including Canada's Kids Can Press, for example.

Potential synergies can be almost as attractive to the acquired company as the financial boon. TV-Loonland AG, a German entertainment company, acquired many companies in the late 1990s and early 2000s. As of 2003 it owned 65.1 percent of Saerom Entertainment, a Korean animation house, and 100 percent of Telemagination, a U.K. animation studio, as well as portions of several other production and distribution subsidiaries, an online company, and a merchandising operation. These acquisitions turned TV-Loonland into a vertically integrated organization with global reach. Many of the subsidiaries continue to operate independently, and all benefit from synergies with the parent company.

A controlling interest can range from 50.1 percent (or even less, if there are multiple ownership partners) to 100 percent. If the ownership advantage is slight, the minority partners can buy back a percentage of the majority owner's holdings with a relatively small amount of cash if things go wrong later. But it's hard to overcome a significant ownership advantage.

Once the decision has been made to put a studio up for sale or to search for majority investors, its executives should study their operations and decide whether they need to take steps to increase the company's value. When Danish company Egmont decided to focus on the Scandinavian market, it planned to sell its animation subsidiary, Egmont Imagination. Before putting the assets up for sale in 2002, it reduced the subsidiary's infrastructure and production slate, but kept the full distribution operation intact. It hoped these tactics would generate more interest from potential buyers.

Public Stock Offerings Going public by offering stock is another method of bringing in funds while retaining control of the company. Not many animation houses take this route—although several Internet content providers tried it during the bullish years of Web-based animation—but some multifaceted entertainment companies with animation among their primary businesses have gone public. TV-Loonland, for example, is listed on one of the German stock exchanges.

Initial public stock offerings can raise a significant amount of money, but being a public company is not without risks. Primary among these is that the value of the company goes up and down based on stockholders' sense of how the company will perform in the future. This means any company announcements can be followed shortly by a stock tumble (or a spike). The company must make many of its activities public, according to the laws of various countries, and it must be careful about how and when it announces its initiatives or plans. The fact that stockholders expect to see results every quarter has an influence on corporate strategy and day-to-day operations; executives feel pressure to take steps that will boost earnings immediately, even if these steps are contrary to what they believe is good for the company over the long term.

The risks of being a public company can be illustrated through examples. When video game developer Square took its company into filmmaking in 2001 its stockholders did not approve, believing that movies were too risky a venture. As a result Square's stock price fell 22 percent in one week. In 2001 Stan Lee Media, an online entertainment company that is now out of business, announced a $2.2-million round of financing that would help it stay alive while waiting for revenues to start coming in from theme park, film, and other exploitation deals involving its online-origin properties. But when the company's stock price fell to under $1 per share, its intermediate-term financing deal fell through, resulting in the shutdown of SLM.

Debt Some studios use debt as a means to secure a temporary influx of cash. They may take out a bank loan, which brings in funds but at the same time increases overhead costs, due to the expense of monthly debt repayment.

Other companies issue bonds. In 2000 Knightscove Entertainment, a Canadian film production company, issued bonds (backed by insurance) to raise $37 million. The start-up company planned to use the money to produce ten to twenty family films with budgets of $3 million to $10 million over four years; it intended to fund up to 70 percent of the production cost of each.

Exhibit 12.4

Potential Revenue Streams for an Animation Company

Work-for-hire project fees (flat fee or hourly)

Commercials

Special effects

Web sites

Corporate projects

Other flat fees

Options from third parties

Exercise fees for options (percent of budget)

Marketing/promotional fees

TV license fees (per episode)

Royalties (including advances and guaranteed minimums)

Merchandise licensing

Home video

Music CDs

Technology licensing

Internet distribution (fee per download)

Distribution fees/commissions from representing third-party properties

Home video distribution

Film distribution

Television distribution

Licensing representation

Back-end participation

Coproductions in all media

Studio films

Option/exercise of properties by third parties

Internet properties

Hewlett-Packard provided New Media Venture Partners, owner of Moon Crescent Studios, a digital-animation and live-action entertainment company, with a $17 million financing package that included $15 million in debt financing and a $2 million equity investment. HP also provided products and services to the company's subsidiaries; much of the debt was connected with the purchase of this equipment.

13

Strategy and Management

Managing an animation studio requires developing an overall business strategy for the company, as well as overseeing the day-to-day operations that keep it going.

Exhibit 13.1

Selected Strategic Considerations for an Animation Studio

Mission/Scope/Structure

    Focus

    Size/corporate structure

    Services and styles offered

    Geographic scope

    Customers served

    "Brand image"

Diversification/Balance

    Styles

    Territories

    Proprietary vs. contract work

    Target customer groups (e.g., special effects for advertising vs. film)

    Animation vs. nonanimation services (licensing, distribution, etc.)

Expansion

    Services

    Geographic reach

    New customer bases

Modes of expansion/growth

    Adding staff

    Purchasing a company

    Launching new offices/subsidiaries

    Strategic alliances

STRATEGY

It is important to set a strategy that outlines the financial and creative objectives for the studio in the short and long term. Creating a strategy involves summarizing the studio's goals in a mission statement (a short paragraph that states the studio's reason for being, around which all planning is focused); studying the studio's competition, analyzing their strengths and weaknesses, and positioning the studio to stand out; researching the characteristics and needs of the marketplace and deciding on which target audience to focus; listing financial and creative objectives for the next year, the next five years, and the next ten years; and outlining the concrete steps the studio will take to achieve these goals in terms of production, marketing, distribution, and pricing. Executives incorporate all of this into the studio's business plan, which they can refer to as they make specific business decisions over time.

Market conditions and the characteristics of a given studio evolve over time. Thus the strategy cannot be set in stone; flexibility is key to survival in today's competitive animation industry. Company executives should review their goals and strategy often, making revisions to reflect the changing landscape while remaining true to the core principles of the mission statement. Some companies review their strategies quarterly or even monthly, but most shoot for an annual review.

Many studios show their business plan to outside experts for input before they finalize it. These may be animation industry participants (but not direct competitors) or executives from allied industries. They may also be businesspeople who are not involved in animation but are well-versed in general marketing and business principles and can give the studio's executives a fresh perspective.

When setting up a studio's long-term strategy, it is also important to develop an exit plan. In other words, the company's founders should prepare for what will happen if one or more of the founders leaves the company or if the studio is sold or goes out of business. Areas to consider include details about remuneration and changes in creative and financial control. Many animation executives don't want to think of these topics during the optimistic early days of the studio, but things happen.

The Core Team

Part of strategic thinking involves deciding how large the core team should be and what personnel should comprise it. That most commonly means keeping the studio "lean and mean," with a small core group of permanent employees supplemented by freelancers, but the precise definition of "lean and mean" varies depending on the company and its objectives.

As noted in chapter 12, some companies have hundreds of employees, while others have a half dozen staffers. These smaller companies look to fill their permanent positions with people who have multiple skills or are willing to be trained and to be flexible when it comes to their daily responsibilities. With each project they may take on a different role. Larger companies or those that operate in a well-defined niche (e.g., special effects) may prefer to hire specialists.

Contrary to industry trends, companies still need to ramp up their full-time staff on occasion, such as when they add a new business or service, or if they find themselves with a constant heavy workflow over a long period and expect that level of activity to continue. Wild Brain, a full-service San Francisco animation shop, expanded its facilities by 10,000 square feet and doubled its roster of permanent employees to fifty in the late 1990s. It still enhanced its staff with thirty to fifty freelancers at times when the amount of work dictated such a course.

Balance

Strategic planning is a balancing act between focusing on and excelling at one aspect of the business—being known as the best at one style or type of project can bring in clients and partners—while offering a palette of services to appeal to customers looking for a one-stop shop. Being too specialized will reduce opportunities, while trying to be all things to all people can spread finite resources too thin and prevent the development of a "brand image."

Exhibit 13.2

Factors to Consider When Hiring an Animator

Education

Four- or two-year degree in animation

Four- or two-year degree in art

Four- or two-year degree in another subject

Certificate program

No degree but some courses in animation or art

Technical skills

Knowledge of and experience in common 2D software packages

Knowledge of and experience in common 3D software packages

Knowledge of and experience in both

Art talent

Strong demo disk

Strong art portfolio

Work experience

Staff positions at recognized studios

Feelance jobs with recognized studios

Internships or other work experience

No work experience but some familiarity with animation (e.g., through schooling)

Contacts

Active membership in animation associations

Attendance at animation conventions and trade shows

Notes: Studios give different weights to each of these categories depending on their needs. In general, art skills and the portfolio or demo disk mean more than technical skills or schooling. However, the stronger candidates are in each category, the more likely they are to be hired, and at a higher salary. Networking is not a job qualification but opens doors, since most hiring is done through referrals rather than want ads or other methods.

Studios must wrestle with the question of balance in many areas of business.

Customers and Type of Work   Some companies specialize in one style or genre of animation, or one type of client. A studio might focus on stop-motion animation, gaming, special effects, or commercial clients, for example. Shops with narrowly focused areas of expertise have become much less common than in the past; most companies prefer to position themselves to serve a wide range of client and partner needs, bidding on commercial and entertainment work, offering a range of styles, and creating everything from direct-to-video productions to webisodic series.

Film Roman, best known for television production, expanded into commercials and into Internet production and distribution in the 2000s, while B.A.T. Produçoes of Brazil, which historically worked in commercial production for television, spread into long-form programming as well as Internet games and entertainment. A digital animation and effects studio, Lost Boys, specialized initially in commercials, TV series, and effects; when it moved into gaming, that sector quickly accounted for close to 20 percent of the company's revenues.

Studios today see themselves as content providers, not creators of film animation or advertising spots. Some areas lend themselves more to specialization—special effects and gaming, for example—but many studios have tried to diversify. In the past, commercial work tended to be a specialty, with some studios focusing only on that area of business. As of the early 2000s, most commercial studios have sought work in long-form entertainment, webisodics, or effects. Few studios can specialize exclusively in sectors such as Flash animation, although some, such as Unbound Studios, focus primarily on creating animation and games for the Web.

Being positioned to provide several types of animation and serve multiple client categories helps smooth out the natural ups and downs of the business. When the commercial production industry is slow there may be a backlog of animated or effects-heavy films in the major studios' production pipelines. There's no standard formula for how a studio should balance its resources, however. One Dallas-based animation studio spent 80 percent of its time on commercial work as of 2001, with the remaining 20 percent devoted to long-form entertainment. Atomic Cartoons, a Canadian studio, started life as a 100 percent traditional 2D animation house, moving to 50 percent Flash and 50 percent traditional by its second year and to 60 percent Flash by its third year, 2001.

Even within one sector of the entertainment industry, most studios are diversified. An MPAA study showed that, in 2001, of $31 million in total revenues associated with film releases (live-action and animated), 40 percent was related to home video releases, 31 percent to television licenses, 18 percent to box office revenues, and 10 percent to pay TV. All media contribute revenues, not just the medium where the property began.

This trend toward diversification has affected postproduction shops, as well, where companies offer multimedia, editorial, and graphic services of all types to clients from the commercial, corporate, broadcast, and film sectors. Meanwhile, companies that have traditionally focused on production services, including Asian studios, have expanded to offer development and preproduction functions such as storyboards, comp drawings, character design, and animatics.

Some studios focus on one area of expertise but diversify within that area. Aardman Animations, for example, is best known for stop-motion work, especially short films and commercials. It continues to specialize in stop-motion using Plasticine, but has expanded into feature films, music videos, and title sequences, as well as online entertainment.

Proprietary Versus Contract Work   As has been noted, most studios balance contract work, which brings in low-margin but steady revenues, and proprietary properties, which offer greater control and profit potential, but at greater risk. Usually studios tend to focus on one or the other of these strategies and consider the other secondary. Those that specialize in proprietary properties take on contract work to smooth out peaks and valleys in income, while those that focus on contract work develop their own properties to keep their staffers busy and fulfilled, as well as position themselves for future revenue streams.

In some cases the split of service versus proprietary work is strategic, while in others it's a matter of serendipity. Pork & Beans, a studio that spent 75 percent of its time on service work as of the early 2000s, made a strategic decision to focus more on in-house–generated projects, with the goal of splitting its efforts fifty-fifty between the two. Other studios move the balance toward service work when those opportunities exist and toward proprietary work when the flow of storyboards slows.

The balance between proprietary and service work varies from studio to studio, of course, but often hovers around the fifty-fifty mark. Mike Young Productions had such a balance in the early 2000s, doing half proprietary projects such as *Butt-Ugly Martians* and half service work such as *Clifford* for

Scholastic Productions. Similarly, 40 percent to 50 percent of Wild Brain's income in the early 2000s was attributed to commercial work, which allowed it to fund its proprietary projects.

International Expansion   Many animation companies are expanding outside their home territories, particularly on the proprietary side where the trend is driven by the rise in international coproductions and the worldwide decrease in TV license fees. Studio B Productions, a Canadian firm, produced 140 episodes in 2002, with three-quarters of those generated internally. Most of those were coproductions with studios in other countries, such as Kapow Pictures of Australia and TV-Loonland in Germany, which meant that the shows had a global audience, required global marketing strategies, and brought in globally derived revenues.

On the service side, companies in the United States and abroad are positioning themselves as worldwide animation providers. Indian companies are doing service work for U.S., Canadian, and European networks and production companies, while U.S. broadcast design firms are creating animated logos and IDs for broadcast, cable, and satellite networks in Malaysia.

For proprietary properties, especially films and television series, international revenues can rival or exceed those from North America. This is true of both the major studios and smaller houses whose properties are international in scope.

Distribution, Ancillaries, and Other Businesses   Some studios balance their animation production activity with other, related businesses. They may distribute their programs, and those of other studios, to the television or home video market, or sell and represent properties to ancillary product manufacturers. In 2000 4Kids Entertainment, which is involved in production, distribution, and merchandising, mainly of animated properties, attributed 74 percent of its $88 million in revenues to licensing and merchandising, 4 percent to distribution and 22 percent to production. (The company began life as a licensing agency.) TV-Loonland in 2000 had revenues of $80.2 million: 29.1 percent was from distribution, 68.9 percent from production, and 2 percent from merchandising.

In most cases, one or two of these sectors will predominate, but more studios are attempting to balance these businesses. As of 1999, France Animation's distribution activities brought in about 15 percent to 20 percent of its revenues, but its objective was to double that proportion, taking fuller advantage of its five-hundred-show catalog. Similarly, Decode Entertainment of Canada had been increasing its production of properties in which it had a stake and, in the late 1990s, it launched a distribution arm. It intended to focus on selling its own properties but also represent outside programming.

Of course, not all of these business sectors are successful every year. In one year during the 1990s, 58 percent of Nelvana's revenues were attributable to production and distribution (with over 40 percent of that due to distribution of library programming), while its licensing and merchandising business sustained a loss of $250,000. By 2000 the company attributed 6 percent of its revenues to licensing, and was seeing 45 percent annual growth in that sector.

Some companies are adding live-action properties to their portfolios as a means of diversification. Leading Spanish animation house BRB Internacional moved into live-action production in the early 2000s, focusing on television movies. Up to that point it had produced more than 700 animation hours for television and 20 internationally distributed features.

Corporate Structure

When a new competency or area of business becomes important strategically or accounts for a significant share of revenues, some companies change their corporate structure to reflect that. Setting up a new division or subsidiary focused on that aspect of the business may help the company support it better, or it may be a signal to the industry that it is serious about this business sector.

As studios diversify, they sometimes acquire existing companies rather than setting up new subsidiaries. Others look for opportunities for strategic alliances that will allow them to expand while keeping their own overhead costs and upfront investments in check.

Divisions and Subsidiaries   Creating a new division to oversee a certain portion of a studio's business may be as simple as allocating some existing staffers to become dedicated employees of the new division and sending out a press release to announce the step. At the other end of the spectrum, it may involve a significant investment, either to purchase all or part of another company or to start a division from the ground up, with new facilities, equipment, and staff. In most cases the move falls somewhere along the middle of this spectrum.

Visual effects company Rhythm & Hues, primarily known for special effects and live-action production, set up a division called ToolBox in 2001 for commercial production, focusing on marketing its resources to live-action commercial directors who were allied with other production houses. The company had been involved in this business for several years, but launching the new division showed its seriousness about this market segment.

Foundation Imaging, which specialized in visual effects for science fiction television series, opened a 170-employee commercial-effects division in 2000, marking its official move into commercial effects. Meanwhile, Brilliant Digital Entertainment started in 1996 as a 3D online animation company, but expanded into advertising and music videos, launching new divisions to oversee these businesses.

Cuppa Coffee Animation of Canada had long been involved in commercial animation, broadcast design, and animation for entertainment, but many people in the industry were not aware of the broadcast design sector of its business. In 2001 it announced a broadcast design division, which did not change its day-to-day operations significantly, but gave it the opportunity to tout its abilities as a full-service animation house to colleagues and customers that were under the impression it was a commercial and children's television specialist.

Often companies will set up new subsidiaries abroad to expand their international activity. San Francisco's Wild Brain opened a Munich subsidiary in 2001 called Wild Trixx Media GmbH, as well as a U.K. office, in the hopes of lengthening its roster of European clients for its TV, film, commercial, and Internet animation services. It had received inquiries from potential clients in Europe, but felt it needed a staff on the ground to better handle these requests.

Similarly, French studio Millimages opened a U.S. subsidiary, Millimages USA, in 2001. Its objective was to increase communication between itself and the major U.S. distribution channels and producers who were becoming frequent partners. Toei, the Japanese entertainment conglomerate, launched a subsidiary in early 2000 dedicated to handling its worldwide copyrights as global demand for its Japanese anime series grew.

Distribution is another area that many studios handle through separate divisions, in part because it is a very different business from animation production. Igel Media, a German company, created a subsidiary called Igel Media Distribution in 2001 to focus on global sales of its own shows and those of a French studio, Xilam. 4Kids Entertainment, which was already involved in distribution, production, and merchandising, launched a home video division in 2002 to produce and market home videos and DVDs based on properties with which it was involved; it appointed an exclusive distributor, FUNimation Productions, to handle the new business in the United States.

Traditional animation companies that move into interactive production for gaming or the Internet tend to set up distinct divisions to handle this business, since it is different in terms of production and distribution from the studio's core focus. U.K. animation production company Cosgrove Hall invested $300,000 in a new, fifteen-person division called Cosgrove Hall Digital in 2000 for this purpose; it was expected that the staff would triple in the division's first eighteen months and that Cosgrove would raise another $300,000 in investment to support it.

Acquisitions   Acquiring a company is a common way for a studio to enter into a brand-new business or a new geographic area where it has little expertise and no infrastructure in place. This strategy is expensive upfront, of course, but purchasing an ongoing business brings the studio a ready-made reputation in the new area and a trained staff, and can be less expensive in the long run than building a new division from the ground up.

Entertainment Rights, a production and distribution company based in the United Kingdom, wanted to increase its catalog and become more active in licensing, a sector in which it had limited experience. It acquired Link Licensing, which had 440 hours of programming in its distribution library and long expertise in the United Kingdom and European licensing markets, in 2001 for an estimated $21 million.

Similarly, Carrère, a French animation house, purchased a leading French licensing agency, VIP Production, to help it increase its activity in licensing. At about the same time, it acquired Les Armateurs, a feature-film producer. Together, the merged company was able to acquire European rights for television, merchandising, film, and home video, something none of the companies could have done alone.

U.K.–based production and distribution house HIT Entertainment set out to expand its presence in the United States and to enlarge its portfolio of international brands. To that end, it bought Lyrick Studios, best known for *Barney & Friends*, for $274 million (40 percent in cash and 60 percent in HIT stock), in 2001. The acquisition gave HIT a preschool brand that fit well with its existing portfolio, a U.S. office and expertise, and a video distribution arm. It later purchased Gullane Entertainment, which gave it another key preschool franchise in *Thomas & Friends*.

Vinton Studios is an example of a company that used an acquisition strategy to move into a new style of animation. Vinton is best known for stop-motion animation (it owns the Claymation trademark) but wanted to enhance its 2D capability. It purchased a cel-animation company, Celluloid Studios, in 2002. Celluloid had a good reputation and distinct style, so it kept its name after the merger. The purchase allowed the two companies to join together to bid on jobs requiring a mix of 2D and 3D animation, and allowed them both, individually, to offer 2D and 3D services to their clients.

When Film Roman added visual effects to its portfolio of animation services, it purchased VanHook Studios, which became a division of Film Roman called Forum Visual Effects. VanHook's staff was integrated into the staff at Film Roman's studios and worked closely with Film Roman Digital and other divisions.

In gaming many independent studios want a financial infusion and guaranteed distribution for their games, while larger producer/distributors want exclusive access to content. Both parties often benefit when the larger company purchases the smaller. Such was the case when Sony purchased the independent gaming studio Naughty Dog in 2001.

Strategic Alliances and Partnerships Many companies, especially smaller and medium-size ones, prefer to expand through strategic alliances, which allows them to offer additional expertise and/or capabilities without adding overhead. These partnerships and alliances can take many forms.

Some are broad-based distribution or sales deals. CinéGroupe aligned itself with Lion's Gate in a long-term multiproperty distribution deal that allowed Lion's Gate to expand its animation offerings and assisted CinéGroupe in getting its properties in front of consumers. Pixar and Disney allied for a ten-year partnership (set to expire in 2005) in which they planned to jointly produce five cobranded, computer-animated feature films. The deal brought financial resources and broad distribution to Pixar, while it brought Disney increased 3D content and additional properties to exploit through distribution and ancillaries.

In television, Klasky Csupo has long had an exclusive alliance with Nickelodeon, which gives it a home—and wide exposure—for its properties, while giving Nickelodeon a stream of popular content. A first three-year agreement started in 1996; in 1999 it was renewed for another five years. Viacom and Nickelodeon got exclusive TV rights to all Klasky product and a first look at any theatrical content.

Sesame Workshop partnered with an animation house, Cartoon Pizza, to create at least six children's properties; the studio was allowed to create properties for other producers at the same time. Cartoon Pizza, which was to oversee the creation and production of all the projects, reduced its overhead by moving its operations to Sesame Workshop's offices. Sesame Workshop handled financing, distribution, educational content, and research.

Alliances can help studios expand their services in the work-for-hire world as well. In 2000 Chelsea Pictures created a division called Id, which focused on creating advertising for online distribution. The division was a loose alliance involving several agencies, each with its own competencies. JibJab, a Brooklyn, New York–based studio, was the online animation specialist in the group.

Strategic alignment can also involve facilities or hardware. DreamWorks and Hewlett-Packard announced in 2002 that they were joining together in a three-year pact under which Hewlett-Packard would supply faster, more advanced computers to the studio. For HP the alliance represented a big sale of equipment; it also got marketing and product placement rights in Dream-Works's productions as well as the right to use the phrase "DreamWorks's preferred technology provider."

Alliances can also extend the partners' reach geographically. In 2000 525 Studios, a visual effects and postproduction house, partnered with a French 3D and visual effects house, Buf Compagnie. Buf had already done some work for U.S. and Canadian shops but wanted greater exposure in North America. Meanwhile, 525 wanted to add more 3D animation and effects capabilities to its offerings.

DAY-TO-DAY OPERATIONS

There are a number of considerations involving the day-to-day running of an animation studio. Legal issues, the setup and maintenance of systems, marketing and customer relations, and other administrative duties all play into the establishment and maintenance of a successful operation.

Systems

It is important that a studio have efficient systems, computerized and otherwise, in place to ensure timely billing, meeting of deadlines, and communications. Spending adequate time and money upfront to create appropriate systems will ensure a smooth operation.

Communication   Studios must have the ability to send artwork and animation at various stages—animation tests, character drawings, animatics—to their partners and customers via the Internet, although the old-fashioned method of overnight shipping still applies in some cases, especially when it comes to approving the finished product. High-speed Internet connection allows partners and clients/suppliers to shave days off the length of the production process compared to what it used to be, enabling them to complete all approvals, until the last step, online. E-mail allows quick communication to rectify mistakes or miscommunications, or relay changes, immediately. It also reduces the challenges associated with time differences and language barriers.

E-mail cannot and should not replace face-to-face meetings. For example, before taking on a new client or hiring a new service bureau, it helps to visit the customer's or vendor's facilities and meet its staff. During the creative process, especially the development phase, it makes sense for coproducers and animators to talk through issues in person. At contract studios abroad, on-site supervisors from the hiring studio help communicate, act out scenes, and explain humor, none of which can be done adequately over the Internet.

On the downside, the Internet has made it easier for infringers and pirates to steal artwork and animation, enhancing their ability to market rip-off versions of films or other entertainment properties simultaneously or even before their release. Therefore, aside from putting a high-speed Internet system in place, such as a T1 line, one of the most important objectives for a new studio is to create a digital security system. There are many ways to accomplish this: passwords for authorized users, logging users off if they leave the computer unattended (a signal of possible unauthorized downloading), making only nonreproducible art available, etc. The amount of security depends on the studio's budget, the desires of their clients, and the types of projects with which they're involved.

Administrative Systems Setting up administrative systems for paperwork and especially digital assets may seem less important than other start-up duties, but in fact is an important component of launching an efficient operation. Digital and paper assets have to be easy to find and retrieve in cases of referral and reuse, or the company will be spending unnecessary time and effort during the production process simply trying to track down information.

A studio needs a good system for production management so it can monitor the progress of projects, both on the computer and in paper backup, as they make their way through preproduction, production, and postproduction. The production process is complex, with many separate but interdependent tasks being completed simultaneously by a large number of artists, animators, and technicians. A producer needs to be able to find out in a moment where things are, who has signed off on various scenes, and other information. Every project, proprietary and work-for-hire, must be tracked from beginning to end.

Despite the rise of the computer for production and organization, the animation process still leaves a paper trail. Physical tracking sheets accompany the project, with each person involved signing off as scenes are completed, although the information is eventually input to the computer. Producers need to have a system to file these for future reference, backup, and storage.

It is also important to have systems in place for daily backup of digital files in various media. Studios need to ensure their work isn't lost during the production process; having to redo a scene because of a misplaced or damaged file can make it impossible to stay within the budget. Animation houses must also save digital assets for possible reuse in sequels, ancillary products, or unrelated productions, and because digital files have monetary value as an asset.

Finally, animation houses need efficient filing systems for financial, legal, and other daily communication and documents. Not being able to invoice a client in a timely manner or track the receipt of payment will create cash flow problems that affect the entire operation. Not having the proper contracts or legal paperwork at hand will stand in the way of solving disputes easily and assigning responsibilities quickly. While setting up physical and computer-based systems for such documents often seem trivial in comparison to the studio's core tasks, these functions are important contributors to a successful business.

Personnel

Personnel issues, including hiring and training of permanent staffers and freelancers, are among the top priorities for anyone running an animation studio.

Hiring   Studios have different strategies when it comes to hiring, depending on the characteristics and levels of experience they're seeking. Some recruit at the leading animation schools, such as Sheridan College in Ontario, Canada, and CalArts in Santa Clarita, California. (See appendix 2 for a partial list of animation schools.) Many of these houses are involved with the schools on an ongoing basis, not only recruiting but lending facilities, teachers, and guest speakers, and offering internship opportunities. Canadian studio Nelvana has established long-term relationships with many of the leading Canadian animation schools, including Sheridan.

Animation companies often use recruiters to keep an eye out for animation professionals who might be a good fit with the studio. For example, Animated People Recruitment has specialized in placing 3D animators in the United Kingdom. These recruiters have relationships with animation schools and fine art programs and maintain contacts with working animators and executives.

Some shops use traditional methods of seeking employees, such as classified advertisements in *Variety* or *Animation Magazine,* although the bulk of hires tend to result from contacts or industry recommendations. The animation industry is a close-knit community where individuals' work is noticed by their competitors, possibly leading to future job offers or freelance opportunities.

A few studios reach out to the community in innovative ways to unearth new talent. For example, they might run a contest encouraging animation professionals or the public at large to send in animatics, storyboards, scripts, or online animation clips. JustKidsMedia sponsored an online storyboard contest that was open to students and amateurs as well as animation professionals. While it offered $600 as a prize, one of its objectives was to seek out new talent. Associations also hold regional competitions; ASIFA-Central, for example, has one for members located in the midwestern United States.

While some studios are looking for employees with specific expertise, the prevailing view is that "house styles" and software facility can be taught, but innate art talent cannot. Therefore studios often favor someone with a strong fine-art portfolio and little direct animation experience over a candidate who is adept at Maya software but whose demo disk shows no flair. Similarly, a studio can train a candidate who has a strong classic animation background in the basics of 3D, but can't teach art to someone whose aptitude is CG software. In addition, smaller operations—and to an increasing extent larger ones, too—look for animators, artists, technicians, and executives who can perform many duties and/or are willing to be trained in tasks outside their experience. For them, flexibility is a key attribute in a new employee.

Some studios require a certain level of education, such as a degree from a three-year art program, or from a reputable animation school like Sheridan or CalArts. Others may look for a candidate who has completed a certificate program in animation, or who has an unrelated degree from a college or university with some training in character design and/or animation.

Many studios are more likely to favor candidates with a strong demo disk or portfolio, no matter what their educational background, if any. Some may prefer a familiarity with the animation process but will consider an inexperienced candidate with a great portfolio. A new hire with a relevant degree would start out with a higher position or salary than one without, as someone with both 2D and 3D experience would over someone whose expertise is narrow. Inexperienced animators may even be hired as gofers, administrative assistants, or production assistants and use what they learn to work their way up the ladder.

Studios not only look for animators but also graphic development specialists, designers, story artists, technicians (some requiring an artistic background), writers, and a range of other creative and support professionals.

Getting Hired   Experienced animation professionals sometimes use a management company such as AniManagement to manage their careers. Or they may seek out an agent to assist them or use their network of contacts developed through participation in industry events and associations. Since the animation business is cyclical, most animation professionals are hired and fired (or let go at the end of a specific project) numerous times throughout their careers, so they keep marketing materials handy for a quick update of their resume, disk, and Web site.

Less experienced animation professionals must go through the routine of sending out their materials to studios of interest. Prospective employees can research studios on the Internet, where company Web sites offer information about studio operations and clients, as well as by watching productions in which they had a hand. It also helps to read industry trade publications for a sense of hiring trends and which companies might be a good fit. Most young artists don't need agents; agents help people who are already in high demand negotiate the best compensation package. In fact, it's hard to secure agency representation without much experience; contacts are as important a factor in finding representation as they are in finding a position.

Reps or agents handle experienced animators, storyboard artists, and all types of animation specialists. They allow busy animators to work on the creative side of their careers while they take over the business side. Artists tend to be viewed as having more credibility if they're represented after they achieve a certain level of success. (Agents take a commission of 10 percent to 15 percent on all work the artist does while they're representing him or her, even if they didn't have a hand in it.)

The contact person to approach at a studio varies. At larger studios the director of human resources or the vice president of recruitment might be the first place to start, while at smaller studios the executive producer or producer, or a creative director, might handle hiring. As always, the best way to find out who to contact first is to call the studio or check its Web site.

Most shops want to see a cover letter stating what sort of position the candidate is looking for, a one- to two-page resume of work experience and education, and a three- to five-minute CD-ROM "reel" featuring a few examples of the applicant's best work. If no demo disk is available the candidate can substitute a portfolio of fine or graphic artwork. The CD or portfolio should demonstrate the artist's ability in different styles, if possible, but still give some sense of where he or she excels. The disk should outline specifically what the applicant's role was on each shot.

Animation professionals, whether early or late in their careers, should not be discouraged when they hear "no" in response to an inquiry about a job. The business is cyclical, and every three months or so the workflow of a studio can be reversed, opening up freelance positions or even staff jobs that weren't available just weeks before. Therefore, it makes sense to stay in contact with companies that showed interest but had nothing available upon first discussion.

Getting an education in art or animation can be a way to get a foot in the door at an animation house. When taking this route it's important for would-be animators to choose a school that fits them. Factors to consider include the curriculum, degrees offered, who's on the faculty, what the specialty is (e.g., 3D or 2D), if any, what industry connections and career placement services are available, the types of guest speakers who come to campus, what opportunities exist to produce work worthy of a demo disk, and costs.

One method of gaining experience early in a career is by being an intern at a studio. Several animation houses offer internship opportunities—sometimes with a small salary—that not only help train and teach about the workings of the industry, but also give the interns a sense of whether they'd like to work in animation and/or at that company.

At any time in an animation career contacts are important, including at the beginning. Both experienced animators and recent grads benefit from attending animation conferences, software user groups, chapter meetings of student organizations, and association get-togethers. In fact, while all studios accept resumes and demo disks and file them away, most say their hires come through industry contacts rather than through unsolicited mailings. Studios receive a huge stack of resumes and CDs each year, so it is difficult for any one to stand out.

Many studios go to schools to recruit, or attend recruitment fairs specializing in animation, which occur mainly in cities where animation is a big industry and at animation markets and events. Some do training seminars for people interested in animation and find new employees from particularly talented students. They also use want ads in local papers, union newsletters, and industry trade magazines.

Management and Business Staff   In addition to its artists and technicians, an animation company needs business personnel—to varying degrees depending on the size of the operation—responsible for tasks such as marketing, licensing, promotions, legal, financial, general management, and administration. The ideal candidate for these types of positions would have animation or entertainment industry expertise, but the qualities that make a good animator are not necessarily the same as those that make a good businessperson. Therefore, a person's business expertise takes priority over his or her animation knowledge.

This is true for CEOs and other top executives as well as those in the lower ranks. While studios are founded by animators, there comes a time when they need to bring in someone to handle business strategies, tactics, and operations. The CEO handles these duties in consultation with the founders, while the founders have the upper hand on creative decisions, sometimes with input from the business side.

The company's business decisions and operations support the creative development of the animation. While many of the company's business staff act in a behind-the-scenes capacity, they are in many ways as important to the success of the company as those who perform the creative functions. Therefore, studios should take as much care in hiring the right people for legal, marketing, and other business positions as they do on the creative side.

Training   Most studios have some form of training system to familiarize their new hires with not only technology but corporate systems, house styles, and other topics. In addition, specific productions may require dedicated training, as was discussed in chapter 2. In many cases ongoing training systems are informal, with the new hire learning about the organization from another employee or several employees in the company or department. Other studios may employ a mentoring structure, with senior employees offering new hires guidance on their specific jobs and on more general career decisions.

Other studios have implemented formal training systems. Nelvana puts its new employees through an in-house training program, as does Pixar, which calls its program "Pixar University," and Disney. Several overseas studios have training programs as well. This is particularly true in countries where animation is a growing industry but not part of the culture, such as India; studio employees must be trained in timing, storytelling, and other creative and technical facets of animation, in addition to hardware, software, and company systems.

Unions   Major studios and some smaller production companies have contracts with the unions that represent workers active in animation. These companies must follow union rules for minimum salaries and benefits; all employees or freelancers working with these companies in jobs covered by the union must become members within a month or so of being hired. If the employer doesn't have a union contract, union rules do not govern the employees who work there.

As noted in chapter 2, the major union representing animators is IATSE and its Motion Picture Screen Cartoonists locals in L.A. (Local 839), New York (600), San Francisco (16), and Orlando (843). Most of the larger studios, including Disney, Warner Brothers and Universal, have agreements with IATSE, as do ILM and Digital Domain (the latter with a limited agreement), but many smaller independents do not.

Union members agree not to work for nonunion companies but, because most animators must move from company to company in order to stay busy, and relatively few houses are union, they sometimes violate the rules. Some union members frown on such activity, but penalties are rarely imposed.

Other unions in addition to IATSE govern work on animation properties. Most actors belong to the Screen Actors Guild (SAG) or the American Federation of Television and Radio Artists (AFTRA), with the former focusing more on film and the latter on television. (As of early 2003, the two were in talks about a possible merger.) The Writers Guild of America (WGA) began representing animation writers in 1990s—its Animation Writers Caucus has 350 members—while technical positions such as sound recording engineers and editors are often members of their respective guilds. Other unions, including the Directors Guild of America (DGA), do not specifically cover animation.

Customer Relations and Marketing

Meeting the day-to-day needs of existing customers and mining new ones, both directly and indirectly, account for a significant percentage of an animation studio's time and effort. In addition to meeting deadlines and budgets, and corresponding/invoicing in a timely manner, customer service in large part means keeping the lines of communication open, informing clients of changes, giving them regular progress reports, and simply touching base whether a project is in the works or not.

Many studios have an ongoing system of marketing communications in place, although for others marketing themselves is a somewhat haphazard affair. As noted in more detail in chapters 6 and 11, regular marketing activities can include attending trade fairs and conferences, joining and participating in associations, running regular image advertising, entering contests and competitions, and having a PR campaign in place.

Marketing also involves keeping promotional and advertising concerns in mind during the production process, especially when it comes to proprietary projects. Creating additional footage, providing samples such as animatic excerpts, and supplying screen shots, demo disks, video presentations, behind-the-scenes film, and other materials while production is in progress allows marketing and publicity personnel to do their jobs and keeps marketing expenses down.

These marketing and PR procedures are important in both peak and down times. In fact, periods when work flow is slow are good times to make contacts with existing clients, prospect for new ones, take a look at strategies and tactics, and otherwise improve the business.

Legal and Financial Systems

A wide range of financial and legal details come up in a typical day at an animation studio.

Financial   One key financial task of an animation studio is to monitor actual costs versus budgeted costs, using cost or variance reports. This task is often handled by the production staff for a large proprietary production, but may be done by a studio's finance or business affairs department for contract projects or, at smaller studios, for proprietary projects.

In addition to creating and monitoring budgets for proprietary and work-for-hire productions, a few of the other financial and accounting tasks ongoing at an animation studio include acquiring and maintaining insurance;

making and monitoring investments; negotiating financing deals with co-production, distribution, and investment partners; working out acquisition and merger deals; daily accounting including receivables and payables; payroll; compiling quarterly and annual financial books; calculating and paying taxes; ordering supplies; and more.

Producers on specific projects are sometimes involved in these tasks, particularly budgeting, as are other company personnel, but in most cases dedicated financial and accounting personnel are responsible for the bulk of this work.

Legal The legal tasks involved in running a studio are many. They include everything from setting up the partnership or other legal structure when the company is launched to settling disputes. Two of the most important and time consuming tasks are 1) negotiating contracts with all types of companies and individuals and 2) legally protecting a company's proprietary properties against infringement.

Contracts There are a significant number of contracts that a studio enters into on a regular basis. They can include submission/nondisclosure/confidentiality agreements; employment and freelance contracts; licensing contracts with manufacturers, promotional partners, and retailers; contracts with overseas and domestic subcontractors; contracts between production partners; financing deals; mergers and acquisition deals; distribution agreements; strategic alliance contracts of all kinds; work-for-hire agreements with clients; contracts with vendors such as postproduction houses; noncompete agreements; confidentiality agreements; and many others, depending on the nature of the studio's work.

Each contract usually starts with a boilerplate version submitted by one of the partners. All points are negotiable; the partners discuss the points until each is satisfied with the end result. Negotiations can take a year or more for complex deals. In many cases parties to an agreement will sign a "deal memo" or "deal-point memo" outlining the main points of agreement first. This document is not legally binding, but can be used as a good-faith basis on which to proceed with production even while the attorneys finesse the fine points. In some cases development, preproduction, or production must move forward in order to meet deadlines, even if the final deal isn't in place, although this is rare. The deal memo allows the partners to feel as if there's less risk in going forward.

Exhibit 13.3

Types of Contracts Involving Animation Houses

Agent/rep representation agreements

Attorney representation agreements

Cofinancing agreements

Confidentiality/nondisclosure agreements

Contracts with freelancers

Coproduction agreements

Deal-point memos (short form contracts)

Distribution agreements (home video, film, television, etc.)

Employment contracts

Equipment rental agreements

Insurance contracts

International distributor/foreign sales agent agreements

Investment agreements

Lease agreements

Letters of intent

Licensing agent retainers

Licensing contracts with manufacturers

Licensing contracts with retailers

Marketing agency retainers

Marketing deals with partners

Merger or acquisition papers

Musician/composer agreements

Noncompete agreements

Option exercise deals

Options and option renewals

Overseas supervisor deals

Property purchase agreements

Public relations firm retainers

Publisher-developer agreement for electronic games

Publisher-distributor agreement for electronic games

Purchase orders

Service contracts for software

Strategic alliance deals

Subcontractor agreements

Union agreements

Vendor contracts (e.g., postproduction houses)

Work-for-hire contracts with client

Note: This list is not exhaustive.

All contracts are different depending on the type of deal, the objectives of the partners, and other considerations. A licensing deal will not contain the same terms as a television distribution agreement. But all include certain common components. These include, in no particular order, the term (duration) of the agreement, the names of the parties, what rights are being granted (rights to sell, produce, distribute, manufacture, etc.), what type of payment is changing hands and what compensation/reward is due each partner, what properties are involved, what all the partners are bringing to the deal (financing, services, sales expertise), what geographic area is involved (worldwide or one territory), warranties that both parties are able to provide what they say they will, options to extend the deal, and/or whether the agreement is exclusive or nonexclusive. The more detail, the better; clarity upfront will help prevent disputes later.

The agreement alone, no matter how detailed and clear, does not guarantee the success of the partnership. The document is irrelevant if the parties cannot deliver what they've promised. Choosing the right partner is more important than the deal itself; the deal simply outlines and clarifies what each partner brings to the table and what each expects to get back. It serves as a basis to resolve disputes that come up later.

Legal Protection   Before a studio can market its animated properties to the trade and consumers it must legally protect these properties to reduce the chances of theft or infringement. (In a work-for-hire situation the client is responsible for any trademark or copyright protection.) The two major types of intellectual property protection that affect the animation industry are copyrights and trademarks.

Copyright protection is automatic upon creation of the property, although registration with the U.S. Copyright Office of the U.S. Library of Congress provides additional protections. Copyright prevents outside parties from stealing the expression of an idea (e.g., a script, storyboards, animatics, or a final production), not the idea itself. Through agreements with other countries and major copyright conventions, registering a copyright in the United States effectively protects it in nearly all other countries in the world where business will be done, and vice versa.

Trademark law protects logos, designs, and other elements of a property that are used to identify a brand in commerce. Studios that want to extend their properties into branded items sold in stores, including videos, DVDs, sound tracks, books, comic books, and licensed merchandise, must protect them through registering them as trademarks. A property can be considered a trademark if it appears on commercial items sold in stores or through direct response, doesn't infringe any existing brands, and is clearly identified as a trademark (with the ™ symbol before registration and the ® after). The trademark has to be used in commerce in order to maintain the trademark rights. In other words, products tied to the brand must be sold, otherwise the trademark rights can be lost. Trademarks should be registered with the U.S. Patent and Trademark Office for full protection; most tie-in partners will want the property to be registered or at a minimum the process started before they'll consider doing business with the property.

A property owner must register various elements of a trademark in each product category and in each country where it will be used. Each registration costs over $300, so fully registering a property (including several elements, 25 countries or more, a dozen product classifications, and so on) adds up fast. Studios and their legal representatives must weigh the benefits and costs until they come up with a strategy on how to best protect the property from infringement without overspending. Trademark registration, including conducting a search to see if the proposed or any similar brands are already registered or in use by other parties, is complicated as well as costly; studios should enlist the assistance of an attorney specializing in intellectual property.

The partners involved in a production need to decide up front who will hold the copyright and trademarks (joint ownership is possible) and who will register it. If the property is based on an existing property, such as a book, the partners and the underlying rights holder must decide which elements of the animation will be owned by the original copyright or trademark holder and which by the animation studio and/or their partners.

While copyright and trademark are the primary protections for animation properties, there may be other areas of the law that can provide additional protection in certain cases, such as right of publicity (which covers celebrity likenesses), patents (inventions, technology, and product design), or trade dress (the overall look of packaging).

The World Market

Animation houses in any country need revenues from international markets to break even on their proprietary properties, no matter whether the property resides in the film, television, online, gaming, or video segments of the industry. Many of the major studios peg 50 percent or more of their revenues from both distribution and ancillaries to global markets. In television, finding partners abroad is nearly essential in order to finance a program; in addition, a series can succeed in international markets alone, without ever finding a home in the United States. And, thanks to the Internet and other international news sources, word of individual animation properties travels fast around the world, preparing consumers to embrace new productions as they make their way from country to country.

A decade or two ago the United States dominated the entertainment market on a worldwide basis, but that is no longer true. Locally produced animation properties can succeed not only in their home territory but abroad as well, including in the United States. This is particularly true of television, but also applies to online, video, gaming (where Japan has always been a power), and, to a lesser extent, film properties. Several Japanese animated feature films have been released in the United States to great critical acclaim and lots of publicity, if not to particularly strong financial revenues to date.

Consumers in most areas of the world like animation. At the same time, animation travels well. Compared to live-action entertainment properties, it is relatively easy to tailor most animated properties to the tastes of individual markets. While the importance of international markets has been discussed throughout this book, this chapter takes a closer look at animation trends, consumption, and production in specific markets.

THE WORLDWIDE ANIMATION MARKET

Trends in animation worldwide vary depending by market sector.

Film

The animated film business traditionally has been dominated by the major U.S. studios; while some films from other countries can do business globally, most have their greatest success in their domestic and nearby markets. U.S.–origin films remain the most likely to achieve worldwide status.

Non-U.S. markets have become more important to the major studios, however, and now can account for about half the overall revenues for many films, especially when merchandising and other ancillaries are factored in. Disney/Pixar's *Monsters Inc.,* released in 2001 in the United States, generated $504 million in worldwide box office receipts by April of the next

Exhibit 14.1		
Populations of Top Entertainment Markets Worldwide		

North America

United States	287.4 million
Canada	31.3 million

Latin America

Brazil	173.8 million
Mexico	101.7 million

Europe

United Kingdom	60.2 million
Germany	82.4 million
France	59.5 million
Spain	41.3 million
Italy	58.1 million

Asia/Pacific

Japan	127.4 million
China (mainland)	1.28 billion
Australia	19.7 million

Source: Population Reference Bureau, World Population Data Sheet, 2002

---

year, with more than $251 million of that (slightly less than 50 percent) traced to international territories.

In general, the pace of international roll-outs of animated films originating in the United States is quicker than in the past. Some films are launched almost simultaneously around the world, or at least within a six-month period of their U.S. release (with premieres pegged toward holidays and peak moviegoing periods in each country).

A 2000 sales survey of independent, U.S.–based film distributors, conducted by KPMG for the American Film Marketing Association (AFMA), shows how the relative weight of different media associated with film properties varies by region. It found that 61.88 percent of independent U.S. film distributors' international sales were to Western Europe. Of that, 31 percent was from theatrical distribution, 20 percent from video, and 49 percent from TV licenses. On that other hand, in the second largest market, Asia/Pacific (excluding Australia/New Zealand), which accounted for 17.57 percent of sales, 38 percent was from theatrical distribution, 25 percent from video, and 37 percent from television licenses.

Television

The global nature of the animation business is especially evident in the television industry, where coproductions are becoming the norm, with the exception of some programs fully owned by U.S. studios or global TV networks. Falling broadcast license fees, difficulties in securing financing, and the need for as many revenue streams as possible has made coproductions and international sales critical for most producers.

Programs originating outside the United States are gaining distribution and finding financial success in the United States, something that was rare a decade ago. U.S. broadcasters not only consider but actively seek out productions from Europe, Australia, and Japan. U.S. networks view properties with commercial track records abroad as less risky; they also like the fact that they're complete and expenses are limited to dubbing and slight editing. At the same time, the U.S. market is not the be-all and end-all it once was. In fact, the United States is considered secondary for many shows with strong international sales; they can make money from sales in Europe alone.

The TV market is becoming more fragmented and more competitive all around the world. New channels (cable, satellite, broadcast) and increased privatization of media in developing countries have given producers more places to sell their programming. But these developments have also split the viewing audience into numerous small groups, making it difficult for a single show to succeed. Countries such as the United Kingdom and Germany, as well as the United States, have been especially affected by this trend.

Home Video

Home videos of popular films can succeed abroad, just as they can in the United States. A factor that affects home video success, however, is the penetration of VCRs in homes in each country. This figure varies significantly; some countries have not embraced home video, while others have robust per capita sales. In Japan, home video is among the most vibrant media of all, for all genres of animation and all demographic groups. Many Japanese animation properties are launched as original videos and those that come from other sectors, such as electronic games or television, count home video among their top revenue-generating ancillary categories (along with comic books).

Within Europe, Germany, France, and the United Kingdom together account for 68 percent of all home video spending, according to *Screen Digest*. Japan dominates the Asia/Pacific region, of course, with 61 percent of all spending there. In Latin America, Mexico and Brazil together account for

77 percent of video spending; in Africa, South Africa accounts for one-third; and in North America, the United States accounts for 92.5 percent.

DVDs have grown in significance in the United States in the early 2000s, becoming an important medium for secondary distribution of films and TV series. But, like home video, DVD has not been embraced equally around the world. Worldwide shipments of DVD players and recorders was expected to approach 60 million units by the end of 2002, according to researcher In-Stat/MDR. The United States is the largest market, but Europe's growth rate exceeds that of the United States, and its purchases of DVD players are likely to exceed the United States' by 2004. China's purchases are likely to pass those in the United States by 2006.

Gaming

According to *Screen Digest,* the global market for interactive software for leisure use was $17.7 billion in 2000. The United States at $6.3 billion accounted for the largest segment of that, followed by Europe with $5.8 billion and Japan with $3.4 billion. Within Europe the United Kingdom was the top market for console software, with sales twice as high as in either France or Germany. Many of the giants in the industry, including Nintendo and Sony, are based in Japan, which has long been dominant in the gaming industry, although key companies are located elsewhere, such as Electronic Arts in the United States and Infogrames in France.

The fast pace of technological change impacts this sector more than any other. Computer and console technologies are constantly being improved, resulting in the release of new versions and new platforms. Each introduction requires new versions of existing games, and is usually accompanied by several brand-new titles. Game developers and publishers must support each new platform as well as continuing to produce games for consumers that remain with their older systems.

One trend in gaming is the increased tendency for owners of animation and other types of licensed properties to grant developers, publishers, and/ or distributors licenses for multiple platforms—sometimes all computer and console platforms—on a worldwide basis. Not all licensees can afford this type of deal, but it makes sense from a strategic point of view.

The Internet

The Internet is by its nature a global medium. Any computer user almost anywhere in the world can access any site, although individual sites are not marketed equally in all countries. With search software, however, a computer user can find sites in any country.

Computer penetration, online and high-speed access levels and costs, and Internet usage vary from country to country. A 2002 survey by eMarketer found that the Asia/Pacific region was the world's largest Internet market as of the end of 2001, with 165 million users. Most of the usage was concentrated in three Asian nations, Japan, China, and South Korea, the last of which is one of the world's largest single-country Internet markets.

South Korea has one of the highest broadband penetrations as well, with nearly 20 percent of the population having high-speed access as of the early 2000s, according to researcher point-topic.com. Canada has 10 percent access, compared to almost 5 percent for the United States and almost 4 percent in Japan. European countries tend to have lower broadband penetrations, with Germany the top nation in the region with slightly over 3 percent and France and the United Kingdom at about half that. All of these percentages have grown exponentially since that study; in the United States, for example, 30 percent of computer households had broadband by 2004.

Wireless technology is emerging around the world as a potential distribution channel for animation (in its simplest form). As of the early 2000s, only Japanese consumers have embraced this technology in a big way, however; there, the use of wireless technology in the form of i-mode phones has exceeded Internet usage by a significant factor, although consumers are starting to focus on using the phones for calls and e-mail and using them less to download animation. Wireless has been more of a factor in the gaming market than in animated entertainment.

MARKET CHARACTERISTICS

Each country's animation industry has its own characteristics. More important, each nation has its own local tastes, distribution infrastructure, retailing tiers, and legal and regulatory environment, all of which affect how animation is distributed and enjoyed.

North America

Both the United States and Canada are home to dedicated children's and animation networks that account for a large proportion of animation hours viewed. A decade ago the three broadcast networks dominated animation in the United States, but as of 2003 historically animation-heavy time periods, such as weekday afternoons and Saturday mornings, have all but disappeared on many networks. Meanwhile, cable channels run animation at all hours of the day and night, and most of the big success stories in both viewership and revenues have come from Nickelodeon or the Cartoon Network, as well as PBS, in recent years. (There are some exceptions, such as *Pokémon* on the WB network.)

In terms of production, the major Hollywood studios distribute virtually all the top animated films on a worldwide basis (and produce or coproduce many of them), as well as a significant number of television series with global reach. The United States also has a number of animation studios of various sizes on both coasts, and some scattered around the interior of the country. They supply animation for proprietary and service projects, from corporate applications to special effects. It is also a center of Flash production for both entertainment and corporate Web sites.

Canada hosts a variety of small and midsize studios, many of which are key players in worldwide television production and distribution. The Canadian government supports its indigenous animation industry in a number of ways. It has coproduction treaties with dozens of countries around the world; requires that at least 50 percent of all television programming on Canadian networks be locally made; and offers TV producers up to 50 percent of their budgets through incentives administered through Telefilm Canada. Major animation studios in Canada include Nelvana, Cookie Jar (formerly Cinar), Mainframe, and CinéGroupe, to name just a few; all are involved in both proprietary and contract work. Due to favorable exchange rates and strong government support, many productions have moved away from the United States and into these Canadian studios.

While many animation properties succeed in both the United States and Canada, it's important to remember that the two are separate countries with different market characteristics and different tastes. European properties can do well in Canada, particularly those originating in France, and many of these make their way to Canadian airwaves, particularly in the form of Canadian-French coproductions.

Asia/Pacific Rim

Japan is the main animation-consuming and producing country in Asia and among the top in the world for most segments of animation, with home video and gaming particularly strong. For example, according to *Screen Digest,* Japan accounts for 61 percent of all spending on home video in the Asia/Pacific, versus 8 percent for Australia/New Zealand and 31 percent for all other territories. Japan's population is six and a half times that of Australia's.

Japan   Franchise marketing is alive and well in Japan, where most animation properties extend into TV, home video, film, gaming, licensed products, and publishing (especially comic books, or *manga,* which account for 60 percent of all book sales in Japan). The various media are interconnected and cross-promoted. Per capita sales of licensed merchandise based on hit properties in Japan far exceed sales in other countries, including the United States. Many properties surpass $1 billion in retail sales of merchandise in Japan—something relatively few U.S. properties do—even though its population is 44 percent the size of the United States.

Whereas most countries are dominated by children's animation properties, this is not true in Japan. Animation here extends into every age group and subject matter, including nonfiction, with styles and content ranging from cute and sugary sweet to violent at a level not seen in any other country. Many of the softer children's properties become long-term franchises, lasting for years and having numerous iterations in all media. One such property, *Doraemon,* has been successful in Japan for more than thirty years, supported by 100 million comic book sales, 1,800-plus half hours of television, 23 feature films and myriad home videos, merchandise, and promotional and advertising activity.

Properties for older children, teens, and adults tend to have a short but vibrant life, generating hundreds of millions of dollars in sales of videos and merchandise over the few months they're available and saturating all media during that time. Some of these endure to become longer-term franchises (*Akira* is one example), but many come and go quickly. Even children's properties with franchise potential tend to rise quickly; Shogakukan's *Hamtaro* was launched in Japan in July 2000 and had already generated more than $2.5 billion in retail sales of merchandise by early 2002, when it was introduced to international audiences. The concept was based on a series of storybooks first published in 1997, but it was the TV series *Tottoko Hamutaro* that sparked the franchise. (Japan is the second largest TV market in the world; 60 new television titles air each week and 90 percent of content is Japanese.)

Because Japan has a robust domestic animation industry, as well as a homogeneous culture, properties from other parts of the world have a difficult time entering the market and succeeding. Local properties dominate, although gentle preschool animation, mainly from Europe, can gain a foothold.

Cute properties intended for young children are embraced as a fashion accessory by girls and young women, while the teen boys and young men drive the violent, action-themed market segment.

Local films account for most top animated releases at the box office. The occasional U.S. film, such as Pixar's *Monsters, Inc.*, can reach the top box office echelons, but local producers—which released 27 animated films in 2001— see more success. The top example is Studio Ghibli, which has given the world *Princess Mononoke (Mononoke Hime)* and *Spirited Away (Sen to Chihiro no Kamikakushi)* and whose films nearly always reach the top of the charts in Japan, setting records along the way. *Spirited Away* earned over $150 million at the box office in Japan (this with less than 10 percent the number of screens that exist in the United States). With the exception of Studio Ghibli's offerings, most top films are components of multifaceted animation franchises, such as *Doraemon, Pokémon,* or *Akira.* Despite all this activity, the average moviegoer in Japan sees only one film per year, lower than in the United States, Europe, or Australia.

Unlike in other countries, original animated videos (OAVs) account for a huge segment of the video market in Japan. Many franchises get their start as OAVs, which also represent a major component of franchises originating in other media. Gaming is another integral aspect of entertainment franchises in Japan, even more so than in the United States or other countries. Major franchises originate in video games (*Pokémon, Super Mario,* and *Sonic the Hedgehog* being just a few prominent examples.)

In terms of production, there were an estimated 300-plus animation (anime) houses in the country as of 2001, producing about 600 episodes of animation per year. Many of these focus on service work for the domestic market (and, in rare cases, for studios abroad), but some produce proprietary properties for Japan and, increasingly, global markets. Examples of studios with a global reputation include Toei Animation, the largest house and the leader in exportation of animation (responsible for *Digimon, DragonBall,* and *Sailor Moon,* among others); Nippon Animation, the second largest studio; Bandai, also a major toy and gaming company; Tsuburaya; and TMS. Animation budgets for the average Japanese TV episode are approximately one-fourth the size of those in the United States. This means producers rarely need to participate in coproductions, although this is changing as studios start to target the international market.

While exportation of Japanese properties to the U.S. market is a relatively new phenomenon, animated television series from Japan often do well in other parts of Asia, as well as in other regions including Brazil, Spain, and Italy.

Other Asian Territories   The greatest percentage of television fare in most Asian markets comes from Japan, with U.S., European, and Australian properties also available. Animation from any country that has a worldwide following can gain popularity across the region, although not equally in all nations. Some countries are more avid animation consumers than others.

Differences in local tastes, government regulations, penetration of entertainment equipment including television sets, disposable incomes, and other factors all play into the size and potential of individual markets. Some countries promote domestic entertainment through quotas; Korean programming must account for 50 percent of all air time in that country, for example, and 25 percent of animation must be local. Other countries, such as Singapore and Malaysia, heavily censor content.

Mainland China is the fastest-growing animation market in Asia (and the world). It historically has allowed mainly domestic properties but, as it begins to open its borders to trade with the rest of the world, it is starting to embrace foreign animation fare, especially for television. Non-Chinese producers and property owners making inroads include Disney, Warner Brothers, United Media, EM.TV, and Cookie Jar.

Several countries in Asia have strong animation production industries, focusing on providing service work for international studios but starting to develop their own properties. South Korea once commanded about half of the worldwide market for service work, although that proportion has decreased as competition has grown and assignments have moved to lower-cost countries. Akom, one of the largest of Korea's 100 animation studios, saw demand for its service work reduced from 200 half-hours in the late 1990s to less than 100 in the early 2000s. The Korean government has started to offer financial aid to the industry; Korean studios can usually get only 5 percent to 10 percent of their production budgets from the local broadcast license fee and have been at the forefront among Asian animators in selling their properties to a worldwide market.

A significant amount of animation production has moved to greater China (including Hong Kong and Taiwan, which have long done animation service work). Mainland China, in particular, has been aggressive about positioning itself as a lower-cost alternative for producers assigning 2D contracts. The government has launched its own animation organizations, including Shanghai Animation Telefilm Group, a studio established in 2000, and the Shanghai Animation Institute, the first higher-education center focusing on the craft. Labor costs in mainland China are about a third of those in Taiwan or Hong Kong, which have comparable costs as nearby countries such as Singapore.

There were more than 120 animation houses in China as of 2001, according to the China Animation Association, with China Central Television (CCTV) and Shanghai Animation the two largest. (The latter accounted for close to 40 percent of all the domestic animation aired in China, most of which was broadcast on CCTV.) Chinese studios doing business internationally include Hong Ying (in mainland China), Jade Animation (Hong Kong), and Wang Film (Taiwan). Taiwan created a program in 2002 to provide development money for digital animation projects.

The Philippines has been another historically strong country when it comes to producing contract animation for U.S. and European studios, with Philippine Animation Studio Inc. (also known by its initials, pasi), Fils Cartoons, and Toon City among the companies based there. Other countries in the region, such as Singapore, Malaysia, and Vietnam, are lesser-known animation producers, but their activity as lower-cost alternatives has been growing. Indonesia has 250 domestic animation studios, which mainly focus on providing service work to Japanese companies.

India has been trying to position its animation industry as a low-cost, high-quality provider for the global marketplace. Costs in India are lower than in almost any other nation, and while Indian studios still face some image problems, their workload is increasing. By some estimates, India accounted for 10 percent of all the animation service work in Asia in 2000. UTV Toons is the largest animation house in the country; a total of 70 studios were in business in India as of 2002, with approximately 20 of those involved in the global animation market, according to the Association of Indian Producers of Animation (AIPA).

Like animation studios throughout the world, formerly all-service studios in Asia have been developing their own properties. Sunwoo, one of Korea's largest animation studios, developed *Milo's Bug Quest* for the international market; other Korean-origin properties, all 3D, include *Cubix, Top Blades,* and *Run-Dim.* Both Taiwan and Korea have a strong market for Internet animation, and several Web-origin characters have gone on to become multimedia success stories. Korean examples include *MashiMaro, Julla-man,* and *Woobiboy.* Malaysian studios released their first animated feature film, *Putih,* in 2000, while India's Pentamedia released *Sinbad: Beyond the Veil of Mysts,* a $20-million movie distributed by Warner Brothers, and Crest Communications a $50-million film, *Automata,* for Columbia TriStar.

Australia/New Zealand   Most entertainment properties that are popular internationally, whether from North America, Europe, or Japan, also find success in Australia and New Zealand, although, due to the small population (19.7 million in Australia and 3.9 million in New Zealand), total sales, attendance, and viewership are small compared to other territories. Yet per capita entertainment usage is high; moviegoers, for example, attend films 3.7 times per year on average, more than in most territories outside the United States. Australia in particular embraces properties that incorporate edgy humor, such as *South Park* or *The Simpsons.*

Although the two countries are often considered as one territory when it comes to distribution or ancillary deals, there are differences between Australia and New Zealand in terms of tastes, distribution, culture, retailing, and other factors. New Zealand traditionally has leaned more toward English properties and Australia more toward American, especially those that reflect its beach/surf culture, to name just one difference.

Australia has a well-developed animation business, fairly small but long active on a global scale. Costs for animation are high (although lower than in Europe or the United States during much of the 2000s, due to the relative value of the Australian dollar) and domestic license fees are low, covering only about 15 percent to 20 percent of budgets. Therefore, virtually all studios, which include EM.TV/Yoram Gross, Energee Entertainment, Disney Australia, Animation Works, and others, are involved in international coproductions. They are also frequent customers of Asian subcontractors, as they look for ways to keep costs down.

Because of the difficulty of competing on the world market, several formerly independent Australian studios have merged with global companies. Yoram Gross is now part of Germany's EM.TV, while Energee merged with RTV Family Entertainment, also of Germany. These deals have allowed the companies more access to global markets, especially in Europe, and have given them the financial strength to produce additional content.

Australia requires that 55 percent of program hours be devoted to shows from Australia and New Zealand; New Zealand has no domestic programming quotas. The Australian government also supports its animation industry; an Australian coproduction partner can access up to 60 percent of the production budget from local sources if a series is sold to an Australian network at a premium license fee. Each state has its own funding body as well.

Europe

The United Kingdom, Germany, and France are the leading animation markets in Europe. In many cases properties that become popular in one country (whether indigenous or from outside the region) expand across Europe, although their level of success varies from country to country. Despite the changeover to the European Union, there are many differences from one nation to another.

Most importantly, tastes remain unique in each country, which affects ratings levels, moviegoing, sales of home videos and interactive games, and all other aspects of a property. Because of cultural differences, there are many properties that are popular primarily in one or a few countries only, such as *Astérix* in France or *Tabaluga* in Germany.

Several countries in Europe have active animation industries, with a focus on creating properties for the television market. According to a 2000 report by CARTOON, a European animated film association, and *Screen Digest,* France produced 275 hours of animation for film and television from 1997 to 1999, Spain 124 hours, Germany 75 hours, and Denmark 12.5 hours.

The European Union has promoted animation across the region with a plan called Media Plus. Media Plus allowed for nearly $350 million in funding earmarked for developing and promoting EU content, starting in 2001. (The funds don't go toward production costs.) The EU also implemented a Broadcasting Directive that encourages members to devote at least 50 percent of their programming time to European fare. The wording was somewhat loose, however, and countries within the EU have interpreted it in different ways. Eight European countries have prohibited marketing on television to children.

Since 1926, with the release of *The Adventures of Prince Achmed,* Europe has produced 183 animated feature films, according to CARTOON. Fifty-one films were released from 1997 to 2001, and 33 were in production as of 2002. In home video, according to *Screen Digest,* the United Kingdom accounted for 35 percent of all spending within Europe, followed by France at 20 percent, Germany at 13 percent, Scandinavia and Italy at 7 percent each, and Spain at 5 percent. The United Kingdom, France, and Germany are the biggest markets for all types of animation product, although their per capita spending varies from medium to medium. Those three countries are the most populous in Western Europe: Germany has 82.4 million inhabitants, the United Kingdom 60.2 million, and France 59.5 million.

United Kingdom   The United Kingdom is strong in the production and consumption of television and home videos for the preschool market, such as *Bob the Builder* or *Postman Pat.* Many of the productions have literary roots. The United Kingdom is often the first market targeted abroad by U.S.–origin animation properties, partly because of the shared language, but also because

British consumers tend to embrace many of the same global properties as U.S. consumers do, as well as their own, homegrown productions.

In films, the top box office draws are usually American films, at least in animation. While the British film industry is strong, it is limited primarily to live-action productions, with the notable exception of Aardman Animations, producer of the DreamWorks-distributed *Chicken Run*. Of course, Aardman's *Wallace & Gromit* is among the most beloved British animation properties for any age, and has earned fame in other countries.

The United Kingdom has about a dozen major animation companies, many of which target worldwide markets, and approximately 300 overall, including many boutique operations. In addition to Aardman, major studios include Cosgrove Hall, Telemagination, Entertainment Rights, and the largest, HIT Entertainment, as well as several, such as Loose Moose, specializing in commercial production, broadcast design, and effects. The U.K. government offers its industry some tax breaks on feature films and television series, but they can be impractical for many producers. Seventy percent of the budget and 70 percent of the payroll must be spent in the United Kingdom to qualify; it is often cheaper to send production to Asia than to stay in the United Kingdom, even with the tax breaks, which would contribute about 8 percent to the overall budget. The trade organization PACT has lobbied to change this situation.

The United Kingdom is a major source of interactive games within Europe, according to the European Leisure Software Publishers Association (ELSPA). U.K.–origin games account for 35 percent of the domestic market, versus 31 percent for Japanese and 25 percent for U.S.–origin titles. A third of all PlayStation titles sold in Europe originated in the United Kingdom in 2001.

Germany   Germany is Europe's largest TV market and third largest animation producer, and German animation fans support both global and homegrown properties. The country is often combined with Austria and Switzerland into a single German-language territory when it comes to deal making. German properties that have made a mark domestically and, in some cases, abroad in recent years have included *Werner,* a comic book property that was translated into three top-attended and widely licensed films, and *Die Maus,* the star of the 25-year-old property *Die Sendung mit der Maus.* Both have inspired merchandise, audio, and video/DVD sales, the first to an adult audience and the latter to preschoolers.

In addition to EM.TV, which, as of 2003, is financially troubled but still a significant player, other German animation producers include TV-Loonland, a multifaceted entertainment company; RTL, which owns networks and finances productions; RTV, a multiterritory broadcaster; Ravensburger, a puzzle and game company with a television distribution arm, and Trickcompany and Hahn Films, both specializing in movie production. Most of the larger German studios are involved in international coproductions and cofinancing, usually retaining distribution and merchandising rights for the German market.

German funding for animation is controlled by the regions (Länder) rather than the national government. But private funds such as the Berlin Animation Fund, Cartoon 2000, and the Victory Media Group, created through tax breaks to investors, have contributed more to the German animation industry than government funds have.

France France has traditionally been a difficult market for animation producers from other countries, except those from Canada and Belgium. The country has steep local content quotas, requiring 60 percent of programming to be European and two-thirds of that to be French. French studios create most of the programming embraced by French viewers but, conversely, often find it difficult to export their productions to other countries. Many of the top classic TV animation properties are based on French and Belgian comic books, including *Astérix, Lucky Luke, Tintin,* and *Marsupilami.* In the early 2000s several French-produced animated films saw success domestically, including the $4-million *Kirikou* (1999) and the $11-million *Chateau des Singes* (2001), a French-German-British coproduction. *Les Triplettes de Belleville* hit international theaters in 2003, earning an Oscar nomination in the United States.

France is the most prolific animation producer in Europe. Its animation houses, including the largest studio, Millimages, are frequent coproduction partners, especially with Canadian studios, and this fare accounts for most of their animation exports.

One reason for the growth in animation is France's strong system of subsidies and tax breaks. French animators, according to the Centre Nationale de la Cinématographie (CNC), can, on average, get 11 percent of their budget from the CNC, 17 percent from fee deferrals and reductions, and 19 percent from a French broadcaster. This is a 47 percent total contribution from French sources. The remainder is filled by coproducers and cofinancers (mainly international distributors). By bringing such a large portion of the budget to the table, French studios are able to keep a significant ownership stake in the coproductions with which they are involved.

France has become an important source of titles in the worldwide inter-active gaming market since the mid-1980s. French companies Infogrames, Havas Interactive, Ubi Soft, and Titus were all, as of 2001, ranked among the top 15 video game makers in the world. They generate 80 percent of their sales and revenue from abroad, since just 8 percent of total worldwide sales for interactive games occur within France

Other Territories   Spain is an important territory for animation, both in terms of audience size and TV production. Viewers have long had many options for animation viewing, including global properties—U.S. shows historically have accounted for half the animated offerings on the air—and those from its indigenous animation houses. Spain is the second most pro-lific animation-producing country in Europe, after France, producing nearly 150 hours in 2000.

Spanish studios, which do not receive government support, include long-time powers D'Ocon and BRB Internacional and newer entries Neptuno Films, Anima 2, Filmax/Bren Entertainment, Planeta, and Cromosoma. Some of these operations also produce animated films, mostly for the domes-tic market. Spain, which has two animation trade associations, AEPA and APIA, offers the lowest-cost animation production of any European country, with budgets about 60 percent of those in France as of the early 2000s.

Italian consumers embrace many television animation properties, in-cluding Disney characters and Japanese anime, although Italians watch less television per capita than in many other countries. The Italian government is working on getting more of its own animation on its airwaves. Its big television players, including RAI, the state broadcaster, which produces more than 100 animated hours a year, are helping satisfy market demand for local properties such as *Lupo Alberto*. RAI contributes up to 30 percent of an Italian TV show's budget, including its license fee.

In 2002 Italian broadcasters implemented new rules to ensure that after-noon programming from 4 P.M. to 7 P.M. is sex- and violence-free (with some exceptions for news programming.) In addition, shows airing during prime time that are unsuitable for children must feature a warning.

Italy is starting to become more active in animated feature films (for the-atrical and home video distribution) as well as television animation. RAI joined with U.S. studio DIC in the early 2000s for *Monster Mash,* believed to be the first Italian-U.S. coproduction of a feature film. Italy is also host to Car-toons on the Bay, one of the world's leading animation festivals and markets.

The Benelux countries, Scandinavia, and Eastern Europe are all consumers of animation, although to a lesser degree than the nations already mentioned. Animation fans in the Benelux countries (the Netherlands, Belgium, and Luxembourg) tend to like programming from the United States and other parts of Europe, which dominates the airwaves and the movie screens, but both the Netherlands and Belgium have several animation studios. Miffy is one Dutch animation property popular throughout Europe and in Japan.

Scandinavians (inhabitants of Sweden, Norway, Denmark, and Finland) tend to prefer less violent programming than other parts of the world, often embracing British and European properties for young children over edgier fare. Scandinavia, too, has several local animation companies, including Happy Life and Filmtecknarna; many focus on properties for the domestic market. Television advertising isn't allowed during children's programming in Sweden, Norway, or Denmark.

Eastern Europe, a fast-growing but still underdeveloped television and consumer market, is hungry for all kinds of animation and often purchases packages of classic TV series from the United States and Western Europe. Its populations had not been exposed to these properties the first time around, due to their closed borders. As nations such as Poland, the Czech Republic, and Hungary become more developed economically, and as media and entertainment markets, they'll demand more original properties. Eastern Europe has several studios that are active in service work, including Varga Studios of Hungary, and some are joining in on international coproductions.

Latin America

The market for animation in Latin America consists largely of television series from producers in the United States, Europe, and Japan. Classic properties, such as the Looney Tunes and Disney characters, have made a name there, as have properties associated with global networks available in Latin America, such as Cartoon Network. Latin American consumers were fans of anime properties long before that genre's surge in popularity in the rest of the world during the late 1990s and early 2000s.

Latin America is often viewed as a single territory and is the target of pan-regional licensing and distribution deals. But culture, tastes, retailing, business norms, and other characteristics vary from country to country, albeit not as signicantly as in Asia or Europe. Brazilians speak Portuguese; while all other Latin Americans speak Spanish, their dialects and idioms differ. "Pan-Latin" deals must, as pan-regional deals in any territory, be tailored to the needs of each nation. Brazil accounts for half of South America's population, with 173.8 million inhabitants; Mexico has a population of 101.7 million.

The number of TV channels and networks in Latin America grew significantly in the late 1990s and early 2000s, and continues to do so. All these outlets are competing for viewers, subscribers, and advertisers, creating a fragmented landscape that makes it difficult for animation properties to succeed. Another challenge in Latin America is the economy, which has been volatile for years. The economic status of Brazil and Mexico tends to drive the performance of the whole region, but any shaky economy (and there are many) affects all nations.

Historically, there have been few properties originating in Latin America outside Brazil, although this situation is starting to change. Brazil, on the other hand, has a well-developed television market and has long been a source of indigenous entertainment properties. In the animation sector, the biggest source is Mauricio de Sousa Productions, which has released many television series, videos, and films based on its key franchise, *Monica's Gang,* and others. It also has an Internet presence. Its television series have aired on Brazil's Globo television network for years.

Mexico and Brazil are the two top countries for consumption of most media. For example, in the video market Mexico accounts for 46 percent of the Latin American spending and Brazil 31 percent, according to *Screen Digest.*

Other Regions

Almost every country in the world has some animation production, albeit not to the extent of the countries mentioned above. Most studios in these nations produce animation for local commercials or effects, or animated films or TV series for their domestic markets. Even the most undeveloped animation markets are seeing increased activity from local studios.

Africa has few indigenous animation productions, for example, but the number of productions is starting to pick up. AnimationAfrica, based in South Africa, produced a 3D animated series called *Tails* in 2002. The 13 10-minute episodes targeted children aged two to six and were produced in English, with dubbing planned for export. *Tails* represented one of the first series created in Africa for the global marketplace.

Meanwhile, Sunrise Productions in Zimbabwe released what is believed to be the first animated feature film produced in Africa, also in 2002, although many animated shorts had been produced on the continent. The film, *The Legend of the Sky Kingdom,* featured stop-motion animation.

ENTERING THE GLOBAL MARKET

Before taking an animation property into a new geographic territory it's important to study the market. Not only will its inherent characteristics affect which properties succeed there, but they will play a role in how the property is distributed, which type of entertainment vehicles and merchandise are appropriate, and how best to enter and do business in that territory.

Market Factors to Consider

It helps, first of all, to ascertain the size of each nation's entertainment business on a sector-by-sector basis. Some countries' populations consist of avid moviegoers who generate significant per capita box office totals but don't play many interactive games; other nations might exhibit the opposite characteristics. Markets such as Japan embrace original animated videos, while many others prefer secondary-market video releases of theatrical productions only. Analyzing these types of criteria helps determine which types of entertainment vehicles make sense in a given country.

Many governments have instituted regulations on the amount of local content that must air on television. Those with high domestic-content requirements, such as Indonesia (which dictates that 80 percent of programming must be of Indonesian origin), obviously will be difficult to target.

As noted in the market summaries above, cultural differences and tastes vary in each territory, even within a single, relatively homogenous region such as Latin America. In territories such as Asia, this cultural fragmentation is significant. Not only do small-population countries differ significantly from their neighbors in terms of tastes, but also one ethnic population's habits will often differ from other populations' in the same country. India alone has fourteen official languages, and each linguistic group has its own tastes. Cultural factors dictate fashion choices, types of entertainment that succeed, types of premiums coveted, and all other facets of life, all of which help determine what entertainment, marketing, and distribution decisions will work in that region.

Demographic and psychographic data about a country's population are also critical in formulating an entertainment marketing and distribution strategy. Average age, number of children in different age brackets, education levels, economic factors, and literacy rates are among the characteristics that play into how a property is sold and advertised, and which types of ancillary merchandise might work.

Studios must determine the specifics of how entertainment vehicles are

---

Exhibit 14.2

Checklist for International Market Analysis

Population

Total size and growth

Average age and size of age segments

Demographics by segment

Psychographics by segment

Population density

Subpopulations (e.g., by ethnicity or language)

Entertainment distribution and infrastructure

Number of film screens and frequency of moviegoing

Total box office

Number of television stations (broadcast, pay, cable)

TV viewership levels and relative ratings

Television penetration (broadcast, pay, cable)

Internet and broadband penetration

Computer and video game console sales and usage

VCR and DVD player ownership and growth

Size of home video/DVD market (includes sales vs. rental, OAV market)

Privatization vs. government ownership of media/entertainment outlets

Size of publishing market (books, comic books), by format

Size of music market (soundtracks)

Advertising market by type of media

Retailing structures for entertainment products

Typical roll-out and timing strategies

Literacy rate

Economic and political factors

Average disposable income, total and by population segment

Currency exchange rates and fluctuations

Income trends

Inflation

Average pricing for entertainment products

Stability of government

Changeability of laws and regulations

Telecommunications and transportation infrastructure

Trade agreements and quotas

Competitive situation in relevant industries

Regulatory and legal issues

Taxes

Import and export duties

Intellectual property laws (e.g., trademark and copyright)

Enforcement of laws

Amount of infringement and counterfeiting

Exhibit 14.2

Regulatory and legal issues (Continued)

Domestic content regulations for television

Consumer product safety and liability

Packaging regulations

Direct response legislation

Product standards

Advertising

Promotional and premium regulations

Privacy laws

Cultural and taste issues

Language(s)

Preferences for local or imported products and properties

Sizes and fashion preferences

Product specifications

Promotional and premium techniques that work

Holidays and weather

Selling seasons

---

distributed in each market. What are the number of television stations and their ratings? What is the penetration of cable and satellite television? What times of day is television the most watched, and which demographic groups watch at certain times? How many movie screens are there? Is the Internet or wireless a viable distribution channel for entertainment? What technical specifications are required?

The retailing infrastructure in a given territory will affect how sound tracks, comic books, novels, home videos, and licensed merchandise are sold to consumers and at what price. France relies on mass market distribution in hypermarkets (large-scale food/discount store combinations), while Italians shop mostly at mom-and-pop retail stores. Different types of outlets sell and/or rent entertainment products in each market.

In terms of marketing campaigns, some countries emphasize tactics such as direct mail, while others focus on in-theater advertising. Advertising regulations and the effectiveness of various media vary, as do traditional methods of advertising and the messages conveyed. Many countries have rules regarding advertising to children; some Scandinavian countries ban it altogether. In France, Warner Brothers created a special movie poster for its film *Iron Giant*, since it felt the original poster, used in other markets, would put consumers off by being too scary for a children's film.

Regulatory and legal environments not only affect advertising. There are consumer product safety laws, privacy laws regarding direct mail, regulations on promotions and premiums, TV content quotas, trade regulations, and many other rules that affect the entertainment industry in each territory.

The competitive situation in each country affects a given property's chances of success. Is there a strong domestic animation industry? Do local populations prefer domestic films and series over productions from other countries? How saturated is the market for games, videos, and merchandise featuring local and global animation properties?

Analyzing a market thoroughly even means unearthing differences in how day-to-day business is done. In Japan, negotiating a business deal requires a long period of formal discussion and polite back-and-forth, including personal meetings; once the deal is signed it tends to be exclusive and enduring.

Adapting a Property

Based on the criteria outlined above, animation properties often must be adapted to fit market needs. Some dubbing is nearly always required if a production will be marketed internationally. This simple form of adaptation requires a new script for each language (a loose translation with words that match lip movements) but no further editing.

A small group of actors in each country or language handles most of the dubbing duties involving international films and television series. These professionals are cost-effective and professional, but using their services makes a production sound identical to others in that country. In some cases, it may be worth the extra cost to hire actors with distinctive voices.

In some cases—rarely for TV, but sometimes for films—the revoicing process is sophisticated and expensive. Rather than having local singers record versions of songs, for example, the songs might be rerecorded in multiple languages by a global superstar. This may be a boon from a marketing standpoint, since the internationally known recording artist will be a draw for the film, as well as for ancillary production such as soundtracks or books about the behind-the-scenes process of making the movie.

Simply deciding how many languages to dub into takes some strategic thinking and a cost-benefit analysis; several countries have multiple official and unofficial languages spoken by large populations. Dubbing usually leads to more viewers or attendance in the case of children's animation, but sub-

---

Exhibit 14.3

Methods of Adapting an Animation Property for Foreign Markets

Dubbing

Subtitling

Editing out scenes

Editing scenes to replace signage, etc.

Creating a new story for all or part of the production, to eliminate cultural references that are offensive or don't make sense

Rerecording music

Reversioning (using parts of existing animation in conjunction with locally produced segments)

Note: Some episodes or properties require more than one of these methods for a given country, or a mix from country to country.

---

titles are more cost-effective, especially for languages spoken by small populations. Most strategies involve a mix of dubbing and subtitling.

In addition to being translated, some properties need further editing, such as changing names of characters and places to reflect the culture or eliminate insensitive words; altering humor to capture the local sense of what is funny; eliminating difficult-to-translate techno talk in science fiction properties. In addition, some countries may dictate that violent or sexually explicit scenes are edited out. If editing is extensive, new scenes may need to be added for local markets, but this is usually only worthwhile for the biggest territories, and not always then.

The cost for dubbing and editing an animated television episode for a new market varies. Bandai sold three shows to Cartoon Network in the early 2000s; each show cost $15,000 to $20,000 per episode to edit and dub for U.S. audiences.

A more sophisticated type of localization, used in television, is called "versioning" or "reversioning." A studio, using local creative staff, creates a show for its own market using elements from the international production (under the watchful eye of the original producer) combined with new elements. This technique is often used for children's television shows that have an educational slant; early childhood education requirements and standards differ around the world. Reversioning can also be a relatively inexpensive way to create local content to meet government quotas.

Reversioning often involves using internationally applicable animated segments, which are dubbed, and interspersing them with live-action wrap-arounds involving local talent and content. Sesame Workshop uses this strategy with *Sesame Street,* as do the respective licensors of *Noddy, Teletubbies,* and other preschool series. Sesame Workshop supports twenty localized co-productions that integrate animated and puppet vignettes from the producer's archive into live segments with local actors, puppets, and content. It also offers dubbed versions in some countries.

Afterword

Many of the trends discussed in *The Animation Business Handbook* should continue as the industry moves deeper into the twenty-first century. As new technologies emerge and practitioners in all media look toward animation to help them stand out in a continuously competitive market, there will be more opportunities for both work-for-hire animation projects and proprietary properties. At the same time, competition among animation studios, especially as they diversify into new markets, will remain intense. The animation industry will continue its global drive, and creativity will be the watchword when it comes to deal making.

Animation studios and independent animators will need to think flexibly and creatively in order to succeed. As this book has shown, there are few hard and fast rules to running a studio, marketing a property, or securing contract work. Those practitioners who can identify new ways of doing things that satisfy all partners will be able to succeed.

Another predictor of success will be the ability to combine knowledge, expertise, and talent—the components that drive the artistic process of creating animation—with business sophistication and technological know-how. Those who can integrate all three spheres—creativity, business, and technology—to come up with solutions to meet the needs of clients and partners will be well positioned in the marketplace.

Flexibility is an attribute whose importance cannot be overstated. The world of animation is in a constant state of flux. Market conditions, competitive landscapes, methods of distribution, business tactics, consumer tastes, and technological tools change at such a rapid pace that the creation, marketing, and distribution plans surrounding a single production can require course corrections several times, from the beginning of the development process to the end of the postproduction stage and beyond.

In order to think creatively, remain flexible, and integrate all the facets of the animation process, studio executives and animators must stay educated about industry trends and developments. Networking, perusing printed and Web information, keeping an eye out toward competitors, and maintaining a high profile are all critical, not just to allow a studio to stand out from the crowd, but to keep a handle on the current landscape and find its own way.

Maintaining a network of trusted advisors can help a studio succeed. It makes sense to look toward respected colleagues with complementary knowledge for advice on running the studio. It also makes sense to get a fresh perspective by talking to others outside the animation industry. Their experience in marketing, distribution, sales, or other facets of their own industries may help a studio look at its own business in a new way.

Innovation will become ever more critical if a studio is to stand out. With trends changing so fast, just keeping up with what the rest of the industry is doing will not necessarily be enough. It will be important for companies to take the lead and set out in new directions that allow them to stand out. The guidelines set forth in *The Animation Business Handbook* will help them do that.

Appendix 1: Glossary

2D animation. Flat animation form created by hand, using cels, or by computer.

35 millimeter. Common exhibition format for theatrical feature films.

3D animation. Computer-generated style of animation with more depth than **2D animation.**

3D CGI. Short-hand description for computer-generated **3D animation.** CGI stands for computer-generated imagery.

50/50 net deal. In home video, an agreement where the producer and distributor of a home video split the profits after deducting expenses from gross revenues.

Above the line. Direct costs deducted from revenues to derive gross profit. Includes producers and directors and associated costs, as well as all costs related to the script and voice recording.

Accounts. 1) Clients. 2) Financial books.

Acetate. In the case of 2D animation done in the traditional manner, material used for animation cels.

Acquisition. 1) In the case of a broadcaster, cable network, or distributor, the purchase (via a license fee) of a property to air for a given amount of time. 2) The purchase of another company as a means of business expansion.

Acquisition budget. The annual amount reserved by a broadcaster, cable network, or distributor for purchasing or licensing existing properties. Part of the programming budget.

Acquisitions executives. Management-level employees at a broadcaster, network, studio, or distribution company, in charge of seeking properties to add to the company's roster of offerings.

Action figures. Important ancillary products for animated properties targeted at boys and young men. Can be collectible or meant for play.

Actual expenses. Expenditures made in the process of producing an animated property. Productions must track actual expenses to ensure they stay within budget and have enough financing to cover costs.

Adaptation. The process of tailoring a property, usually for a new geographic or consumer market. Adaptation for international markets can include dubbing, editing, subtitling, and/or **reversioning**.

Added value. Extra services offered by an animation studio to its customers.

Adjusted gross proceeds. Gross revenues associated with a property, less certain expenses. Often the basis for participation shares. The definition of adjusted gross proceeds varies from production to production and should be carefully specified in contracts.

Administrative costs. Expenses associated with the overall management of a production or studio. Can be attributed directly or included in overhead.

Advances. Upfront payments. Usually a portion of royalties, commissions, distribution fees, or other later payment streams.

Advertising. 1) One means of raising and maintaining the profile of a studio or property. 2) A work-for-hire opportunity for an animation studio.

Advertising agency. An organization retained by an advertiser to handle creative executions, strategy, and media buys. The advertising agency's creative director is responsible for hiring an animation studio, if needed.

Advertising channels. Media vehicles for advertising. Major advertising channels include newspapers, magazines, broadcast television, cable, and the Internet.

Advertising industry billings. The total amount invoiced by advertising agencies, usually in a year. The level of billings is an indicator of the health of the advertising industry, which affects the number of commercial opportunities available for animation studios.

Advertising-supported business model. For an Internet site, a reliance on advertising sales as a main source of revenues. Not usually viable as a standalone strategy.

Affiliate label. A distribution structure in which an interactive game publisher/distributor sells another publisher's titles to retailers.

Affiliated Web sites. Internet sites that license a given property. Granting rights to several affiliated sites creates a network, allowing a studio to sell advertising based on aggregate audience size.

Affiliates. Television stations associated with a network or Web sites associated with an online property or content provider.

AFM. See **American Federation of Musicians (AFM).**

AFTRA. See **American Federation of Television and Radio Actors (AFTRA).**

Agency commissions. Percentage of revenues taken by an agency as compensation for services. Commissions vary depending on the type of agency, with advertising agencies taking 15 percent and licensing agencies 35 percent to 40 percent, for example.

Agents. Outside representatives that handle selling duties for a studio. Agents specialize in one type of service, such as licensing, promotions, marketing, pitching properties, advertising, etc.

Air date. The date a television show premieres.

Allocation. A division of costs or revenues. Overhead costs, which are not traceable to a single production, are allocated to all productions within a studio.

American Federation of Musicians (AFM). The major union for musicians performing live music for films or other animation productions.

American Federation of Television and Radio Actors (AFTRA). One of the unions governing voice-over actors.

Amortization. The process of spreading expenditures over several productions or years. Large equipment expenditures may be amortized.

Analysis. The process of breaking a production down into its smallest components in preparation for creating a budget or production plan.

Ancillaries. Products and services tied to a production. Ancillaries bring in additional revenues in addition to those from the production itself.

Ancillary categories. The major classifications of ancillary products and services. They include home video, sound tracks, toys and other licensed merchandise, and interactive games.

Ancillary departments. Departments within a studio or company responsible for ancillary categories such as licensing.

Ancillary merchandise. Licensed and other tie-in products tied to an animation production.

Ancillary revenue stream. Cash flow attributable to ancillary products, usually in the form of a royalty.

Ancillary revenues. Total cash receipts from licensed merchandise and other ancillary products. The promise of ancillary revenues helps attract investors to a property.

Animated property. An animated franchise with a presence in film, television, and/or other media.

Animatic. A reel that shows the progress of an animation property through various stages of production.

Animation. An entertainment medium consisting of drawings or computer-generated images in motion.

Animation art. Collectibles consisting of materials used during the production of an animation property, including cels, maquettes, drawings, etc.

Animation cel. One frame of an animated production, on acetate. Cels are popular collectibles but are becoming rare as productions go digital.

Animation clips. Short excerpts from an animation production. Used on a demo disk or for marketing purposes.

Animation director. The lead person charged with overseeing the animation team. May also be the lead director, or may be a separate position, in which case the animation director works with the lead director.

Animation producer. The producer charged with overseeing the business concerns surrounding the animated portion of a live action/animated production.

Animation production. The process of animating a project, from **key framing** to **ink-and-paint**.

Animation studio. A company that specializes in the creation of animation. Can be a small company with a few people or a large firm with a thousand or more employees.

Animation style. The look of the animation. Styles include 3D animation, 2D cel-style animation, stop-motion animation, etc.

Animation Writers Caucus. A group within the **Writers Guild of America** that includes writers specializing in animation scripts. The AWC lobbies on behalf of animation writers so they can earn similar compensation to live-action writers.

Animator. An artist specializing in creating moving images for video, film, or digital media.

Anime. The Japanese word for animation. In English, used to describe Japanese-style or Japanese-origin animation properties.

Annual advertising budget. The amount of money devoted to image and property-specific advertising campaigns within one year.

Approval. The act of reviewing animation footage or products to ensure that they achieve desired objectives or quality.

Approval rights. Authorization to monitor quality control. Approval rights are one element negotiated when putting together a financial package for an animation production.

Arcade games. Large, standalone, video-style games played in a retail location. Creating animation for arcade games is a work-for-hire opportunity for animation studios.

Arrangers. Personnel responsible for creating a score for a film, television, or other animation production. Usually hired on a contract basis rather than being on staff.

Art director. Person responsible for overseeing the creation of an animation production's overall visual look.

Art house circuit. A small group of theaters, mostly located in major cities, that focus on exhibiting titles appealing to an upscale, intellectual audience.

Assistant animator. A lower-level position in the animation production process. Several assistant animators are usually assigned to a given production, depending on length and complexity.

Assumptions. Set of theoretical circumstances used as the basis for forecasting.

Attendance. The number of people who see a film or live theatrical event. Used as a gauge of success.

Authoring tools. Technology needed to create an interactive game.

Authorized licensee. Officially licensed manufacturer or interactive game maker.

Automatic option. The contractual right of a distributor, licensee, or other partner to renew an agreement at the end of the term if certain performance milestones are met.

Average production cost. The mean range of expenses associated with different types of animation productions. Used as yardsticks by which to compare a property and its costs versus those of the competition.

Awareness. The amount of recognition a property has among its target audience. Marketing iniatives are intended to boost awareness.

Back-end participation. Share of income associated with a property after the recoupment of expenses. Back-end participation is a matter of negotiation in any financing or production deal.

Background keys. The main paintings showing background scenes on top of which the action occurs.

Background painter. An artist charged with creating the environments on top of which the action occurs in an animation production.

Backstory. The historical events that happened to characters prior to the start of the action. Backstory may be highlighted in ancillary products such as books or comic books or in a prequel.

Backup. A copy of a digital file. Digital files are among the most important assets associated with a production; systems must be in place to back them up.

Balance. A strategic issue for a studio. The balance of work-for-hire versus proprietary projects, freelancers versus staffers, domestic versus international work, and 3D versus 2D animation are among the issues a studio's executives must weigh.

Bank loan. One method of covering an animation production's budget. Usually not a preferred method but may be viable for certain productions, especially films.

Banner advertising. A type of commercial message featured on a Web site. Can incorporate motion graphics created by animators.

Barriers to entry. High costs or other factors that make it difficult for new companies to enter a particular industry. There are high barriers to entry in the interactive gaming market.

Barter syndication. A method of selling television productions to individual stations. The syndicator and the stations split advertising time and each reaps profits from their portion. The syndicator sells its time to national advertisers on the basis of the aggregate audience for the show.

Base pay. The salary paid to an animator or other employees, exclusive of benefits and other perks.

BECTU. See **Broadcasting Entertainment Cinematograph and Theater Union (BECTU).**

Behind-the-scenes footage. Film or video of animators doing their jobs. Used for marketing purposes.

Below the line. Indirect expenses associated with an animation production. Includes all expenditures outside of those related to the producer, director, script, and voice recording.

Benefits. Health insurance and other compensation on top of an employee's base pay. Full-time staff are entitled to benefits; freelancers are not.

Bible. The blueprint for an animation production, including the concept, themes, character profiles and designs, basic story line and story arc over time, and the environment in which the action takes place.

Bid preparation. The process of creating a proposal and price estimate, based on client specifications, for a work-for-hire job such as a commercial or special effects.

Bid solicitation. The process of calling for proposals and estimates for animation projects, undertaken by the client.

Big Three networks. ABC, NBC, and CBS. These three broadcast networks were the only television outlets for decades, before the advent of cable networks and upstart broadcast networks such as Fox.

Big-budget features. Theatrical films with budgets over $50 million.

Biographies. Profiles of creative personnel or executives associated with a studio or production. Used for marketing purposes.

Board flow. The number of storyboard sets coming into an animation studio from potential clients as part of the bid-solicitation process. A measurement of the health of the work-for-hire portion of the industry.

Boards. Short for **storyboards.**

Boilerplate. A standard, prewritten contract, sometimes used as a first step in contract negotiations.

Bonds. A means of raising cash. Sometimes used by larger studios to raise funds for expansion or specific projects.

Bonus compensation. An extra payment due if a certain milestone is reached or action taken. In a syndication deal, bonus compensation may be due if stations run a program during a certain **daypart.**

Books. An ancillary product category. Important because it helps develop characters and story lines outside the core entertainment, as well as generating revenues.

Bottom line. Profit after all expenses are deducted from revenues.

Boutiques. Small studios or service facilities. Boutique firms often specialize in a niche of production or service provision.

Box office. Gross revenues from ticket sales to a film.

Brand image. Characteristics associated with a brand or property in the eyes of consumers. Some brands are "family friendly" while others have an "edgy" image.

Branding strategy. Marketing or business plan covering all facets of an entertainment or animation franchise.

Brands. Term sometimes used to describe entertainment franchises.

Breach of contract. Violation of the terms in an agreement between two parties. Can be grounds to terminate the deal.

Broadcast design. The process of creating an on-air or on-screen brand positioning for a network and/or Web site, using consistent colors, logos, catchphrases, station IDs, and programming **opens**.

Broadcast networks. Television networks that air their signals over terrestrial airwaves, as opposed to via cable lines or satellites.

Broadcast partners. Cofinanciers in a production agreement. Broadcasters help fund the production through distribution advances in their territory.

Broadcast sales. The act of licensing a program to a television network. Can be part of a cofinancing deal or a straight distribution arrangement.

Broadcast schedules. The times at which programs air on a given network.

Broadcasting Entertainment Cinematograph and Theater Union (BECTU). The union governing animators in the U.K.

Brochure. A printed selling tool containing information about a studio and its work.

Budget. The amount of money expected to be spent on an animation project, based on known specifications and assumptions.

Budget components. All the tasks, services, and supplies included in a budget.

Budget coverage. The percentage of a budget for which funds are promised by the various partners. Preproduction cannot begin until there is 100 percent coverage.

Budget cuts. Reductions in planned spending on animation, on the part of clients. Client budget cuts squeeze profit margins for animation suppliers.

Budgetary constraints. Creative or other limits dictated by the size of a project's budget.

Budgeted expenses. Costs included in a budget for an animation project.

Bumpers. Short entertainment or promotional pieces that air between programs or before or after commercials. Often animated.

Bumps. Increases in compensation at preagreed milestones.

Business affairs department. The group of people charged with legal and business tasks associated with a studio or production.

Business model. A studio's strategy or strategies for generating revenue streams and profit.

Business plan. A written document that summarizes a studio's mission, positioning, objectives, strategies, and tactics.

Business strategy. A plan for achieving one or more business objectives.

Buyer executive. The manager at a network or major studio charged with overseeing an animation project acquired or coproduced by the company.

Buzz. Positive word of mouth about a property or studio.

Cable networks. Television networks whose signals are delivered over cable lines rather than over the air.

Cancellation. The termination of a television series. A risk for tie-in partners of an animated TV program.

Cannibalization. A situation that occurs when two similar properties, studios, products, or marketing strategies negatively affect each other. For example, the existence of two similar toys based on an animated show could cannibalize each other's sales.

Cap. A maximum level over which expenses or deductions cannot go. Producers may cap the expenses a distributor can take off of gross revenues before remitting the remainder.

Capturing names. Using a Web site or another direct-response marketing mechanism to add potential customers' contact information to a database that can be used for future marketing efforts.

Career placement. A department at a college or university that helps students secure positions at animation studios after graduation.

Cash deficit. Difference between a production budget and the funds at hand to pay for actual expenses. The deficit has to be eliminated before production can get under way.

Cash flow. The amount of money coming into and going out of a studio at a given time. Incoming cash flow should be adequate at any time to cover expenses, including overhead.

Cash reserves. The amount of money a studio has, above the cash flow from day-to-day operations. When cash inflows are low, cash reserves may be needed to cover overhead expenses.

Casino games. Electronic games found in gambling casinos, often containing animated sequences.

Casting director. The person charged with hiring the primary and secondary voice talent for an animated production.

Catalog. A studio's backlist of finished productions sold to networks as reruns, usually in packages.

Cel animation. Traditionally made 2D animation.

Celebrity likenesses. Depictions of celebrities in animated form. Productions featuring likenesses need approvals from the celebrities, except in certain cases of parody. Celebrities increasingly provide voices for their animated versions.

Cell phones. Wireless telephones that allow for downloading of content, including simple animation.

Censorship. Deleting scenes, depictions, or language that are considered offensive. Some countries censor animated content before allowing it to be exhibited.

CG animation. Short for computer-generated animation. Often refers to 3D animation, but much 2D animation is done with computers as well.

CG animators. Artists specializing in moving images done on computer, usually in 3D. Three-D animators are in demand for gaming, television, and film, as well as other applications.

CG special effects. Photorealistic or stylized imagery combined with live action in films, television entertainment, and commercials.

CGI animation. A synonym for **CG animation**. CGI stands for computer-generated imagery.

CGI supervisor. The person charged with overseeing computer-generated special effects in live-action or animated entertainment or commercials.

Character designer. An artist who creates the look of characters during the preproduction stage. Their designs are given life by animators during the production process.

Character development. The process of creating a character, including its look, background, traits, and story lines.

Chart of accounts. A system that assigns each cost associated with a production its own number. These numbers are compiled to create the production's income statement, used for accounting purposes, and to track actual versus budgeted expenses.

Checkpoints. Various milestones during the production process where executives and partners approve the work done so far.

Cinematics. Animated sequences appearing in interactive games to further the story or reward gamers for achieving milestones.

Circular production process. A production process that goes back and forth between production and preproduction, rather than preproduction being finished and then moving into production. Three-D animation and film animation tend to have circular production processes.

Clay animation. A style of **stop-motion animation** using clay figures.

Cleanup artist. The animator responsible for taking the key animators' work and creating clean lines of final quality.

Clearances. 1) The number of markets and/or homes in which a syndicated show will be available. 2) The acquisition of permissions and rights.

Click-through rate. The number of computer users who click on an advertisement or link. A measurement of the success of an Internet promotion.

Clout. Negotiating power. Partners with more clout have more weight when it comes to meeting their objectives in a negotiation.

Cobranding. The pairing of two complementary brands, franchises, or properties to maximize marketing value.

Codirectors. Members of the directorial staff that assist the lead director by heading up certain functions or sequences.

Cofinanciers. Partners in a production that provide funding through distribution advances or other investments but do not take part in the physical production.

Cofinancing. The act of providing partial funding to an animated production.

Cofinancing partner. See **Cofinanciers**.

Cold call. Contacting a potential customer without having a previous relationship to help open the door.

Collaborative. Describes a process or task that requires several different people performing interrelated functions. Animation is a collaborative art.

Collectibles. Products sought after by fans of an animated property as mementos or for investment. Animation cels and other materials used in the production process become collectibles.

Comic book specialty shops. Small stores specializing in retailing comic books; can also carry animation products including videos.

Comic books. Ancillary products tied to some animation properties targeted toward teen and young adult males. Also a source of underlying properties that can become the basis for animation productions.

Commission. 1) A percentage of revenues taken as compensation by an agent. 2) The purchase of animation services on a work-for-hire basis.

Commercial animation. A sector of the work-for-hire animation market focusing on completing projects for television advertising.

Commercial production houses. Studios that specialize in creating live-action or animated commercials. Commercial production houses may subcontract with separate animation studios as needed.

Compensation. The means by which partners, employees, or freelancers are paid for their contributions to an animation project or studio.

Compensation package. The combination of revenues, salary, hourly wage, return on investment, benefits, and/or other components that make up the payment or return for a partner, employee, or freelancer.

Competition. Other properties marketed to the same audience or other studios operating in the same sphere. The amount of competition in a market at a property's launch affect its chance of success.

Competitive bidding. A process by which several studios are asked for proposals and estimates for a single project.

Competitive landscape. The amount of competition in a given territory at a specific moment in time, such as at a property's launch.

Complexity. The sophistication of an animation project in terms of the number of elements, the number of layers, the number of special effects, or other factors. The complexity determines the size of the budget and personnel required.

Complexity analysis. An examination and breakdown of all the elements of an animation property to determine the labor, time, and money needed to produce it.

Composers. Writers of scores or songs for an animated production. Used more for film projects than television or other types of properties, but can be involved with any project. Usually paid a fee on a work-for-hire basis rather than being on staff.

Computer animation. Using a digital rather than traditional production process to create an animated project. Most animated productions in the 2000s are created with computer animation.

Computer games. Interactive titles meant for use on a PC or Macintosh computer rather than a console.

Computer households. The number of homes in a given territory with personal computers.

Computer-generated animation. See **CG animation**.

Computer-generated imagery (CGI). See **CG animation**.

Concept. An idea for an animated property, usually expressed through a treatment, bible, or other written form.

Conceptual artist. The person charged with creating the overall look for characters, backgrounds, or other elements of an animated project during the preproduction stage.

Conceptual paintings. Detailed and colored renditions of the overall look of characters, backgrounds, or other elements of an animated project, based on preliminary sketches.

Confidentiality agreement. A document signed by a potential customer before being pitched a new animation concept. Many customers will not sign, in order to prevent frivolous lawsuits.

Consignment. The sales of a product to a retailer on a returnable basis. Ancillary products such as home videos and books are sold on consignment.

Console video games. Interactive titles meant for use on a dedicated gaming machine rather than a computer.

Consultants. Outside companies retained by a studio, production, or other company to offer advice on a particular subject area. Underlying rights holders may act as consultants on a production.

Consultation rights. The ability and authorization to offer advice at various stages of production. Consultation rights of the parties involved are one element negotiated as part of a production agreement.

Consumer campaigns. Marketing initiatives targeted toward fans and potential customers.

Consumer marketing. Promotions, publicity, and advertising directed at fans and potential customers.

Consumer press. Print and broadcast media targeting fans and potential customers, rather than the **trade**.

Consumer product safety laws. Legislation governing the way products can be made, in order to protect consumers. Laws in different countries affect the licensed products and premiums that can be sold there.

Content plays. The number of times an Internet production is downloaded or viewed. A measure of success and awareness.

Content providers. Animation companies that provide entertainment productions for the Internet and other media.

Content-driven. A licensed product that depends on the content of an animated production rather than just its graphics. Books are content-driven.

Contest. A marketing technique in which fans enter to win prizes. Helps fans feel a personal interaction with a property and allows marketers to capture names of potential customers.

Contingencies. Unexpected occurrences during an animation production that put actual expenses over budget.

Contingency fund. An extra 5 percent to 10 percent added to a budget to account for **contingencies**. A normal component of proprietary and work-for-hire budgets.

Contract. An agreement between two parties.

Contract animation. Another term for work-for-hire animation, where the studio completes a job for an agreed-upon price and the client retains all rights.

Contract negotiation. Discussion over the various elements in an agreement until the final deal is satisfactory to both parties. Typically done by or in consultation with an attorney.

Contract obligations. Responsibilities of each party in an agreement, as dictated by the written deal.

Contract projects. Work-for-hire animation jobs in which the studio provides services for a fee and retains no rights.

Contract violation. Nondelivery or breach of a term in an agreement. Possible grounds for termination of the deal.

Contribution. The input of each partner into a production agreement. Can be a financial investment, services, or other valuable elements.

Controlling interest. Majority ownership in a property or company.

Conventions. Trade gatherings where studio executives can raise awareness, pitch properties, and meet potential clients or partners.

Convergence. The interrelationship of mainstream media and the Internet. Online and off-line components of a property work together to raise awareness and direct fans back and forth between the two media.

Convergent Web sites. A Web site connected to a mainstream entertainment property such as a television show or film.

Co-op fee. A cash payment, sometimes a percentage of sales, that goes into a marketing budget used by retailers. Licensees and interactive game publishers may pay a co-op fee to the licensor or distributor to help pay for retailers' marketing initiatives.

Coproduction partner. A participant that contributes production services. A coproduction partner may also add financing, distribution, or other elements of value.

Coproduction treaties. Agreements between two countries that facilitate efforts by studios in the two nations to work together. Canada has coproduction treaties with dozens of countries.

Coproductions. Animation productions involving more than one company contributing creative services.

Copyright. A means of protecting the expression of a creative idea. Scripts, treatments, and animation productions are all protectable under copyright law.

Copyright conventions. Treaties among countries that extend copyright protection for a property created in one country to other signatories. A copyright registered in the U.S. is protected virtually worldwide due to copyright conventions.

Copyright registration. Filing paperwork with the U.S. Copyright Office that documents the creative expression of an idea protected under copyright. Filing affords added protection, although copyright protects expressions of ideas upon creation.

Core entertainment vehicle. The originating entertainment upon which a franchise is based. The core entertainment vehicle for *Aladdin* was a film, although the franchise extended into most other media.

Core fans. The most avid group of consumers of a property.

Core team. The main group of people responsible for producing an entertainment project.

Corporate family. Various companies within one entertainment conglomerate that take advantage of synergies with one another.

Corporate sites. Web sites that promote a company's products, services, and businesses. Many use animation for entertainment, demonstration, or design purposes.

Corporate structure. How a company is configured in terms of number and organization of people and businesses.

Corporate underwriters. On public television, companies that provide funding for a program and receive time for a promotional message before and after each episode.

Corporation for Public Broadcasting. An entity that provides financing for public television programming.

Cost estimates. Forecasts of expenditures associated with an animated production, based on assumptions. Used to formulate a budget.

Cost of entry. The amount of upfront expenditure required to enter a new business area.

Cost per minute. A way to compare costs of different animated projects.

Cost reports. Documents recording actual expenditures associated with a production.

Cost-benefit analysis. A process of assessing the costs and potential gain from a project or new business to see whether it will be beneficial for a studio or company.

Cost-effective. A measurement of value versus cost. Animation studios look for the most cost-effective means of getting a project done without sacrificing quality.

Cost-plus. See **Cost-plus-fixed-fee**.

Cost-plus-fixed-fee. A means of bidding for a work-for-hire project in which each actual cost is billed to the client, along with a flat fee representing the studio's profit. Used in situations where project specifications are apt to change during production.

Creative concerns. Issues having to do with the content and look of a property. Each partner in a production deal wants its creative concerns addressed.

Creative consultants. Credit describing outside parties who advise on a production.

Creative control. Decision-making power regarding the look and content of a production. One of the points of negotiation in putting together a partnership deal for an animation property.

Creative director. At an advertising agency, the person reponsible for putting together the artistic execution of a commercial. The person to which the animation studio reports.

Creative executive. Sometimes the title of the manager at a network or other purchaser of animation charged with overseeing development.

Creator-led television series. A TV program where the creator of the concept has artistic control, rather than network executives. More common on cable than broadcast.

Creator. The person who originated a concept for an animation property; the underlying rights holder.

Credits. Titles describing each person's role in an animation production. A matter of negotiation.

Criteria. Measurements used to evaluate a decision or assess performance.

Cross-collateralization. A situation in which revenue streams are combined to allow partners to recoup their investment. Cross-collateralization favors investors who are paid back first; those with back-end participation must wait longer for any remuneration.

Cross-couponing. Including marketing messages on related licensed or entertainment products that allow customers who purchase one to get a deal on another.

Crossover potential. The ability for a property to enter different media or appeal to new audiences.

Cross-promotion. Using two products, entertainment vehicles, or partners to promote each other. A frequent marketing technique to support a licensed animation property.

Cult television shows. Programs that appeal to a small but avid audience. Can be new or nostalgic.

Cultural factors. Tastes, regulations, and other characteristics of a country that affect how a licensed property will perform there.

Currency fluctuations. The relative value of currency in one country versus another. Affects compensation in situations where studios from multiple countries are involved in a production.

Current executive. Sometimes the title of a network executive charged with overseeing an acquired or coproduced property.

Customer relations. The ongoing service provided to a company's clients. In a competitive market, strong customer relations will position a studio well against its competitors.

Customer service. See **Customer relations.**

Cut. A commission or share of revenues taken as compensation.

Cybercelebrities. Digitally animated hosts of a television or Internet entertainment or news program, sometimes created in real time.

Cyberhosts. See **Cybercelebrities.**

Cyclical. The up and down nature of the animation industry or other businesses. Cyclicality means revenue streams are not steady and studios must have reserves in place for slow times.

Database management. Using the computer to store and retrieve files including records and digital assets.

Day-to-day operations. The ongoing administrative business of a studio.

Daypart. The time of day in which a television program runs. Prime time is one daypart.

Daytime. The **daypart** in which most children's programming runs on the broadcast networks.

Deadlines. Milestones during the production process when certain tasks must be completed. Missed deadlines affect a property's ability to launch on time, and therefore its success, on a global basis.

Deal memo. A short-form preliminary contract that summarizes the main points in a deal but is not legally binding. A precursor to a long-form contract.

Deal-breaker. A disagreement that makes a contract between two parties impossible.

Debt. A means of gaining cash through borrowing. Sometimes used to cover the last part of a production budget, but not a preferred method in most cases.

Dedicated site. A Web site devoted to one property.

Deficit. The difference between cash on hand or promised, through investment or distribution guarantees, and the funding needed to produce a property. New sources of financing must be found to cover the deficit before production can begin.

Delivery date. The point at which a final version of an animated property is due to the customer.

Demo disk. A CD-ROM containing animation samples that illustrate a studio's or animator's capabilities. Used during the pitch and hiring processes.

Demo reel. A VCR tape containing animation samples that illustrate a studio's or animator's capabilities. Used during the pitch and hiring processes. Largely replaced by the **demo disk**.

Demographic characteristics. The age, income, race, and other traits associated with a target customer group.

Demonstrations. A technique to show how a product or service is used. Animation is often a means of demonstrating a product on an e-commerce Web site or in training situations.

Desktop animations. Short animated sequences that can be downloaded for use on a personal computer.

Destination site. A Web site where people can go for entertainment. Many destination sites have not been able to find viable business models to allow them to stay in business.

Detailed budget. A budget showing every line item. Used for monitoring and planning purposes and to develop a summary budget distributed to partners and financiers.

Developers. The personnel or companies charged with creating a video or computer game.

Developing markets. Geographic territories that are economically emerging. They are difficult markets in which to succeed but have great future potential.

Development. The process of getting an animation property ready for pre-production. Includes creating story lines, fleshing out characters, and attracting financing. The first step in a production process. Since there is no guarantee the production will get made at this point, funds spent may not be recouped.

Development costs. The amount spent during **development**. Not always recoupable.

Development executives. Management at the network or other purchaser charged with overseeing the development process on an acquired or coproduced production.

Development stage. The first stage in the creation of an animation project, in which the creative and financial packages are put together.

Development tools. Technology needed to produce an animation project, especially in gaming.

Differentiation. A means of promoting characteristics that make a property or studio stand out from its competition.

Digital asset sharing. Use of digital animation files in more than one production. Digital asset sharing can help recoup development costs by amortizing them over several projects.

Digital assets. Electronic files used in the production process.

Digital printouts. Output of an electronic animation file, sometimes created as a collectible in cases where cels are unavailable.

Digital production company. A studio that specializes in computer animation, often for gaming or the Internet.

Digital security system. A means of preventing theft of digital assets, particularly as they are communicated or shared on the Internet.

Digital television. Television where signals reach the set digitally instead of in traditional analog form. A relatively new technology with low penetration.

Dilution. A situation where a brand message or property characteristics are lost due to too much competing information. Something to remember during the pitch process, when providing too much data about a property might dilute its core message or essence.

Direct costs. Expenditures that can be tracked directly to a given production. In animation, includes the director and producer and their teams, as well as costs associated with casting, voice recording, and the script.

Director. The leading creative person on a production, whose vision is translated into animated form.

Direct-response advertising. Advertising messages that allow the recipient to respond via mail, telephone, or Internet. Direct-reponse mechanisms are valuable because marketers can track results and capture names for future initiatives.

Direct-to-video productions. Original animation productions that are distributed first on video and/or DVD. Usually based on a high-profile franchise, but can be completely new.

Display materials. Signage and other printed materials used in-store or on-site to promote a property or marketing message.

Distribution. A means of getting an animation property in front of consumers or viewers. Home video, television, film, and the Internet are among the possible distribution channels for animation.

Distribution channel. A vehicle whereby an animation property reaches end users. Film is one distribution channel for animation.

Distribution fee. Compensation for distributing a property, usually in the form of a commission or royalty.

Distribution guarantees. Minimum payments due to the producer from the distributor, based on forecasts.

Distribution rights. Authorization to sell an animation property in a certain territory or territories in a certain medium or media.

Distribution strategies. A combination of selling methods used to get an animation property in front of as many viewers as possible.

Distributors. Companies with expertise in selling animation properties in a given medium and territory.

Diversification. Adding services, styles, or customers to decrease reliance on one business segment.

Division. A corporate structure that oversees one style, service, or customer segment.

Division of labor. The distribution of creative rights and responsibilities and production services among partners of an animation production.

Domestic content requirements. Government regulations dictating the amount of local entertainment product that must appear on television stations. It is difficult for foreign properties to succeed in countries with high domestic content requirements.

Domestic distributor. A company specializing in selling animation to one or more medium, operating in the same country as the producer.

Domestic release. The means and timing of a property's premiere in the producer's home country. Usually refers to theatrical or home video/DVD distribution.

Download. The acquisition of a digital file over the Internet. The number of downloads is a means of measuring the success of a Web-original production.

Dubbing. A means of adapting a property for foreign markets by using existing animation footage but rerecording the script in a new language.

DVD. Digital video disk. A fast-growing sector of the home video market.

E-commerce. Selling products, including entertainment or licensed merchandise, over the Internet. Niche properties are particularly applicable for sales through e-commerce.

Editing. 1) Part of the postproduction process. 2) A means of tailoring a property for foreign markets, such as by deleting inappropriate content.

Editorial department. The group of people who maintain the animatic and/or story reel, usually a central focus during the production process.

Education. One method of assessing a potential new hire. Some studios look for educational background, while others look for pure art talent, regardless of education or experience.

Educational software. Computer disks that teach concepts, usually for young children. An opportunity for animation service work, since most titles contain simple animation.

Effectiveness. Results of a promotion or distribution technique.

Effects animators. 1) Animation personnel specializing in moving objects other than characters. 2) Animation personnel specializing in adding animated sequences to live-action productions.

Effects-heavy. A live-action film, television episode, or commercial that relies on special effects to depict the action or environment in a large proportion of frames or shots.

E-mail. A means of communicating over the Internet. Can be used for marketing messages as well as communication among partners.

Emerging. A technique or market that is in its early stages of viability, but growing fast.

Employment agreement. A contract that keeps an animator or other employee at a studio exclusively for a period of time.

Employment contract. See **Employment agreement.**

End user. The ultimate fan of a property. Often used to describe fans of gaming or the Internet.

Engineers. Technical staff on a production that troubleshoot, develop new plug-ins, and otherwise enable the artists to achieve their goals.

English-language rights. Rights to a property in the United States, Canada, the United Kingdom, Australia/New Zealand, and other English-language markets.

Entertainment conglomerates. Corporations that oversee entertainment activity in all or many media.

Entrepreneurs. Solo animators who usually offer their services on a contract basis.

Episode director. A director that oversees one installment of a television show, reporting to the series director.

Equal joint ownership. A situation in which partners share equally in all copyrights and trademarks associated with a property.

Equity investor. An entity that provides funding for a production in return for an ownership stake.

Established property. An existing entertainment production upon which new projects can be based.

Event marketing. The use of live events to promote a property to fans or the trade. Often one component of a marketing strategy.

Exclusivity. The granting of rights to one licensee or partner. Exclusivity can be broad (including many media, territories, and/or retail channels) or narrow.

Executive producer. A top executive on a production. Usually the title given to a person who created a concept or brought in significant financing.

Exercise price. The prenegotiated price paid when an optioned property is approved for production, after the development process is complete. Often stated as a percentage of the production budget.

Exhibitors. Companies that take booths at a trade show to promote their products, properties, or services.

Exit plan. A strategy for what happens if a company shuts down or one of the partners leaves. Should be part of any partnership deal.

Expansion. The act of entering new geographic territories, providing new services, targeting new customer groups, adding new styles, building new facilities, etc.

Expenses. Costs that are charged to a given production as they occur.

Expertise. Knowledge, skills, and/or experience. Relative expertise levels are a factor in the division of rights and responsibilities in a partnership deal.

Exploitation rights. The ability to distribute or merchandise a property in a given medium and geographic area and reap the revenues from that activity.

Exposure. The amount of awareness generated by a given marketing initiative or property.

External funds. Financing from an outside company not involved in the creation of the concept.

Extras. Additional content added to a DVD, often animated.

Facilities. The physical building used by a production or studio.

Fact sheets. A list of information about a property or studio, included in marketing or press packets.

Fans. The consumers of an entertainment property.

Fantasy effects. Special effects depicting situations that could not occur in real life.

Farming out. The act of subcontracting certain services associated with a production.

Feature film. A full-length production of about 90 minutes, usually intended for theatrical distribution but sometimes for television or home video/DVD.

Fee reduction. A cut in compensation for production services, as an alternative to a cash contribution. A fee reduction helps fund the production by reducing the size of the budget.

Feedback. Comments from fans or partners. Feedback may encourage a producer to adapt or improve a property.

File sizes. The number of bytes used in a digital animation file. Large file sizes prevent fast downloading and are a barrier to a wide audience for an Internet property.

Film festivals. Gatherings where films are screened for the trade or consumers. One means of exposing a property to potential distributors or generating buzz among fans.

Financial backer. An entity that invests in a production or studio; usually refers to an outside investor.

Financial institution. A bank or venture capitalist. A source of financing for a few animation productions.

Financial package. The total investment from various sources to cover a production budget.

Financial penalties. Payments due if promised tasks or responsibilities are not completed on time, on budget, or up to expected standards.

Financial risk. The amount an investor stands to lose if an animation production for which it provided financing fails.

Financing. Investment that goes toward covering an animation production's budget or a studio's ongoing expenses or expansion.

Firm bid. A method of pricing for work-for-hire projects in which costs are estimated and a profit margin added to create a price. That price remains in effect even if actual costs change.

First-run syndication. A method of distributing a new television program by selling it to individual stations to aggregate a national audience. A difficult way to distribute an animation property in the current market.

Fit. A match between objectives, product and property, property and network, or other elements. A good fit between various components is a precursor to a successful promotion, property, or partnership.

Flash software. Software created by the Macromedia company for Internet animation. The primary software used for Web-based entertainment, due to its small file size and ease of use.

Flat fee. A means of compensation for a contract animation project or as part of the reward structure for a financial investment. The fee remains unchanged even if sales, costs, or other variables are flexible.

Flexibility. The ability of a studio or production to adapt to a changing marketplace or other variables.

Flyer. A marketing sheet that summarizes the characteristics of a property or studio.

Footage. An excerpt from an animated production.

Foreign sales agents. Companies that specialize in selling properties for distribution in various media around the world.

Format. The specifications of a property in terms of style, distribution platform, length, or other variables.

For-profit funds. Entities that provide financing for animation projects with the goal of making a return on their investment.

Fourth quarter. The period from October through December. Generally the main sales window for products such as toys or children's home videos.

Fragmentation. The segmentation of a market into small audience groups. Fragmentation makes it more difficult for an animation property to succeed widely.

Frames-per-second. A measurement of animation quality. More frames per second results in a smoother final product.

Franchise. An entertainment property that is available in multiple media and product forms.

Franchise backing. A situation in which a new entertainment project is based on an existing property, giving it marketing and recognition advantages.

Franchise development. A strategy in which a new entertainment project is viewed as a potential franchise with viability in several media outlets.

Franchise marketing. A strategy in which all facets of a multimedia franchise are promoted for the benefit of all.

Free services. 1) The inclusion of no-charge tasks, which would normally come at a cost, in a work-for-hire bid. An incentive to choose one studio over another. 2) One possible contribution to a coproduction or cofinancing deal.

Freelance pool. The number of freelancers available for a project when needed.

Freelancers. Animators or other personnel who are hired on an hourly or daily basis, and paid a wage based on time worked, without benefits.

Frequency. The number of times a program airs or a marketing message reaches consumers. Greater frequency leads to more exposure.

Fringe costs. Taxes and other expenses associated with an employee above the base salary.

Full-service. A term describing a studio or facility that offers many services to its clients, making it easier for the customer to use just one facility to complete a job.

Full-time staff. The number of people employed by a studio. Usually complemented by freelancers during busy times.

Funding. Investment needed to cover a production budget or a studio's initiatives.

Game animation. Animated sequences incorporated into an interactive entertainment title.

Game designers. Artists charged with creating the look of an interactive entertainment title.

Game developer. Company that specializes in creating games for interactive systems.

Game discs. The physical software on which console or computer games are distributed.

Game distributor. A company that sells interactive games to retailers on a consignment basis, taking a commission on revenues.

Game publisher. A company that produces, finances, and markets interactive game titles.

Gamers. Users of interactive game titles.

Gantt chart. A visual representation of an animation production's schedule, showing the times when various personnel and departments are needed and the overlap among various tasks.

Gap. Another name for the deficit between production funding needed and cash in hand.

Gatekeepers. Companies that stand between a property and its fans, including theater distributors, retailers, and the like. Producers must market the property to gatekeepers as well as consumers.

Genre. The type of content. Action-adventure is one animation genre.

Geographic rights. An ability to distribute a property or exploit a property for merchandise within a certain territory.

Geographic scope. The total number of countries in which a property is available to consumers.

Giveaway. A free premium to consumers or the trade to help promote a property.

Glitches. Unexpected challenges that arise during the production process.

Global broadcasters. Television networks that are available on a worldwide basis, but usually acquire programming on a localized basis.

Global delivery schedules. The deadlines at which broadcasters or other distributors around the world need delivery of a finished production.

Global marketing strategies. The plans for promoting a property on a worldwide basis, keeping the message consistent while localizing tactics.

Government incentives. Tax breaks and subsidies offered by a government as a means of boosting its local animation industry and local content offerings.

Government subsidies. One form of incentive by which a government provides funding to animation productions using local content and personnel.

Governmental funds. Financial pools overseen by governmental bodies to boost the local animation industry through financing.

Grant of rights. A statement of the rights being allocated to a company or individual as part of an agreement. Includes factors such as exploitation rights, territory, properties included, etc.

Green light. A go-ahead for a property to leave development and enter pre-production.

Gross participation. A compensation structure in which a partner is remunerated from gross funds rather than net. A means of recouping an investment earlier in the process than back-end participation would allow.

Gross profit. Revenues less **direct expenses.**

Gross ratings points. In television the total number of ratings points available during a specific **daypart.**

Gross revenues. Revenues before some or all expenses are deducted. Gross revenues are defined in various ways depending on the production.

Guarantees. Promises of minimum levels of services or payments.

Guilds. Unions governing the personnel involved in an animation production. Productions that have a deal with a guild must follow its minimum wage and other guidelines.

Hard contribution. An investment of money, as opposed to services or other contributions.

Hardware. The computers and other machinery needed to produce an animated project.

Head shots. Photographic portraits of creative or business executives involved in a production or studio, used for marketing and publicity purposes.

High-budget films. Theatrical releases with budgets over $50 million.

High-profile property. A production or franchise with significant levels of awareness among the trade and/or consumers.

High-speed Internet. An Internet setup where content is delivered via T1, DSL, or cable. A necessary infrastructure for studios that need to communicate and send animation art over the Internet to partners and clients.

Hit. 1) A successful property. 2) A single access of an Internet site by a computer user.

Holidays. Celebration or vacation days that tend to be high-usage periods for entertainment. Vary by country.

Home video. Entertainment delivered on VCR cassettes or DVDs. One possible distribution channel for animation.

Human resources department. A group of personnel at some studios charged with hiring and overseeing staffing issues.

IATSE. See **International Alliance of Theatrical Stage Employees (IATSE).**

Image advertising. Print or broadcast messages that promote a studio in general rather than a specific property, initiative, or service.

IMAX. The leading company in the large-format theatrical film distribution market.

i-mode. A wireless device/phone marketed by DoCoMo in Japan that allows consumers to download small packets of information, including animation.

Impressions. The number of people who see a property or marketing message multiplied by the number of times they see the property or message.

Inbetweener. An animator who creates the drawings that cause the scene to move between key frames or poses.

Incentive. A means of encouraging a client or consumer to purchase or sample a product or studio.

Income streams. Various means of generating a profit. Most studios rely on multiple income streams to survive.

Incremental costs. Expenses that are additional to what would normally be spent, with the additional amount attributable to a given property or initiative.

Incubator. A means by which a property can develop and gain a following before achieving wider distribution. The Internet can be an incubator for properties before they are sold to mainstream media.

Independent agents. Outside companies that assist a studio in certain functions such as sales, licensing, or distribution.

Independent concept creators. Artists who come up with an idea for an animation project but do not have the means or expertise to produce it.

Independent contractor. A company that provides services on a work-for-hire basis.

Independent distributors. Companies that are unaffiliated with the major Hollywood studios and sell animation properties in certain media and territories.

Independent producers/studios. Companies that create animation properties and are unaffiliated with the major Hollywood studios.

Independent video stores. Small retailers focused on selling or renting home videos and DVDs that are not outlets of one of the major chains.

Indies. Another name for independent studios, distributors, or retailers.

Indirect costs. Below-the-line expenses. In animation, any expense outside of directors and producers and their teams, casting and voice recording, and the script.

Individualization. Tailoring a property for a single customer or territory.

In-flight programming. A distribution channel, usually secondary, for animation.

Infrastructure. The hardware, software, facilities, and other equipment owned or controlled by a studio. A solid infrastructure must be in place for a studio to maintain a certain level of production.

Infringement. The unauthorized use of a property by a party other than the copyright or trademark holder or their licensees.

In-game animation. Animated sequences that appear in a video or computer game.

Inherent lifespan. The amount of time a property is likely to exist. Some animation productions are faddish and short-term, while others have the potential to endure.

Initial public stock offering. A means of raising funds by going public and selling stock in the company.

Ink-and-paint. The last phase of the production process, where color is added to the drawings.

In-kind contributions. An investment in a production that consists of services or other soft contributions, rather than money.

Installed base. The number of machines in households or businesses. The installed base of a given video game platform is an important predictor of sales.

Installments. Partial payments due at various points during the production process or at various milestones during the course of a distribution or merchandising agreement.

Intangibles. Elements of compensation that cannot be quantified in terms of monetary value. Creative control is an intangible form of compensation.

Integration. An interrelationship between various components and partners involved in a marketing initiative.

Integrity. In animation, the essence of a property. Merchandising concerns can be addressed during preproduction, but any changes should respect the property's integrity.

Intellectual property. A brand or concept protected by trademark or copyright laws that can be exploited by the owner in various media and product categories. A production's most valuable asset.

Interactive entertainment. Animation or other entertainment that allows the user to manipulate the property. Usually refers to computer or console video games or Internet entertainment.

Interactive rights. The right to exploit a property in interactive categories such as video games or online gaming. A video game manufacturer might help fund an animation property in order to secure interactive rights to that property.

Interactive software. Educational, gaming, entertainment, or other titles meant for use with computers or video game consoles.

Interactive story books. Book-based software titles that allow children to explore a story interactively.

Interactive television. An emerging technology that allows viewers to manipulate television content. A merging of computer and television technologies.

Interdivisional licensing deals. Licensing agreements that take place between sibling companies within an entertainment conglomerate.

Internal funds. A studio's cash reserves, which can be used to finance all or part of an entertainment budget.

International Alliance of Theatrical Stage Employees (IATSE). The union governing most animation workers in the U.S. through its **Motion Picture Screen Cartoonists locals** in various cities with significant animation industries.

International coproductions. Animation properties produced and funded by several partners located in different countries.

International distributors. Companies that sell properties in various media within their own territory. A producer must work with many international distributors to gain worldwide coverage for its property.

International presales. The act of selling a property in various international territories in advance of production, using the advances and distribution guarantees to fund production and attract additional financing.

Internet access. The ability to log onto the Internet from a home computer. The level of Internet access in a given geographic market determines the viability of launching a Web entertainment vehicle there.

Internet component. An element within a promotion that involves the Internet, such as a contest where consumers enter by filling out an online form. Marketing initiatives supporting animation properties often include Internet components.

Internet exclusive. A property that is available only on the Internet.

Internet-origin property. A property whose first exposure is on the Internet, although it may extend into other media later.

Internship. A short-term position with an animation studio that allows a recent grad to gain experience and a sense of what it is like to work in animation. Some are unpaid, while others have a small stipend.

Interstitials. Short animation pieces that appear on television or online before and after programming or commercials.

In-theater advertising. Commercial messages shown on a movie screen before the feature begins.

Inventory. The amount of programming or products in a library or warehouse. Includes previous and current properties or products.

Investment. A financial contribution to a property or studio.

Investors. Financial contributors to a property or studio. May be allied (partners, distributors, etc.) or outside contributors.

Job titles. Descriptions of the various roles in an animation production or studio. The tasks associated with a given job title vary from project to project.

Joint bid. A situation in which two or more studios band together to submit a proposal and estimate for contract services.

Joint venture. A business structure in which two companies both contribute financing and other up-front services and split the revenues after recoupment.

Key animator, key frame animator. The animator responsible for drawing the main poses in a sequence.

Kinematics. The science of creating the skeleton and musculature for a 3D-animated character and the process by which it moves.

Knockoff. A property or product that closely emulates a popular existing property in the hopes of riding its coattails.

Labor. The personnel required to produce an animation project. Labor is the largest single cost associated with most productions.

Labor hours. The number of people required to complete a task or production, multiplied by the number of hours required of each.

Large-format distribution. A large-screen production and exhibition format for films. IMAX is the leading company in this industry.

Late delivery. Missing a deadline, particularly for shipment of the finished production. Causes problems for distribution, marketing, licensing, and other departments and may be associated with financial penalties.

Late fees. Penalties due if a delivery date or milestone is missed.

Lawyer. An important member of the team supporting an animation property. Attorneys assist the production by negotiating contracts and protecting intellectual property, as well as performing other business-affairs tasks. Lawyers may be on staff or retained.

Lead times. The amount of time necessary for production or preparation before the delivery date. Lead times required by various partners may differ, and all must be taken into account when scheduling.

Lean and mean. A structure in which a studio keeps few people on staff and relies on freelancers for much of its labor requirements. Keeps overhead low and helps the studio survive slow times.

Leave-behinds. Marketing materials given to potential clients after a pitch presentation to enhance or support the pitch content.

Legal counsel. See **lawyer**.

Legal department. An in-house group of attorneys and support staff, usually at a larger studio.

Length. One of the specifications to be determined during development of an animation property.

Libraries. Archives of past productions offered for sale.

Library programming. Episodes done in the past that are available for sale to secondary channels, often as a package.

License. An agreement that grants distribution or merchandising rights for a period of time in return for a payment.

License fees. In distribution, payment for the right to offer a television show or film in a geographic territory for a period of time. Payments range from hundreds to millions of dollars, depending on the grant of rights and the production's budget.

License terms. The details about a license agreement, including properties involved, geographic territory, length of the license, etc.

Licenseability. The potential for an animation property to be licensed for merchandise categories. Licenseability can help attract financing partners, since it increases the chances for a return on investment.

Licensed merchandise. Products tied to an animation or other property. Can include everything from toys to apparel, depending on the nature of the property.

Licensed products. See **Licensed merchandise.**

Licensee. A manufacturer, distributor, network, or other partner that holds a license to merchandise, distribute, air, or otherwise exploit a property.

Licensee summits. Meetings that bring together all the manufacturers licensed to create products based on a particular property.

Licensing. The act of leasing the rights to a manufacturer to create products based on a property for a given amount of time in return for a royalty on each item sold.

Licensing agent. An individual or company that sells merchandising rights to manufacturers on behalf of the property owner in return for a commission on revenues.

Licensing executives. In-house employees of a network, studio, or other company responsible for selling merchandising rights to manufacturers.

Licensor. The owner of the rights to an intellectual property.

Lifespan. The length of time a property endures in all media.

Likeness rights. Rights granted by a celebrity to use his or her depiction in an animated property and/or associated merchandise, usually in return for a fee.

Likenesses. Depictions of celebrities.

Limited distribution. Sales of a production or product in a small number of outlets.

Limited exclusive. An exclusive deal in a narrow channel of distribution or for a short period of time.

Live pitch. A pitch presentation done in person, usually after the potential cutomer is familiar with the property through a written proposal.

Loan. A method of generating funding through borrowing. An uncommon means of gaining financing for a production.

Local content. Television programming created in the market where it is broadcast.

Local content quotas. Minimum amounts of domestic programming broadcasters are required by law to air.

Localization. The process of tailoring productions, properties, or products so they will succeed in a geographic territory.

Logline. A one- to two-sentence description of an animation property.

Logo-driven. Describes products that feature graphics from a property but do not incorporate content. Apparel is logo- or graphics-driven.

Long-form contract. A detailed agreement between two parties.

Long-form entertainment. Television, film, or other productions of a half-hour or more in length.

Long-term partnerships. Alliances between two or more companies that are intended to endure for longer than a standard contract, usually for multiple years.

Loss leader. A production or project sold at below cost in order to bring in future work. The cost of the loss leader is recouped through subsequent or other higher-priced productions or jobs.

Low-budget pictures. Usually defined as films with production budgets of $10 million or less.

Made-for-video projects. Animation productions distributed first on home video and/or DVD.

Main model pack. A type of style guide for 3D animation, showing characters, backgrounds, and other elements of the production.

Mainstream advertisers. Companies that target a wide consumer audience or customer group with their commercial messages.

Mainstream media. Print or broadcast media, as opposed to the Internet or other "alternative" media.

Major. See **Major Hollywood studio**.

Major Hollywood studio. One of the **vertically integrated** entertainment conglomerates based in Hollywood. The majors usually handle distribution in all media on a worldwide basis for the properties they fund.

Major studio. See **Major Hollywood studio**.

Majority owners. Stakeholders that control 50.1 percent or more of a property or studio.

Make-good advertising. Free commercial messages that run if the original ad message reached less people than expected (e.g., during a show that had lower-than-promised ratings).

Mall-based touring show. A live production featuring characters from an animated series, usually targeting young children. The shows take place in a retail mall setting.

Management company. A firm that specializes in managing the careers of creative people, including some animators.

Manager. An individual retained to manage the career of a creative person, in return for a commission on revenues. Relatively few animators have managers.

Manga. A Japanese word for comic book. Integrally related to **anime** in Japan.

Maquette. A sculpture that shows how an animated character looks from all sides.

Market conditions. The competitive situation in a geographic or product market at a given point in time. Market conditions affect the chances of success for an animation property.

Market contraction. A situation in which some companies go out of business or are merged into other companies, resulting in a market with fewer players. Can also apply to markets with declines in sales or number of properties.

Marketing agencies. Companies retained by a studio to assist in promotional and marketing initiatives surrounding a property or properties.

Marketing budget. 1) The annual funding devoted to a studio's promotional and advertising activity. 2) The amount devoted to creating marketing programs for an individual property.

Marketing materials. Supporting documentation such as fact sheets, brochures, and animation clips that can be used in promotional efforts.

Marketing message. The main theme that all marketing activity surrounding a property is meant to convey. All partners should put forth a consistent marketing message.

Marketing plan. A document summarizing objectives, strategies, and tactics to support a property or studio.

Marketing support. Money and other contributions that back a marketing strategy.

Marketing synergies. Complementary contributions brought by various partners to a marketing initiative surrounding a property with which all are involved.

Markup. 1) The profit margin added to a work-for-hire bid. 2) The difference between the purchase and selling price of a product at retail, representing the retailer's profit on the item. 3) A position in CG animation that is required to create virtual worlds and 3D characters.

Marquee names. Celebrities who perform a voice-over role and whose connection with the property can be highlighted in marketing initiatives.

Mass merchants. Large retailers that sell a high volume of product at a low price and with a low per-item profit. Wal-mart, Kmart, and Target are the major mass merchants in the United States.

Master toy licensee. The primary toy manufacturer creating products associated with a property. A key partner because of the marketing clout and potential revenues it brings to the property.

Measurable. Describes a marketing tactic for which the results can be quantified.

Mechanical licensing. The process of acquiring the rights to a song from the publisher for purposes of reproducing it on a CD offered for sale.

Media expense. The cost of purchasing space or air time for a commercial message.

Media kit. 1) A packet of information about a studio or property for the press to use as background. 2) A packet of information about a publication or broadcast outlet for advertisers to use when deciding whether to advertise. Includes a **rate card.**

Media release. A one- to two-page article about a newsworthy item sent out to the press.

Medium. 1) An entertainment vehicle. Media for animation include film, television, the Internet, electronic games, and home video/DVD. 2) A type of animation, such as cell or stop-motion.

Merchandisable. Having qualities that lend themselves to licensed products.

Merchandising. 1) A synonym for licensing. 2) The act of displaying and promoting merchandise on the retail floor.

Merchandising participation. A share in licensing royalties as part of the return for investing in an animation property.

Merchandising potential. The chances of a property to be successful in the licensing market. Strong merchandising potential helps attract investors to a production.

Merchandising rights. Authorization to exploit a property for licensed merchandise in a certain geographic territory. A possible means of compensation for investing in a production.

Merger. The purchase of one company by another.

Milestones. Points within a production process or other contract periods where certain performance levels must be reached or deadlines met.

Minibible. A document that describes the characters, premise, and story lines associated with a property.

Minimum guaranteed royalties. In licensing, an amount of money due each year or accounting period. The "guarantee" is measured against actual royalties; if royalties exceed the minimum, more money is due, if they do not reach the minimum, then the minimum payment is due.

Minimum salaries. Guild-dictated wages for each position, below which employers with union agreements cannot go.

Minimum wage requirements. See **Minimum salaries**.

Mission statement. A short synopsis of the focus and objectives of a studio, included in the business plan.

Mo-cap. See **Motion capture**.

Monetization. The ability to generate cash flow and profit from a business model. Many Internet companies have not found a way to monetize their activities.

Motion capture. A 3D animation style where humans' motions are plotted in the computer through the use of special equipment.

Motion Picture Association of America (MPAA). An association representing the major Hollywood studios. Feature film releases are registered with the MPAA.

Motion Picture Screen Cartoonists locals. Local affiliates of the **International Alliance of Theatrical and Stage Employees (IATSE)** that govern animation workers.

Multifaceted franchises. Properties that have incarnations in various media and product outlets.

Multifaceted programs. Marketing initiatives that involve several promotions, partners, and media vehicles.

Multipartner programs. Marketing initiatives that involve two or more partners. Some partners may be involved with the animation production being marketed, while others are outside companies that want to be associated with the property.

Multiplayer games. Video games or computer games that allow two or more players to compete. Online versions allow thousands of players to compete against one another.

Multiterritory deals. Licensing or distribution agreements that cover two or more geographic territories.

Multiyear promotion. A promotional alliance or iniative that goes on for two or more years to support ongoing franchises.

Music researchers. Employees charged with researching rights holders and costs of musical pieces needed for an entertainment property.

Music videos. An opportunity for contract animation work; many music videos contain animation or special effects to make them stand out visually.

Musical recordings. An ancillary product category that includes sound tracks and musical albums inspired by an animation property.

National coverage. The aggregation of households across the country to form a national audience for a syndicated television program sold to local stations.

National distributor. A distributor of interactive games or other products that sells to national retail chains.

National Program Service. An arm of the Public Broadcasting System that offers programs to PBS member stations.

Negative pick-up. A form of financing for films in which domestic distributors and international broadcasters purchase distribution rights before the production of the film. Their advances and distribution guarantees help finance the production and allow producers to generate additional financing from other sources.

Negotiated rates. Compensation percentages that are preagreed by the partners in a deal. Most compensation rates are negotiable, rather than being standard throughout the industry.

Negotiation. The process of discussing the various components of a deal between two parties. Negotiation of contracts having to do with animation can take months or even years.

Net profit. Bottom-line income after the deduction of expenses. Different studios define net profit differently, so the definition should be negotiated and spelled out in the contract, especially when a partner's compensation is based on net profits. In film there are often no net profits after the deduction of expenses, due to accounting procedures.

Network executives. Management-level employees at a television network charged with overseeing development of acquired, coproduced, and proprietary content.

Networking. Building contacts through presence at associations, organizational functions, trade shows, and other industry events. An important marketing tool.

Networks. Cable and broadcast television channels. Important customers for proprietary animation properties. Increasingly, they take an ownership stake in the properties they air.

News release. See **Media release**.

Niche productions. Animation projects that appeal to a narrowly focused target market.

Noncompete agreements. Documents between freelancers or employees and studios by which the freelancer or employee agrees to not work for a studio's competitors for a period of time.

Nondisclosure agreement. A document where a potential customer agrees to keep a property shown to it by the seller confidential. Many clients will not sign such agreements on the advice of their legal counsel.

Nonexclusives. Agreements that allow the partners to form similar deals with other companies.

Nonprofit groups. Organizations that may provide funds for an animated production that supports themes promoted by the nonprofits.

Nonsalary compensation. Intangibles that form part of a compensation package. Can include creative control, credits, or other components.

Novelizations. Books that tell the story portrayed in a film or other animation property. Ancillary products.

OAVs. Original animated videos. The term used for direct-to-video productions in Japan, where OAVs comprise a big consumer market.

Objectives. The goals of a studio for its business or for an individual production. All strategies must work toward these objectives; the objectives of the various partners must complement each other.

Official licensee. An authorized manufacturer of merchandise tied to an animated production.

Off-line. In the Internet world, any medium outside of the Internet. The opposite of online.

Off-network syndication. Secondary runs of television programming sold through **syndication.**

Offshore production. Sending all or part of an animation project overseas for the production process, typically from key framing through ink-and-paint.

Off-the-shelf software. Nonproprietary software that can be purchased at retail. Allows studios more flexibility than proprietary packages and usually at less cost.

One-off projects. Stand-alone animation projects without franchise backing.

Online animated trailers. Animated promotional pieces that run on the Internet to promote films, television series, or comic books.

Online auctions. Sales of collectible merchandise that occur on Internet-based auction sites.

Online distribution. Exhibition of an animation property on an Internet site or sites.

Online film festivals. Exhibitions of short films created for the Internet. Can be online or in theaters.

Online gaming. Video games played over the Internet that allow multiple players to compete against one another.

Online music videos. An emerging entertainment form similar to a traditional music video but intended for online distribution. Often includes 3D animation.

Opening sequence. The portion of a television or Internet series that stays the same from episode to episode, containing titles, credits, and other content. In film or home video the opening section containing titles and credits. Also known as the "open."

Opening weekend. The first three to five days (depending on the inclusion of holidays) that a film is exhibited. A large audience on the opening weekend can make or break a film, since there is usually a steep dropoff thereafter.

Open. Short for **Opening sequence.**

Opportunistic. Describes a strategy that takes advantage of opportunities that present themselves, rather than planning for these eventualities.

Option. The right for a company to develop a property owned by another rights holder in return for a payment and the promise of future payments if the property goes into production.

Option payment. A cash payment that allows the payer to acquire the right to develop a property for a period of time.

Option renewal. A payment that allows an entity developing a production based on an underlying rights holder's property to extend the development time. The renewal fee is usually about half that of the original option payment.

Original online series. An ongoing group of short episodes meant for distribution over the Internet.

Original video productions. Another term for **direct-to-video productions**.

Outside investors. Financial partners that have no synergistic relationship with the property outside the provision of cash for production.

Outsourcing. The act of sending all or part of a production to another studio on a subcontract basis.

Overages. Actual expenses that exceed budgeted levels.

Overexposure. A situation in which a property has too much awareness, often generated through marketing initiatives, causing potential customers to get sick of it and often shortening its life.

Overhead. Studio costs not attributable to a given production. A studio's overhead is allocated to all the productions at the studio during the accounting period.

Overruns. Actual expenses that exceed budgeted levels.

Overseas studio. An animation house, often located in Asia, that completes animation production on a subcontract basis at less cost than can be achieved domestically.

Overseas supervisors. Independent contractors on site at an overseas subcontracting studio who monitor the production on behalf of the hiring studio.

Overtime. Labor hours performed on top of the scheduled forty-hour work week. Most productions require some overtime, adding to the projected cost.

Ownership advantage. A majority stake in a studio or production.

Ownership stake. The percentage of a studio or property owned by each partner.

P&A budget. See **print and advertising (P&A) budget**.

Package. An assemblage of inputs by various partners, and their respective returns, that enables an animation production to be funded and produced.

Packaging. The eye-catching wrapping or box surrounding a video, sound track, or licensed product. An important part of the marketing mix.

Page views. The number of pages within a Web site that consumers have looked at over a given period. A measurement of the success of a site.

Panregional promotion. A marketing effort that extends across several countries. The overall message is generally the same throughout the region, but tactics are tailored to each country.

Panregional strategy. A plan for marketing, distribution, or licensing that extends across several countries. The strategy includes a mix of message consistency and tailored tactics.

Paper trail. The documentation recording each step along the production process. Helps track a production and enables producers to find information later if needed.

Parent company. A firm that owns a studio or other operation.

Partial funding. A contribution of financing that covers some of a production budget.

Participation points. The percentage of gross or net profits a partner gets as full or partial compensation for its investment in a property.

Partners. Companies or individuals involved in an animated property, providing services, financing, or other elements of value, and getting monetary rewards of various types in return.

Partnership deals. Contracts that outline the contributions and compensation of each partner involved in a production as well as other details of their relationship.

Partnership. An alliance of two or more companies for a production or marketing initiative, with each providing some contribution and receiving equitable compensation.

Patent. A means of protecting a technology-related intellectual property.

Pay cable. A cable channel that requires a monthly fee on top of the basic cable subscription. An early window for television distribution.

Pay-per-view. A pricing method where consumers or subscribers pay each time they see an animation property. Has been used on cable and satellite television; some Internet providers are attempting experiments in this area.

Payroll. The total compensation for all labor associated with a production or studio.

PBS Plus service. One of the services the Public Broadcasting System uses to distribute shows to its members.

PDAs. Personal digital assistants. Wireless devices on which consumers can record and download information, including simple animation.

Peak of production. The point in the production process when the most output is being created and the most labor hours are being used.

Penetration. The percentage of households in an area that possess a certain technology, such as cable or home computers.

Per capita sales. The sales per person of an entertainment product in a given territory. A means of comparing the success of a property in different nations with diverse population sizes.

Per episode costs. The expenses associated with one installment of a television or webisodic series.

Performance milestones. Levels of sales or viewership that must be achieved, as per a contract. Missing these milestones may be a grounds for discontinuing the partnership or may require a financial penalty.

Permissions. The act of granting another party the right to use a likeness or other intellectual property. Permissions usually are accompanied by a fee. Animation producers must get permission for the use of existing content in a new production.

Perpetual rights. The ability to exploit or distribute a property forever. Most licensors do not want to grant perpetual rights, or want at least to tie them to performance.

Personal digital assistants. See **PDAs.**

Personal interaction. A mechanism that allows fans to participate more closely in a property, such as by meeting voice actors, attending a fan fest, or being animated into an episode. Marketing components often include some opportunity for personal interaction with the property.

Personnel. The people involved in creating and providing business support for a property or studio.

Personnel hours. The number of people involved with various creative tasks associated with a property multiplied by the number of hours each spends on each task.

Photo-realistic effects. Special effects done with a computer that emulate real life.

Pilot. A speculative first episode of a television series used to sell the property. Not employed as frequently in animation as in live action, due to the expense.

Piracy. Unauthorized copying of an entertainment product.

Pitch. A presentation meant to sell a property to a potential client.

Pitch presentation. The personal meeting where the pitch is delivered. The pitch presentation is the most important element in the process of selling a property to a potential customer.

Pitch process. The development of a pitch, including researching customers, preparing the property, creating marketing materials, making first contact with a proposal, and doing the pitch presentation.

Planning. The act of preparing strategies and tactics for production, marketing, distribution, and other facets of an animation property. Adequate planning can prevent costly problems later.

Platforms. The vehicles or outlets where an entertainment or animation property can be distributed.

Play pattern. The way children interact with toys. Animation productions that suggest a strong play pattern will lend themselves to toys as ancillary products.

Plug-ins. Technological additions meant to work with existing software and enable additional tasks or creative results.

Portfolio. A sampling of art images. Used in the hiring process, especially to evaluate artists without animation experience.

Portfolio of services. The range of production and other tasks offered by a studio to its clients.

Positioning. The relative standing of a brand, property, or studio compared to its competitors. Includes factors such as brand image, target audience, popularity, track record, and style.

Post houses. Postproduction facilities.

Postproduction. The last phase of the production process. Includes music editing, picture editing, compositing, color correction, and other tasks. Usually outsourced to a postproduction facility. In live-action production animated special effects are added during postproduction.

Postproduction supervisor. A member of the production staff, usually in-house, that oversees all postproduction tasks, both outsourced and internal.

Preliminary bid. A proposal and estimate submitted to a potential client for its review and approval before finalizing. May be changed before the final bid is set.

Premiere. The first time a production is shown to consumers.

Premiums. 1) Products given away or sold to consumers as part of a marketing initiative. 2) An extra monetary amount added to a fee or price in return for providing additional value.

Preproduction. The first phase of the production process, after development is finished and financing is in place. Tasks include visual design, honing of scripts, and voice recording.

Presentation materials. Print, video, or digital support to enhance a live pitch presentation.

Press conferences. Events to disseminate news about a production or studio to the media.

Press release. See **media release.**

Primary distribution channel. The main and usually first media vehicle for an animation production.

Primary television markets. The geographic territories that are the most important for television sales. In Europe, Germany, the United Kingdom, and France are primary television markets.

Prime moviegoing period. Times of year when people in a given country see the greatest number of films. Usually coincides with holidays or long vacation periods.

Prime time. On television, the period between 8 P.M. and 11 P.M. (U.S. Eastern time). The most viewed television **daypart** for adults.

Principal cast. The voice actors who record the lead characters in a production.

Print and advertising (P&A) budget. Costs associated with creating and duplicating the final negative after the finish of production and of advertising a film.

Privacy laws. Legislation governing how a company can market to consumers, especially regarding direct response. Local privacy laws affect the marketing techniques that can be used in different regions.

Privatization. The process of transferring from government to private ownership. Privatization of television in a country indicates more opportunities in the long run, but may make sales difficult in the short term.

Producer. The lead person on a production team responsible for noncreative aspects of the project, including financing, scheduling, hiring, and tracking progress.

Product categories. Groups of ancillary merchandise. Toys comprise one product category, which consists of individual products including action figures, plush figures, board games, dolls, etc.

Product development. The process of designing an ancillary product.

Product placement. A marketing technique where a branded product appears in an entertainment production. In animation the product is drawn into the production.

Production budget. A total accounting of expected costs associated with an animation production. Once the budget is set, producers strive to keep actual costs within the budget, since the budget dictates the amount of funding secured.

Production company. A firm specializing in creating programming for entertainment or advertising. Some production companies specialize in animation, others hire animation houses as needed.

Production design. The overall look of an animation project, created during the development and preproduction stages.

Production executive. A management person at a buyer's company, especially a television network, with oversight over shows or properties in production at a given time.

Production phases. The four major stages of an animation production, including development, preproduction, production, and postproduction.

Production plan. A document that summarizes all the details of an animation production, including labor needed, scheduling, supplies, etc. Used to prepare the budget and track the progress of the production.

Production stages. See **production phases.**

Production volume. The amount of footage being produced at a given time. A means of tracking a production's progress.

Professional associations. Networking organizations for creative or business personnel. Being active in professional associations is a means of marketing and image building.

Profit. The money left over after all expenses have been paid.

Profit margin. The amount of money left for the studio after expenses are deducted from revenues (or from a project fee). Usually stated as a percentage of revenues. Most studios try to build in a profit margin of 15 percent, but it may be lower, depending on various factors.

Profit participation. The share of profits owed to a partner. Most partners look for profit participation as one means of compensation for their investment in a property.

Profit potential. The chance of making a profit on a property. Productions that seem to have little profit potential will not be made.

Programmers. 1) In television, the executives that make decisions on what should run on the network and when. 2) In gaming, the personnel charged with creating the technology to enable the director's creative vision.

Programming blocks. A series of shows running during a certain time period. Many networks have run multihour children's programming blocks on Saturday mornings.

Programming budget. The amount of money a network or other distribution company devotes to purchasing and producing content for its current and future schedule.

Programming division. The group of personnel at a network that makes decisions regarding what programming will air and when.

Programming executives. Managers at a television network responsible for deciding what shows will air and when.

Programming niche. A narrowly focused content specialty that appeals to a defined target audience. Many cable networks and Internet sites focus on defined programming niches.

Proliferation. An expansion of distribution channels, products, properties, or other items. Proliferation can create more opportunities for animation studios at first, but ultimately leads to more competition and market fragmentation.

Promotional deal. An agreement between two parties, usually a property owner and an outside company, to promote a property, franchise, or production.

Promotional fee. The amount paid for the rights to use an animation property in marketing efforts.

Promotional IDs. On-air logos that identify a network or show.

Promotional partner summits. Meetings that bring together all marketers associated with a given property, to exchange ideas, keep informed, and work on cross-promotional opportunities.

Promotional partners. Companies that work together on promoting a property and each other.

Promotional programs. Initiatives comprising various marketing techniques in support of a property or brand.

Promotional tool. A marketing technique that helps increase awareness for a property, studio, or brand.

Properties available. The brands, franchises, or productions a property owner is offering for licensing or promotions.

Property characteristics. Traits associated with a property or production. A property's characteristics determine where it will be distributed, how marketed, and to whom it will appeal.

Property positioning. The standing of a franchise or production compared to that of its competitors, in terms of awareness, characteristics, distribution, etc.

Property-specific ads. Commercial messages that promote an individual production or franchise rather than a studio in general.

Proposal. A sales document that introduces and explains a property or initiative to a potential customer.

Proprietary properties. Productions or franchises in which the studio maintains an ownership stake.

Proprietary software. Technology developed internally by a studio that owns all intellectual property rights.

Proprietary technique. An animation style or service offered by a studio exclusively.

Public Broadcasting System (PBS). A programming organization that offers shows to its members, U.S. public television stations.

Public company. A company owned by stockholders. A few animation studios are public companies.

Public relations. The act of promoting a company, property, or initiative by generating interviews and articles in the press.

Public stock offering. The initial sale of stock to the public; the process of going public.

Publicity. See **Public relations**.

Publicity agent. An individual or company who represents a studio in its public relations efforts.

Pure distributors. Partners that distribute a property but do not maintain any ownership of it.

Pure-play operations. Companies that are in business entirely on the Internet, without any retail or other presence. Pure-play operations in entertainment are getting rare, as they have not been able to find a business model that will sustain them.

Quality-control process. The steps taken to ensure an animation production meets expected standards. Includes approvals by various partners at specified points throughout the production.

Quotas. Minimum amounts. Some countries have quotas dictating the amount of domestic content that must air on television.

R&D. See **research and development**.

Ramp-up. The process of building up systems, facilities, and personnel until a production is at its peak.

Rank. A determination of relative position. Contributors to a production are ranked in terms of how early they will recoup their investment compared to other partners.

Rate cards. Brochures or lists that set forth prices for various tasks. Postproduction houses and magazines have rate cards for customers and advertisers, respectively. Prices on a rate card are often negotiable.

Ratings. A measurement of the number of viewers watching a television show.

Realism. An animation or effects style that emulates life.

Realistic effects. Special effects in a live-action production, created by computer, that look as if they were filmed on location.

Reciprocal distribution agreement. A deal in which two partners in different countries or entertainment sectors agree to sell each other's programming in their respective geographic territories or media.

Recommendations. Positive referrals from an associate or colleague. Many studios hire new employees primarily through recommendations.

Recoupment. The process of earning back an investment in a production.

Recruiters. Outside or internal people who help with hiring.

Recruiting department. An in-house group of people in a larger studio charged with screening and hiring new employees, as well as temporary staffers and freelancers.

Reel. A VCR tape containing animation samples. Largely replaced by CD-ROM demo disks.

Reformatting. Adapting a property for different geographic territories, distribution methods, or audiences.

Regional networks. Television channels operating in two or more countries.

Registered users. Visitors to an Internet site who give information about themselves to the site in return for permission to log on. The number of registered users is a means of tracking a site's success and traffic.

Regulatory environment. The rules and laws in place in a geographic territory. The regulatory environment in a country affects an animation studio's ability to do business there.

Reinforcement. The process of ensuring that consumers see a marketing message several times, increasing the effectiveness of the effort.

Relaunch. Premiering an animation property after a previous attempt. Successful properties are relaunched for new audiences; unsuccessful properties are sometimes reconfigured and relaunched.

Release schedules. The dates at which a property will premiere in different countries or different media.

Rental. The portion of the home video/DVD market where consumers pay a fee to watch a video for a short time. Also describes a theatrical distributor's lease of a film to show on its screens for a limited time.

Rental market. The portion of the home video/DVD industry focusing on titles that are rented, rather than sold, to consumers.

Rent-a-system. A means of film distribution where the producer handles advertising and duplication of prints and the distributor handles selling only. More expensive up front for the producer, but it may be the only means of gaining distribution. Also allows the producer to retain all rights in the film.

Reproduction. A copy of an animation cel or digital file sold as a collectible product.

Request for proposals. A call by potential customers of animation for bids from studios.

Rerecording. The act of redoing voice recording on sections of an animated production that were less than desired on the first round, or where dialogue was changed during production.

Research. The act of discovering information about a potential client, customer, distributor, market, or partner before contacting them or selling a property to them.

Research and development. The process of creating or acquiring software for a particular task or tasks.

Reserve for returns. A portion of revenues held back by a distributor to cover returns when products such as books or interactive games are sold on **consignment**.

Residuals. Payments to actors and sometimes other participants in a production for each time the production airs, after the airings (usually two) included by contract in the original payment.

Responsibilities. The actions partners are contractually required to take. Each partner in a production has specified responsiblities, ranging from delivery of funds to approvals to provision of services.

Retailers. Stores or catalogs that sell entertainment products to consumers.

Retailing tiers. Types of stores, segmented by price and volume. Specialty and department stores make up one retailing tier, mass merchants make up another.

Retain. To keep rights or ownership. Most partners want to retain certain rights in a property with which they are involved.

Retainer. A monthly payment to outside companies that gives the payer the right to consult with them any time during the month. Attorneys and publicists often require a retainer.

Retakes. See **rerecording**.

Return. The financial compensation owed in return for a company or individual's monetary or nonmonetary participation in a property.

Reuse. The ability to exploit a digital asset or scene more than once. A cost-saving device.

Revenue streams. Sources of cash for a production or business. Many partners or studios rely on multiple revenue streams in order to succeed.

Revenue sharing. A split of revenues among two or more partners. In one type of revenue-sharing arrangement, Internet producers receive a percentage of sales from distributors or destination sites as compensation.

Reversion of rights. A situation in which rights that were granted to a partner go back to the property owner at the end of a contract or other specified period.

Reversioning. Tailoring a production to a new market, usually by combining clips from the original production with locally produced segments.

Revoicing. See **rerecording.**

Right of publicity. A body of law that protects a celebrity's right to control his or her own likeness for commercial uses.

Rights. Ownership or permission to exploit a production, such as for distribution, ancillaries, etc.

Rights acquisition. The purchase of the right to exploit a property for a certain period of time in a certain geographic area.

Rights clearance. The process of acquiring permissions and paying fees to use existing content, such as music or likenesses, in a new production.

Rights holders. Parties who are able to exploit certain facets of a production, either through ownership or an agreement with the owner.

Risk. Uncertainty. Partners in any animation production face the risk that they will not recoup their investment.

Rollout. The schedule and strategy for expanding into new media, customer groups, or geographic territories.

Royalties. A percentage of revenues per unit sold. The standard compensation for a licensing agreement allowing a manufacturer to sell tie-in merchandise.

SAG. See **Screen Actors Guild (SAG).**

Sales. The number of entertainment or ancillary products purchased and their monetary value. Sales are a gauge of success for an animation property.

Sales forecasts. Estimates of potential sales levels for various facets of an animation property. Helps partners decide whether to join the production.

Sales representative, sales rep. An agent who represents individual animators in securing work or studios in securing jobs or selling projects.

Sales sheet. A marketing tool that lists positive attributes of a property or studio.

Sample footage. Excerpts from an animation property. Used for marketing and approval purposes.

Sampling. An opportunity for consumers or potential viewers to try a product or property. Premiums are one means of encouraging sampling.

Satellite television. TV signals distributed through satellite rather than cable or terrestrial broadcast.

Scheduling. Creating a plan summarizing when various staffers are needed, when various marketing initiatives will launch, and other timing issues.

Score. The music accompanying an animation property.

Screen Actors Guild (SAG). One of the two leading unions representing the interests of actors, including those providing voices for animation productions.

Screenings. Exhibitions of animation productions for the trade or consumers. A marketing tool.

Script development. The process of moving from treatment to final script. Can involve several scriptwriters, each with expertise in a certain facet of scripting, such as dialogue or plotting.

Season. 1) A group of thirteen or twenty-six shows in television. 2) A retail selling period.

Seasonality. The cyclical nature of a business in which the bulk of sales or activity occurs at certain times of year.

Secondary distribution channel. Media outlets that are less important or come after the core distribution of a property. Secondary distribution channels for films range from television to airlines.

Secondary market. An audience, consumer group, or geographic territory that adds incrementally to a property but is smaller than the primary market or markets.

Secondary sales window. See **secondary distribution channel.**

Second-run syndication. Sales of already-aired television series (reruns) to individual stations to aggregate a national audience.

Segmentation. The division of a market into sectors, such as by consumer group or distribution channel.

Self-distribution. The act of distributing a film without the help of a distributor. A costly and difficult method, but one that allows the filmmaker to retain all rights to the production.

Self-produce. To create a production using internal funds.

Sell-off. The process of getting rid of certain acquired rights by sublicensing them to other parties.

Sell-through. The portion of the home video/DVD market that focuses on sales to consumers rather than rentals.

Sequels. Entertainment productions that continue the story begun in a past production. Does not have to be in the same medium.

Series. A group of productions broadcast on a periodic basis featuring the same characters and concept. Television and the Internet are the primary distribution channels for series.

Service bureau. An outside facility that handles tasks for a production on a subcontract basis.

Service studios. Animation houses focusing on providing production services on a contract basis.

Shared employees. Studio staffers who work on more than one production at a time.

Shelf space. The retail presence of a property. The need to generate shelf space is one reason for the importance of marketing; a greater amount of shelf space correlates with increased sales.

Shop. An alternative term for an animation house or studio, especially a small one.

Short films. Entertainment, usually of less than a half-hour in length. May be distributed theatrically, such as at a film festival, or on television, home video/DVD, or the Internet.

Short-form contract. An agreement that summarizes the key points in a deal and serves as a precursor to the long-form contract. Usually not binding, but may be enough to begin preproduction or product development in a time-sensitive situation.

Short-form entertainment. Usually defined as productions of less than half an hour.

Sibling companies. Separate firms that operate under a single corporate umbrella.

Signage. A display that promotes a product or service, usually in a retail or live-event environment.

Silent partners. Investors that are not involved in the day-to-day operations of the studio or production.

Simultaneous release. Premiering a property in more than one territory or more than one medium at once.

Sister companies. See **sibling companies**.

Site-based media. Entertainment distribution vehicles that are located in public areas. Closed-circuit television at a retail store is a site-based medium.

Soft contribution. An investment in a production other than cash. Providing services at a reduced fee would be a soft contribution.

Software. 1) The tools required to produce a digital animation production. 2) A distribution medium for animation, particularly in gaming.

Sole proprietor. A one-hundred-percent owner of an animation production or studio.

Sound track. 1) The music that accompanies an animated production. 2) An ancillary product that features songs from a film or other entertainment project.

Special effects design. The creation of special effects for an entertainment or commercial production.

Special effects. Computer-generated additions to a production. In live action they portray actions or events that cannot occur in real life or would be too expensive or dangerous to film; in animation they include any moving objects or atmospheric devices outside of the characters.

Specialization. A focus on one aspect of the production process or one style or service. More studios are diversified than specialized.

Specialty catalogs. Direct-mail devices that include entertainment or ancillary products focused on a narrow customer group.

Specifications. The format, length, and other traits of an animated property.

Speculative investment. A financial contribution without a guarantee of a return. Much investment in the animation process, especially during the development stage, is speculative.

Spin-offs. Another name for ancillary products or entertainment.

Spokescharacter. An animated creation that is associated with a brand in a marketing campaign. Tony the Tiger is a spokescharacter for Kellogg's Frosted Flakes.

Sponsorship. An association with a production as a promotional tool. The sponsor reaps a marketing benefit from the connection, while the producers receive a fee.

Sponsorship fee. The payment for the right to associate a brand with a production. The fee often helps pay for the production.

Staffing requirements. The amount of labor needed for a production, when, and for how long.

Stakeholders. Parties who maintain ownership in a property.

Standalone business model. A situation in which a company relies on a single revenue-generating activity to stay in business.

Start date. The time when a property or promotion launches. Scheduling is created based on the start date.

Start-up. A studio or production in its early stages after launch.

Start-up costs. The direct, indirect, and overhead expenses, plus one-time expenditures associated with the launch, that accumulate for a new studio or production. Many of these costs accrue before cash flow from operations is adequate to keep the company in business.

Start-up financing. The investment required to cover **start-up costs** before a studio or production's cash flow can cover them.

Station groups. A number of television stations in different markets owned by the same company.

Stock price. The value of a share of stock at any given moment. A variable that affects publicly held studios.

Stop-motion animation. A style of animation in which photographed objects move from frame to frame.

Storage. A system for organizing and maintaining in-use and archived files, either physically or digitally.

Store traffic. The number of people who come into a retail location during a given period. A measurement of the effectiveness of a promotion.

Story arc. The direction of the plot over several episodes.

Story reel. A work-in-progress version of an animation production that helps track the creative process and enables producers to see how the project is shaping up.

Storyboard. A visual depiction of the story and action contained in an animation production. The creation of the storyboard is part of the preproduction process.

Strategic alliances. Long-term partnerships between two companies with complementary expertise, experience, or resources.

Strategic planning. A process of planning future business steps to achieve corporate objectives.

Strategy. A broad plan of action to achieve corporate objectives.

Streamlining. A process of simplification. Studios may streamline their full-time staff or the specifications of a project as a cost-cutting measure.

Strip. A television show that is aired Monday through Friday.

Studio system. The situation that exists in entertainment production and distribution, particularly in regard to films, in which a handful of major Hollywood studios control distribution, financing, and ownership.

Studios. Companies that specialize in the production and/or distribution of entertainment productions.

Style guide. A document that contains the specifications of a property, including its look, character attributes, backgrounds, themes, summaries of how characters can act, logos, etc.

Stylized effects. Special effects that are in a fantasy style, as opposed to photorealistic.

Subagent. An individual or company retained by an agent to handle certain aspects of the business, such as a geographic territory or product category.

Subcontractors. Companies or individuals that handle certain aspects of production or other services for a fee.

Sublicense. A grant of rights by a licensee for certain areas under its jurisdiction. A U.S. licensee might sublicense another manufacturer for certain overseas territories, with approval from the licensor.

Submission forms. Documents that property owners can fill out to give a production company or distributor a sense of whether it would be interested in pursuing the property. Often available online.

Subscription. A form of payment for cable programming or some Internet programming. A fee entitles the subscriber to unlimited access for a period of time.

Subsidiaries. Companies that are owned by parent companies.

Subsidiary rights. Rights to exploit a property in secondary distribution channels.

Subtitles. An on-screen text translation. The simplest means of adapting a property for a new market, and an alternative to dubbing.

Summary budget. A document containing an overview of planned expenses for a production used to help secure financing. A more detailed budget is also prepared for tracking purposes.

Supporting cast. The voice actors playing secondary roles in an animation production.

Sweepstakes. A contest where consumers enter for a chance to win a prize. A technique often used as part of a marketing initiative to support an animation property.

Synchronization license. An agreement authorizing a producer to use existing music in an entertainment production.

Syndication. A means of television or Internet distribution where a program is sold to individual stations to aggregate a national audience, which allows commercial time to be sold to national advertisers.

Synergies. Complementary services or expertise.

Synopsis. A summary of a plot or concept used to help sell a production.

Systems. The mechanisms and infrastructure in place to allow and/or track production, financing, archiving, and other processes associated with an animation project.

Tailoring. Adapting a property to new geographic markets, consumer groups, or media vehicles.

Target audience. The proposed viewership for an entertainment property or ancillary product.

Tastes. Preferences in terms of property and product attributes. Tastes vary between different geographic territories.

Tax breaks. Incentives offered by some governments to encourage the local production of animation.

Tax implications. The effect on each partner's tax payments on a production. Some countries offer tax incentives that can reduce a production's budget.

Team bid. A proposal and estimate for work prepared jointly by more than one vendor.

Teams. Groups of staffers responsible for a single facet of an animation production, such as a sequence, episode, or special-effects shot.

Tease. A subtle marketing message ahead of the release of an animation production meant to encourage interest from potential viewers.

Technical crew. The staffers responsible for maintaining and developing the hardware and software needed to complete the production. Duties include problem-solving and trouble-shooting during preproduction and throughout the production process.

Technology licensing. A means of generating revenue by authorizing outside companies to use technological tools developed by a studio in return for a fee.

Television windows. The respective television channels to which a producer can sell a property, including pay and basic cable and broadcast television in all countries.

Tentpole release. The most high-profile, well-marketed release by a studio in a given year.

Term. 1) The length of an agreement. 2) A point within or element of an agreement.

Termination. The end of an agreement.

Terrestrial broadcaster. A television network or station whose signals are broadcast over the airwaves rather than via satellite or cable.

Territory. A geographic region. Can include one or more countries.

Test. A narrow distribution of a product or property to gauge consumer interest.

Textless version. An animation production that excludes the soundtrack, used for international distribution.

Theatrical. A distribution channel involving the exhibition of films in a movie house or playhouse setting.

Theatrical play. A live performance. Sometimes a secondary or ancillary entertainment channel for an animation property. Disney's *The Lion King* was adapted as a theatrical play.

Theme park rides. Attractions at amusement parks, often incorporating animated scenes through which the rides can travel.

Thin margins. Profit margins that are smaller than desired because of higher-than-expected expenses or the desire to get a job.

Three-dimensional animation. See **3D animation**.

Tie-in partners. Companies that are associated with a production promotionally or for a marketing or licensing effort.

Tie-in products. Another term for ancillary products.

Tie-in publishing. Licensed books or comic books based on an animation property.

Timing. The schedule of releases, marketing initiatives, expansion, and other actions surrounding an animation property.

Title animation. Creating motion graphics for the title sequences in a film or other entertainment production.

Total net receipts. Revenues from an initiative, less certain expenses. The definition varies from deal to deal and should be spelled out in the contract.

Toy. An important ancillary product for a children's property.

Toyetic. Qualities that add to play value. A property that is "toyetic" lends itself to licensing in the toy category.

Track. To monitor progress or results.

Track record. A history of sales or performance. A strong track record helps sell a studio or property to potential partners.

Trade campaigns. Marketing efforts that target industry partners such as retailers, distributors, studios, etc., rather than consumers.

Trade component. An element within a consumer marketing campaign that targets trade partners, such as retailers or distributors, to encourage them to promote the property to consumers.

Trade dress. The look of packaging. Can be protected under U.S. law.

Trade partners. Companies that work together to produce or support a property. An exclusive retailer carrying licensed products based on a property would be a trade partner of the studio producing the property.

Trade publications. Magazines or newspapers targeting businesspeople. A vehicle for advertising messages aimed at trade partners.

Trade regulations. Laws governing the import and export of goods. Trade regulations affect launch strategies in new territories.

Trade shows. Gatherings of companies involved in an industry. A good place to network with potential and current partners and customers, as well as promote a studio and its wares.

Trade, the. Companies involved in or allied with the business of animation.

Trademark. A means of protecting an intellectual property that will be marketed as a brand. An important step for animation properties that will be available in some form at retail, such as home video/DVD or licensed merchandise.

Trade-offs. The give-and-take required to put together a production. A studio might have to trade off certain creative elements in order to arrive at a budget that would be able to attract financing.

Traditional acquisition strategy. In television a process of purchasing existing programs, paying the producer a license fee. Many networks are getting involved as coproducers or cofinanciers of properties, rather than acquiring them the traditional way.

Traditionally animated. A production created through 2D-cel animation. Few productions are traditionally animated as of the 2000s, although many use a style that makes them look as if they were.

Traffic. 1) The number of people who go to a store or log on to a Web site in a given period. 2) The process of tracking the elements of a production and sending scenes to different departments.

Trailers. Excerpts of an entertainment property used to market that property prior to the release. An important promotional technique for films.

Training. A process of teaching new hires about a property, technology, and/or corporate systems.

Training videos. A teaching tool used in a business or school setting. Training videos often incorporate animation for entertainment or demonstration purposes.

Treatment. A summary of the story in an animation production. An early step on the way to the final script.

Troubleshooting. An action done during development and preproduction to try to prevent glitches, especially having to do with technology.

TV households. The number of homes in a given territory that possess televisions.

Two-dimensional animation. See **2D animation**.

U.S. Copyright Office. The governmental department that records copyright registrations.

U.S. Patent and Trademark Office. The governmental department that evaluates and records trademark and patent registrations.

Underbid. A situation in which a studio submits an estimate that is not adequate to cover costs. May be on purpose as a means of securing a new customer, or due to inexperience.

Underdeveloped territory. A geographic region where animation or a specific property is relatively unknown.

Underlying property owners. The parties that own the rights to a concept or property on which productions are based. Often the creator of the property, but can be an early exploiter of rights in the property.

Unexploited concept. An idea that has not been developed or produced as animation.

Union contract. An agreement between a studio and a union by which the studio agrees to follow union rules, including minimum wage schedules.

Union regulations. Rules created by a union regarding wages, benefits, and work conditions. Must be followed by studios that have agreements with the union.

Unions. Organizations that support the rights of individuals working in certain industries and that work to improve conditions for workers. IATSE's Motion Picture Screen Cartoonists locals represent animators in the United States.

Unsolicited submission. The act of sending a proposal to a partner, distributor, customer, or other party with which the studio has no previous relationship.

Up-front fee. A payment due at the beginning of a production or relationship, usually upon the signing of a contract.

Upside potential. The profit a studio and its partners may be able to generate through their association with a property.

Valuation. The process of placing a monetary figure on various contributions to a production. Compensation packages depend on valuing each partner's input.

Variables. Elements of a production that may change and for which producers cannot plan accurately.

Variance reports. Documents that detail actual costs associated with a production. Also called cost reports.

Vehicles. Distribution or media outlets for an animation production.

Venture capitalists. Investors that finance start-up businesses with the expectation of a significant and early return. A rare source of funding for animation studios.

Versioning. See **reversioning.**

Vertically integrated. Description of companies that control all of or many points along the entertainment distribution chain. For example, they have divisions overseeing production, television networks, film distribution, home video/DVD, publishing, and/or other businesses.

VHS. The leading home video format, but one that is shrinking as the popularity of DVDs grows.

Video distributor. A company that sells videos to retailers on behalf of producers, paying the producer a royalty on sales in return for manufacturing, marketing, and selling their titles.

Video game. An interactive entertainment title played on a dedicated console made by companies including Nintendo, Microsoft, and Sony.

Video-on-demand. A type of pay-per-view system that allows consumers to view a production when they want to, for a fee.

Viewership levels. The number of people who see a given entertainment production.

Views. A measurement of the number of people that access pages of a Web site.

Vignettes. Short animated pieces often used as interstitials.

Viral marketing. Using e-mail or instant messaging to create positive word-of-mouth about a property.

Virtual instructors. A training technique in which an animated character in a televised or video production is used to teach principles or methods. For example, a video featuring a virtual instructor could be used to teach home-owners how to repair a hole in a wall.

Visual development. The process of creating the look of a production, character, background, or other element of an animated project.

Visual effects. A technique used in a live-action film to create a scene that cannot be filmed cost-effectively or safely. Matting a scene into a background is one type of visual effect.

Visual script. A description for a series of storyboards.

Visual style guide. A document that summarizes all the elements relating to how a character or production should look.

Voice-acting specialists. Actors that focus on providing voice performance for animation, commercials, and other productions. Most animation productions are voiced by a small group of these specialists, but some are voiced by marquee-name actors known for their live-action work.

Voice cast. The actors who record the dialogue for an animated production.

Voice-over. Spoken narration.

Voice recording. The process of creating the dialogue track for an animated production.

Voice talent. See **voice cast**.

Voice track. See **voice recording**.

Volume. A measurement of sales, usually at the wholesale dollar level. A measurement of success for an animated production or ancillary product.

Web-based advertising. A vehicle for commercial messages over the Internet. Banner advertising and interstitial advertising are two types of Web-based commercial formats.

Webisodes. Short installments of an entertainment series distributed over the Internet.

Webisodic. An ongoing series of **webisodes**.

Web site. An online area dedicated to a subject, corporation, or property. Many Web sites contain animated content.

Word of mouth. The spread of buzz about a property from person to person, often without the aid of a marketing campaign. Many promotional initiatives hope to spur word of mouth.

Work flow. The number of projects or properties in a studio at a given time.

Work for hire. A project done on a contract basis for a fee with no retention of ownership.

Worldwide distribution rights. Authorization to sell a property all over the globe in one or more media.

Wraparounds. Locally produced or separate vignettes that appear before and after an existing entertainment clip in a repurposed or reversioned show.

Writer. An important member of the production team, responsible for creating the script.

Writers Guild of America (WGA). The guild governing entertainment writers, including some who specialize in animation. Actually two groups, WGA East and WGA West.

Appendix 2: Resources

BOOKS

Baumgarten, Paul A., Donald C. Farber, and Mark Fleischer. *Producing, Financing, and Distributing Film: A Comprehensive Legal and Business Guide*. New York: Limelight Editions, 1992.

Blumenthal, Howard J., and Oliver R. Goodenough. *This Business of Television*, 2nd ed. New York: Billboard Books, 1998.

Clark, Barbara, and Susan J. Spohr. *Guide to Post Production for TV and Film: Managing the Process*. Boston: Focal Press, 1998.

Cones, John W. *43 Ways to Finance Your Feature Film: A Comprehensive Analysis of Film Finance*. Carbondale, Ill.: Southern Illinois University Press, 1998.

Curran, Trisha. *Financing Your Film: A Guide for Independent Filmmakers and Producers*. New York: Praeger Publishers, 1987.

Editors of *Animation Magazine*. *Animation Industry Directory*. Westlake Village, Calif.: *Animation Magazine,* annual.

Editors of *The Licensing Letter*. *The Licensing Letter Sourcebook*. New York: EPM Communications, annual.

Goodell, Gregory. *Independent Feature Film Production: A Complete Guide from Concept Through Distribution*. New York: St. Martin's Press, 1998.

Johnston, Carla Brooks. *International Television Co-Production: From Access to Success*. Boston: Focal Press, 1992.

Kanfer, Stefan. *Serious Business: The Art and Commerce of Animation in America from Betty Boop to Toy Story*. Cambridge, Mass.: Da Capo Press, 2000.

Kent, Steven L. *The Ultimate History of Video Games: From Pong to Pokémon*. Roseville, Calif.: Prima Publishing, 2001.

Lee, John J. *The Producer's Business Handbook*. Boston: Focal Press, 2000.

Levison, Louise. *Filmmakers and Financing: Business Plans for Independents*, 3rd ed. Boston: Focal Press, 2000.

Litwak, Mark. *Contracts for the Film and Television Industry*, 2nd ed. Los Angeles: Silman-James Press, 1999.

————. *Dealmaking in the Film and Television Industry—From Negotiations to Final Contracts.* Los Angeles: Silman-James Press, 1994.

Lutz, Edwin George. *Animated Cartoons: How They Are Made, Their Origins and Development.* Bedford, Mass.: Applewood Books, 1998.

Moore, Schuyler M. *The Biz: The Basic Business, Legal, and Financial Aspects of the Film Industry.* Los Angeles: Silman-James Press, 2003.

Raugust, Karen. *The Licensing Business Handbook,* 5th ed. New York: EPM Communications, 2004.

————. *Merchandise Licensing for the Television Industry.* Boston: Focal Press, 1995.

Roncarelli, Robi. *The Roncarelli Report on Computer Animation.* Toronto: Pixel, annual.

Vogel, Harold L. *Entertainment Industry Economics, A Guide for Financial Analysis,* 3rd ed. Cambridge: Cambridge University Press, 1994.

Wiese, Michael. *Film and Video Financing.* Studio City, Calif.: Michael Wiese Productions, 1999.

Williams, Richard. *The Animator's Survival Kit: A Manual of Methods, Principles, and Formulas for Classical, Computer, Games, Stop Motion, and Internet Animators.* London: Faber & Faber, 2002.

Winder, Catherine, and Zahra Dowlatabadi. *Producing Animation.* Boston: Focal Press, 2001.

Wolf, Mark J. P., ed. *The Medium of the Video Game.* Austin, Tex.: University of Texas Press, 2002.

PUBLICATIONS

Animation

3D
www.3dgate.com/magazine/

Animation Journal
912-352-9300
www.animationjournal.com

Animation Magazine
818-991-2884
www.animationmagazine.net

Animation Report
818-346-2782
www.awn.com/anireport/index.html

Animation World Network
323-606-4200
www.awn.com

Animatoon
82-2-400-2566
www.animatoon.co.kr/

Art Byte
212-988-5959
www.artbyte.com

Cinefex: The Journal of
Cinematic Illusions
909-781-1917
www.cinefex.com

Computer Graphics World
603-891-0123
cgw.pennnet.com/home.cfm

Imagine (formerly Animation UK)
44-117-9902-9966
www.animationuk.com

Entertainment and Ancillaries

Advertising Age
312-649-5310
www.adage.com

AdWeek
646-654-5420
www.adweek.com

Boards
416-408-2300
www.boardsmag.com

Cinefantastique
310-204-2029
www.cfq.com

DVD Premieres
www.videopremiereawards.com/

Entertainment Marketing Letter
212-941-0099
www.epmcom.com

Film & Video
914-328-9157
www.filmandvideomagazine.com

Hollywood Reporter
323-525-2000
www.hollywoodreporter.com

Kidscreen
416-408-2300
www.kidscreen.com

License!
212-951-6707
www.licensemag.com

The Licensing Letter
212-941-0099
www.epmcom.com

Licensing Today Worldwide
44-1384-440591
www.a4publications.com

Millimeter
818-563-2647
www.millimeter.com

Post
212-951-6600
www.postmagazine.com

Screen Digest
44-207-424-2820
www.screendigest.com

SHOOT
800-634-6810
www.shootonline.com

Sight & Sound
44-20-7255-1444
www.bfi.org.uk/sightandsound/

Variety
323-857-6600
www.variety.com

Video Age International
310-914-4450
www.videoageinternational.com

Video Business
323-857-6600
www.videobusiness.com

Videography
323-634-3400
www.uemedia.com/CPC/
 videography/

FESTIVALS AND MARKETS

AFI Fest
323-856-7707
www.afionline.org

AFI Los Angeles Film Festival
323-856-7707
www.afifest.com

American Film Market (AFM)
310-446-1000
www.afma.com

Anima Mundi
55-21-2541-7499
www.animamundi.com.br

*Annecy International Animated
Film Festival*
33-4-5010-0900
www.annecy.org

ASIFA-Hollywood Animation Expo
818-842-8330
www.asifa-hollywood.org

Banff Television Festival
403-678-9260
www.banff2003.com

Cannes Film Festival
33-1-5359-6100
www.cannes.fr/Francais/fiffr.html

*Cannes Lions International
Advertising Festival*
44-020-7291-8444
www.canneslions.com

Cartoon Forum
49-331-706-2700
www.cartoon-media.be

Cartoon Movie
49-331-706-2700
www.cartoon-media.be

Cartoons on the Bay
39-06-3749-8315
www.cartoonsbay.com

CineAsia
646-654-7680
www.cineasia.com

Comdex
800-472-3976
www.comdex.com

Electronic Entertainment Expo (E3)
877-216-6263
www.e3expo.com

EPM Entertainment Marketing Conference
212-941-0099
www.epmcom.com

Game Developers Conference
415-947-6000
www.gdconf.com

Imagina
377-93-10-40-60
www.imagina.mc/index.php

Independent Feature Project Market
212-465-1828
www.ifp.org

International Consumer Electronics Show (CES) and Digital Hollywood
703-907-7600
www.ce.org

L.A. Screenings
310-914-4450
www.videoageinternational.com

Licensing International
203-882-1300
www.licensingshow.com

MILIA
33-14-190-4479
www.milia.com

MIPCOM
33-1-41-904-563
www.mipcom.com

MIP-TV
33-14-190-4416
www.miptv.com

NAB
202-429-5300
www.nab.org

NATPE
800-NATPE-GO
www.natpe.org

Promax & BDA Conference
310-788-7600
www.promax.tv

SIGGRAPH
312-644-6610
www.siggraph.org

Sundance Film Festival
310-328-3456
www.sundance.org

Tokyo International Anime Fair
03-5320-4786
www.taf.metro.tokyo.jp/

VSDA Conference
212-886-3681
www.homeentertainment-expo.com

World Animation Celebration
818-991-2884
www.animationmagazine.net

ASSOCIATIONS AND NETWORKING/RESOURCE GROUPS

American Association of Advertising Agencies (AAAA)
212-682-2500
www.aaaa.org

American Film Institute
323-856-7600
www.afi.com

American Film Marketing Association (AFMA)
310-446-1000
www.afma.com

Animation Nation
www.animationnation.com

ASIFA-Hollywood
818-842-8330
www.asifa-hollywood.org

Association of Independent Commercial Producers (AICP)
212-929-3000
www.aicp.com

Broadcast Designers Association (BDA)
310-712-0040
www.bda.tv

California Lawyers for the Arts (CLA)
415-775-7200
www.calawyersforthearts.org

CARTOON, European Association of Animation Film
49-331-706-2700
www.cartoon-media.be

Entertainment Software Association (ESA)
202-223-2400
www.theesa.com

European Leisure Software Publishers Association (ELSPA)
44-1386-830-642
www.elspa.com

Motion Picture Association of America
818-995-6600
www.mpaa.org

National Association of Broadcasters
202-429-5300
www.nab.org

NATPE
800-NATPE-GO
www.natpe.org

PACT (U.K.)
44-20-7331-6000
www.pact.co.uk

Promax
310-788-7600
www.promax.tv

Special Interest Group on Computer Graphics (SIGGRAPH)
312-644-6610
www.siggraph.com

Video Software Dealers Association (VSDA)
818-385-1500
www.vsda.org

Visual Effects Society
310-315-6055
www.visualeffectssociety.com

Women in Animation
818-759-9596
www.womeninanimation.org

UNIONS

American Federation of Musicians
www.afm.org

American Federation of Television and Radio Artists
www.aftra.org

Broadcasting Entertainment Cinematograph & Theater Union (BECTU)
www.bectu.org.uk

IATSE Motion Picture Screen Cartoonists Local 839
www.mpsc839.org

SAG Screen Actors Guild (SAG)
www.sag.com

Writers Guild of America East
www.wgae.org

Writers Guild of America West
www.wga.org

SCHOOLS

CalArts
661-255-1050
www.calarts.edu

Sheridan
905-845-9430
www.sheridanc.on.ca

Index